WALKING
TO
GUANTÁNAMO

Richard Fleming

Commons

Commons
greekworks.com
New York, NY
info@commonsbooks.com
info@greekworks.com

Book design by Chris Frieman.
Jacket design by Viktor Koen.
Maps by Jonathan Wyss, Topaz Maps Inc.

Library of Congress Control Number: 2008929246

Fleming, Richard.
Walking to Guantánamo
p. cm.
Includes bibliographical references and photographic insert.
1. Cuba 2. Travel 3. Descriptions
I. Title

ISBN-10 0-9814579-1-6 (cloth)
ISBN-13 978-0-9814579-1-8

For John and Joan, my parents

PART ONE
Walking to Guantánamo

Uno
Arrival

The line to check in for the twice-weekly flight to Havana was hot, long, and not moving. In front of me was a short man of obscure ethnic origin, all wiry muscle, like a marathon runner. He didn't look Cuban, and there was something about his carry-on luggage that announced he was not American.

We were waiting for the flight to Havana in the airport in Santo Domingo. I was on my way to cross the length of Cuba on foot, sure that I would emerge from the trip with a unique understanding of America's closest island neighbor. I would write a deep and nuanced account of the journey and kill my incipient midlife crisis dead in its tracks. From a journalistic perspective, I felt I should start meeting people as soon as possible, but all I could think of as a conversation starter was, *Do you live in Cuba?* Under the circumstances, this struck me as a stupid question.

I thought for a moment.

"Do you live in Cuba?" I asked the man in Spanish.

"Yes."

"But, are you Cuban?"

"No, Hungarian. My name is Alfred Herzka." That explained the faint guttural edge to his Spanish. We shook hands.

"On vacation in Santo Domingo?"

"No, I am a journalist. I was working on a story in Haiti. Also, I had to leave to get another Cuban visa."

We spoke of *Santería* and *Vodou* in Haiti, where he had just been and I had spent a lot of time. Alfred had lived in Cuba for nine years, some of that time with a proper journalist's visa, but he had kept his activities more clandestine of late, leaving the country every two months to get a new tourist card, sometimes entering the country on a Hungarian passport and sometimes on one from a country in which he had naturalized. This interested me because I had calculated that it would take about six months to walk across Cuba and I wanted to stay as far off the radar as possible. I knew I was going to have to leave Cuba at least twice to renew my own tourist visa and I had already fretted many hours away over the prospect of breaking the long walk into fragments. Getting in and out of the country smoothly was a major concern. Alfred had a great deal of experience in this department. It seemed a fabulous stroke of luck, our meeting this way.

"It would be better not to speak in Spanish," he said in guttural English when I asked him to tell me more about visas. "*They* might have people here, in the line."

"What?" I looked about us. As much as his whispered suggestion of Cuban operatives spying on us here in the Santo Domingo airport it was my new friend's Hungarian accent that made me paranoid. He spoke English like an interrogator in a World War II B-movie. Was he serious? I looked at him. Alfred seemed to be sweating: his face was covered with a moist sheen. He nodded, grave. I peered around cautiously and managed only to confirm that we were indeed standing in a line in an airport. It seemed as if no one could care less about what we had to say. I suggested to Alfred that we speak in French. I realized I was sweating profusely. My scalp itched. For a moment, I wondered why the cathedral-like architecture of airports ignores the air-conditioning challenges posed by tropical climates. Now the line was moving; we were nearing the counter. I mopped my brow and decided it was a bad idea to check in with a man with two passports and a funny accent.

As we taxied down the runway, billowing clouds of steam frothed out of the vents into the compartment of the Ilyushin 62M jet. Through the fog, I could just read small Formica signs glued to the yellow fiberglass panels overhead. *No Smoking! Fasten Your Seat Belts!* Noisy Dominican students on the way to an international youth congress ignored them, bouncing up and down the aisles and snapping photos of one another as if they had never been on a plane before. Then they all demanded glasses of ice water while the plane was still on the ground, as if accustomed to flying first class. Stewardesses strolled the aisles with trays of boiled sweets. I waved to Alfred, who was seated a few rows behind me. The upright tray tables were made of genuine wood. Antique Russian wood. Cubana is one of the most dangerous airlines in the world. *Calm down.* After a whining sprint down the runway, we were off and flying above the clouds blanketing Hispaniola, the sun so bright white on their puffy upper surfaces that it hurt to look out the window.

The flight is longer than it would be from Miami, but we were quickly across the Windward Passage and over Cuban territory, following the northwest thrust of the island. Looking down through brief gaps in the clouds, I saw patchwork rectangles of cultivation cut by the occasional road. There were a few distant hills, but no sign of the coastline. I tried to picture myself walking through the endless agricultural landscape unfolding below. Cuba is a very big island. Even as we started our descent into Havana's Jose Marti International airport, there was still no trace of the city, just endless rows of green crops against the brown earth. "Look at all the lettuce around here!" yelled one of the more boisterous Dominican youth. "Me quedo aqui, con Fidel!" I'm staying here, with Fidel!

The moment the wheels were on the ground, Alfred was on his feet in the aisle next to me. "We must hurry," he said. "We must go quickly to immigration. The difference between those first in line and the last can be many hours." But it was impossible to hurry. The passageway was already crammed with people wrestling their carry-on items toward the doors, and we were among the last to get on the bus at the bottom of the gangway.

"It's okay," said Alfred. "This is a good place to be, we will be the first off the bus." As we sprinted into the terminal toward a long wall of immigration booths, he called out to me: "Don't worry, just tell them you are here to work on studies of *Santería* and *Vodou* in Cuba. They love those cultural affairs." Moments later, I was alone in a sort of walk-through closet, sliding my passport and tourist card across a high Formica counter to an olive-clad Cuban official.

"Do you speak Spanish?" he asked.

"Si, mas o menos," I said. He smiled a dry, thin smile that suggested I should pull up a chair and get comfortable. I asked myself why I always had to show off my linguistic accomplishments. The counter was very wide, and it was impossible to see what was going on behind it, but the officer was fussing about performing some series of tasks involving my destiny.

"Uh, please don't stamp my passport," I said. I had been told that Cuban immigration was happy to oblige Americans who wanted no record of their visit to haunt them later, upon their return to the United States, but that it was advisable to mention it to the officials when entering the country.

"How long are you going to be in Cuba?"

"I'm not sure." The moment the words left my mouth, I knew that this was the wrong answer. "It all depends on whether I can generate interest here in a bird-observation project I have in mind." Rumors persisted that the ivory-billed woodpecker, thought to be extinct, still lurked in the deep forests of eastern Cuba. Seeing it would be the crowning glory at the end of the foot-powered odyssey upon which I was about to embark. But perhaps it had been unnecessary to share this exciting prospect with the immigration officer. I considered whether it was too late to forget how to speak Spanish.

"May I see your airplane ticket please?" I handed it over. He raised his eyebrows at my open return. How is it possible not to know how long you will remain in the country? You are a tourist, no? Are you alone? What are your plans? Have you no job? What is your job? I could summon up no adequate answers to these questions, a few of which I had asked of myself, many times.

"I hope to investigate the differences between Haitian *Vodou* and the *Santería* that is practiced here in Cuba," I offered. *La cultura de aquí.* Even to me, this sounded lame and unconvincing.

"Do you have a letter of introduction? Are you affiliated with any institution? No?" He looked at me. Then he handed me my passport and ticket. He could only have concluded that I was too stupid to work for US intelligence. "Welcome to Cuba," he said.

I had made it through immigration with breathtaking speed. The baggage claim was a desolate wasteland. Spotless, modern, state-of-the-art, and empty. It reminded me of the Jacques Tati film in which Hulot wanders bemused and alone for two hours through a world of glass and chrome. Other passengers trickled in as they completed the immigration process, but after fifteen minutes there was still no sign of any luggage. Then Alfred appeared.

"You see that guy over there?" he asked in French, making a Tourette's-like jerk of the head that failed to indicate any particular direction. "Don't look, don't look! He is plainclothes, the secret police *en civile.* They move through the crowd listening to conversations." A man was indeed moving through the handful of people now clustered around the baggage carousel, edging toward us.

"Shh, shh, il écoute, il écoute," said Alfred. We stopped discussing him just fast enough to appear suspicious, and both stared down at our carry-on bags, as if to reaffirm their existence. The man stood not far off and gazed at the carousel, still devoid of luggage.

Alfred went to the bathroom for a very long time while I watched his bag for him from a discreet distance. Soon, the inexorable rotation of the baggage carousel began to have a hypnotic effect. I felt sure that it had been turning around this way since the dawn of time. The agent moved away. Another man, short and mustached and wearing a floral print shirt, slid up beside me and whipped a folding leather wallet out of his pocket. He opened it fast at waist level with both hands and I caught a quick glimpse of a picture on an ID card before he crammed it back into his pocket. This was exciting. I had never been badged before.

"Permit me your passport, please. Your ticket, sir?" The man was terrifying in his politeness, but I survived a brief interview, managing to avoid both African religion and birdwatching as topics. By the time Alfred returned, a few bags had even begun plopping out onto the belt.

"Does it make sense to share a taxi into the city?" I asked in French. We kept lapsing in and out of various languages.

"Only if you want to wait for me. They stopped me over there and told me they are going to go through my luggage." Alfred was glum. On the way to the bathroom, he had failed an interview. If his luggage ever materialized, he was to wait off to the side for his turn to be searched. I looked over toward this purgatory of vinyl-upholstered chairs, where a few dejected travelers were already sitting against the wall.

"Just the wait can take hours," Alfred said. Muttering in a low voice, he began to catalogue the suspect items he carried in his luggage.

I tried not to gloat. "Sorry to hear that," I said. "They just interviewed me, didn't seem to be much of a problem." Over Alfred's shoulder, I saw my bag rolling off the conveyor belt and onto the carousel. "Look, I think I'll just grab a cab, you know, rather than wait, but give me your phone number. Maybe we can get together later in the week for a drink. Once I've settled in and things. It's been great meeting you."

Just then another undercover operative appeared.

"You are together?" he asked me.

"No, uh, that is to say, we've only just met. In the airport. What I mean to say is, the airport in Santo Domingo."

"What is the purpose of your visit to Cuba?..."

I collected my bag and went and sat down with Alfred, near the others.

"When they search, they are incredibly polite but extremely thorough," he said. (Much later, I was to meet a Canadian sex tourist in Cienfuegos who described the customs inspectors opening each and every individual sliver of his Wrigley's chewing gum.) Although the claim area was once again empty, the baggage-inspection process had not yet begun. Furthermore, since we were among the last ones chosen for inspection, we now would have to wait for everyone else to complete the process.

"This is very bad," said Alfred. He was worried that he had a suspicious number of cameras, too many for a tourist. He had many "texts," but these, he felt sure, were mainly about Haiti and ought to be okay. In case things got really grim, he was carrying what journalists call a "flasher," in this case a letter from a Hungarian newspaper formally requesting an interview with Fidel Castro. "I have only had to use it once," he said, "but the guy I showed it to picked up my bags like a porter, carried them outside for me, and made sure I got a taxi."

A sixtyish customs agent in a mustard-colored uniform came and sat nearby and began to interview two businessmen who were traveling together. He made one of them move away to the seats across from us so as not to hear what his friend had to say. Another agent escorted a couple and their bags off into a little room at the end of the customs hall.

I tried not to think about my luggage. Rolled up inside my sleeping pad were half a dozen large-format photocopies of topographic maps, the entirety of Cuba at 1:500,000. Maps of this scale are useless for walking, but they were the only ones I'd been able to find at the Princeton University library. At the time, I had found it hilarious that they had been prepared decades earlier by the US military. Now, I hoped very much that the corner of each map—which read "United States Navy Air Reconnaissance"—had fallen off the edge of the copies. I also had a handheld eTrex® GPS satellite receiver, which could tell me my precise location at any point on the face of the globe. Were I ever to become lost in the Cuban forests, I planned to take it out and try to figure out how it worked.

It was now mid-afternoon. As yet another official walked past, Alfred leaped up from his seat beside me and accosted him. He appeared to have lost his mind.

"This is unacceptable, I've been here for over an hour," he said, almost shouting. "You can't treat tourists like this. I have people waiting for me." The official looked stunned. He was holding his palms out in a gesture of supplication, or defense. "This is bad for tourism," Alfred screamed, advancing on the official while waving in my direction, as if I were the economic future of Cuba, about to jump up and get back on the plane to Santo Domingo. I massaged my forehead, kneading my temples, as I stared down at the linoleum. "Here is my luggage," screamed Alfred, gesticulating like a madman. "Go ahead, look through it, let's get this over with, I need a telephone, why am I sitting here?"

They led him away. His outburst was like a stain blotting out my last hopes of leaving the airport before nightfall. I pictured the customs officials squeezing out all his toothpaste, then all my toothpaste, and then doing other, much more horrible, things. Then, moments later, Alfred reappeared.

"This guy is not like the others, he's not a problem. He has a brain of his own and understands you can't welcome people into the country this way." He leaned in close to me as he picked up his suitcase. "I told him not to search your bag," he whispered. "I'll wait for you outside." Then he strode out through the big red double doors into Cuba.

I felt very lonely. It was all so incomprehensible. Had Alfred whipped out his Fidel flasher letter? Was he not what he appeared to be? Should I begin to yell and scream and cause a stink of my own? My interrogator asked me to wait for a moment, went away, and then returned from some deep inner sanctum with my passport. He sat down and flipped through it.

"What do you do for a living?" he asked.

"I am a sound recordist for films and television."

"Have you done any films I've seen?"

This is the question everyone always asks when meeting a soundperson. The answer is no, although I once worked on a straight-to-video sequel, *The Substitute II*, an action-adventure bloodbath that a few people may have seen while taking long Mexican bus trips.

"I doubt it," I said. I was weary of conjuring up all the wrong answers to their questions. I looked down. I was wearing a T-shirt promoting our sound department on the film, *La Ciudad*, David Riker's beautiful neorealist examination of the hard lives of recent Latin American immigrants to New York, which almost nobody has seen. "This film," I said, "won a prize at the Havana film festival a few years ago."

The interview was over. "Here are your papers, *disculpe la molestia*— please excuse the bother—I hope you enjoy your stay." I went through the exit doors and into the main terminal. After the relative isolation of the previous hours, it was strange to find it full of people. I wandered through the crowd, but I couldn't find Alfred Herzka anywhere.

In the taxi, the driver sang "Cienfuegos," the classic song by Beny Moré about his first arrival in the big city capital of Las Villas. We barreled past a huge billboard that read "Three Anti-Imperialists," and I recognized Che Guevara but not the men in the other two high-contrast illustrations. This advertisement for Cuba's dead heroes was the only billboard I saw, and the ride into Havana was most notable for the lack of signage along the route. The waving palm trees, sunbleached cinderblocks, and the way people on the sidewalks kept to the shady side of the street to hide from the afternoon sun, all identified suburban Havana as the outskirts of a tropical Latin American city, but there was none of the screaming hodgepodge of awnings and mismatched, brightly painted facades of auto-body specialists, dry-goods bodegas, paint and hardware stores, cassette vendors, and locksmiths that clog every artery leading into San Salvador, Guayaquil, or Miami.

We arrived in the Vedado section and pulled up in front of a large white Victorian mansion, the "casa particular" I had located on the Internet and selected for my first night in Cuba. *Casas particulares* are private homes that accept paying guests, much like bed-and-breakfasts. A recent phenomenon, they have emerged in the post-Soviet relaxation of Cuba's once strict laws against private enterprise. This house had an excellent reputation. The front yard was an explosion of tropical plants. An old woman with carefully tended white hair was sitting in the foyer behind the big glass doors as if she had been waiting for me. When she got up to greet me at the door, I saw that she was tall, with the bearing of a Spanish aristocrat. I pictured myself sitting in the garden late into the evening, sipping *mojitos* while I wrote in my diary.

"Please come in and sit down. Would you like some coffee?" I dropped my bags and sank onto the settee. She was at least seventy. "We received your e-mail from Santo Domingo," she said. "Unfortunately, we have no rooms available at the moment. But don't worry, I will call a friend."

A few minutes later, Miriam came to get me, limping up the ruined sidewalk. She had black hair framing a strained, pale face. A single woman in her fifties, she had been a prominent academic, but she told me that her leg and a variety of family problems had speeded her early retirement. She insisted on carrying one of my bags. "It's only a few blocks," she said, but, after fifty yards, she was struggling, and I took the bag back, embarrassed to have let her take it to begin with.

"The Vedado" she said, "is full of architectural marvels. Perhaps one day you would like to go for a walk around the district and I will explain them to you."Even the few blocks we had walked were full of contrasts. A neocolonial palazzo with a sweeping marble veranda and overgrown park-like front yard butted up against a dilapidated sandstone apartment house, from which ragged laundry flew like flags. On the next block, a ruined diminutive castle was just visible through clogs of ivy, while, next door, a soft-cornered art deco kidney bean of a building might have, like the Jetsons spacecraft it resembled, just flown in from Miami Beach. Before the revolution, the Vedado had been a posh district, the residents frantic to outspend one another in the construction and appointment of their homes. Now, the opulence had a decayed charm.

We crossed a wide boulevard and the character of the neighborhood changed at once from a delicious but absurd variety into utilitarian tedium. Miriam led me to a two-bedroom apartment at the back corner of a towering concrete block. The inside had claustrophobic ceilings and was dimly lit. She showed me a cramped room with two twin beds mashed together and windows that looked up into an airshaft. The apartment was halfway below street level, and what little light there was filtered in through dense strands of laundry hanging outside. Somewhere up above children were shouting and clanging on the metal railings. I let Miriam show me the bathroom, which she and I were to share, hoping to find something so horrible that it would excuse my not staying.

"I'm trying to get the money together to put in an air conditioner, but first I want to redo the floor in here," she said. She offered a sad, thin smile. "I know it's not very nice."

"It looks just fine," I said. It would be all right for a night. I took my bags into the room, threw them on the bed, and sat down with Miriam at a small glass table in the main room. There was a lot of paperwork to be done: the date; the country from which I had arrived; my name, nationality, and passport number—all went into a journal of registered guests, ready for inspection by the immigration authorities. Miriam said they could appear at any time. Another copy had to be delivered to the immigration office the next day. A separate receipt was for me. My signature was required.

Miriam gave me a set of keys and I went out into the last of the day, walking down streets that sloped toward the sea. I was as unprepared physically to walk across Cuba as I was in every other way, and I had decided that I would walk as much as possible while in Havana, going on foot for any errands that needed to be run and thereby reaching my peak fitness level over the course of the next three or four days, just in time to leave for Pinar del Río and prance across the mountains of the Sierra del Rosario like a mountain goat.

There really were half-century-old American coupes and sedans parked along every street. Many were up on blocks, with Cubans underneath them, tinkering. One house had a very old sign in cracking red paint tacked to a tree: "please do not disturb, we have no oranges." People sat on their stoops, chatting, and old women peered out the open windows.

Near the water were clusters of high-rises badly in need of a coat of paint, and the sun shone orange, warming the salt-blasted patina of their towering surfaces. Turkey vultures and tiny, twittering Antillean palm swifts exploited the updraft where the ocean air dodged over the buildings. I crossed the six-lane highway that divides the *Malecón* from the city and peered over the seawall into the Straits of Florida. Other than to make my way to the western city of Pinar del Río, put on my backpack, and walk the thousand or so miles it would take to reach Guantánamo Bay, I really didn't have much of a plan.

I admit now that it was a strange idea. In my late thirties, I had, back home, a wonderful girlfriend who loved me and with whom I shared life in a funky, downtown Manhattan apartment. We carved as much time as we chose out of our freelance lives to take relaxing, extended vacations. My career as a sound recordist was thriving and included more exciting travel than most people ever dream of. But although I was desperate not to lose these things, and feared any threat to the life I had built, an equally desperate feeling of stagnation and unfulfillment had begun to grow, to nag and threaten. I had spiraled into depression. Marriage and fatherhood loomed over our relationship, terrifying me. I felt in my bones what it once said on my eighth-grade report cards: *Not living up to his potential.* I slept badly and was plagued by abstract aches and pains and maladies until what I perceived as the nightmarish mediocrity of my existence assumed life-threatening proportions. Returning home from exotic trips as if from any other daily grind, I would dump my gear on the kitchen floor after weeks away and sink into an armchair with the newspaper. If Cynthia was lucky, I'd greet her listlessly and respond, "I don't want to talk about it," when she asked how the job had gone.

Gloom like this is the worst reason to travel, but the idea of walking across Cuba had gathered dust in my brain for years. So I finally decided to brush it off in that frantic, desperate grasping at a solution that only happens in the midst of a deep and solid depression. I equated the upcoming trip and the life-changing book I would write about it with salvation. "I just have to do this," I told Cynthia.

Cuba was fascinating and mysterious, and I suspected that what I read in the United States about the island bore little resemblance to reality. Every viewpoint was poisoned by political venom. As a child, prejudice and propaganda had literally tinted my view of the communist bloc gray. I had imagined that there were no colors or trees behind the Iron Curtain, only black mud and snow, gray overcoats, and buildings made of unpainted cement. I was sure that similar, subtler distortions colored my adult image of Cuba, the last gasp of world communism and a tropical paradise that combined many of my various interests: the country is the indisputable cradle of Latin music, with an endless array of rhythms; as a lifelong birdwatcher, I hoped to see the numerous endemic bird species that live on the island; and, after becoming interested in Afro-Caribbean religions while working on a documentary about Haitian *Vodou,* I wanted to see something of *Santería.* This nation, right next door to America but so little known, was my perfect subject. It seemed ideal to walk, to go into the countryside. By doing so, moreover, I'd avoid the political baggage and escape the developing tourist economy of Havana to share the lives of normal, average people.

The idea first came to me while working on a film in Haiti, after reading about the desperate transport shortages that had developed in Cuba after the Soviet bloc collapsed, ending decades of cheap, subsidized fuel and inexpensive truck, tractor, and bus imports. In Haiti, where transportation was equally dire (there were almost no roads to speak of), I had backpacked in the hills on a free weekend. There, the most remote mountain trails were clogged with merchants and farmers carrying their produce ten or fifteen kilometers over the hills to market. To walk the countryside in Cuba, I was sure, would be to share the paths and highways with average citizens of all ages walking to work, to their fields, or between their villages. I would learn the realities of the country firsthand.

Over the course of a few months, this dream developed into an obsession. I insisted that I couldn't imagine what else to do. Cynthia supported me but decided not to stay in New York, missing me. She found a house for rent on a Greek island and we sublet our apartment.

Along the *Malecón*, waves crashed against the jagged limestone, sending a fine spray of salt over the seawall onto the passing traffic. A lone, brown pelican cruised above the waterline, following the curve of the roadway, while tiny crabs scurried in the seaweed. Two fishermen walked by wearing short-sleeved wetsuits rolled down to the waist and carrying spearguns, flippers, and a solid string of snapper. The *Malecón* is a spectacular collision of city and sea. On one side of the wall swim bathers who know from years of experience just where to climb over and safely enter the water; on the other side rise the teeming warrens of Centro Habana, blocks and blocks of crumbling apartment buildings that divide the historic old port district from the Vedado.

Farther along the *Malecón*, a young guy in a shredded red golf shirt and greasy brown leather baseball cap caught up with me. "D'donevye?" he said. His accent was so heavy that I was unsure what language he was speaking. Since I had been told that no foreigner walks two blocks in Cuba without someone asking, "Where are you from," I guessed that this was the question.

"Estados Unidos," I answered. He gave a broad smile, shook my hand with enthusiasm and said something else unintelligible. He sounded as though he spoke through a mouthful of large ball bearings. After I begged him to repeat himself three or four times, I understood that his brother lived in Hialeah. A few more blocks established that he was a *pulpo* fisherman who fished the harbor, and that his brother had sent him the baseball cap he was wearing a year and a half ago. It had a large metal plaque on the front that read, "Boy of London." He seemed eager to know about the outside world.

"Is it true," he asked, "that this same model of cap is now available in white leather?"

When I let myself back into Miriam's, I found her on her knees on the granite floor, lighting a candle with a butane stove lighter. She murmured a prayer and then dribbled a few drops of wax onto the ground to hold the candle firm. Being a solid woman, with no apparent muscle, getting up off the floor seemed rather a chore.

"How was it?" she asked.

"Nice. I walked down by the water."

"I didn't expect you back so soon. I was just going to do a little sorcery in the house."

"You were? Are you a *santera*?" Miriam had struck me as a sort of sedate domestic type. She was also white. I realized I had a racist preconception that she would not know about anything so exciting and African as *Santería*.

"I hope to 'make my saint' this year, but it's very expensive."*

A little glass table held a bowl of something like cake batter. Next to it was a rock of talc. "What's that for?"

"It's for a purification ceremony, for my prosperity in the business with my house."

Upon closer inspection, the mixture looked more like spoiled milk, with a pasty solid mass floating on top. "What's in it?"

"Aha!" she said. "You look red and white to me, but I see already that you have a dark side, a black interest in witchcraft." I presumed she was referring to my red Irish beard and rosy English complexion. "It has seawater, crushed chalk—you can use eggshells if you don't have any chalk—indigo, perfume, *aguardiente*, *vino seco*, milk, and one egg white," Miriam explained, as if we were on the set of a cooking show. She said that she was going to spread this concoction around the corners of the apartment with *lengua de vaca*, cow's tongues, the long spatulate leaves of the common ornamental houseplant. I wondered what effect it might have on the vague odor of mildew in my room.

"Isn't religion sort of frowned upon by the government?" I asked.

Miriam explained that she had only been a believer for about five years and that, until recently, overt expression of religious belief had been a career-stopper, unacceptable for a member of the party faithful like herself.

---

* *Hacer su santo*, undergo the *Santería* initiation process.

She had been an atheist and a "militante del partido," a party militant, who had gone into the countryside in the early 1960s as part of the massive literacy campaign, one of the teenagers and students who went out from the cities to teach reading and writing to crusty old farmers and laborers who had never been inside a classroom. Things had changed since the implosion of the Soviet Union. Miriam said that there was no longer any reason for the Cuban government to toe the international communist line on religion. "Because of the necessities that one feels now, the tendency is to grow closer to religion," she said, referring to the so-called *período especial en tiempo de paz*, "the special period in peacetime"—or, more commonly, *período especial*, "special period" of austerity and revolutionary sacrifice that has continued unbroken since the Soviet Union collapsed.

Miriam dashed my hopes that she was about to collect up some leaves and start spreading batter around the apartment, saying that she planned to do the purifying the next day. She turned on the television, and we watched *Palmas y cañas* (*Palms and canefields*), a sort of musical revue for country folk that offers hefty women in cowboy boots belting out rootsy Cuban favorites for a geriatric studio audience. The Sunday evening program aims to recreate the ambiance of a kind of Cuban jug-band hoedown known as a *guateque,* at which oldtimers used to gather at the close of market-day for a little *décima* poetry, music, and spit-roasted pig. The smiling, white-haired series audience sang along and clapped primly after each number. Between acts, a male-female presenter duo traded feeble banter in front of a backdrop reminiscent of a high-school pageant. The program is about as unhip as television can get—the grand finale and highlight is a poetry competition in which a couple of poets backed by a twelve-stringed lute take turns trading mild rhyming insults and tame double entendres. With an arrogant, media-savvy smirk, I declared it the greatest show ever produced. Miriam replied that she thought it was pretty much a program for hicks and rubes but that her father was a legendary *decimista* and *laúd* player from Havana province. Sensing a journalistic opportunity, I said I wanted to meet him. Would it be all right if I stopped and visited him on my walk from Pinar del Río?

Dos

Those first tentative steps

Tengo de todo en mi estancia,	On my ranch I've got it all,
aves, ganado, lechones,	fowl, cattle, plenty of porkers
muchos potros redomones,	a whole lot of half-wild colts,
mucha vianda en abundancia	vegetables, abundant crops
cuido con perseverancia	I guard my farm with perseverance
mi finca desde temprano	rising in the early morn
y en mi bohío de guano	and in my humble thatched hut
respiro y vivo sabroso	I live and breathe easy
porque me siento orgulloso	because I feel most proud to be
con ser guajiro cubano.	called a Cuban *guajiro*.
—Clavelito, *Soy Guajiro*	

Four or five *Pinareños* leaned over a low, chainlink fence, waving business cards at me as I got off the bus in Pinar del Río. The few other passengers remained on board to continue on to Viñales across the mountains, and I found myself standing in the depot surrounded by urgent offers of hospitality. Pickings were slim for the *casa particular* proprietors of Pinar del Río. I announced that I already had a place to stay, *muchísimas gracias*, but one woman was so desperate and upset after yet another wasted and humiliating trip to the bus station that I took her card anyway, with the feeble promise that, if I didn't like the house I was going to, I would not hesitate to come by.

"How much are you paying at the address you have?" The bus had already pulled out of the terminal but she was still holding a handful of business cards like a tiny fan. "Mine is much cheaper," she went on, although I had not answered. "It has air conditioning." I wrestled with the backpack, finally managing to hoist it onto my back. "I make an excellent breakfast," she called out, making her final plea as I headed for the exit.

A friend who had been to Pinar del Río a few months before, had recommended the house of Laura Valdes, a few scorching blocks' walk along the main street. Halfway up the dark stairway to the second-story home was an ominous chainlink gate like that of a Bowery flophouse, but, once buzzed in, I found myself in a comfortable and huge living room, every inch of the wall covered in bookshelves of dark wood.

"There are 50,000 volumes," said Laura. "My late grandfather's collection; it may be the largest private library in Cuba."

"It's incredible," I said. "They were like vultures down at the bus station. There must not be very many tourists."

"It's terrible," she said. "I hate it when I have to go there and look for travelers, but I am just starting with this business. Sometimes you have nobody, and you still have to pay the tax at the beginning of the month, guests or no guests. *No es fácil.*" It's not easy. After only a few days, I already recognized this phrase as a Cuban mantra, an all-purpose equal-opportunity summary of life's hardships.

The late Dr. Batlle had been an inveterate world traveler and keeper of scrapbooks: an entire wall of the library was filled with bound collections of periodicals and clippings, many stored in homemade files made from boxes that had once held Kodak and Agfa X-ray film. The Kodak boxes dated his collections to the period before the embargo. The labels on the boxes read: "Painters of England #1"; "Africa"; "First World War"; and "Deserts and Dry Areas." He had been a man who kept tabs on the world.

An Australian construction worker, on a cycling holiday, was just leaving. He had bicycled west along the north coast and down from Viñales. "Any pointers?" I asked. "Did you have any problems out there?"

"I don't speak a word of Spanish," he said, "and there are no signs anywhere, that's probably the worst thing. But the people are fantastic. They think you're mad, of course, but the moment you stop, people come out and offer to fill up your water bottles."

"I'm leaving tomorrow morning to walk to Viñales."

"What, on foot? I don't much fancy that, mate. Well, drink lots of water, it's hot like hell out there and it just pours off you. On the bicycle, I've been drinking seven or eight liters a day."

I went to my room to fuss with my backpack. I had the vague notion that if I distributed the weight carefully in the pack, I would barely notice I had the thing on. As soon as everything was unpacked and spread out on the bed, however, I felt overwhelmed and lay down on my back surrounded by piles of clothes and socks, a hammock, a mosquito net, film, cameras, a water filter, maps, and an ambitious quantity of blank notebooks. I was badly depressed. I stared up at the ceiling. The room was what I had hoped to find on my first day in Havana, with bizarre quasi-antique built-in wood furniture and tall, tall windows that opened like narrow cathedral doors onto little railings over the street. The headboard of the bed held infinite tiny drawers and on a side table was an ancient Ilmenau tube radio with a deco panel that offered the "K-band" of channels. When I switched it on, a tiny lamp slowly illuminated to a soft and dusty green, although it was impossible to coax any sound out of the radio.

I went out for couple of beers at the bar down the street to cheer me up. A red light bulb screwed into the bottom of an ineffectual ceiling fan cast its dim glow on a scene of such institutionalized squalor that I was forced to abandon my cherished belief that, of all the earth's citizens, I am the very weariest and most downtrodden of all. The only other patrons were four dejected, stubbly tobacco-workers grafted onto their stools, hands curled permanently around their glasses. To lift their drinks and even to take a sip was an onerous, joyless task. They drank *aguardiente*, a cheap cane liquor dispensed by a barmaid who would have seemed sad and ruined in any other context but came across as positively bubbly compared with the rest of this bar's inhabitants. She poured grimy glasses of the clear liquid out of an old plastic gallon jug that might once have held cooking oil. A small blackboard listed cheap poisons in smeared chalk. Other clients came in with various to-go containers, old plastic Pepsi bottles, and pre-owned rum flasks for the barmaid to refill. From somewhere in the dingy recesses of the adjoining *comedor* blasted, with vicious intensity, the worst sort of energetic British dance pop, complete with senseless chipmunk vocals. Nobody paid the slightest attention to the deafening music or to each other or to the stranger in their midst, and we all liked it that way.

I went to bed early in preparation for the big day, the debut of my epic hike. Sleep did not come easily. It was Saturday night. Reveling couples and mufflerless motorcycles passed under the window. Mosquitos hummed at my ears and drank my blood. I got up, balanced the oscillating fan on a chair, and turned it on full, pointed straight at my chest. This cyclone was too much for the mosquitos, but, within moments, I was freezing to death, huddled in a ball in my lone sheet, teeth chattering in the balmy tropical climate. I am 6'4" tall and 225 pounds, statistics that are not out of place on a *Monday Night Football* broadcast, and the hardier vampires soon discovered how to avoid the fan's gust by drifting up from the leeward side of the bed into my considerable wind shadow and darting in to suck at my back through the sheet, like swallows drinking from a pond.

In order to get an early start, I had crammed everything back in the pack before going to bed, but I now dragged myself up and pulled out the mosquito net again, scattering the remaining contents on the floor. After years untouched on the "camping shelf" at home, the net was fusty with mildew. The new coil of utility cord bought at a camping store collapsed in my hands in a tangled mess of knots, but, hopping and swatting, I at last managed to construct a lopsided grid across the room, attaching cord to various shutters, a nail, a picture hook, and a doorknob while the mosquitos honed in on my shins. I tied the net to this web of string with great care, but, as I lifted the edge to crawl back into bed, a nail pulled out of the wall and the entire mess collapsed.

I fought a mounting, hysterical fury. Tucking the mosquito net under one side of the mattress and lying along the extreme edge of the other side created a semblance of sanctuary. The mosquitos whined disconsolate on the other side of the mushroom-scented barrier. As I felt sleep finally starting to descend, a rooster crowed from the rooftop next door. It was morning.

"How did you sleep?" asked Laura, coming in to see what I wanted for breakfast. When she saw the aviary of ropes and netting crisscrossing the room, she burst into laughter. She marched over to the headboard.

"Why didn't you just use this?" she asked, producing a tiny electronic plug-in mosquito repellant from one of the hundreds of little drawers.

Hiking along the road out of town to the turnoff to Viñales, I saw bicycles everywhere. Most had a large plastic milk crate mounted over the back wheel and a heavy load of something. One carried a stack of bricks; another had a small chest of drawers strapped to the back rack. Not a single person was walking, but one curious guy stopped riding his bike and walked it along beside me for a while.

"Difficult to get a car to Viñales at this late hour," he commented. I hadn't left quite as bright and early as I had hoped.

"I'm walking," I pointed out.

"What, you don't want a taxi?"

"Then I wouldn't be able to meet people like you and have a chance to talk with them." *Real authentic Cubans.* He considered this for a moment.

"Estás loco," he said. You're crazy. "But good luck, anyway." He rode off.

At the crossroads, a dozen people were lounging on the grass in the shade, waiting for rides up and over the mountain. They looked at me as if at an apparition as I waved, turning the corner and hiking away from the city. A green and white sign (exactly like the road signs in the United States) said: "Viñales 25km." The sun was already quite high in the sky, but I felt I was moving along well and it seemed that only moments had passed when I reached another sign: "Viñales 22km." I realized the whole proposition was going to be much easier than I had thought.

I passed tiny three-room wooden houses with front porches just big enough for a rocking chair or two, and seedlings sprouting in old tin cans out front. Most had corrugated iron roofs, but a few were still tiled, Spanish-style, with baked orange clay. One front yard full of seeded wildflowers had a yellow-faced grassquit singing its buzzy little reel from among patches of purple, orange, yellow, and maroon flowers that shifted in the breeze. It was much flatter than the map suggested and I kept expecting the road to start its inevitable slope up toward the mountain pass.

The shoulder straps on the backpack began to chafe. I decided to take my first rest. I drank an entire liter of water with no trouble at all, slathered myself with sunblock, and got out my towel and tucked it under my baseball cap in the manner of a Foreign Legionnaire, to protect against the relentless sun. It was unpleasant putting the pack back on, but I managed to get back underway. Around the next bend, I came to another road sign: "Viñales 23km."

Down the road, a woman was sweeping the dirt in front of a low white house constructed of rough-hewn boards. "Ven, ven," she called to me. "Come, sit down and drink a coffee." Her name was Nieves. She was in her sixties, but strong, as if she had never stopped working all her life. We went around back and she introduced me to her daughter, Betty, and grandson, Adrian, who was about four. He was sitting under a tree in the dust, buck-naked. A little piglet was tied to the tree and a few chickens were scraping around. At the end of the yard was an outhouse on the brink of collapse. Beyond that, the yard gradually merged into swamp.

Nieves brought me a coffee, half an inch of black, sweet liquid in the bottom of a glass. "What a beautiful towel," she said. "It's a marvel." It was one of those small, badly printed squares that one buys for $1.99 on the boardwalk after arriving at the beach and discovering that the towels have been left at home. She took me by the arm and led me to the family towel, a gray threadbare rag hanging on the clothesline. It was more holes than fabric.

"Very expensive," she said. "These things, clothes, soap, everything, has to be paid for in dollars." Nieves fingered her tanktop, which had once had a touch of embroidery around the collar but was now stained and almost as full of holes as the towel. "Food is no problem, but our clothes are falling off our bodies. Here, have a banana. Would you like a plate of *ajiaco*? You must be hungry. We just killed a pig recently."

I could barely fit inside the house, but I sat down and enjoyed the rich stew, thick pork gravy full of chunks of malanga and plantain that Nieves served with white rice. In the living room was an ancient Soviet television. A stylized portrait of Fidel hung on the wall.

"Delicious food," I said.

"*Sabroso*, fresh pig meat," said Nieves.

I got up and stood in the doorway. Out in the yard, Adrian had a firm grip on his little wiener and was carefully spraying a fine stream of toddler marinade.up and down the back of the piglet tied to the tree.

I wish now that I had given Nieves the towel, which was later stolen from me in Ciego de Ávila, but the first lunch of the first day of the walk seemed no time to be giving things away. Instead, I pressed a dollar into her hands and dug out my bar of Ivory soap and cut it in two and gave her half. She seemed very pleased. "Maybe you could send me the towel when you get to Guantánamo," she said.

The hills began not far beyond her house. The smallholdings and tiny farmhouses with their patchwork fields petered out and gave way to scrub oak and brush growing on steep slopes. The earth was brick red. The sensation I had been having earlier, that my ankles had been struck with hammers until shattered, migrated upward, settling in my knees, which twinged bitterly at the climb. Here, the few oncoming cyclists rushing down the hill were going too fast to safely lift a hand off their handlebars. Instead of waving, they gave a whistle and a little sideways dance of the head in greeting as they flew by. Jagged clumps of white limestone thrust out of the land, and soon there were pines, the *pinares* for which the province is named, scattered across the hillsides. I began to see wilderness birds that only live in forests of quality, avoiding man, like the brilliant turquoise and blue red-legged honeycreeper, with a velvet black upper back and flashes of yellow under the wings.

Near the top of the pass the view behind me was magnificent. Beyond the foot of the rolling hills were a vast lake and a hint of the city. The Caribbean Sea was just visible at the farthest edge of the hazy horizon, more imagined than real. To the east, the Sierra grew fiercer and steeper, while an unbroken vista of pine-clad hills stretched to the west. A mint black Studebaker glided down the mountain road. I felt a tremendous sense of personal accomplishment. I had walked all of fifteen kilometers.

Over the top of the ridge on the last curve down into Viñales, I found another spectacular view of fields, farms, and the oddly shaped limestone towers called *mogotes* that make this valley so picturesque. Like miniature buttes, dozens of these bulbous natural sculptures rise without warning from the flat valley floor. I stopped to take a photograph of the landscape and down my last half-liter of water on a little spur of weedy field above the valley. Tobacco drying sheds, majestic palms, and green hedgerows sliced up the red and brown patchwork of fields. Small footpaths wound from one farmhouse to the next. North Florida might have looked like this a hundred years ago.

Beside me a *guajiro* was driving his pair of oxen out onto the road, pulling a wooden sled piled high with the local sweet potato called *batata*. He sang to his beasts of burden as he turned up the hill, and gave me a subtle nod of greeting. Moments later, there was a screeching of brakes. I thought he had been hit. Out on the road, a passenger van had stopped suddenly. A handful of tourists were scrambling out of the car as if at a game park. Cameras in hand, they jogged up the hill alongside the oxen, snapping away at the bemused farmer like *paparazzi*.

The *guajiro* is a Cuban icon, a noble peasant who works and lives off the land. A quasi-mythological archetype much like the American cowboy, the Argentine *gaucho*, or the Puerto Rican *jibaro*, he is a man more comfortable out in the fields chatting to his animals than in the company of city slickers and fast talkers. In a country where seventy percent of the population lives in cities and towns, the *guajiro* is the ultimate rural guardian of the revolution. The *guajiro* was once white, but, in today's Cuban consciousness, the image typifies the racial mixture essential to the new national identity: part Spanish, part black African, and perhaps even some strains of the pre-Columbian Taíno Indian. This first true *criollo* son of the island poured his sweat into the soil, carving pastures and canefields out of jungle and thorn. He dripped his blood onto the battlefields of both revolutions, first when Spain was vanquished and then when Castro and his *barbudos*, the bearded ones, sent the traitorous dictator Fulgencio Batista running to Miami.

In the United States, where the Marlboro Man is under attack as a corrupter of children and the Wild West has long ago been fenced into submission, the closest thing that remains of the romantic ideal of the cowboy is a rodeo star who flies light planes and buys a new F-150 pickup truck every other year. In Cuba, however, the *guajiro* lives on, plucking tobacco off his own bushes for a quick home-rolled smoke, conversing with his cows, and shimmying up the all-providing Royal palm trunk to collect *palmiche* berries to feed the sow, or cut fresh fronds to thatch his *bohío*. When out weeding the bean patch, he still wears the olive-drab shirt of the revolutionary soldier, farming in fatigues, ready to leap into battle at any moment.

I walked down the hill into Viñales. The town has been earmarked by the government as a tourist destination, and at least every third house along the tree-lined main street displayed the blue and white sign on the door indicating a state-licensed room for rent. A town of three short streets, Viñales has ninety *casas particulares*. It looked a charming place, but I had walked myself into exhaustion. I found bed and dinner with a warm but reserved couple, showered, and collapsed.

The next day, I hiked all morning through forest and limestone hills, walking east on a well-worn path devoid of people. I watched birds and wondered where all the Cubans that I had planned on sharing the road with were. Finally, I reached San Andrés, a village the size of Viñales, but with none of the shady colonial charm of the latter's pine-lined main boulevard. It was early afternoon; I had made excellent time, but my feet were an agony of blisters. It was impossible to imagine walking farther. In contrast to the glut of visitor housing in Viñales, however, San Andrés offered no lodging of any kind.

"That's a Viñales thing," said one man, emerging out of the shady interior of his house in response to my question about looking for a place to stay. "We don't have that here." Across the street, three guys sprawled on the ground under a tree in a little schoolyard waved me over. They were very drunk and too friendly for the cautious town of San Andrés.

"Have a drink. What you looking for? A room?" said one, sloshing some *aguardiente* into the jagged bottom third of an old beer can and lifting it up to me. "How much you gonna pay?"

I said it was maybe a little early for a drink. All I wanted to do was dump my pack, take my boots off, and have a look at my feet. "How much would you charge?"

He got up unsteadily and shook the dust off, ready to talk business.

"Fifteen *fula*. With food."

I had never heard the word *fula* before, but my would-be host had a take-it-or-leave-it delivery like a hardened gangster selling a carton of cigarettes in a prison film. Renting a room without a license was a criminal enterprise, and he wanted to be sure to convey that he was the right man for the job. I imagined spending the rest of the afternoon and evening with these worthies, as they got more and more bold and amicable and drunk.

"Thanks, but I was really hoping to get a few more kilometers under my belt before calling it a day," I said. My feet were raw cubes of flesh. I plodded joylessly onward.

By the time I got to Cayo Hueso, I was resigned to sneaking off into the woods, slinging the hammock between two trees, and dining on a tin of sardines, but after spending the entire morning hiking in complete isolation past dozens of excellent campsites, I now could see nothing but houses. In fact, San Andrés and Cayo Hueso seemed to be one long town stretching without end in a strip along the road. Finally, I stopped a woman and turned to shameless hinting.

Marixa was sturdy and square-shouldered. She spoke with me for a long time, assessing various options and inviting passersby into the dialogue to see what we could come up with, but she was really assessing me. It was already clear to me that my demonstrating the desire to walk even as far as the next corner indicated a severely troubled personality. Every tourist was correctly perceived to have unimaginable riches. Most sensibly drove about in rented cars or hired drivers. What's more, as an American,

I came from the land of serial killers, a country where, Cuban television constantly pointed out, armed prepubescents made a daily routine out of spraying the halls of their schools with automatic weapons-fire. I protested that I didn't want to take a car or a bus to a nearby town where there might be a hotel.

"I think I understand," said Marixa, after we had been talking for ten minutes. "You actually enjoy walking." The dam had broken. "My sister's husband died two months ago, suddenly. So my mother moved in with her. I'm on my way to visit them right now. My mother's house is just sitting empty; we'll ask if you can use it. If not, you can come to my place and put your hammock in the yard."

We walked through little alleys between cinderblock houses and along the edge of a small field. It was simultaneously densely populated and rural; small yards butted back to back, each with a handful of rows of vegetables.

The house was full of women. Marixa's mother, Señora Toledo, had a badly infected left leg that was swollen from just below the knee down to her ankle. She wore a cracked white plastic sneaker on her bad foot and a black canvas hightop with a purple puffy sock on the other. Marixa's older sister, Migdalia, the recent widow, was wiry and tough, with short-cropped hair. She clearly ran the show, but now, in her time of need, the house had filled with supportive characters. A very pregnant neighbor sat in the living room with another cousin who lived in a house nearby. There was a brief conference while I stayed out on the porch and then suddenly everyone was bringing me things and sitting me down and telling one another to get the bathroom ready for me to bathe. They gave me gritty bread from the *libreta*, the monthly government ration book. The bread was smeared with hot, oily tomato paste. A *refresco*, flat and incredibly sweet, was a homemade cola infusion with half an inch of undissolved sugar at the bottom of the glass.

Marixa said she had to leave or she would miss the only *guagua* to Entronque la Palma, and Migdalia took me over to her mother's old house, all of fifty feet away. She showed me how to wedge boards up against the wooden shutters from the inside so that nobody could open them in the night, as there was no glass in the windows. The house had three white-washed rooms, with one shelf unit made out of a few boards and some cinderblocks and a sheet of plywood for a table. She demonstrated how to lock the door, by twisting a bent nail to latch with another one that was nailed into the doorframe, and pointed out the outhouse in a corner of the yard.

While I was stringing my hammock up across the living room, they brought over a fluorescent tube for the ceiling and an ancient industrial fan, the most terrifying appliance I had ever seen. The motor had been pirated from some kind of light industrial lathe or other woodworking tool, the blades had no cage around them, and there was no plug, just two stripped wires that Migdalia suggested I jam directly into the slots in the wall socket. I was sure that it was the only fan between the two households and I felt overwhelmed by their hospitality and kindness toward me.

"You rest, and when you want your bath, come over to the house," said Migdalia, and they went out and left me, thankful to be alone with my feet.

In the morning, Señor Toledo arrived. Having heard the news that a gringo visitor had stopped down at his ex-wife's place, he wanted to see for himself. I was busy taking goodbye pictures of all the ladies posed on their porch, a large production that involved everyone changing into their best clothes. He tied up his horse nearby, but didn't approach the house, and Señora Toledo immediately went inside without greeting him. It was an uncomfortable situation.

"Migdalia, Migdalia, come have a picture taken with me," he said, calling to his daughter. I avoided him, angered that he thought that I should take his picture. Where had he been the night before when the *señora* he had abandoned was cooking me a huge meal of beans and rice and serving me her infrequent meat ration? Señor Toledo was a classic *guajiro*, a barrel-chested guy in a battered straw cowboy hat and a long-sleeved khaki-green army shirt. As nobody was inviting him up onto the porch, I finally asked him where he wanted his picture taken.

"Con la yegua," he said. With the horse. The photograph shows Migdalia and Señor Toledo on either side of his horse. Migdalia looks grim. Señor Toledo stands upright and proud, holding the reins, his hand on the back of the horse's neck, his face obscured by a patch of morning haze or a flare on the camera's lens.

The red soil around Cayo Hueso is prime tobacco-growing country. Heading overland back toward the mountains and La Güira, I walked through fields of fragrant leaf. The sweet smell seeped out from big drying barns, drifting over the land in elusive pockets of scent. These big triangular peaked barns, really just two roofs leaning together in a squat A-frame, held tons of leaf hanging and waiting to be turned into the world's most famous cigars.

The fertile bowls of tobacco land nestled among the *mogotes* soon gave way to the mountains as I headed south again, climbing a steep ridge that circled a massive limestone bluff. For more than an hour, the view to my left was of this looming, craggy outcrop, white rock stained and streaked with orange smears, and pockmarked with holes and caves. It was too hot even for the vultures, which, instead of soaring around the peak, sat draped over bare trees in ungainly lumps like wind-snagged garbage bags. At the very top, in a pine forest of the tallest trees I had seen yet, the altitude almost eased the heat. I followed up a turning to the left marked "Centro Turistico," to an abandoned and forlorn handful of decrepit cabins in the forest, where a young Dutch couple was sitting on a log eating cheese. They were staying in San Diego de los Baños and touring the area on brand-new bicycles, one towing a trailer with their baby daughter nestled in it. I said I hoped to see them later in town. They said I had a long way to go yet; in fact, it was another five and a half hours' walk down the mountain. By the time I got there, my feet were so raw that even when I knew I was close, one or two kilometers before reaching San Diego, I had to stop and take off my boots and socks and stand undignified, massaging my toes by the roadside.

"De los Baños" means "of the baths" and San Diego was reputed to be rather like a Cuban version of Lourdes or the spa at Evian, a relaxing town where one went to "take the waters" for a spell. As the day's grueling walk dragged on, I envisioned the sulfur baths of San Diego as an earthly paradise for the feet, which, when dipped in the magical waters, would be healed, restored, and even strengthened. I decided to take my first day off from the eastward march and spend it lounging in steaming pools at the foot of the mountains. The very thought of it gave me strength as I limped into town. At a tiny hotel across from the baths, Adelaida and Alfredo, a septuagenarian couple from the city of Pinar del Río, were staying in one of the rooms for their annual two-week cure. The proprietor, Julio, said the "hollandeses con bicicletas" were staying in another. Julio had run the place as a guesthouse for bathers since "before the triumph of the revolution." His wife was away, in the middle of a five-month trip to Miami to visit their son, Julio Jr.

Julio's living room doubled as the dining room and lounge for the guests. The television was permanently on. I sat with Adelaida on a ruined green couch. She had been to Miami twice to visit her sister and quite liked it, she said. Last January 12, she had gone for the interview to get her third visa, but, on the twenty-eighth, she had received a phone call from Florida to say that her sister had died, so she didn't go.

"The one place I would really like to go before I die is Spain," she said. "Just to see it. It is unjust, everything needs dollars, but unless someone is sending them to you, you can't get any."

"No es fácil," I said, trying to commiserate like a Cuban.

On television, a reporter stated that the Group of 77 was meeting in Havana and cut to Castro talking about the problems of the Third World in the face of globalization. He illustrated the gross over-consumption of the United States with some statistics and called for varying gasoline prices in different countries to reflect a disparity in per capita income of over 500-fold between the richest and poorest countries. By the time Fidel began a convincing attack on neoliberalism, I had forgotten I was watching the news.

On some nights, Castro is the news. He does not speak in sound bites, and sometimes hours go by before the newscaster reappears onscreen. One evening broadcast I saw consisted of Castro delivering, in its entirety, a speech almost three hours long. At the very end, after some final shots of Fidel acknowledging the crowd and descending from the podium, there was a cut back to an archetypal newsdesk and a reporter who simply said, "That's the news for today."

In the morning, I did laundry and watched lizards. There were at least four or five different varieties in Julio's yard. Back by his little laundry shed was a pile of junk lumber overgrown with weeds, and lizards were everywhere. One was a rich and dusty dark brown with the tail, probably regrown after some earlier narrow escape, tacked on like an afterthought. The tail spiraled laterally as if it had grown sideways, and the lizard did pushups off its splayed front feet, alternately pumping the tail and flexing its dewlap, a huge white disk round and flat as a knife-blade, out from its throat. I saw a slim, fine-featured, pale-green lizard with a cream stripe down the spine, and one jet-black, very shy, with impossibly long toes, leaning timidly around the corners of the logs. Another, at least eight inches long, had a long and narrow head, pointy and snakelike. Bright green, grading to blue on the forehead, it leaped from the vertical concrete wall onto an old chunk of pipe and slowly rusted, melting into its background before my eyes.

In the afternoon, I went to take the waters with Mark, Mariska, and Vera, the Dutch family. The baths were in a building with an oppressive, institutional feel, like an American elementary school of the 1960s. The vast complex offered acupuncture, massage, steam rooms, and hydrotherapy. We sat in a lounge full of wicker armchairs waiting to check in, feeling rather as if we were in a hospital. Instead of "No Smoking" signs, each table held a life-size ceramic sculpture of the lungs of a smoker, glazed in vile olive and eggplant hues and spouting a variety of severed tubes. Beside it was a matching ashtray.

A nurse led us down a spiral ramp deep into the ground. The stench of sulfur grew stronger the farther we descended into the earth. The vague sense of being in a hospital gelled into the certainty that we were in an asylum. Soon the walls were blistered and peeling from the onslaught of the humid fumes. Many stories down, there was a small version of the upstairs lounge with more wicker furniture. We were handed off to another nurse-like attendant who told us that the men and women would have to bathe in different areas.

Mark and I changed in a huge, sodden subterranean changing room crowded with gray lockers and booths made of glass brick before descending still farther into the baths themselves. The room was steamy and dim with tall walls painted ochre. I had lost track of how far underground we were. There were three tiled swimming pools, one with a foamy slick of sulfurous scum on the top, one empty, and the largest milky white. A male attendant stood watch over the pools, although there was only one other man in the bath, holding his swollen ankle up to the spigot where the water poured in. The woman who had brought us went away saying she would be back in fifteen minutes, the maximum time permitted. Although we seemed to be at the center of the earth, the water was sadly not hot enough to leach away the muscle fatigue and bruises on the balls of my feet. But the sulfur was narcotic. After a few minutes soaking in the water, the institutional oppression was forgotten; the thought softly crept into my mind that the attendant was there to make certain that the bathers didn't relax into mush and dissolve in the pool.

Our warden returned in what seemed like no time.

"That was never fifteen minutes," I mumbled, dragging myself out of the pool. Getting changed and going back up to the lobby was like trying to push an enormous mound of jello up a mountain.

Tres

Neither here nor there

Tu Amor es un periodico de ayer (Your love is like yesterday's newspaper)
—Tite Curet Alonso

Walking is for losers, I thought. After marching only a kilometer, the balm of San Diego's subterranean hot springs was already a distant memory. Blisters and ankle pains were again tweaking my resolve, and I was looking for a nice place to take an early rest when a man pulled alongside driving a two-wheeled wagon pulled by a harnessed horse. "Subete," he said. Climb up.

I wavered, but only for a moment. In the five years since first having the malformed idea to walk across Cuba, I had often imagined myself basking in glory as I told of how I had walked every step of the way. Now, I quickly revised my description to include the timeless elegance of a horse-and-buggy ride. Negotiating the one little metal rung in front of the wheel took me so long that I thought the man was going to retract his offer. As I clambered up to the seat, the lopsided, top-heavy backpack almost yanked me backward onto the bed of the wagon. The horse shifted uneasily, sensing the incompetent extra weight thrashing around behind him. Serafim and his son, Juan, were on their way to take care of Serafim's father at the old family house. As we clip-clopped along, Serafim told me he was sixty-four years old, one of ten brothers. His father was ninety and his youngest sister twenty-eight. He nodded with raised eyebrows while I did the math.

The sister nearest Serafim's age lived in Miami. She had abandoned

Cuba soon after the revolution. "Aqui está mejor," he said. It's better here. "We have tranquility. Money is difficult, but I've got my horse, I've got my wagon, *yo resuelvo mis problemas.*"*

I was beginning to understand the extraordinary amount of space that Miami occupies in the collective Cuban mind. The city is the focus of disgust mixed with longing, home to counterrevolutionary traitors who also happen to be beloved sisters and sons and uncles, a land of violence and depravity that provides desperately needed dollars. On Cuban television, the nightly propaganda assault against the morals, values, and leaders of the grotesque city and nation looming just to the north prevented anyone who might have wished not to think of Miami from ever forgetting about it; the city was portrayed as the source and root of all of Cuba's problems, dating back at least to the Bay of Pigs. It was a place of horrifying evil, engraved by propaganda onto the souls of all Cubans. Alternately, it was where your brother, daughter, or best friend lived. The barrage of official negativity was softened and contradicted by visiting long-lost cousins, its credibility eroded by grandmothers coming back from visiting their grandchildren— senior citizens, their role in the economy complete, were among the only Cubans who could easily obtain the necessary permission to visit the US and return—until the constant, contradictory conceptions of a universally mythologized Miami developed into a national schizophrenia.

Once adjusted to my extra weight, the horse pulled the cart fast and steady along the pavement, and we soon arrived at the crossroads with the old *carretera central*, once the automotive spine of Cuba. I dropped down to the ground. Serafim turned off and headed down a dirt track, waving goodbye. On the fourth day of my hike, I had sold myself out for a two-kilometer lift.

Walking along the *central* was a marked contrast to the solitude of the mountains. Like the roads I had followed over the *cordillera*, it had very little traffic, but there were houses all along it and many people in the road to greet and wave to. Once they had lived beside the busiest road in Cuba, the lone highway reaching from one end of the country to the other, but

---

* The verb *resolver* has a very particular connotation in the Cuba of the post-Soviet era. It means to solve, or to resolve, to find a solution or way out of a bind or problem. Cubans use it constantly, and it sometimes (but by no means always) implies the kind of mutual backscratching that allows society to function outside the confines of the regime, suggesting barter or storing away a favor for later use.

a superhighway had replaced it for almost half its distance and, like some stranded segment of Route 66, it felt abandoned and forgotten.

I passed the Maxim Gorki Rural School and the Yuri Gagarin Goose Farm. Down the road, Frederico Valverde caught up with me. He had just gotten off a truck from Los Palacios out on the *autopista* and was walking home. He was the first Cuban I had met who didn't think that my walking was symptomatic of a grave mental illness.

"Oh, *Estados Unidos*," he said, "you come from the land of Lincoln, Martin Luther King, Malcolm *Equis*, and George Washington! Lots of beautiful history to your country. *Me gusta mucho bilal y sus cometas!*"

"What?"

"*Beelaylee, beelaylee*, you must know about him."

I finally understood that he was talking about Bill Haley and his Comets. Frederico had fought in Ethiopia and had chunks of a landmine in his knee and thigh from two tours of combat duty in Angola. Cuba has sent troops to wars I've never heard of. He took me to his house a bit off the highway and gave me a *chirimoya*, a misshapen fruit of the custard apple family that looks like a pale squashed soursop but is sweet as candy. I set to eating the flesh, which tastes like gritty *crème caramel*, spooning it out like an avocado, as Frederico rushed around the yard, collecting an armful of mangos and several kilos of grapefruits for me to take on the road. I had known him all of five minutes, but when I set off down the road again, I was laden with fruit. "Ya tu sabes," he called out to me. "Now you know, if you ever come by this way again, you got a place to stay and all the fruit you can eat."

After a few more kilometers of plodding along the old central highway, I arrived in El Fierro. On the map, it looked like a town, but it was nothing more than a minor crossroads along the central highway. A faint breeze blew puffs of red dust over the road but did nothing to relieve the extraordinary heat. I took off my pack and leaned it against a little sandwich shack. I bought a slice of ham on dry rounds of white bread and a *refresco de fresa*—cold, red sugarwater of no particular flavor. On the other side of the road was an open-air bar selling fingers of rum to a handful of daytime drinkers shaded from the sun by a narrow awning. All eyes were on me, and I experienced that cliché moment from a western, when the stranger rides into town. I pulled on my hat and hoisted the pack back up onto my shoulders. As I was cinching the waistbelt tight, disaster struck. I heard a horrible sharp, cracking sound, and the plastic buckle broke cleanly in half. "This is very bad," I said in Spanish, as much to myself as to the lady in the sandwich hut. I plodded down the highway, like a wounded dog slinking off into the bush. With no waistbelt, it was only minutes before I could feel every last grapefruit, notebook, and pair of socks cutting twin furrows into my shoulders. I stopped by the side of the road to think things over.

When Lázaro and Papito stopped and offered me a ride to the outskirts of San Cristóbal, I didn't hesitate. Papito thought it was hilarious that I was breaking my back walking around Cuba. He was a big, beefy, outspoken guy with sunburned biceps. He said right away that he had put his name in for a visa at the American interests section. Twenty thousand US visas are raffled off each year in the visa lottery known everywhere in Cuba as *el bombo.* "If I lived up there, I would sure as hell never come here to 'walk around,'" he said, incredulous. We were bouncing along in a huge orange tractor, the three of us jammed into the open cab. "There's no life here, all I want to do is get out."

They were apiculturists, on the way home from a day tending bee-hives. Lázaro was skinny, with olive skin and a trim black beard. He waited a minute before speaking. "I love my country," he said. "I think I would like to go over there just to see how it is, but I don't want to leave."

The two were good friends, co-workers who commuted together each day, but their views spanned extremes of sentiment that divide families, friends, and even couples in Cuba. It was easy to picture Papito in Miami joining the ranks of the rabid anti-Castro contingent while Lázaro kept on tending to the bees, trying not to feel betrayed. They pulled up at Lázaro's house and he went in to look for a bit of hardware with which he thought I might be able to rig a belt repair. He emerged with a rusty iron figure-of-eight big enough to tow a car.

"This is not going to work," he said. "You need an upholsterer or a saddlery."

The lobby of the only hotel in San Cristóbal was like a mausoleum, but the sullen girl behind the counter assured me they were full to capacity. I knew she was lying. I had read that when confronted with an obvious tourist, the state hotels invariably claim to be booked solid. There are a variety of official excuses for this policy, but the reason for it is obvious: the govern-ment wants to steer all tourist cash to the dollar hotels and resorts where it can extract the maximum of foreign exchange.

I was nonetheless enraged. That I was being discriminated against for being too wealthy did not solve the problem of having nowhere to stay. I fumed, but had no constructive response. "Oh, really, you're full, are you? Well, that's…that's just wonderful," I said, turning away.

A cobbler set up with a portable roadside stand said that my backpack problem was out of his league, but a young black guy who was hanging around with him offered to take me to a place to sleep and we set off for the plaza. Just off the main square, he banged on a high, wooden colonial door. Eventually, a wizened old white man with a hooknose and white hair opened a little peephole in the door to see who was there. My situation was explained, and he let me in.

"Who the hell was that?" he asked me, when my guide had departed.

"Just a guy who brought me here, I don't know him," I said.

"Never seen him before," said Valentin, taking me out through the parlor into the courtyard of the house, a sprawling riot of cracked cement tiles and potted plants in rusting tin cans. Along one wall under an awning was a bar with a few empty bottles on the shelves behind it. A few old magazine clippings of girls in swimsuits were tacked up on the wall, but the sun had leached every speck of color from the paper. "How long do you want the room for?"

"Just tonight," I said.

As Valentin's wife, Yolanda, set about changing the sheets in the room, she told me that Valentin had desperately wanted to emigrate to the United States in the first year of the revolution but that her aging parents forbade her from going. Valentin had stayed in San Cristóbal out of love.

I sat on a little, white iron chair near the bar waiting for the room to be readied while Valentin made endless trips across the patio carrying buckets of water from a burbling spigot to a huge blue plastic water tank. The spigot had no handle and was wrapped with rags in a vain attempt to stem the flow, but it dripped fast enough for a bucket to fill in a few minutes, and Valentin would shuffle out and carry it to the tank. "You never know when they're going to turn off the water around here," he said as he passed by for the twentieth time. I asked what he had done for a living before he retired and he gestured toward the bar.

"Both of us were in *astronomía* our whole lives," he said. This seemed unlikely. Two retired astronomers running a hotel out of their house. I pointed up at the purpling sky. A few stars were just becoming visible overhead. "Everything that has do with the heavens?" I asked. Valentin cackled. "*No, no, gastronomía,*" he said. "That bar is my shrine to the food service industry."

At seven the next morning, I was on the toilet. Instead of toilet paper, it is common in Cuban households to find neatly cut-up squares of newspaper—usually *Granma*, "the official organ of the Communist Party of Cuba"—hanging from a nail in lieu of a roll. While I was wiping up with an article vilifying Janet Reno, Valentin knocked on the door. Given my temporary indisposition, I called to him through the window to find out what he wanted.

"You have to get going," he said. "Yolanda is making your breakfast, then you have to go to get your backpack fixed."

I pulled myself together and opened the door. It was an early hour for eviction, and I was not ready for a sudden departure. The entire contents of my pack were still strewn across the floor. I had taken everything out the night before while looking for a solution to the belt problem.

"I have a couple coming at eight," he said, whispering. In case I hadn't caught his meaning he gave a bizarre and abstract sexual wriggle, holding his fists out from the elbows and doing a little boxer's dance. This vague, hunched thrusting seemed particularly obscene coming from a man his age. I tried not to laugh. It was a one-room, hot-sheet hotel.

I packed quickly and Yolanda gave me breakfast. The couple watched me eat, sitting nearby on a pair of chairs welded together from bent rebar, with seats ingeniously made from old wire refrigerator shelving. "There's something we want to ask you before you go," said Yolanda. Shy and conspiratorial, she looked around as if someone might be listening over the garden wall. They leaned in closer: "Is Miami really as nice as they say?"

Cuatro

The Darwinist and the animist

"**C**on esto tu puedes cinchar un buey," said the saddlemaker. You could strap down an ox with that. He had sewn two rusty old iron rings into the webbing of the backpack, but they were strong. The belt held well and I left San Cristóbal behind me to the south, crossing the superhighway in pouring rain and walking up the shoulder. An open-backed truck whipped by, full of hitchhikers crouching forward against the cab and huddling together in wet mounds like kittens to avoid the heavy drops. Cutting overland toward the *sierra*, I circled a huge, almost dry reservoir on a dirt track along the top of the embankment. Thunderheads rolled in from the plain and jousted with the mountains. It was desolate but beautiful, with distant views of gold and emerald sugar-cane fields that glowed bright with an inner light, defying the storm.

I soon climbed up to Soroa, another of the villages dubbed a "touristic site" by the Cuban government. It wasn't really a village at all, just a sprawling one-story hotel with the garish color scheme of a Howard Johnson's set down in a field in the middle of the cloud forest. A bar-restaurant devoid of custom sat beside a burbling brook and a gated trail with a sign demanding an entrance fee. There was nobody there to collect it.

Nestled in the forest behind a copse along the road, I found a woman who rented out half of her two-room wooden cabin. I hung sodden socks from a line on the porch and collapsed on the bed. The room was decorated with collages of European liquor and jewelry advertisements cut from glossy magazines, along with some empty plastic bottles that had once held various shampoos. From these tourist leavings, Sandra had crafted a shrine to goods and glamour that did not exist inside her Cuba, a fantasy world of black cocktail dresses and glistening, whiskey-soaked ice cubes. I found this profoundly depressing.

Sandra knocked on the door timidly. "Richard, Richard," she said, "I am very sorry to disturb you, but an unfamiliar car has stopped in the road below and I need you to put your backpack in the room. I've already taken your socks around to the back." She had no license to rent out the room and was afraid someone might see my stuff on the porch. The fine if she were caught was the unimaginable sum of $1,500, roughly ten years' salary in Cuban pesos. "I rent anyway," she said, defiant but cautious. "What can they take from me?"

I tiptoed out onto the porch to snatch up my gear and then went around back.

"What's the idea behind this walking?" asked Sandra.

"I'm on my way to San Antonio de los Baños to learn about *décima*." I had tired of the resultant incredulity whenever I announced that I was walking to Guantánamo.

"My mother is a poet," said Sandra. She said her mother had written many *décimas* about life before the revolution, to explain to her younger relatives that things now were not as tough as they could be. She promised to mail some poems to me at Miriam's the next time she visited her mother. She did, along with a note that simply said, "My mother wrote them down for you in her own hand; please pardon any mistakes, she only has second grade."

Décimas *for my niece Janet*

Dicen que aquí no hay comida.	They say there's no food here.
Yo como todos los días.	I eat every day.
Cuando niña no tenía	When I was a girl I had none;
mi niñez fue entristecida	my childhood was full of sadness,
y me sentía abatida	I felt beaten down
con hambre y pasaba frío	by hunger, and I was cold.
y con yuca y caspia	Gleanings, and the cassava
que mi padre lo sembraba	that my father planted
ese sustento nos daba	were our only sustenance.
son tristes recuerdos míos.	These are my sad memories.

El muchas veces regó	He often watered
el surco con su sudor	the furrows with his sweat
y con cariño y amor	and with love and tenderness
todos sus hijos crió.	he raised all his children.
Pero recuerdo que yo	But I remember
un vestido no tenía	I had no clothes to wear.
mi pobre madre salía	My poor mother went out
y muy dispuesta enseguida	and soon afterward,
trabajando en escojida	by picking through the leavings,
entonces lo resolvía.	she managed to get me some.
Y si mi padre hacía diez	And if my father harvested ten furrows,
surcos con hambre y fatiga	hungry and exhausted,
el capataz enseguida	soon the overseer came
venía a quitarle tres.	to take away three.
Yo se que mi padre fue	I know that my father
trabajador ejemplar	was an exemplary worker.
no se podía dudar	There is no doubt
el muchas cosas sembraba	he planted many things,
pero en la tierra que estaba	but in the land where he lived
no era fácil trabajar.	it was not easy to labor.
Y yo voy a continuar	I am going to continue
haciendo todo el relato	telling you the whole story.
yo no tenía ni platos	I didn't even have plates
para poder almorzar	to be able to eat lunch,
y cuando me iba a acostar	and when I went to go lay down,
eramos cuatro en la cama	there were four of us in the bed,
y yo estiraba con ganas	and when I tried to stretch out,
un pié para descansar	there was no room to try and rest.
y entonces iba a chocar	My foot would go banging
con la vieja palangana.	right into the old washbasin.
De yagua era mi casa	I can't forget the house was of palm trunks
y de guano que no olvido	and thatched with fronds.
piso de tierra y hoy vivo	The floor was dirt, but now
en una buena y con plaza	I live in a good one, there's a plaza;
carnicería y que pasa	I have a butcher, and what else?
tengo bodega también	A grocery, and a store,
tiendecita y atelier	a workshop, a clinic
consultorio y hospital.	and a hospital.

Ya tengo lo principal	So now I have the essentials
lo que quería tener.	I always wanted to have.
Yo doy gracias a Fidel	I give thanks to Fidel
con todo mi corazón	with all my heart
amo la revolución	I love the revolution
y agradecida estoy de él.	And I'm thankful to him.
Hasta la muerte soy fiél	Until death I'll be faithful
porque recuerdo aquel día	because I remember that day
que estando en la casa mia	when I was in my house
vinó la guardia rural.	and the rural police came
Me botó al camino real	and threw me out into the street
con cuatro hijos que tenía.	with my four children.

—Ramona Campos Martinez

In bed that night, I fussed with a small, shortwave transistor radio that was in the room, but it did nothing but pop and sizzle and make watery, static noises. At last, one station resolved for a moment and I heard a British accent say, "On Wall Street today, the stock market crashed." That was all, just that one sentence before the station retreated behind a whining barrage of white noise. No matter how carefully I edged the knob across the band, the world outside remained hidden.

By the end of the next day, my knee was in open revolt, twinging with every step. I spent a squalid night on a mildewed, sheetless mattress: the bed of a night-watchman at a rest stop beside the highway. He had been in the army. In the morning, he said, "Walk on the grass at the side of the road, and you might actually make it. It's much easier on the feet than walking on pavement. I learned that during my military service." It seemed a bitter irony that, unfit as I was, I had survived the mountains only to have trouble walking the flat. I tried to deny that anything was wrong with my knee for as long as I could, but by the time I approached Artemisa, I was stopping every few hundred meters and sitting down on my pack in the dust to massage my knee. I began limping and, with three kilometers to go and the town in sight, tenderness gave way to sharp, stabbing pains. I hobbled along, cursing to myself in Spanish.

A slim guy with a tidy mustache and an immaculate red bicycle pulled up alongside me.

"¿Qué pasa?" he asked.

"It's not going so well."

"Put your bag up on here." He patted the handlebars.

"I can tell you take good care of that bike, and this bag is pretty heavy."

"Don't worry about that."

He dismounted and walked the bicycle, and I balanced the backpack across a milk crate bolted behind the seat, steadying it with one hand.

"Where are you going?"

"I don't know, with this leg. I have to be in San Antonio de los Baños tomorrow." *I have an urgent appointment with a poet*, I thought.

"You can't walk there."

"Why not?" I responded. "I walked here from Pinar del Río," but I had little pride left.

"Look at you, you can't."

I was leaning into the Soviet bicycle, using it as a crutch, more or less hopping down the road.

Ernesto took me to his sister Fredis's house.

"This is Richard, he needs to rest his knee, maybe lie down for a little while," he explained. "I have to go now," he said to me, "but I'll come back later and take you around the town."

I sat in the front room with Marta, Fredis's aunt. She was a hefty black woman, her distinguished sweptback hair streaked with white. She had one foot in a cast and was staying in the house while her own was under construction around the corner. We sat in matching rocking chairs, two invalids. I wrapped my knee with an Ace bandage. Fredis brought cold water on a tray, then a cola.

"I would love to go on an adventure like yours," said Marta. "I walk everywhere; if I didn't have this cast on, you wouldn't even find me."

Fredis laughed. "It's true, she is so full of energy you can't keep her down."

Marta was a biology professor at the local high school. She had a warm and patient smile, which had never wilted, I thought, despite enduring countless generations of students. There was not a wrinkle on her face. She told me that the Sierra de los Organos, the mountains I had crossed twice in the last week, were the oldest range in Cuba and the first part of the island to emerge from the sea. The *mogotes* were the result of erosion, and very near Soroa, she said, was the dividing line between these ancient mountains and the sharper, younger Sierra del Rosario. I loved Marta. When she spoke, she shared her enthusiasm. She didn't sound like she was teaching, and her words alone made places fascinating.

"You must walk through Matanzas. You would love it. I did my field work there in the Valle de Jumurí; it is a place with many endemic plants." She exhaled audibly, frustrated. "If only I didn't have this cast on, I would go with you." Marta talked about the endemic orchids that I had seen in Soroa and told me to look out for *Eleutherodactylus limbatus*, "the world's smallest frog."

Fredis came back from the kitchen again.

"I was just putting sheets on the bed upstairs and I made you some lunch." she said.

While I was eating, they left me alone in the kitchen. There was a great hubbub in the front room of noisy greetings and cackling laughter. A new, loud voice dominated the house and came booming down the corridor behind me. I heard footsteps.

"Come out here and let me get a look at you!"

A woman near Marta's age, but with her hair died jet black and just coiffed, burst in. She was wearing bright orange, platform flip-flops and had beefy arms and improbable ledges of fat jutting out like shelving at the back of her shorts. She tapped a pair of oval gold-rimmed sunglasses to her pursed lips.

"What have we here? You're very big." She put her hands on her hips and fixed me with a stern gaze.

I felt small, sitting at the low kitchen table. I had become a member of the family the moment I arrived, but this new woman made me feel like a guest she wasn't sure about. She filled the room.

"Uhhm. Yes. I'm Richard. Ernesto brought me. Fredis has been very kind to invite me and all that."

"So I can see. How is the food? Fredis is an excellent cook. I am Esther, the mother of Fredis. I live in Santos Suarez in Havana. Marta is my sister."

Esther could not have been more different from Marta. She commanded attention, and while Fredis and Marta had welcomed me into their home without even a question, Esther was inquisitive and skeptical, with the big features of Celia Cruz. She flew about the place. Marta sat still, of course, because of her leg. I wanted to hug Marta and go on a biology field trip with her. Esther's brash big-city ways scared me.

I finished eating and went back into the front room.

"Your sister is kind of a hurricane," I said to Marta.

"She wasn't always this way. You wouldn't believe it, she had such terrible asthma that she almost died."

"I could barely walk," said Esther, charging into the room, and the conversation. She reminded me of a bulldozer.

"But since she 'made her saint,' she has had no problems at all. Even though I am *en esto* [in this religion], I was surprised."

Four years earlier, Esther had undergone the *Santería* initiation ceremony, receiving *Yemayá*, La Virgen de Regla, as her saint. She had worn only white clothing for a year, and made a pilgrimage across the country to El Cobre, a shrine near Santiago that is the most important religious site in Cuban *Santería*.

"Richard, which saint is urging you along on your Mission in Cuba?" Esther asked.

"I'm sure I don't know."

"Surely you don't imagine that you are doing this walk because you want to. It is definitely a Mission."

"I'm not sure I know what a Mission is, really. I got very sick while working on a job in Haiti, and then spiraled into depression. I needed a change in my life. I decided to come here. It was probably a stupid idea."

"I think you have a strong spiritual side," said Esther. "And a powerful attraction to this religion."

While Esther was injecting Marta with some antibiotics for her foot, a colleague from Marta's school arrived. Artemis was tiny and skinny, with red hair. She was about a third the size of either of the sisters, whom I now thought of as the Darwinist and the animist. Esther hadn't made a believer out of me yet, but Artemis's arrival was something like a miracle. She was the school's swimming coach and physical therapist. Within minutes, I had my trousers off and was sitting in the middle of Fredis's living room in my boxer shorts while Artemis poked and prodded my knee.

"Is that painful?"

"No."

"This?"

"Aaah. Shit, that hurts."

"That's good news. You have muscle pain, nothing more. The muscle may be tearing a little bit. Just rest a few days and you'll be fine."

"You must stay here for the night," said Marta. "Fredis has a room made up for you upstairs."

Artemis went and got a jar of electric green goo labeled, *Tropical Gel Para Masajes Anti-Celulitis* and started working some of it into my quadricep. She put my Ace bandage back on, showing me how I had wound it incorrectly the first time.

I called Miriam in Havana to say that my knee was a mess but that I would be arriving at her father's house the next day one way or another. She was very concerned. "It's fine," I said, "and I am with some wonderful people, two sisters, one is a *santera* and the other is an expert in Cuban botany. It's perfect for me."

Later, I went out into the evening to test the knee. Artemisa was laid out on a grid. It was just getting dark, and the town was a voyeur's paradise. In Cuba, life is lived on the street, or between the street and the kitchen. All the houses were one story tall and had the shutters and doors open wide, offering snippets of daily life to passersby. In one house, a family was sitting down to eat under neon tubes that made the pale green kitchen walls glow cold and blue. Next door, the kitchen was painted pink and an old dangling bulb suffused the room with orange light. A woman was bent over a table stripping beans out of the pod. Children hunched over their homework, and somewhere somebody was practicing on a clarinet.

Televisions were on everywhere, the color ones flashing blue up the walls like lightning. The old black-and-white Soviet sets sent bursts of sepia flickering out onto the pavement. I heard the theme music for the nightly news come on, booming out of twenty nearby sets into the street where I stood.

Like the commercials on American television, the opening sequence of the Cuban news is much louder than the program it accompanies. The purpose is similar. They both say, *Pay attention, this is your society.* The volume of the commercials in the United States rouses viewers from their entertainment-induced stupor and, if they've dozed off, wakes them up, thereby reaching every possible customer. The hectic strains of the lead-in music for the Cuban news, which play for a good two minutes, are both a rallying call and an announcement that nothing has changed. The situation is stable, blares the music, come and see what the regime has done for you today. *Advertising* is a bad word in Cuba, while *propaganda* is not. The two words have connotations precisely opposite from those in common usage in the US. The first is officially considered an evil and manipulative tool of capitalism, created by devils to enslave the public, while the second exists to encourage the people, give them a needed pat on the back for a job well-done, and sing the praises of the glorious revolution they have built.

When I went downstairs in the morning, Esther grabbed me in the hallway before I had even said good morning.

"I couldn't discuss this with you yesterday with all the hubbub, but I wanted to tell you that you have a very strong Arab spirit."

"What, you mean, from Arabia?"

"*Si,* Richard, because not all of the spirits are black or white. I also think you are going to be very prosperous when you go back to your country, you must write to me and tell me. Your saint is *Obatala.*"

"I don't understand. I have a spirit and a saint?"

"I'll try and explain it to you, but later, I have to give Marta her injection."

Esther went to get a needle and antibiotics for Marta's foot. I went into the living room.

"You have your very own *curandera,*" I said to Marta. A *curandera* is a doctor who works with herbs and roots, drawing on the knowledge of her forefathers to cure and heal. In Haiti, they are literally known as *doktè fey,* leaf doctors. Esther returned and I asked, "Do people still go to the *curandero* here?"

"Baah, of course," said Esther. "More than ever, with the price of drugs what it is, but they always go to the doctor first."

"Meaning people believe that modern medicine works the best, but then if that doesn't work, they turn to plants?"

"No, that has nothing to do with it. They might not even want to hear what the doctor has to say, but if you don't go and then you die, there is nobody to sign the death certificate." She laughed her huge laugh. "The family can't go to the authorities and say, 'We took him to the *curandero.*'"

"That is my specialty, the study of medicinal plants. Many of them work very well, I mean from a scientific point of view," said Marta. "In fact, I wanted to ask you, if you think there is a way that I would be able to use the Internet to present my resume? Maybe there are companies out there looking for this information."

"That's what the Internet is perfect for. Do you have access through the school?"

"Not yet, but maybe one day."

I told Marta I had heard of adventurers going into the rainforests of Ecuador and Bolivia on behalf of large pharmaceutical companies to steal cures from shamans. After they came out, they applied for patents on this ancient pharmacological knowledge and made millions.

"I understand that some of these things work, but how did the shamans or the *curanderos* first learn which plants to use for what remedies? Especially here. An African healer or witch doctor or whatever who was brought here as a slave must have been surrounded by plants that were totally unfamiliar."

"Yes, but they used their intuition," said Marta. "They looked around and found plants that had the same curative effects as the ones they knew at home. And I think it is possible that the spirits also helped. When they came down in the ceremonies and mounted people, they gave information and counsel about which plants to use."

I had been hoping to stir things up a little bit between scientific Marta and spirited Esther, since, for me, they embodied a Cuban version of the debate between creationists and evolutionists, but I realized that I had invented the contradictions between the ways they looked at the world.

"I'll tell you a story that our mother told me," said Marta. "She had alopecia, she was losing all her hair, and she didn't know what to do about it. But someone, somebody already dead, came and spoke through another person to tell her the cure, a solution made with wild vervain."

Later, when I was alone with Esther again, she told me that her spirits never mounted her; instead, they spoke inside her head, while she was awake. "For instance, they could come now, while I'm having a conversation. But my sister, the one with the bad foot, the spirits come down and they ride her." In *Santería*, as in *Vodou* in Haiti, it is considered bad form and sensationalistic to describe people as "possessed" by spirits. Instead, both cultures use the metaphor of horseback riding, the earthly body the steed, mounted by a spirit jockey.

Ernesto came to take me to the taxi stand and we said our goodbyes and took photographs. Esther wanted one of her dog. Looking at the pictures now, I see that her smile is every bit as warm as Marta's. I took Esther's address in Santos Suarez and promised to visit. "Stop at El Rincón on your way back into Havana," she said. "Your knee will get much better."

The stand for *colectivos* was on a shady boulevard near the edge of town. These taxis follow fixed routes, like buses, and don't leave until full. There were a few drivers on an island between the lanes, lounging on the grass next to fifty-year-old Chevies and Dodges. The special period has seen many of these vast old cars converted into collective taxis because they accommodate so many riders. We stuck my pack into the cavernous trunk of a black Cadillac so enormous that it swallowed eight passengers before the driver slipped behind the wheel and turned the ignition.

Cinco

El Rincón

G oing up Miriam's childhood street, I walked right past her son, Rodolfo, sitting on a stoop. He had a look I recognized: crushed and depressed. On the next block, I saw a number on a house and turned back, realizing I had gone too far.

"I thought that might have been you," he said, in English. "I was out here waiting for you. Please come in."

It seemed odd that he hadn't said anything as I walked by wearing my huge backpack.

"Your English is fantastic. Did you spend time in the United States?" I asked. But I remembered Miriam saying something about her eldest son being damaged in some way and "never amounting to much."

"No, I taught myself. With a book I had."

"Really?"

"I had a dictionary I used to read."

"Well, it's excellent."

"No, I know it isn't. I don't have anyone to talk to."

Rodolfo's T-shirt said *New York* on it in blue, tall letters like skyscrapers. "Diego," he called, switching to Spanish, "our guest has arrived."

Miriam's father was crinkled and tiny with age. Everything about him had shrunk except for his ears, which stuck out from the sides of his head like great leaves of cabbage. He was wearing a brown polyester gimme cap, a checkered western shirt, and black canvas sneakers.

"Welcome," he said. "You're the one who wants to learn about *décima*." He sighed. "I haven't played in a long time, you know. Arthritis. Once I played *laúd* with all the great poets. Back then, everybody wanted me to accompany them. *Pues*, many of them have died now."

Rodolfo went and got the *laúd* for him. I couldn't figure out if Rodolfo took care of Diego, or the other way around. It looked like a little bit of both, with Miriam paying the bills out of her Havana apartment rentals. She had told me Diego was eighty-one years old and Rodolfo had "nervous problems."

"I'll be in my room," said Rodolfo.

"You don't like *décima?*"

"I like Led Zeppelin, Chicago, Craydensay Clerrwetter. I have some tapes." From the way he pronounced Creedence Clearwater, it was obvious that he had never heard the words spoken aloud.

The *laúd* was horribly out of tune but Diego strummed a few bars. Within moments, a guy stuck his head in through the open door to the street. "What's going on here? I was just going by. I haven't heard that sound coming out of this house in years."

"The young man wants to learn about *décima*," said Diego.

"I'll sing one," said the newcomer. He came in and sat down next to me on the vinyl-covered couch. "Go ahead, play. I'm ready. This is one of my grandfather's. José Marichal Negrin." Diego strummed. His fingers strained to bend around the neck of the miniature twelve-string guitar. Arsenio Negrin began to sing, then abandoned the effort.

"Can you tune that up; it's got to be higher. I have to sing high."

There was a horrible, whiny, twanging sound as one of the strings snapped and flew up the neck of the *laúd* to dangle, bobbing in an ugly coil.

"I'm so sorry," I said, "maybe this isn't such a great idea."

"Forget it," said Arsenio, "go ahead and play." He was pumped up and sweating, sitting forward on the couch with his hands balled up in fists as if waiting for the starting-gun of a sprint. Diego began again, on the now eleven-stringed instrument. The thought came to me that this was his final performance; the broken string would never be replaced.

Arsenio turned toward me. With his sweaty face inches from mine, he sang at the top of his lungs, perhaps the only way he knew how, knitting his brow. His eyes closed and I could see his teeth. He was almost crying, with effort or emotion. His singing was deafening and as out of tune as the *laúd*. I tried not to recoil, but it was as if I had my head stuck out the window of a moving train.

Después de una temporada	After a period,
bastante larga por cierto	actually quite a long time,
he retornado al concierto	I've returned to performing
de la décima cantada.	the sung *décima.*
Dejé mi cómoda almohada	I've left my comfortable pillow,
donde mis tristezas lloro	where I cry out my tears,
para incorporarme al coro	to join the choir again
con la mayor lealtad,	in utmost loyalty
porque se que l'amistad	because I know that friendship
vale mucho mas que el oro	is worth much more than gold
—José Marichal Negrin	

"That was great," I said. I felt shell-shocked. "Have you ever thought about performing?"

"Never, are you kidding? I fucking hate *décima*. But when I heard Diego playing, I remembered my grandfather. I couldn't help myself, it's in my blood."

Miriam arrived with Nestor in his white Lada, "the only thing he ever got from his father." Nestor was salty blond and muscular, with a polo shirt and tropical print shorts. He looked like he worked at a marina on Martha's Vineyard. It was easy to see what had happened to Rodolfo. While his younger brother was getting the girls, the car, and a job on a boat, he sat in his room with his cassettes, reading a dog-eared English dictionary over and over again. He was like one of those guys who never stop playing *Dungeons and Dragons* until the day he realizes all his friends are married and have jobs. Rodolfo wanted so desperately to visit the America of his imagination—not the land of career opportunities and unimaginable wealth envisioned by so many Cubans, but his own, invented classic-rock subculture—that he couldn't even bring himself to ask me about my country. He was an émigré of the mind.

Miriam showed me around the house as if I hadn't arrived hours earlier. "I bought this television for them," she said. "Out of money from the apartment. I had to buy it. If you don't have a television here, you die of boredom." Rodolfo skulked around and watched and smoked cigarettes like a bag lady, hunched over with his elbow folded close to his body and his fingers curved around the shape of his mouth, as if someone might try to steal the smoke. Diego made coffee, which he called "the black nectar of the white gods." When he brought it, he said:

Yo no tengo capital	Although I haven't got any scrip,
pero si le doy con gozo	I will still with pleasure give thee
el café mas delicioso	of the most delicious coffee
que un hombre puede tomar.	a man could ever hope to sip.

I declined a cigarette. "I've been smoking for seventy-five years," said Diego, "I started when I was six, out in the fields, planting tobacco. There you were, with the plant, and you just rolled some up right on the spot and smoked it when nobody was looking." We spent the afternoon transcribing Diego's *décimas*, although he protested that he was known as a *laúd* player and that his dead friends were the real poets. He recited poems from memory and explained that the Moors brought a two-stringed version of the *laúd* to Spain during the Islamic conquest. After the instrument arrived in Cuba, either from Spain or via the Canary Islands, the neck was shortened, Diego said, to match the tuning of violins. Although generally translated as *lute*, a Cuban *laúd* does not have the deep-bellied pear shape of the lute. Instead, it is a tiny guitar the size of a viola, flat-backed, with the curlicues of a violin. Any man larger than shriveled, octogenarian Diego cannot play it without appearing to have stolen a child's toy.

The next morning, my knee was feeling much better. Returning to Havana in the back of Nestor's Lada seemed like a huge defeat, however, so to salvage my pride and the walk (*my Mission*, I thought) I decided to follow Esther's suggestion and walk to El Rincón. I would beg San Lázaro to strengthen my knees and legs for the rest of the journey across Cuba. Miriam explained it all over dinner and asked me to light a candle for her when I got there.

San Lázaro is the patron of travelers, the sick, and the lame. He is the syncretic expression of the *Santería orisha Babalu Ayé*, and his shrine at El Rincón is the most important religious site in Cuba after El Cobre. People go there to pray for a cure, making a *promesa* to return if their condition improves. Going has an element of sacrifice and pilgrimage, and it is said to be best to arrive on foot. Each year on December 17, faithful worshipers make the trek, some crawling, as Afrocubaweb describes it, "on their knees, with bricks tied to their feet."

The chapel at El Rincón was a whitewashed church with three great dark wooden doors set beneath a squat belltower and a cupola as on an Eastern Orthodox church except that, painted flesh pink, it looked like a single great Amazon breast. Inside, groups wandered between various small altars, clutching handfuls of lit candles. (One woman had too many to hold and looked as if she might start a fire at any moment.) The altar designated to San Lázaro was attached to a gift shop with some religious calendars and cards with prayers printed on them. There was a man behind the counter whose main job was to accept armfuls of flowers and lay them around a small, glass-fronted cabinet with a San Lázaro statue in it.

"I'd like to buy a candle, please," I said to him.

"Please take your hat off."

I scrambled to remove my baseball cap. "I'm very sorry. Could I just get one candle, *por favor?*"

He looked at me as if I had just asked him to sell me a package of condoms. "The candles," he said, "must be purchased *outside.*"

Unwilling to arrive at Miriam's without having lit her candle, I went back outside, down the drive and past the gates, stopping to give a few dimes to a beggar stretched out on the sidewalk. Salesmen were lined up along the road. By Cuban standards, it was an orgy of commerce. I hadn't seen so many things for sale since leaving New York. Three pushcarts were stacked high with cut flowers of every description and color, a candle vendor sold lumpy homemade candles for five pesos each, and four card tables covered with ceramic religious statues were set up on the shoulder of the road.

Figurines of the seated Buddha and of an American Indian in a lurid yellow codpiece sat beside pale blue Virgins and red Santa Barbaras. They were cheaply made and grotesque. The San Lázaros looked like anorexic action figures dotted with unconvincing leprous wounds and clumpy, plastic-looking gray hair. While excluding herself and her own newfound faith, Miriam had explained that religion was on the upswing because times were hard. Times had to be very tough indeed for people to be putting their faith in these dismal objects.

As I knelt and mumbled the prayer to San Lázaro writ large on the front of the altar, my sore knee twinged. I asked for health and firm legs in the days ahead. All the altars had signs that warned, *Do not place candles here.* The etiquette was to blow them out and give them to the gift-shop attendant at the end of the visit. He was happy to receive spent candles even if selling new ones was unthinkable. Somewhere in all this was a thriving recycled wax business.

El Rincón is nestled in the fertile fields beyond Havana's airport. I couldn't see the city, but the air-traffic control tower was obvious, so I crossed scrubby fields toward it, soon running into train tracks, two steel ribbons that headed straight and unbending toward the terminal in Habana Vieja. I walked the tracks for hours. The fields eased into the suburbs and the suburbs became the outskirts of the city.

For several kilometers, the tracks followed the edge of an armory or military base, surrounded by a daunting double fence. A grid of barbed wire several meters tall and a chainlink fence inside it protected a no-man's-land between. I pictured snarling German shepherds patrolling this modern-day moat, but the only visible security system was a cluster of tin cans hanging from the razor wire every few meters. *Beef Luncheon Meat*, it said in English on the long red cans. I thought of the money the American taxpayer might save were the US military to adopt this *Just Married* defense system.

Where the train tracks converged with a multilane highway beyond the airport, a man was selling dollar boxes of rice and pork chops out of his garage and I stopped for lunch. He had a dual-burner gas range set up beside a picnic table, under a pea-green roof of wavy plastic. He said the first stop on city bus Route 190 was only a few blocks away. It went right through the Vedado.

At the bus stop, a few university students were milling around and sitting under an awning.

I asked one of them, "Is this the stop for the 190?" He nodded.

A moment later, another student arrived.

"Quién es el último?" Who's last?

Nobody said anything.

"You are waiting for the 190, aren't you?" he asked the group in general. "So who's last? *El último? Por favor.*"

The one I had asked if I was in the right place gestured at me. "I think he's last."

"Oh, I guess I'm last," I said.

"Who goes in front of you?" asked the newcomer.

"I'm sorry, I don't know."

"What, you mean you didn't ask who was last?"

"No," I said. "I didn't know."

I had failed to take advantage of Cuba's civilized solution to the country's endless opportunities for waiting in line. Under this homegrown system, passengers need only determine who is in front of them in the line. Once this is settled, they flee the hot sidewalk to lounge beneath trees, wander off with friends, or even go run errands. In case the person you are keeping tabs on should never return, it is considered prudent also to ask who goes in front of the *último*. When the bus arrives the line snaps back into existence and the passengers board in strict order.

Instead of the triumphant march into Havana that I had pictured, I made my return to Miriam's crammed onto the back of the 190 bus, amid a crush of passengers.

Seis

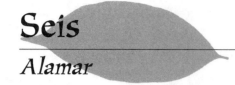

Alamar

La construcción socialista no es ni hermosa ni fea, es completa o incompleta, válida o no válida. El resultado de un proceso organizador, una valoración meramente estética no es applicable.

Socialist construction is neither beautiful nor ugly; it is either complete or incomplete, valid or not valid. Since it is the result of a process of organization, a solely aesthetic evaluation is not applicable.

—Hannes Meyer, *Marxist Architecture*

Miriam's apartment was so depressing that I considered moving once again. After just a few hours there, I felt stultified and immobile. In the dark living room, the television was always on unless Miriam was so gloomy that she couldn't bear the distraction. Then she would lay herself down on her narrow daybed with her plump white arm draped across her eyes and her bad foot on the floor. She was fifty-five, single and lonely, with only this dismal apartment to show for her years of struggle. I was never sure if she would have been miserable anywhere, or if Cuba was as horrible as she said it was.

A slap from an old friend hurts much more than one from an enemy, which is why the television was showing a live demonstration against the Czech government. Streams of people drifted past the Czech embassy protesting a Czech-sponsored UN resolution condemning Cuba for human-rights violations. Helicopter shots of the route showed a ribbon of humanity winding through Nuevo Vedado. Huge titles flashed onto the screen, as if the population was being urged to chant along at home. *TRAIDORES, LACAYOS, MARIONETAS. A CUBA SE RESPETA.* (Traitors, Lackeys, Puppets. Cuba demands respect). Flotillas of schoolchildren in match-ing uniforms and bands of workers from the Centros de Trabajo, all in the same red and white T-shirts, marched past the embassy and the cameras for most of the afternoon, shouting at the shuttered building.

"They have them programmed," said Miriam, "they don't think any more." It was a masterful display of propaganda. I should have jumped out of my chair and rushed out to see it, but demonstrations like this were on television every week. I was already numb to the spectacle.

Night after night, the evening news presented the extended highlights of yet another demonstration that the same channel had only just finished broadcasting live in its entirety, like a post–Super Bowl newscast making the winning team the lead story and showing all the touchdowns just one more time. With nothing else to watch, all of Cuba waited for the news to end and the soap opera to begin. *El rey del ganado* (*The king of beef*) was the national passion. On Mondays, Wednesdays, and Fridays, it was a near certainty that the news would run late, postponing the start of the *telenovela* as the captive audience tuned in and waited.

One evening, while I was waiting in line for a street-corner pizza, two women arrived and established who was the *último*. The waiting dragged on. After fifteen minutes, I had watched three rounds of pizzas prepared, cooked, and sold with agonizing deliberation. The woman making them moved at a glacial pace. The small lumps of farmer's cheese seemed to fall one by one on to the pie as she tapped them from a minute plastic scoop. Someone in front had ordered five of the tiny pizzas at once, requiring one complete baking cycle just to fill the order. The women behind me grew anxious. One paced the sidewalk; the other, like me, watched, riveted, as the geology of the process unfolded. Finally, they could take it no more.

"Oh," said one, "I was so hoping for a pizza. But it's not possible."

"*Mira*," said the other, "I'm sorry, but we don't want the pizzas any more. The *novela* is going to start any minute." They rushed off.

El rey del ganado, a Brazilian production dubbed into Spanish, depicts the multigenerational family feud between the Berdinazzis and Mezengas, Italian immigrants turned land barons. Political influence, social injustice, lurid passion, sweeping vistas of coffee plantations, and thousands of head of cattle are the chief ingredients. Miriam devoured every episode.

I wandered back through the Vedado to the apartment. Sounds of tele-vision drifted out onto the street and unruly trees cast somber shadows on the inky blue pavement. There was a great commotion at Miriam's door. A *babosa*, a monstrous ovoid slug, was sucked up against the floor of the entryway. Two guys were prodding at it with a stick, trying to coax it into a jar. Miriam watched as if in shock.

"What's going on around here?" I asked.

"Oh, my God," said Miriam. She rarely swore. "I forgot to tell you. About ten days ago, I was limping down the sidewalk as usual and a woman I don't even know stopped me and asked me what was wrong. I told her I had just been to the doctor to have an ultrasound. I have a bone spur, a sharp bone that is putting pressure on my instep when I walk. So she told me, 'What you have to do is get yourself a *babosa* and let it slime and slither all over your bad foot. Then take it and put it in a jar,' she said, 'but don't kill it.'

"So anyway, my friend got the slug for me and it was so revolting I couldn't go near it. Plus, it was Thursday of Holy Week and who could do that kind of black magic then? I couldn't face it. That was about five days ago. I took the slug and threw it away in the garden. *And now it has come back to my door.* I have no choice, I have to do the cure."

The *babosa* safely stored back in its jar, I called Gonzalo Vidal, a Chilean expatriate photographer. He had fled Chile during the Pinochet dictatorship, at the peak of the disappearances of Chilean citizens in the 1970s. A friend in New York had given me some black-and-white film and other unavailable-in-Cuba photo supplies to give him. "He's kind of an aging hipster," Alex had said. "But no matter what, he's guaranteed to show you a good time." At the other end of the phone line, a woman said, "just a moment," and then I heard footsteps and doors banging and loud cries of "Gonzalo." I waited a good five minutes. Finally he came on the line.

"It's the walker! How are you? Sorry, man, it's not my phone; I live five flights up, and I was really just getting up. Last night was kind of a heavy one. *Mira*, when are we going to get together?"

"Any time, just tell me where to be."

"You know Alamar?"

"No, but I'll get there."

"It's just outside of the city. Come tomorrow for lunch. I live in Building A39, Apartment 26. Take the camel. The pink one, it leaves right from the Vedado."

Camels are huge long buses named for a dip in the middle where the doors are. They are pulled by tractor-trailer cabs. At least two hundred people were at the bus stop. A peanut vendor was doing a brisk trade and someone else was offering pizzas and *refrescos*. Finding the *último* among the throng was a challenge in itself. Although *camellos* are huge, it looked as if the bus was going to begin its journey full. After half an hour, no buses had arrived and the little lane was packed with people. At last, a bus came. The conductor got off and handed out slips of paper to the first thirty people, something like ten percent of the line. Then, they opened the bus doors. The *último* system had collapsed in the heat of the day, and crowds charged the bus, scrabbling at the folding doors. But without a slip of paper, there was no getting on. This ugly scenario was repeated three or four times over the next hour until I received my slip of paper and boarded, some two hours after arriving at the bus stop. Then, less than a block later, the bus stopped again and the vast *camello* filled completely. I had mistakenly been standing in a line for people who wished to be guaranteed a seat.

After winding through much of Havana for the next hour, the bus barreled under the tunnel at the end of the *Malecón* and headed toward Alamar, a geometric army of apartment blocks. Identical five-story wedges of concrete stretched as far as the eye could see. The only organic touch were the wavy, reddish stains streaking down the bare gray cement from rusting iron balconies. It is housing built with the efficiency and style of shopping-mall parking, a concrete city of 30,000 that sprang from nothing in the 1970s along a rocky stretch of coast east of Havana. There were huge water tanks on the roofs of these projects. On one, it said E43-Z29.

"Excuse me," I asked a woman next to me. "Can you tell me which stop I want for Building 39A?"

"What's the zone number?"

"I don't know, my friend didn't tell me anything except *Edificio* 39A."

"Pffft. Honey, if you didn't ask the zone number, you're lost." She turned to address the rest of the bus. "*Mira*, anybody know Building 39A?"

"What zone is it in?" asked someone I couldn't see.

A girl a bit further up the bus wriggled her way back toward us.

"I live in 36A, it's the second-to-last stop. I'll show you, just watch where I get off."

When we got off, the bus was almost empty. As it pulled away, I could smell the sea. On one side of the road was an endless vista of chipped concrete edifices, on the other, a scrubby wasteland strewn with rubble, and the Atlantic Ocean beyond. The sense of alienation increased as we made our way among the buildings. Every space between the complexes gave nothing but glimpses of other more distant identical structures. The next revolution starts here, I thought.

"This is my building," the girl said after we had walked awhile. We had not spoken since descending from the bus. "If you continue this way and then bear left, the second Building should be 39." She pointed down a canyon of apartments.

I made my way to a courtyard of brown grassy stubble. A few floors up, a man was leaning over the metal railing of the stairwell.

"Hi there, excuse me, I'm looking for Building 39, Apartment 26."

"Who are you looking for? That's my apartment." This was a miracle. This one building of hundreds must have had fifty apartments in it.

"Gonzalo Vidal."

"I don't know him."

"Do you have a phone?"

"Yeah, you have a number? We'll give him a call."

I relived the first phone call, a woman screaming up the stairwell, Gonzalo padding down five flights of stairs.

"What happened to you?"

"Well, the bus took a little longer than I thought. And I seem to be at your apartment, but not really."

Gonzalo sensibly asked to confer with the owner of the phone. When I got back on the line, he said, "*39A is not the same as A39.* I'm in Zone 4; you went much too far. Take the bus back and ask to get off at El Golfito."

I couldn't face the *camello* again and I thought I'd hire someone to drive me to Gonzalo's door. But here, in these highrises, there was none of the street life of Havana. Except for laundry hung out to dry and a few cars parked along the curving access roads, Alamar seemed abandoned, post-apocalyptic. At last, a lone, antique Polish motorcycle, complete with side-car, sputtered up the drive behind me and I stuck out my thumb, the universal gesture the Cubans call *la botella* because, with the thumb upright, the outstretched hand looks like a bottle. The driver pulled to a stop.

"I'm a little bit lost, I'm trying to get to El Golfito."

"That's pretty far." He unscrewed the gas cap on the tank between his knees and peered in to gauge the fuel level. "I think I can make it, climb in."

I had never ridden in a sidecar before and didn't realize just how low it rides to the road. It was like sitting on the pavement itself. We retraced the bus route through the morass of buildings and then turned back toward the ocean to a park where there were a couple of rum shacks and some couples sitting on benches.

"This is El Golfito." There were no buildings anywhere.

"How much do you want?"

"Give me whatever you like." Cubans were always reluctant to talk business. I gave him a dollar and he sped off.

The first building I reached walking back from the park was Gonzalo's.

"Ah, wonderful, come in; finally, we can eat lunch," he said, greeting me at the door. He had a huge black walrus mustache and long black hair with streaks of gray, thinning on the top, which he wore in a ponytail. He looked like a guy in the music business. He showed me his darkroom in the bathroom and his archive of photographs in the bedroom and introduced me to his friend, Antonia. "She came over last night and she's still here," he said with a guffaw. "We might take some pictures later." Gonzalo brought his work for me to look at while he heated up the lunch. "This is my ongoing series called *Frutas tropicales*," he said. There were stacks of black-and-white images of female nudes posed with papayas, grapefruits, or bananas.

"I think I can see what you're trying to say here," I yelled into the kitchen.

"Some of those are of me," said Antonia, but I thought it perhaps inappropriate to go through them again trying to find ones that might be her.

"They're very beautiful." I didn't know what else to say. I was overwhelmed by the enormity of the cliché. But Gonzalo didn't give a damn. His attitude was, who in their right mind doesn't like naked women and fruit? He was the quintessential party guy.

"Why do people in other countries work so hard?" he asked over lunch. "For what?" Cuba had given him political asylum, and his Alamar apartment.

"It's ridiculous," I agreed.

"Look, nobody here can travel, or at least they can't afford to, and they ask me about how great it is elsewhere, and I say to them, *then why do I live here?*"

"Are there still a lot of Chileans here from the Pinochet days?"

"No, hardly any, I'm the last one, or one of them. I went back to Chile not long ago, just to see it. Everybody has forgotten any idea of struggle, things are booming, it's just sell-sell, work-work. Nobody talks about the horrible things that happened, in case it might upset the economy. It's terrible, I would never live like that."

"I could never live like this, Gonzalo, in these apartments, all identical, one after the other. At least yours has a view of the park."

"You have to compare it to what they had before," he said. "Many of these people were trapped in a house with their parents, or living in the countryside with no electricity, no running water."

We drank beer out of an old half-gallon soda bottle. Gonzalo called it *chopp*, a Latin American term for tap beer. After lunch, we went down to El Golfito and bought a bottle of rum and waded out across some jagged coral to an island in the tiny bay. The warm, tropical Atlantic was at our backs, and the waves lapped at our little islet and shimmered in the late afternoon sunshine. Turquoise, red, and orange fishing boats bobbed in the harbor.

"Aah," said Gonzalo, taking a swig of rum. "You see the fucking repression we're living under in this horrible country? So oppressive." He chuckled and lay back on a warm rock. Antonia was paddling her toes in the tide pools. "They're just so beautiful."

"I'm sorry?" I was starting to think I might have a little snooze.

"Her legs, man, aren't they divine?"

Across the shimmering inlet, the village of Cojímar glowed ochre in the sun. Ernest Hemingway had kept his fishing boat in this very harbor, venturing out in pursuit of marlin and other great manhood-challenging fish. Hemingway remains a huge figure in Cuba, especially now in the age of tourism, and several bars in Habana Vieja owe their popularity to their Hemingway-drank-here status. Nevertheless, he had left Cuba in 1960, the year after the revolution. Cubans who had left at this time, no matter how famous, were regarded as traitors. Most were relegated to the ashcan of history.

"Why is Hemingway still such a hero here?" I asked.

"How many really famous—internationally famous—writers has Cuba had?" said Gonzalo. "He chose to live here, and this was where he wrote his greatest books."

"Okay, but wasn't he the 1940s version of a sex tourist, taking advantage of all the things the revolution opposed?" I had always considered Hemingway the worst sort of macho gringo.

Gonzalo wavered between cynical cool and defense of a local hero. "Sure," he said, "but look across there." He pointed toward Cojímar. "Under that little dome is a bronze bust of Hemingway. Supposedly, the people of the village got together and had it made in his honor. Without any government money. It's made from melted-down boat propellers. They really liked the guy."

"Sure. Aah, Mister Hemingway, so glad to see you. Would you like to buy some fish?"

"They called him Mr. Way. Like: Hey *Meester Way*, where you been? Africa! *Asere*,* what about you give me some money and I go buy us a bottle?"

---

* *Asere* is a streetwise urban salute. Apparently derived from the Abakuá secret society and popularized in prison, it is used by hip Havana street kids both to greet one another and hail tourists.

Siete

Walking the line

Aprendimos a quererte
desde la histórica altura
donde el sol de tu bravura
le puso cerco a la muerte.

We learned to love you
from the historical heights
where the sun of your bravery
blocked the path of death.

Tu mano gloriosa y fuerte
sobre la historia dispara
cuando todo Santa Clara
se despierta para verte.

Your glorious and powerful hand
fires shots across history
when all of Santa Clara
wakes themselves up to greet you.

Vienes quemando la brisa
con soles de primavera
para plantar la bandera
con la luz de tu sonrisa.

You come, burning the wind
with suns of springtime
to plant the flag
with the light of your smile.

Tu amor revolucionario
te conduce a nueva empresa
donde esperan la firmeza
de tu brazo libertario.

Your revolutionary love
leads you to another task
where they are awaiting the strength
of your libertarian hand.

Seguiremos adelante
como junto a ti seguimos
y con Fidel te decimos:
¡Hasta siempre, Comandante!
    —Carlos Puebla

We'll continue onward
the way we did beside you
and along with Fidel we say to you:
Forever, Commander!

That's guerilla action you got there!" I looked up. Two *guajiros* were working their way toward me through dense brush on the other side of the barbed-wire fence I was snagged on. Both had dogs, and machetes. They were the first people I had seen in hours.

I had left Miriam and Havana behind a few days earlier, and set off again, following the tracks of the Hershey light rail line, which lead to Matanzas. What looked on the map like an easy shortcut from the tracks to the coast had turned into a frustrating bushwhack through thorn scrub, interspersed with ponderous clambering over endless strings of barbed wire.

"That's guerilla stuff," the elder *guajiro* said again, gesturing at my backpack.

"No, no, not guerilla stuff, I'm only trying to get to Santa Cruz. And I'm lost." *Please, I'm just a tourist.*

"I'm telling you, that is a whole guerilla rig," he said. "Why didn't you take the road?"

"I wish I'd seen a road," I said. "What road?"

Instead of dragging me off before the local Committee for the Defense of the Revolution, they laughed and gave me directions down a ravine and up the other side, pointing to a water tank on the horizon. There, I found a dairy. An overwhelming bovine odor hung in the air. A man was mucking out a cattle stall.

"Don't take the road," he said. "It's far. Go across that field and turn left at the big tree." He pointed out a radio tower he said was on the hill above Santa Cruz.

Once there, I *felt* like a guerilla, standing in front of another unguarded installation doubtless vital to Cuban national security. To describe the tower as being on top of a hill was something of an understatement. It was atop a cliff, with the city and the ocean at the bottom. I walked around and around the radio tower and peered over the edge, but there seemed to be no trail leading down to the town. The least steep bit was just shy enough of vertical for weeds and wildflowers to grow, and I set off down it on a diagonal, leaning into the slope like a skier and grasping at tufts of grass. Several hundred meters below me at the bottom was a baseball diamond with a game underway, and I pictured myself losing my footing and plummeting down into the infield. At any moment I was sure someone would look up and raise the alarm: *Look, a foreigner up on the radio tower, with guerilla things!*

At the bottom, I slipped through a fence and out into a lane with as much nonchalance as I could muster, brushing burrs and chaff off my shorts and T-shirt. At once, a most unlikely jogger ran up behind me and stopped, panting. He was stout and round and bald, with sweat pouring off his bright red face onto his already soaked shirt. I was certain he was about to have a heart attack.

"Whew," he finally said, when he could speak. "I'm on an exercise kick."

"You should be careful not to overdo it."

"It's only my first day. Look at me, I'm too fat, I have to get out here and do something."

He was the computer-accounts administrator for Havana Club rum, which has a huge distillery in Santa Cruz. He walked with me to help me find a place to stay.

"It's my duty to help you," said Gerardo. "You're a stranger in my town." He asked where I was from and when I said New York, he replied, "Oh, *la Gran Manzana* [the Big Apple] and Buffalo! And Syracuse! But the capital is Albany."

The hospitality I encountered everywhere in Cuba was so intense and genuine that it had started to embarrass and shame me to rely on it. In the United States, land of the gated community, we have forgotten what hospitality is. We think it's having a dinner party or being offered a free cup of coffee in a hotel lobby in the morning. Confronted with Gerardo, who ended his run early to lead me all over town in an increasingly desperate search for lodging, I was forced to consider the time and energy that the average American would likely spend helping a sweaty, bearded stranger wearing a backpack and speaking English with a Cuban accent.

We went to a friend of Gerardo's who he thought might rent, and then a place recommended by a man on the street. It was another hot-sheet house, renting to Cubans who needed a trysting place. At the door, a woman took one look at me and said, "Come in, come in, but hurry." She was nervous and didn't want to rent to a foreigner. "Eso es candela," said Maria. *Candela* means fire, as in: this is just too hot for me to get involved in. The second in command at the police station lived right across the street and if he saw me going in and out, forget it. Maria's husband, Abelardo, proposed an expensive drive to the next coastal village, which had a beach and therefore, they thought, a couple of licensed *casas*.

"I walked all the way here from Pinar del Río; I'm trying to make my whole trip on foot," I said, stretching the truth a bit. "If I go out tonight, I'll sneak through the garage."

"He's a good guy," said Gerardo, "I could tell right away when I met him; he's not going to give you any trouble."

"All right," said Abelardo, "but if the police come, you must tell them that I invited you, that you met me in Havana on a previous visit, when I was a bandleader." We agreed that I'd get in the back of the Buick in the garage in the morning and hunch down until Abelardo had driven a few blocks away from the house. Gerardo left, but invited me to dinner.

Once Maria and Abelardo had decided to rent to me, they were warm and welcoming. The kitchen opened right out onto the yard with no back wall, the way a good tropical kitchen should. I sat with Abelardo eating mangos picked from a tree in the corner.

"I'm sorry about all this," he said. "You should know that the Cuban doesn't *want* to steal and be a liar and a cheat, but he is forced into it. *No es fácil.* Any little thing you do to try and get ahead, they come and make a rule that you can't."

"I bet your friend is doing okay," said Maria. "The ones who work at the factory all walk out of there with barrels full of rum to sell on the black market."

Abelardo had been a saxophone player. "I was the sax, but also the bandleader," he said. "We used to play at all the big hotels, the Havana Libre, the Capri, in Varadero Beach. I loved to play music."

"What happened?"

"I gave it up. Too many years of playing in front of posh crowds eating lobster while I blew my heart out. I was up there onstage in my tuxedo, giving the people a good time; I was the one responsible for their fun, but then, when it was the hour for the band to eat, we'd have to go into the back. It wasn't right."

"You don't play anymore?"

"No, I had a Selmer, but I sold it to an Italian for $1,500. To put an engine in the Buick. I would like to play again someday, but maybe just around the house."

"So what do you do now?"

"I take people around in the car." Abelardo was the only Cuban I ever met who had two automobiles. He had a Czech car from the 1970s, with a Lada engine in it, and an enormous red 1960 Buick that he had converted to run on a Toyota diesel engine. "After I put the motor in, the authorities found out I had two working cars, so they confiscated it. I fought and fought, but they said I couldn't have the car. So I made a *promesa* to San Lázaro that if I got the car back, I would drive her to El Rincón every year. And, by some miracle, they gave her back. So, every year, I drive up and light some candles and put them on the hood."

I snuck out of the house and walked to Gerardo's. He lived with his wife and daughter in a building that might have been airlifted in from Alamar. We ate rice and beans, salad, fried plantains, and *papa rellena*, mashed potatoes formed into a ball the size of an orange, stuffed with flavorful ground beef, and then fried. I could see how Gerardo had gotten his figure. He ate in his boxer shorts, as if clothes were, in this heat, only for the working day. His daughter tried out her excellent English on me. Her "job" was to go with drivers like Abelardo when they had tourists and needed a translator. She worked for tips.

From the moment you meet them, Cubans share everything about their personal lives, from the marital to the financial, without even being asked. Gerardo said they were well-off. He was an executive earning 300 pesos, and between that and the translating and another daughter, married and living in Italy, who sent some money home to help out, the household was bringing in around 1,000 pesos a month, the equivalent of fifty dollars.

"We can eat like this every day," he said. His ample figure suggested that they often did. As soon as his wife left the room for a moment, he gobbled some quick seconds.

"Ever had *papa rellena* before?" he asked.

"Only from people selling it in the street, and it was more *papa* than *rellena*," I said.

"It's not the same at all, is it?" he laughed. "In those ones, you have to look for the meat with a microscope."

Gerardo knew the geography of the United States much better than I did.

"What's the most beautiful state?" he asked.

"I haven't seen them all," I said, "but I think perhaps Montana."

"Lots of copper in Butte."

"The copper pit at Butte is sort of the exception to the beauty of Montana."

"But the capital is Helena."

"I believe that's right."

Gerardo said I was like *El Andarin Carvajal,* who had jogged across Cuba from east to west before the triumph of the revolution.

After dinner, Gerardo made *Cuba libres* "with Havana Club rum, of course." He got out a guitar and played while his daughter sang "Hasta Siempre." She had a beautiful voice. There was no self-consciousness as she sang Carlos Puebla's elegy to the fallen hero of world revolution, Che Guevara. I knew the song, but I had never before noticed that it takes and modifies the form of the *décima.*

One of my favorite things about Cuba was that people got together and played music, with friends or even just as a family. In America, we've lost this tradition to television. It was one of the most simple, jolly evenings I spent in the country. When I got up to leave, Gerardo asked only one thing of me. "I would love it if you sent me a postcard from some out-of-the-way place in the United States," he said.

Maria and Abelardo loaded me up with mangos the next morning for the day's walk. I had heard them falling from the tree onto the tin roof in the night. They said the coast was clear; I could use the front door as long as I didn't hang about. A few kilometers outside of town, I almost got arrested anyway. I was picking my way along the jagged limestone coast behind a narrow, wooded strip of bay grapes that separated the sea from the coastal highway when I walked straight into an immaculate, landscaped resort, with winding asphalt driveways and cute little beach houses dotted among the shade trees. It could only be a resort for foreigners, charging in dollars. I continued along, imagining that I would simply walk through and out the other side, when two guys in black polyester vests and peach-colored floral shirts hurried up to me. They looked like waiters on a cruise liner.

"What are you doing here? You're not allowed to be in here."

"I'm sorry, I was hiking along the coast and suddenly walked right in, from just back there." I pointed toward the unprotected scrub behind me. "There was no fence or anything."

"This is for military personnel only."

"No problem, just point me toward the nearest exit, it's an honest mistake."

One of them pointed up the main driveway to a guarded checkpoint at the turnoff to the main road. As I walked toward it, a crisp new Peugeot pulled past me, and I saw a blur of olive drab behind the wheel. At the gate, the driver gestured to the guard with an urgent jerk of the thumb that, even from a hundred meters back, I could see meant, *Check that guy out.*

I prepared my stupid smile and approached the checkpoint. *I'm sorry; I was just strolling along your beautiful coastline when I stumbled into this mission-critical beachfront recreation facility.* But the guard was bored and his questions perfunctory. As he copied out the details from my passport onto a clip-board with agonizing care, I could see that he was only doing what he had been told in case someone came to have a look later.

In the village of Arcos de Canasi, I crossed the train tracks again and asked the first person I saw, an old black woman standing on her front porch, where I might be able to buy something to eat for lunch. She laughed, said "nowhere around here," and invited me in for a fried-egg sandwich, cooking it for me while I sat in her living room. Her name was Fermina. A Pentecostal, she said it was her Christian duty to give a traveler a meal. As I was eating, a young Matanzan couple came through the door. They had just dropped in to say hello to Fermina. They had been on the train back from Havana but it had unexpectedly stopped in Canasi for an hour due to track work. The husband, Luis Angel, was very clean-cut, wearing a striped polo shirt and jeans. He said he was an electrician, but he looked like an options trader on his day off. His wife, Liliana, hung on his arm on the sofa.

"You're from the States?" asked Luis.

"That's right."

"I tried to go, three times."

"They caught you every time? That's really rough. Who got you, the Americans or the Cubans?"

"The first two times it was the Americans, this last time the Cuban coast guard."

"How did you get the boats?"

"I built them all. The first one was twenty-seven feet. I made one twelve and the last about eighteen. They sink them right in front of you, or burn them once they take you aboard."

"You just launched right from the bay in Matanzas?"

"Yes, but not any more; now, I no longer have the right to build boats," he said wryly.

When they got up to leave, I decided to go with them back to the train station to see about sharing the train ride into Matanzas. I was sick of walking, and I rationalized that their boat-people stories were too good to pass up. I wanted to hear more about what would make a young married couple get into a handmade open boat with a couple of gallon jugs of fresh water and a jerry-rigged motor and try to cross 120 miles of the Florida Straights.

On our way out, I asked Fermina if I could take her picture on her porch.

"You don't want my picture."

"I really do."

"La vejez tiene cara de perro," she said. Old age has the face of a dog.

At the station, they told us the train was not to run again that day. I decided to continue hiking rather than go with Luis and Liliana to the highway to try my luck hitching. It was late afternoon and I walked fast along the tracks, sweating, but there were very few houses. At six in the evening, I stopped at one, a *campesino* home made from split royal palm trunks. I yelled through a windowless frame into the kitchen, "Hay alguien?" Is anybody home? Immediately, three strapping youths emerged around the side of the house and Mom and Dad appeared in the kitchen window frame, the whole family staring at me with wide-open eyes. I was somewhat taken aback.

"Uh, the train stopped in Canasi, I'm walking to Matanzas," I said. "Would you mind refilling my canteens?"

The old woman took them through the window.

"Why don't you hurry out to the highway and catch the last *guagua*?" asked one of the sons.

"Well, I like to walk, but then I was waiting for the train but it wasn't running and I came this way. I don't know; it's almost night. Anyway, do you think there is anywhere around here I could put up my hammock?"

There was only one way for them to react to this incoherent and self-contradictory statement. "He's crazy," said one of the brothers to another. *Es un loco!*

I thanked them, grabbed the canteens and headed down the track. The water tasted like cows.

"Asere. Where you going?" I turned and looked up from the tracks. A young guy in navy basketball shorts was calling to me. It was a shock to

hear this quintessential urban hustler's greeting in what seemed to be the middle of nowhere.

His name was Ariel and he struck me as kind of young Havana street punk. He had a tiger's head tattooed on one shoulder and a slick Caesar haircut that seemed out of place, and he was aggressive and brash, not cautious and soft-spoken like country people. He introduced me to his sister, Anabel. "It's my brother-in-law's farm," he said, "but I stay here, too. I like it much better than the city." In fact, he lived in Playa, in Havana, with an aunt and uncle. "But they are sort of bad people," he said, "they steal my stuff." I had the thought that he himself might be hiding out from the law.

The place was very poor, but it was beautiful in the last of the afternoon sun. Every day there was a tremendous glow that suffused all of Cuba with orange before the sun dipped down. The house was a box made of planks with corrugated tin for a roof. A few dogs lay in the sun on the bare earth of the yard and a huge sow on a rope was snuffling in a pail of slops, oblivious to the handful of piglets jockeying for position and sucking urgently at the arsenal of nipples on her underside. The yard was in Appalachian disarray. A shattered cement cattle trough too heavy to move was storage for an old, lidless bucket of roofing tar and a tattered plastic tarpaulin. A rusted-out oil barrel served as a barbeque or perhaps a trash burner, and an old, spindly park bench with no remaining back slats sat on a concrete slab, a little island amid the chickens scratching in the muck. It was a starter home for young *campesinos*.

Anabel said her husband, Pedro, was off chasing an errant pig, but the train to Matanzas ought to be along in a little while. I knew there wasn't going to be a train, but, after the fiasco at my last stop, I didn't invite myself to stay. Ariel said he had been about to take the kids down to the river for a wash and did I want to go for a swim? I leaned my pack up against the house and stripped down to my boxers. Ariel stood right next to me looking into the pack as I dug through everything looking for my flip-flops. My toes were white and wrinkled and soft from being in boots all day. Below the house was a creek and we followed the banks upstream for a couple of hundred meters to a nice swimming hole at a wooded bend.

Ariel's nephews, about five and seven years old, dove and splashed in the water. Ariel picked them up by turns and flung them, howling, into the middle of the pool as I stood hip-deep in the cold water and scrubbed myself.

"I want to get out of here," said Ariel. "There's no work in Havana, just trouble. The life out here is healthier, but I'll never have a farm. I mean, my sister lets me stay, but for how long? I'm trying to learn English first, so I will be ready when I get there."

I realized that something in my attitude toward Cuba had evolved because I didn't tell Ariel that his plan to try and get a boat was senseless and suicidal. He was twenty-two years old, had been ten when the Soviet Union collapsed, and all he knew was boredom and the necessity of the special period. When we returned to the house, I met Pedro, who had returned without finding the missing pig. At thirty-two, he was on his way to becoming a *guajiro*. He was already quiet and reserved, perhaps from solitary days in the fields. He let Ariel and Anabel do the talking. But he had pride in his place, a few acres he had inherited from his dad, and he showed me around a little, pointing out a field where he had plantains and tomatoes growing. "You won't starve to death out in the country," he said. "Not like in the city."

Anabel yelled from inside that the train was coming; I could run and I would catch it. I had been assuming that when the train didn't come, it would be natural for me to stay. Now, I could just hear the train in the distance, a humming in the wires. The last thing I wanted to do was scramble to drag my half-open pack down the hill and onto the train. "I feel comfortable here, I'd rather keep walking tomorrow," I said to Pedro. "What if I put my hammock up and spend the night?"

Anabel made a huge dinner and we ate in front of the television set. They had a battered old black-and-white on its last legs, but no refrigerator. The pork ribs we had for dinner were salt-cured. There was a vast plate of greasy *congris*, tomato salad, and, for dessert, a *dulce de leche* so sweet, and made from a milk so soured and bovine, that I could not eat it. I begged off saying that I would never be able to sleep after all that sugar. This was greeted with hilarity and ridicule. "Sugar puts you to sleep," said Anabel. Chickens wandered into the house looking for rice scraps and the kids shooed them out again.

On television, Castro was talking about US imperialism and the evils of my country. He seemed rarely to speak of anything else. "Do you think the US is going to invade us?" Pedro asked me.

"No, I don't think so, look how many years it's been. I honestly don't think you should worry about it. Only if, after Fidel dies, there are big problems, then they might. They would say they were here to establish security and democracy."

"When Fidel dies," said Ariel, "there is going to be chaos in the streets, all kinds of problems. Because everyone wants to go over there to the US."

"Do you own any cattle up there?" asked Pedro.

"Well, not actually."

"If you did own one, would you be allowed to kill it?"

"I suppose so, I mean, yes. I'm not sure I know what you mean."

"Here if you kill some guy, you go to jail for five or six years," said Pedro. "But kill your own cow and they put you away for thirty. What does that tell you?"

Pedro said that cows, while theoretically private property, were licensed and registered by the state. The government purchased a fixed number of liters of milk per month and, when they deemed it the right time to slaughter, they bought the meat, both at low Cuban-economy peso prices. Pedro said he didn't have any cattle because it was too much of a hassle, too much red tape, and people from the government coming around to check up on your cows.

"I can have as many pigs as I can raise and kill one when I need it," he said.

The *novela* came on TV. *El rey del ganado's* title sequence opens with sweeping helicopter shots of an endless herd of cattle rushing *en masse* across the Brazilian *pampa*, a swirling, churning ocean of beef. Pedro gestured at the television.

"All those cows," he asked, "are those private property?"

I said they were, but he couldn't quite believe it.

After the *novela*, it was bedtime. There were two beds divided by a narrow partition. Pedro and Anabel slept in one and Ariel slept in the other with the three kids. I had set up the hammock outside the front door under the overhanging roof, and Pedro had come outside to try and untie it and have me set it up inside.

He thought I felt I was imposing and that that was why I had put the hammock outside. That I didn't feel welcome. I couldn't tell him that I couldn't imagine sleeping without any privacy at all. Pedro said it would get very cold outside, but I said I was used to it and actually didn't find any weather in Cuba to be cold. I said I wanted to sleep there and look up at the stars. "You're sure?" he asked one more time through the closed door after he'd gotten in bed. The kids murmured and poked at Ariel, and there were vague barnyard grunts from behind the house. In the middle of the night, I woke when the train clanked by, slowly flashing sparks. The telephone poles were black silhouettes against the purple sky and somewhere in the distance was a lone electric light.

Just after dawn, when I was still in the hammock, I saw the kids heading off to school in their red scarves and shorts. They faced a long walk, to a long bus ride. While packing up and getting ready to go, I made a terrible mistake. I tried to give Anabel five dollars. I said, as I always did, that I really wanted to leave a present but didn't have room in the backpack to carry proper gifts for all the people helping me along the way.

"The dinner and the rest of it was from the heart," she said. "Not because I wanted to get something out of it." She was very angry, and her cheeks flushed, as if I had slapped her.

"I know that, please don't think I don't know that. I just would like to help out a little. I thought maybe you could do something for the kids. I'm sorry." I stuffed the money back in my pocket.

She was offended. Much worse than that, she was ashamed, and she never looked me in the eyes again. I could apologize for having given offense, but there was no remedy for my demonstration of pity. I had crushed her pride.

I walked the railroad all the way into Matanzas. The rails warped and wiggled as I looked down the line, undulating ever so slightly like twin silver snakes. It was easy to see why the trains moved so slowly. In places, the railroad ties had been replaced with old sections of rail, cut into lengths. On some of them, I could still read the word pressed into the iron. *Carnegie.* I came to the place where the track work was still going on. Hundreds of meters of electric cable had sagged down to the tracks. Four shirtless men were on top of a pneumatic platform that extended out from an ancient red and yellow tender car like a giant automobile jack. One of them was banging away at a telephone pole with a mighty hammer. It was a socialist realist tableau of silhouetted muscles and proletarian labor under the baking sun. When I waved my camera to show I was going to take a picture, the man hammering thrust his sledge in the air and shouted *Viva Cuba!*

Ocho

The little dolls

An ancient guy with a patchy salt-and-pepper goatee was sitting on a wooden stool in front of his house, sanding the neck of an acoustic guitar. He wore a *guajiro*'s fatigue shirt, grimy with powdered lacquer and sawdust, and Coke-bottle-bottom glasses that gave him a goofy vibe, somehow inviting casual banter.

"What are you doing?" I asked. "This is the city of *rumba*. There are no guitars in the *rumba*."

He squinted at me through his thick spectacles. They had heavy, black, old-school frames, like Buddy Holly's glasses.

"You like music?"

"Very much."

He put the guitar down to shake hands. He had the delightful and improbable name of Dagoberto Manzo.

"Then I'll tell you what I think. Now, I'm not a musician. I make guitars, and I can play a little. And not everybody thinks the same way, but here is what I think. It's all the same thing. Because every musician, every instrument in the world, has to follow the one most important instrument. Or else it's just not music. The one from which all others come. The one most important in the world."

Dagoberto spoke with evangelical fervor. It was just my luck to have delivered myself right into the hands of a proselytizing religious fanatic. I was sure he was in the middle of an extended religious metaphor and was about to exclaim "the Lord, our God." He kept me in suspense.

"What?" I asked.

"Two little sticks. The two little sticks called *clave*. The *guaguancó* has its *clave* and the *punto guajiro* uses *clave*. Any musician in the world that isn't following the *clave* is not a musician."

Dagoberto's examples are the polar extremes at either end of Cuba's rich musical longitude. The *guaguancó* is black, urban, and African, and one of the primary rhythms that underpins the music now known as *salsa;** *punto guajiro* is the backing music for *décimas* sung by rural white poets nurturing an ancient Spanish tradition. Both demand that the rhythm be kept by the two hardwood sticks, one cupped in one hand, the other tapped relentlessly against it. Between the two lie the racial melting pot and the dozens of genres that make Cuban music so rich. Poetry, improvisation, and the *clave* bridge the gap.

Cuba's greatest scholar of folklore, music, and religion, Fernando Ortiz, wrote a 100-page essay on the origins and mystique of the *clave*, considering and then rejecting every conceivable antecedent to this most Cuban of instruments. After ranging from Hawaii's "concussive sticks" to the Mabodé and Abongo tribes of West Africa and the minstrel shows of nineteenth-century America, in which pairs of old bones were clacked together, he concludes that nothing in the world prefigures the sonority of the *clave*, which "gives its humble sound like the solitary and beautiful drop that falls upon the placid surface of the sleeping water."

"I'll show you a very special guitar," said Dagoberto. He went inside and returned with a double-necked contraption straight out of a heavy-metal music video, except that it had the lustrous wood and voluptuous curves of an acoustic guitar instead of jagged angles and chrome trim. The upper neck was a *tres*, the Cuban guitar of the *son montuno*, which has six strings arranged in pairs. The lower neck was a normal acoustic guitar. They shared the same body. "I used to have just one electric pickup for both necks, but I had to change it," he said. "When you played one, the other would hum *wooo*, like a foghorn. It's the only one in the world. Well, I have seen one other, a musician from Guantánamo had one, but his had the necks mounted back to back, not one above the other, so you had to

---

* "Salsa" is really nothing more than a catchall marketing term developed in New York in the 1970s to sell Latin music; it likely diminished the public's appreciation of the multitude of distinct Cuban rhythms. To paraphrase the late *timbalero*, Tito Puente, who refused to accept the term: "Salsa? I don't what that is; to me, salsa is tomato sauce."

take it off and turn it over to switch instruments. All I have to do is move my hands." He fetched his wife for a photo in front of the palm tree on their porch. In it, he holds the double-bladed axe ready for action, displaying just a hint of wry smile that I think shows both pride in this magnificent guitar and acknowledgment of how silly it is.

Farther down the street, toward the plaza, in the smoky afternoon light, men clattered dominoes on the tables behind the grillwork of the Scottish Masonic temple. Oldtimers sat on the tiled stoops in ruined shoes, chewing their cigars into paste and hoping for a hint of breeze. The tall windows were protected by friendly security, iron window guards welded into dense curlicues, floral swirls, and hearts. Matanzas is known as the Athens of Cuba because of its historic reputation as the cradle of Cuban poetry and culture. It was also, for me, a musical Holy Grail, home of the Muñequitos de Matanzas, a legendary group in the pantheon of *rumba* music. *Rumba* is the most hardcore Afro-Cuban good-time music there is, deep, soulful, and funky all at the same time. Invented by black stevedores working on the docks of Havana and Matanzas in the late nineteenth century, *rumba* is pure vocal percussion, still made by singers and drummers and nothing else. The original players had no instruments at all and sat around during slow moments on the docks, beating out rhythms on packing crates. These *cajones*, now made out of pieces of plywood nailed together in the form of a box, are still sometimes played; since its early days, however, the *rumba* has developed into an astonishing, intricate interplay between a core of three conga drums, all rooted in the all-important *clave*. Like the names of other Caribbean genres such as the Cuban *guaracha* and Dominican *bachata*, *rumba* once simply meant *party*. Over time, the music people most liked to hear at their fiestas took over the name. The party was the music.

Back in Havana, I had been to a *rumba* at UNEAC, the Union of Artists and Writers, perhaps the most powerful cultural institution in Cuba. The cover charge was one dollar, and the afternoon was a collision of intellectual glitterati with young, black "street cred." Women in *kente*-cloth turbans mingled with middle-aged Cuban movie stars under the trees, and the guys sitting at the white, wrought-iron garden tables wore the latest Michael Jordan Nike caps backward, or berets and black wraparound shades. Girls in LA gangster-style mini-braids sipped tap beer next to wild-haired, gray-bearded leftist intellectuals. Recent initiates, in the middle of their ritual year of purity, dressed up their all-white outfits into fashion statements. One of these *santeros* wore a crisp, logoless white ballcap over a white do-rag, blindingly starched white Levis, and a white, baggy oxford shirt meticulously untucked in the back and sliding off one shoulder to reveal the only flash of color, his beaded *Santería* necklace. The latest in urban fashions from the North had seeped through the embargo.

A band called Clave y Guaguancó played, and, on the colonaded terrace of the UNEAC building, the largest of the conga drums, the *tumbadora*, sounded like cannon fire. Young black couples danced on the steps, fluid and athletic, combining the surreal joint-snapping moves of breakdancing with sinuous limbo. It had whetted my appetite, and I was determined to seek out the Muñequitos in Matanzas and, if possible, see them play.

I walked across the plaza and crossed over the river to Versalles on an arched footbridge. Turquoise, red, and orange fishing dories were tied up in a row against houses flush to the east bank. The Hershey rail terminal is in the Versalles district, so named because Frenchmen fleeing the Haitian revolution had settled there. Arriving on foot along the rails the day before, I had met an earnest evangelical named Barbaro who walked with me into town. Despite his religious convictions, he had promised to introduce me to a local *santera*, Loretta. He also thought he knew of a drum-maker who might know the Muñequitos. I met up with him again and, on our way to Loretta's house, we ran into another guy he knew from the neighborhood.

"Excuse me," said Barbaro. "I always hear drums when I come past your place. My friend here from America is very interested in drumming, and I know you play. Maybe he could stop by and talk to you about it."

"Sure. What's your interest? Do you want to take lessons?" He was a young black guy named Eddie, with a mustache and warm smile.

"I'm not a musician, I'm just a *rumba* fan. I'm hoping to meet some of the Muñequitos."

"I'm with the Muñequitos. Come to practice tomorrow morning. I invite you."

I scribbled down the details. It seemed an incredible stroke of good luck.

When Barbaro and I arrived at Loretta's, she was sitting in her tiny front room with her two daughters. Although the door to the street was cracked open, the house felt dim and claustrophobic. Once my eyes had adjusted to the light, I saw that this was because the whole of the little house was given over to the *orishas*. Every corner or patch of wall that might have reflected the light was blocked by a statue of a saint draped in silk and lace. In front of these altars, the floor was covered with clay pots and wilting floral offerings. Loretta herself was festooned with heavyset rings, silver bangles, and mighty earrings tugging down at her earlobes—long, hefty strips of silver that scraped her shoulders. She had powder-white hair swept up and back in an immaculate woman's pompadour, and fine black eyebrows penciled on her white forehead. She wore string upon string of color-coded *orisha* beads.

Loretta took me through from the living room down a narrow hallway to the kitchen, showing off her five altars with the casual pride of a housewife describing the finer points of a new interior-decorating scheme to the neighbors. She explained the meaning of her beads: red and white for *Changó*, red and black for *Elegguá*, yellow and amber for *Ochún*, blue and clear for *Yemayá*. When she spoke, I heard fifty years of cigarettes. A shelf in the kitchen was draped with a brilliant multicolored Mexican serape on which perched male and female dolls, black and white, in red shirts or patchwork dresses. These were further representations of the *orishas*. One black, hand-sewn, stuffed doll in a yellow dress was *Ochún*, but I wasn't sure about a black male doll with a cowboy hat, white beard, and mustache, wearing what looked like a white tracksuit and sitting on a miniature plush red chair.

Inside a low cupboard sat an *Elegguá*, a conical blob of gray concrete inset with cowrie shells for eyes and mouth, conch shells for a crown, and two rounded chunks of coral planted on the chest like breasts. *Elegguás* were once carved from stone or coral, but the ease with which concrete can be formed into the squat triangular shape has won out. In the 1950s, anthropologist Lydia Cabrera found a few examples of the cement version, calling them a "modern and capricious invention of Havana Santería," but today the new materials have taken over, and all the *Elegguás* I saw—in Matanzas, Ciego de Ávila, and Santiago—were made of cement.

"Are you from New Jersey?" asked Loretta.

"I am from New Jersey; I live in New York now, but...."

"How did I know?" she asked. She answered her own question by looking at me with a piercing gaze and tapping her temple with a manicured finger, jangling her bangles. "Do you know any of Los Hershey? The family that used to have a chocolate concern here?"

"That's in Pennsylvania, it's next to New Jersey. But no, I don't personally know any Hersheys."

"Would you be able to get a message to them?"

"I suppose so. It's a huge corporation."

"A saint brought you here, you are a wanderer, but you like to do good. Write this down: *This is from the little girl raised by Ramon Acosta on a plantation in San Juan that belonged to Hershey. That this girl is already an old woman, but she needs to communicate with them. The plantation was called El Tanque. Because she is the daughter of a Hershey. She doesn't want anything from them, just to please be in touch.*"

"You think you might be a daughter of a Hershey?"

"There are a lot of reasons, Richard. Many things over the years that add up. First, my name, Loretta, that's no name for a Cuban—and look at me, I don't look Cuban."

It was true. Although Cubans range from Anglo white to the darkest African blue-black, Loretta, stripped of her bangles and beads, could have passed for a Philadelphia Main Line society matron. She rummaged around in a box and pulled out a photograph of herself as a young girl. She was stunning.

"Oh, you were a real *rompecorazones*," I said. A heartbreaker.

"Indeed, I broke some hearts," she said with an ashy laugh. "When I was seven years old, on the farm of the *campesinos* who raised me, we had a visit from a very elegant foreign woman. My grandmother told me that she would be back, that the woman was looking to buy a house, but she never returned. And then I received a package from the United States, with a doll, and a dress—and me not even having any idea where or what the United States was? Imagine. So I got to thinking and thinking.

"The Acostas always said that my parents had died, but once a man in town in a nice suit stopped his car in the street and tried to grab me. I ran away and hid. Now I am convinced somehow that he was my father. Another time, perhaps only ten or twelve years ago, long after I had come here to Matanzas, to the city, I was on the train coming back from Havana, the same Hershey train, and we had some *refresco*, some fruit juice in a bottle. And there was a woman sitting with her son and he was making a fuss and we offered some juice to him. His mother looked at me in surprise like she knew me. She said that in the house of two old women, in the town of Hershey, there was a picture or a photograph on the wall that looked exactly like me. I was all ready to get off the train in Hershey and go with her to the house, but then, at the last moment, I got scared, I don't even know why."

"I don't want to get your hopes up," I said, "but I'll send them a letter."

"That's all I ask. I know I'm not going to die without knowing the truth."

That evening at the house where I was renting a suite in a grand mansion, I had a long conversation with Joaquín DiHigo, a professor at the local university. A member of the intellectual elite who often traveled outside Cuba to academic conferences, a thinker and pro-revolutionary, he was also a member of the reemerging economic upper class, if only by virtue of having a large and charming apartment to rent out. Unlike most Cuban homes I had been in, the DiHigos had nice furniture and antique family china that, like the house, had been inherited from Joaquín's grandfather. In the hard times since 1989, many families had sold off their last family heirlooms to make ends meet.

"In the Eighties and Seventies," said Joaquín, "everyone here was equal, and everything was equally distributed, but now you can start to see some growing differences."

"I think the differences are quite significant; especially where I've been walking out in the country, people are really suffering."

"People may be poor here, but we don't live in the misery people experience in other countries I've been to—Mexico or Venezuela, for example. I don't understand why we Cubans are always comparing ourselves to the United States. We never ever compare ourselves to other countries in Latin America with which we have so much more in common. We ought to be comparing ourselves to Haiti and the Dominican Republic."

This was an excellent point. The people I had met in Cuba were materially better off than poor Jamaicans, Guatemalans, or Hondurans. But there was a resignation in Cubans that I hadn't encountered elsewhere, a sense that the country was treading water. Or treading gelatin that was slowly thickening.

"All the rules and regulations seem to wear people down," I said.

"I'll tell you something," said Joaquín, "and this is not something I would only tell you, I say the same thing at the university. In theory, nobody can deny that socialism is a better system, but, unfortunately, the human race is not yet advanced enough for socialism. Man is always trying to get ahead. We're not ready for socialism."

I invited myself to watch *El rey del ganado* with the family. The neighbors from across the street came, too. The head of the Mezenga clan had crashed his private plane in Amazonia. Meanwhile, his estranged wife was "putting horns on his head" with a scurrilous and preening pimp named Ralph, a character so one-dimensionally evil that we all agreed he would not be long for this world. In fact, a month later, when I arrived in Trinidad, Ralph was found murdered on a quiet tropical beach. (Cubans claimed that the cuckolding was implicit in the name of the series, "The king of beef." The Spanish expression, "poniendo los cuernos," or putting the horns on someone, means to cuckold.)

The Muñequitos's rehearsal was near the main plaza on the second floor of what I took to have once been a warehouse for goods coming in and out of the port of Matanzas. Stuff unloaded from the same docks, perhaps, where the *rumba* was invented. The drums were stored in a locked closet under the stairs. Eddie's younger brother, Noel, was the band's roadie, humping congas, *batá*, and *shekere* up the stairs into the practice studio, a long and cavernous loft. The musicians gathered in the front near tall shutters that opened out onto the street. The dancers controlled the rest of the space, limbering up in the leotards, track pants, and leg warmers that make up a dancer's wardrobe everywhere in the world. I stood with Eddie outside on a narrow terrace. On the matching balcony across the street from us, a naked toddler was gripped onto the metal railing amid a garden of houseplants in rusting cans, peeing blissfully down onto the street below.

Eddie said they were going to begin with the *batá*.

Batá are hourglass-shaped double-ended drums held laterally across the player's lap and played with both hands. They are used in the *toques de Santo*, the religious ceremonies of the Lucumí. There are three *batá* played by a trio of drummers: the *okónkolo*, the *itótele*, and the *iyá*. They are used to play sacred music and invoke the saints, not to play *rumba*, which is an excuse to gossip, hang out in the park, and dance on weekends. The *rumba* is generally played on three congas of different size that are upright narrow barrels held between the knees, with one skin only, stretched over the top surface of the barrel. But because the same drummers often play both *rumba* and *batá*, one might think of *rumba* as secular *Santería* music.

I asked Eddie if the Muñequitos had always played *batá*.

"It's a pretty new thing for us," he said "but since we're considered a folkloric group, we've been bringing it in. People want to hear the music of the *santos*. Especially internationally, there is a lot of demand, so we have made it part of the repertory."

The *batá* lay across the players' laps. They took a ferocious beating at both ends, and the array of rhythm that surged from the three drums defies description. Not only are all six drumheads tuned to make a different tone, but there are countless variations in the way the hands are made to meet the skin: with cupped palm, full on and flat-handed, or thudding into the rim of the drumhead. The result is an infinity of percussive sound.

Beriel, the cantor, led a call and response in Lucumí. A slow and steady shake of the *shekere* set the pace for the polyrhythmic explosion. An African percussion instrument, the *shekere* looks like an oversized, inside-out rattle. Usually made from a huge dry and empty gourd covered with a mesh of fibers, like a loose fishnet, it has large hard seeds or pebbles knotted into the corners of the webbing. When it is thrust downward, these seeds rap against the outside of the resonant gourd, almost but not quite in unison, making a sound something like a shaken cookie jar full of rice, but much louder.

I was sad to see that the Muñequitos used a fiberglass *shekere*, with red plastic beads instead of seeds, manufactured by Latin Percussion, Inc., of Garfield, New Jersey. This company is foremost in the world among the makers of congas, *batá*, *timbales*, and other percussion instruments, but my ethnographic fantasy demanded the organic, rootsy quality of a gourd. I would have preferred, of course, a gourd that had been hand-knotted by a Muñequitos great-grandmother aboard a slave ship, with seeds brought from Dahomey. Real musicians don't have time for this sentimental nonsense, however, or the pretensions of the fan. No baggage-handler can destroy a durable LP *shekere*, nobody makes flight cases to protect lumpy and oversized pear-shaped gourds, and modern technology has distilled and perfected the primeval sound down to a consistent and repeatable essence.

But it seemed a great irony. According to their corporate website, Latin Percussion was founded as a response to the US embargo against Cuba, when Martin Cohen, a photographer and lounge lizard in the New York Latin scene, discovered in the mid 1960s that good instruments from Cuba had become unavailable in the United States because of the new trade clampdown. After making himself a pair of bongos, he soon invented and patented the "Vibra-slap®," after a request from Bob Rosengarden, then the *Tonight Show* drummer, to "replicate the sound of the traditional horse jawbone with rattling teeth." Fiberglass congas and plastic beaded *shekeres* followed, along with celebrity endorsement contracts for players like the late *timbalero* and showman Tito Puente and Cuban expatriate *conguero* Carlos "Patato" Valdez. "Innovation has always been a part of the LP story," reads their company history. "In building his first patented instruments, Cohen used durable modern materials to replace rare and fragile instruments without sacrificing sound quality." Today in Cuba, a band with an arsenal of LP-brand instruments has cachet: their New Jersey drums are a status symbol, proof that they have toured the world and made enough money to buy the best.

Ned Sublette—who, through his record label Qbadisc, singlehandedly introduced the Muñequitos to American audiences, and certainly to me, in the early Nineties—points out that as good as LP *batá* might sound, they cannot be used in religious ceremonies because, being made of fiberglass instead of once-living trees, they are never inhabited by that special spirit, particular to drums, known as *añá*. *Batá* invested with this spirit are a rare and precious commodity. In *Cuba and its Music*, Sublette writes that such drums "are considered living things," and that a set of them "is in many ways more important than the drummers who play it, as though the drums were the player and the drummers the instruments." At the time, however, I was completely ignorant of the concept of *añá*. It was not until much later in the journey, while wandering the back streets of Ciego de Ávila, that I would encounter this particular spirit.

The origin of the instruments, of course, did nothing to diminish the quality of the music. The group's elders left the athletic drumming to the younger generation and stood behind the drums in a loose group while the cantor led the songs. Every few minutes, one of them would stop the rehearsal and suggest a minute adjustment to the rhythm or dancing. The dancers bent at the waist and scraped the floor, rolled their shoulders and flexed to the rhythm in a variety of impossible ways. They did something that looked like the funky chicken. Swallows flew in and out of the loft to their nests in the eaves, swooping low over the floor behind the dancers.

One of the *rumberos* picked up a *campana*, cowbell, and began to beat it with a stick in what seemed a casual and unplanned way, while another added a second *shekere* to the mix. The change in the energy level was palpable, the dancers ratcheted up their frenzy about ten notches as if a switch had been thrown, and sweat was soon dripping onto the green floor tiles. The youngest male dancer, Figurin, had the Nike swoosh stripe tattooed on the front of one shoulder. He moved with an aerobic urgency, making an ongoing threat to spin out of control and fly into bits. Every reach and twist and leap went farther than I would have thought possible, but he never stumbled, recapturing himself at the last moment from whatever invisible force drove him, sliding back into the realm of believable human movement with a thin smile on his face like a challenge. I imagined the *orishas* would descend at any moment.

During the break, I talked with Noel on the little terrace above the street. He told me that once a truck had lost control on the hill above Loretta's house and smashed into the wall, destroying it completely before coming to a stop in the living room. The statue of the Virgin was left standing, inches from the front of the truck.

"She's a very good *santera*," said Noel.

The second half of the rehearsal, the *rumba* portion, was little more than a formality. Asking the Muñequitos de Matanzas to *rehearse* the *rumba* made as much sense as suggesting to some construction workers that they practice going out for a beer after work. As Ned Sublette put it to me, "the idea of practice in this music is a rather different one. They are practicing all kinds of things, including practicing existing as a group; they're practicing like a married couple practices being married every day." Nonetheless, they polished points so fine that I could not distinguish the changes being made, even when the older *rumberos* called for the music to stop and explained the modifications to the drummers right in front of me. They refined rhythmic transitions, suggesting subtle shifts of focus from one conga to another, while the dancers yawned and lounged against the walls. They heard this exquisite music almost every day.

Eddie told me later that dancing to the *rumba* is an easy and casual freestyle, whereas, because each *orisha* has its own particular ritual dance-step, and sometimes more than one, dancers dancing to the *batá* must keep all the rhythms clear in their mind and constantly listen for cues in the drumming.

A *rumba* begins with a *lalaleo*, a vocal solo of abstracted syllables sung by the cantor, a kind of prelude to the main melody of the song. While *Lalaleo* is an onomatopoeic expression, according to Eddie, it is a mangling of the Spanish *tarareo*, which refers to a wordless introduction or interlude in a song. *Rumbas* are sung in Spanish, and the lyrics are often *décimas*. This meeting of fifteenth-century Iberian peninsular poetry with African long-shoreman drumming unites, like the *clave*, the entirety of the Cuban racial and cultural spectrum. In a fascinating article on this cross-pollination, Philip Pasmanick offers a delicious quotation from an elder *rumba* states-man, Havana singer Chan of the group Yoruba Andabo. *Rumberos*, Chan told Pasmanick, are unlikely to incorporate *décima* into their singing if *guajiro decimistas* might be around to hear them "because they might think the *rumberos* are making fun of them."

As he sang the *lalaleo*, the lead singer, Rafael, began playing the *clave*. I had seen him holding the two sticks outside on the street before the doors were opened; all through the *batá* rehearsal, when neither he nor the *clave* were called for, he had held onto them, as if it was too risky to lay them down anywhere. Now, playing them, he used gentle strokes, as if polishing a rare jewel with a soft cloth. The correct and delicious sound of the *clave* comes not from hitting the two sticks together with any force or violence, but from the resonance of the vibrating wood amplified in the cupped hand that holds the lower stick firm. According to Fernando Ortiz, one stick is male, the other, the one cradled in the palm, female. Although almost visually identical, the two are not interchangeable, and the veteran *clavero* will not only always hit the female with the male, but he will always hit it in the exact same spot, seeking the most perfect sound his two sticks have to offer. It is a sound Federico Garcia Lorca called "a drop of wood."* This is why one of Raphael's *clave* had a lone dent, hollowed out over years despite the relaxed, soft way he brought the two sticks together.

After the rehearsal, Eddie and Noel took me to their house in Versalles just down the hill below Loretta's. On the whitewashed living room wall was a collage of photographs of their late father, Titi. He had been the Muñequitos *quinto* player through most of the 1970s and into the 1980s. With the pride and bias of a son, Eddie said that people still referred to him as "the greatest *quinto* player of all time." The photographs were old and had begun to fade, but they showed Titi in blistering action, hands blurred above the surface of the drumskin. He wore a slick, short-sleeved polyester print shirt of the kind that was the latest in hip streetwear in the

---

* According to Ortiz, the male *clave* is eight inches long, the female one a quarter of an inch shorter. The Lorca image is from his poem, *Son de negros en Cuba*.

early Seventies and a grossly oversized baseball cap, from which protruded puffs of afro. On his face was that particular look of sweaty concentration *congueros* get when they are in the thick of it: the head held tilted just up, the eyes focused out and away—in middle space—never looking at the drum because the exact location of its every minute contour is intimately known. Drum and drummer, merged.

The *quinto* is the smallest and highest pitched of the three congas used in the *rumba*, the baby drum, "child" of the *segundo*, the *mamá*, and the mighty *tumbadora*. Eddie said that the *quinto* is the most liberated of the three, entering in and out of the music at will, forging off on solo tangents like a lead electric guitar. As Sublette puts it, the quinto "speaks."

"But the *quinto* always has to follow the improvisation in the lyrics, and it also follows the dancer," said Eddie. The accomplished *quintero* takes cues from the dancefloor action, not the other way around. This sort of circular commentary is common in the *rumba*, especially in the so-called *montuno* section when the lyricist begins to improvise, singing out on subjects like the news of the day or the skills and looks of the *bailarinas*. I had not realized that such importance was placed on the dancer until Eddie, a *segundo* player, explained the different *rumba* rhythms in terms of the dancing.

"There are three rhythms: the *yambú*, the *guaguancó*, and the *columbia*." said Eddie. We were sitting in his tiny living room, dominated by a television set draped with cloth. Unless the TV is on, Cubans hang a piece of fabric over the screen to protect it from the Caribbean sun, which they believe damages the set. This may be true, for nowhere else are such quantities of ancient televisions still in use.

"The *yambú*," continued Eddie, "is slower than the *guaguancó*, and danced in couples, but they keep their distance from each other, there is no *vacunao*. The *vacunao* is only in the *guaguancó*. *El gallo quiere pisar a la gallina, y la gallina no dejarse pisar*." The rooster wants to lay the chicken and the chicken won't let herself get laid. Dancing to the *guaguancó*, the most popular of the three principal *rumba* rhythms, is all sex. However civilized, many of the world's dances boil down to courtship; in the *guaguancó*, however, the stylization of pursuit and capture often verges on an unfettered parody of copulation. The man and woman slither and pose in circles, ostensibly oblivious to one another, but she never quite lets her guard down, for when he senses an opportunity, the man gives a sudden sexual thrust, which the woman must dodge or parry, typically by crossing her hands in front of her genitals. This is the *vacunao*.

The classic *vacunao* is a literal thrust of the hips leaving little to the imagination, but the cutting-edge crowd I had seen at the UNEAC went in for metaphor. One guy danced as if drunk, staggering up and down the shallow marble staircase to the terrace. He wobbled, flirting with disaster, and therefore impotence, but then spun with lucid purpose to confront his partner and flick an imaginary marble toward her. Next, he bent away from her at the waist and flung his arm between his legs, glancing over his shoulder to see if she had "caught" the *vacunao*. Nonexistent baseballs were batted and invisible Frisbees tossed behind the back. All meant the same thing: sperm is flying through the air, and you had better dodge. A *vacunao* can be as subtle and rude as a tongue quickly thrust out of the mouth, or as bold and physical as an overplayed attack-and-thrust verging on public, clothed rape. I'd seen one female tourist ask one of the more agile homeboys for a dance only to find herself driven to the ground and mercilessly humped at the end of the song, until she was beet-red with embarrassment.

"And the *columbia*?" I asked.

"The *columbia* is much faster. It is danced by the man alone, with machetes or knives. It is more to do with the man showing how fast and powerful he is. There is one more rhythm that they used to play, but it has been extinguished. The *jiribilla*; it is much faster even than the *columbia*. I don't know how to play it, you would have to ask the older guys. Maybe Figurin would be able to dance the *jiribilla*, but most anyone else would have a heart attack."

Eddie put on an old tape of the Muñequitos. When his mother heard the music in the kitchen, she came in and sat down beside the television. She was a petite and skinny woman, wiry and strong, although she couldn't have weighed more than ninety pounds. I saw her beating out the *clave* pattern on the arm of her chair, looking at the pictures of her dead husband stuck up on the wall. Eddie said his father was the *quinto* player on the recording. I thought his mother was going to start crying. Finally, she turned away from the photographs toward me and looked down at the floor.

"No es fácil," she said.

Nueve

Mr. Congo and his charms

I had never had my fortune told, but I wanted to see Loretta in action.
"My American friend," she said, "I didn't think I would see you again. I'm so surprised." Her daughters were still sitting in her living room. Loretta's daughter, Ramona, was overweight and ashen, and suffered from a "nervous problem" of some kind. *Nervios* was a common Cuban complaint, which I interpreted to mean depression. Ramona spent a lot of time slouched in her mother's armchair.

"I'm leaving tomorrow, I wanted to have a *consulta* before I left. And I wanted to say goodbye to you."

"I have a terrible headache, I can't work now, I won't be able to see anything clearly."

I said I would try to stop by before I walked out of the city. I told them I needed a big, brimmed straw hat and Loretta's other daughter said she knew someone who made them. She offered to walk me there. We went a long way uphill into the suburbs of Matanzas and finally found the hat woman, at her home. When she opened the front door, a few unfinished hats were visible at the end of the hallway in the sun on the back patio. For eighty cents, she sold me an authentic *guajiro* straw *sombrero* that would protect me from the sun. My neck was still burned red from days of walking the railroad track.

The next morning when I arrived back at her house, Loretta put on a paisley headscarf and wrapped another one around her shoulders in preparation for looking into my future. She had on vast gold hoop earrings. With her blond hair hidden under her scarf, she looked like a gypsy. We sat down at the kitchen table next to the breakfront covered with the dozens of dolls representing African spirit guides and *orishas*. The wall was painted with a naive mural of a marshy lake in front of a distant squiggly line of brown mountains. There was a paper stuck to the wall near a spidery black tree that said, *Please do not bring children with you unnecessarily, the consultation is 10 Pesos.*

She lit a candle and shuffled a deck of worn playing cards. On the table was a small crucifix submerged in a glass of water, like a plant cutting waiting to grow roots. She made the sign of the cross three times over the glass with the cards and dealt three piles. Loretta looked at the three face-up cards and then asked a question or made a pronouncement. She never explained what any card or group of cards meant. It was all very abstract, as if a set of cards did not so much give information as suggest a line of inquiry.

"You're going to move house," she said. "But you have a small problem."

I waited to find out what the problem was, but we were already moving on to the next cards.

"You had an accident as a small child?"

"Hmmm," I said. "I'm not sure."

"You had to go to the doctor?"

"Sure."

"In the place where you live, are there stairs?"

"Yes."

"You want to achieve something, it is a little bit risky, but you will accomplish it." That was walking across Cuba and writing a book about it, which didn't count; I knew she knew all that.

"The cards say Cynthia is painting a painting. It is taking a long time. She's not fat, is she?"

"No, I wouldn't say so at all."

"She loves you, she adores you, and she has lots of faith in you. She has a mascot of some kind?"

"A mascot?"

"Yes, like a doll, or a stuffed animal, something like that."

"Well," I said. "She took our cat, Joey, to Greece with her."

"That's it!" Loretta grabbed my arm. "Richard," she asked. "Who is Susan?"

I racked my brain, but I couldn't think of any Susans. Loretta was looking at me with suspicion, and I felt she was about to accuse me of hiding a secret romance.

"An older woman, Richard, she's already dead." I shrugged my shoulders. She took my pen and wrote carefully on a piece of paper: S-U-S-A-N W-E-R-R-E-L-L.

"I really don't know," I said.

"She's a spirit that protects you. When you are in the house, put a candle with a flower in her name and pray to God. Say an "Our Father." You are very well-protected by spirits, and you must always put lots of flowers in the house."

Loretta gave me a thin slab of something she called *carey* and said that I should build a wooden stand for it and put it somewhere in the house. It was brown-mottled with olive translucent spots, a tortoiseshell fragment from some undoubtedly endangered species of sea turtle, a piece of the undersea world that Loretta said would bring me luck. We hugged one another goodbye.

The new straw hat kept the sun off my neck as I hiked through the southern suburbs of Matanzas, past cinderblock and zinc-roofed houses, along streets that faded into rutted cart-tracks and then lumpy footpaths. Like any Latin American slum, it was a neighborhood that had sprawled faster than the streets it was on. People had just kept on building beyond the end of the road. One day, perhaps, the streets would be extended, giving these outlying homes a new legitimacy. Many Cubans from the Oriente, the eastern provinces of Las Tunas, Holguín, Granma, Santiago de Cuba, and Guantánamo, were making their way toward the comparative opportunities of Havana. *Habaneros* spoke of the Oriente as if it were another country, where the forces of the Great Depression were at work. Life is hard here in Havana, they said, but *there*, they have nothing. To hear them talk, in the Oriente, there were no jobs, farms were turning to dust, and settlers were leaving to make the desperate trek west in search of fictitious opportunity. In these conversations, houses like the Matanzan shacks I passed were always described as belonging to these migrants.

I crossed railroad tracks, not the dinky and charming rails of the Hershey line, but arrow-straight infinities of burnished steel laid into cement ties held tight by fresh white fist-sized chunks of rock. It was murderous walking on the sharp fill, and I crossed down to a narrow lane that turned south. I couldn't find this road on my map, but it flowed over the fields in the right direction.

I headed south, hoping to reach Limonar by nightfall, but I had no particular desire to go there; it was only a place on the map that seemed reachable in a day. A dirt track led across scrub and farmland. After an hour, I arrived at the edge of the vast campus of a polytechnic, where the students milling about on the lawn in their plaid uniforms murmured and whispered to each other as I walked by. After crossing a flower plantation, I ran into the train line again at the Canimar station. The big blue building had a fresh coat of pale blue paint but looked deserted, and its location was just as remote and arbitrary as stations I had seen on the Hershey line. I walked past on the tracks. Two men were sitting on the platform dangling their feet over the edge. One of them was wearing a striped hospital gown.

"What time is the train?" I asked. I was paranoid about being struck down by a locomotive. The trains on this line, I knew, moved much faster than the Hershey.

"There's nothing until five," said the man who wasn't wearing pajamas. His friend ignored me and looked up into space. He appeared to be damaged in some way. It was about one in the afternoon.

"Why are you waiting already?"

"We don't have anywhere else to go. I'm not from here, I just came to collect my cousin from the hospital."

On the map, the rails led straight to Limonar. Soon I was in deep bush, slogging my way along the oversized gravel between the tracks. It was sheer drudgery; there were no houses or even fields in sight, and the landscape on both sides was flat and drab and clogged with thorny, birdless bushes. What the hell was I doing, I wondered. Somehow I had let my triumphant march of cultural exploration regress into an endless plod along the margins of Cuba's railways.

Behind me, I heard a violent chugging like a gasoline mower gone berserk and I leaped off the tracks with a burst of adrenalin onto the rocky, sloping shoulder. I turned to see something like a go-cart flying up the rails. A minute rectangle of plexiglass windscreen was growing larger by the second, and I could see a single great motorcycle headlamp. I had just enough time to throw a finger in the air before they were upon me, but the driver saw my signal and jammed on the brakes. The wheels promptly locked and the tiny train, little more than two slatted seats suspended on a metal frame, slid past at full speed. It was too surreal a ride to turn down. I had only ever seen anything like it in the pages of Edward Gorey, where imaginary creatures in their Victorian frocks and high-top sneakers rode the rails on a hand-pumped version of this conveyance. I jogged to catch up.

There were no introductions or formalities, for the improbable contraption made far too much noise, even idling. I clambered aboard and the driver, a young guy in a brown tanktop with a military skin-fade haircut, released the brake and opened the throttle. I perched precariously on a cardboard box full of glass telephone insulators, those thick bell-shaped caps, grooved on the outside to hold telephone lines, that are sold in antique stores in the United States. The two other phone workers had to scrunch up to make room for me; the entire train was smaller than a Volkswagen Beetle.

It was a terrifying ride. I literally held on to my new hat as canefields and thorn scrub flew past. If I sat up, the air pasted the skin of my face against my cheekbones, so I contorted myself and crouched into a small pocket of calm behind the windscreen. Kilometer markers passed with alarming frequency. We crossed a great ravine on a high bridge over a hundred meters of vertical jungle that plummeted to the waters of the Canimar River. I saw it coming through the plexiglass and hoped the driver would slow so that I could catch my breath. And he did, for a *guajiro* was gathering sticks by the tracks beyond the bridge. So we crept across while I tried not to look down—far, far down. It was like flying a park bench.

We entered an area of open green fields and the driver slid to a stop.

"This is Limonar already," yelled the driver over his shoulder. I was sitting about two feet away.

"Oh," I screamed. "This is it?" There was nothing in sight except tall blades of golden grass waving in the faintest of breezes. On the horizon, a line of royal palms thrust their dark fronds up into the ashy sky.

He pointed along the track. A kilometer further down, I could just see another pale blue building parked lonely beside the rails.

"I can't take you any further," he said, cupping his hands around his mouth to shout at me. "It's not permitted." I screamed a thank-you, jumped down, and off they went.

A *guajiro* was cutting the tall grass next to the tracks with a machete. Several green bundles were laid out on the ground.

"Hola," I said. "Might you be able to tell me where the town is located?"

He seemed entirely unsurprised by my sudden appearance in that place. "I'm going there now," he said. "I'll give you a lift." He pointed down the embankment at a horse and buggy standing in the dirt road.

When he was done collecting up the grass, we stuffed the bundles into the buggy's compartment. I threw my pack on top and joined him on the seat in front. The air was hot and still, and the horse plodded cautious and deliberate between ruts in the road. Thick clouds clogged the sky, white, immobile. A few birds twittered. The timid creaking of the cart and horse was soothing compared to the roar of the telephone repair car. Finally, here was a chance to talk.

"So," I said. "I suppose the grass is for feeding the horses."

"Yup."

"It seems to be quite a distance to travel. You come all the way out here just to cut grass?"

"Not much by my place."

"Live in town, do you?"

"Yup."

We turned up a lane between a freshly plowed field and a small wood. The clouds on the horizon looked wet and heavy.

"Looks to me like it's going to rain," I said.

"Needs it," he said.

"Hasn't rained in a while, huh?" I asked.

He looked at me and gave the horse an instinctive flick of the switch as if he wanted to speed the journey. Perhaps he regretted offering a lift to such a chatterbox. The horse started and raised its head up under the sting of the whip, feigning an increase in pace, but, after a few jaunty steps, it slumped back down and resumed its established weary gait, picking up its limbs as if trudging through hip-deep mud.

"Do we have far to go to reach the town?" I asked, after we had passed by a few more whispering fields.

"Not too far, but then, of course, we're not quite there yet either."

We continued in silence. When we reached the paved highway, the horse instinctively rejoiced, quickening its pace to a dull trot. A few minutes later, we arrived in Limonar.

There was plenty of time left in the day. On the map, a tempting patch of roadless wilderness beckoned from the southeast. I headed south toward the *central* Fructuoso Rodriguez, a vast, rusting agricultural structure with an enormous smokestack that appeared suddenly around a bend in the road, thrusting upward into the sky from a bucolic setting. The *centrales* were typically former plantations that evolved into the ultimate expression of the "company town," where slaves and their descendents worked to feed the sugar monster, living in communities called *bateyes* that were often little more than squalid camps existing only to concentrate the cane-cutters in one place. Despite the end of slavery in the 1870s, the general principles of the system continued. Illiterate laborers, offered basic necessities on credit, began their very first day's work in the field already in debt, hacking at the sweltering cane with a machete advanced against wages. Somehow, as the weeks and months came and went, the work was never quite enough to pay everything off. The system persists in the Dominican Republic, where Haitians are lured across the border by jobs on sugar plantations only to find themselves in permanent debt to the company store.

A cart track wound through canefields in various stages of cultivation. In one field, young shoots poked up from the brown earth. The next was shaved bald, the ground scattered with chaff from the recent harvest. The track left the cane behind and turned east through piney bottoms of gnarled trees struggling into the sky above a dense and thorny scrub dotted with marshy pools. Groups of smooth-billed anis, great black cuckoos that fly floppy and discombobulated as if about to lose their ungainly ovoid tails, leapfrogged through the bush, emitting jarring nasal squawks. Where there was water, a snowy egret or two picked at the edges of the spongy, thickening mud, but many pools were dry and fissured with cracks, waiting for the rains. A ventriloquistic insect whine filled the air in the late afternoon sun.

It seemed that I always found myself in the most remote spots just as dusk was drawing near. I had not seen a soul in over an hour and, after walking some five kilometers through the pine barrens, I was beginning to despair, and to look for a campsite, when I reached a dirt road. While I was trying to decide whether to turn left or right, a man on horseback trotted up. He wore a broad straw hat and the green *guajiro* army shirt and was on his way home from the fields to San Miguel de los Baños. It was only a kilometer or two up the road, he said. We were very close. He had been the cook at the resort hotel at the baths, but the facilities had fallen into disrepair during the special period, and the hotel was now in ruins.

"Tourists used to come from all over the place to enjoy my food and just relax in the baths, but that's all finished. Scientists from the Soviet Union, mostly."

"Is there anywhere to stay now?"

"There's one other hotel, in the plaza, nothing special."

"But it's a hotel for tourists?"

"Well, now, it's mainly Cubans; tourists don't come here any more."

He slowed the horse to walk next to me, and we continued together until a horse and cart came up behind us. The driver was a surly, skinny fellow who mumbled a greeting to the *guajiro*.

"Hey, youngster," yelled the *guajiro* as the cart pulled even with us, "show some hospitality and give this fellow a lift into town. He walked here all the way from Matanzas."

"Well, from Limonar, really," I said.

The cart was full of calabashes rolling around in the back. They were hard and smooth and shiny and round, like green softballs. I climbed aboard. The calabash has no food value, but the hard, woody seed husks are used to make *maracas*, or bowls carved with designs on the outside.

"What are you going to do with the *güiras*?" I asked.

"I sell them to people who do *artesanía*. They make things to sell to tourists in Varadero."

"How much will you get for these?"

"I still have to boil all the flesh off them and clean them out. Then, I can get about a dollar for them."

"Not bad."

"It's not good. It took me all day to collect them."

I had misunderstood. The entire cartload, dozens of calabashes collected from secret trees dotted deep in the scrub, wholesaled for a dollar.

"Look," I said, "I doubt the hotel here will rent to foreigners, so maybe we can work something out."

"They rent to foreigners."

At the hotel, I gave him fifty cents, ten times the going rate for the ride, and then asked him to wait while I saw if there was a room for me. Before I had even reached the lobby, the calabash dealer gave his horse the reins and I heard the hooves clacking away on the pavement. I turned back in time to see my ride disappearing down a side street. Nothing could have made me more certain that the hotel would be "full." Behind the desk, a jowly, watery-eyed receptionist with greasy black hair and an enormous gut straining against his white shirt looked up at me. He didn't even wait for me to ask.

"We don't have any rooms," he said, by way of greeting. I stood there and peered over his shoulder at the dark wooden grid of cubbyholes behind him. None of the slots held any keys, and I thought I could see a cobweb or two stretched across the shelves. It seemed remarkable that this man should even be there, at his post.

"Is there anywhere else?"

"You could try the *cabañas* at La Piscina," he said. He looked down at the desk, as if he might find some task there demanding his attention. He waited for me to go.

"Would you be able to tell me how to get there from here?"

He sighed. "It's complicated," he said. "Just ask anyone for La Piscina."

I went outside onto the lawn and asked two girls where the *cabañas* were. They looked to be in their early twenties. One was black and the other a *mulata*, with *café au lait* skin.

"You're not going to stay here?" asked the black girl.

"They say they don't have any rooms."

"That's impossible," said the other, "there are hardly any guests. Nobody ever comes here."

"This has happened to me before. The hotels for Cubans don't take tourists."

They said they would show me the way to La Piscina, which means swimming pool, and we introduced ourselves. The black girl was named Magda, and her friend was Irena. They worked as helpers in the local old-age home. Magda found everything I said surprising and even shocking. She put her hand to her breast and gasped with affected horror when I told her I was walking across the country. Irena was saucy and bold and took charge of the search for lodging, leading us downhill away from the center of town.

"Are you married?" Irena asked.

"Yes." I had taken to lying in response to this question early in the trip when I discovered that an emphatic pronouncement of married status made Cubans renting out their homes slightly less likely to assume I was a sex tourist.

"So where's your wife, then?"

Irena stopped a guy riding his bicycle toward us and introduced him as her cousin who worked at the *cabañas*. No, he said, they never rented cabins to tourists either; it wasn't authorized. The security measures were not up to the standards needed for tourism.

"We'll have to go and look for Congo, that's the only other option," said Irena. We walked further down the road to a two-story cement house on a hill. "Wait here, I'll go check." She went up to the house as I stood in the road with Magda. After a few minutes, she returned.

"They're going to get some sheets together and meet us up at the house," she said. "Let's go."

Congo's house was next to La Piscina's *cabañas*. A handful of bunga-lows, which had once been painted in lurid Caribbean colors, were gath-ered around a swimming pool behind a chainlink fence. The whole place seemed locked up tight, as if there had not been any guests here either in quite some time.

Irena said Congo was an upholsterer who sometimes rented his place out and then went and stayed at his sister's. The sister, her husband, and Congo arrived, and the husband let us into the house. It was low, built of cinderblock, and almost empty save for some slabs of vinyl fabric draped over a table in the main room. The sister went into the bedroom and im-mediately started ripping off the sheets and making the bed with some fresh linen she had brought with her. Congo, whose real name was Ro-berto, was a short white guy, very fat, and a vicious, nasty drunk. I rarely hate people the moment I meet them, but I hated Roberto. He stumbled through the doorway of his own home.

"Here's the bed," he said. "You better be out of here by seven." He was holding onto the doorframe for support, and a dense cloud of cheap cane spirit followed his words out into the air, so foul and thick I felt I could see it hanging there in space.

"Thank you, it looks fine to me." I wanted to settle things and for Congo to go away.

In the bathroom, a little row of cement blocks set into the floor divided the shower from the toilet area. A few forlorn and mildewed plastic loops that had perhaps once held a curtain dangled from a rusty shower-rod.

"Oh, the toilet doesn't flush," said Congo, as if this defect in his own abode had only just now occurred to him. "You have to throw in a bucket."

"I'm used to that system. I just want a place to sleep and then I'll be out of here. How much do you want to charge me?" *For this dump.*

"Youse speakee spañol?" he asked suddenly in some sort of English, grabbing my arm and spraying sibilant bursts of alcholic saliva into the room.

"Yes, I speak Spanish." I said in Spanish. *What the hell language do you think we've been speaking for the last ten minutes?*

"*Veinte,*" he said, staring at his fat fist for a while, as if trying to calculate how many fingers he should hold up. Finally, he raised two, for twenty dollars, displaying them in a gesture of sullen triumph.

"That's outrageous," I said. He looked offended, as if I had cursed his mother, and he stomped off into the living room, where he began fondling scraps of vinyl seatcover in the dark and fussing about with some spools of thread. His brother-in-law went to remonstrate with him and try and hold the deal together.

Irena rushed up to me and urgently whispered. "Richard, there is nowhere else."

I considered walking back out into the bog I had crossed earlier that day and slinging up the hammock, but it was almost dusk. Putting the pack back on and walking even one more step held no appeal. I knew if I gave Congo the twenty dollars, he would immediately go away to buy alcohol. Hopefully, he'd drink himself to death and I'd never see him again.

He came back in. "This guy better not touch my stuff," he said in a loud voice. "I hold you girls fully responsible if anything is missing."

"Take it easy," I said, recoiling from the renewed onslaught of his breath. "There's not going to be a problem."

"You speakuh spanny?" He asked, spraying more gobbets of booze around the room.

"We've *been* speaking Spanish," I said. "None of us have spoken anything else since I got here." I wanted to slap the man.

"Okay, you stay here with the girls, no problem."

"The girls aren't staying, but anyway, it's a deal."

"*El líquido, el líquido,*" insisted Congo, holding out his hand with threatening impatience. As in most societies, there are dozens of words in Cuban slang that refer to money, but Congo's choice seemed particularly honest and appropriate. *Give me the liquid.*

Irena, Magda, Congo, his sister, and his brother-in-law were now gathered around me in an expectant group in the small bedroom, where I had leaned my pack and the cash in it against the wall.

"Give me a second, okay," I said. The sister rightly interpreted this as a request for privacy and ushered everyone out into the living room long enough for me to get some money out of the belt in the pack. I gave Congo a twenty and he promptly became warm, friendly, and sloppy. If anything, this was more distasteful than his surly and bilious aspect of moments before.

"No probleng, no probleng," he said, trying out his English again and attempting to embrace me in his pudgy, sweaty arms. He solemnly handed me the key and dragged me over to the front door, demonstrating how the lock worked, as if I were an idiot or a small child. When he was finally gone, I put the lesson to prompt use, bolting his own door behind him.

Magda and Irena said the only place to eat was the hotel where I had been denied a room. I had seen little of the town but had already decided that San Miguel was a miserable and accursed place. I could not face going out to forage for food, as I was exhausted. I also felt for the first time in Cuba that the house was insecure. I invited the girls to go and buy dinner and beer and return to dine with me.

"Lock the door and don't let anyone in except us," Irena said as they were going out.

After a shower, I dragged a sort of Adirondack chair out onto the rectangle of polished cement that served as a front porch. Sitting outside in my boxer shorts and writing in my notebook, warmed by the pink setting sun, I felt my foul mood begin to lift. But after ten minutes, a man in a military uniform roared up the road on a motorcycle and skidded to a dusty stop on the track in front of the house. I thought: busted! What does the prison look like in this horrid town?

But he stayed on the bike and yelled: "Congo?"

"He's in the other house, down there," I yelled back, waving vaguely in the direction of his sister's house. This seemed to satisfy him and he drove off without another word.

Nonetheless, I decided I had best go back inside. Mosquitos materialized in the gloomy interior, whining out at me from every dank corner of the house. I pulled on long pants. Hurrying to set up the mosquito net over the bed, I discovered foil-wrapped packets of condoms tucked under both corners of the mattress by the headboard. Had these been put there as part of the rental agreement or were they left over from former trysts? I tried not to think about this too much as there was nowhere else but the bed to hide from the mosquitos. I got under the net and lay there wondering if I was ever going to see the girls again, or if they had run off with the five dollars I had given them to buy food. I had just convinced myself that I'd have to lie there in squalor eating a can of sardines for dinner when there was a knock at the door.

The girls had tarted themselves up. Magda had changed into a pale-blue denim skirt and a white crocheted vest, and Irena wore black clogs with a synthetic velvet miniskirt the color of orange sherbet and a red tanktop with black spaghetti straps. Her chest was floury with talc. Both of them were daubed with metallic pink lipstick and lurid eyeliner, and Irena had put on pink blush, giving her creamy coffee-colored skin a flushed and feverish cast. They had bought four cans of beer and a huge plate of greasy *arroz congris* with some fried slabs of processed ham. We moved Congo's upholstery supplies onto a chair and sat down at the table. Quickly, it became obvious that the girls had conferred in their absence and agreed that Magda was to do all she could to promote my assignation with Irena.

Magda got up and played waiter, going into the kitchen to serve our takeout onto whatever plates she could find. Irena slid her chair much too close to mine. She smiled, looked up into my face, and literally batted her eyelashes at me.

"Do you have any children?" she asked.

"No, not yet."

"I'd like to have one with you."

I squirmed. Magda returned with plates of food and a beer for each of us.

"Look how nicely she got dressed up for you," she said, sitting down.

"You both look lovely," I said.

"She's got the eyes that can kill," continued Magda, as if she was selling a car.

I gazed into Irena's limpid pools and then turned away with a start, in mock horror, as if to confirm their danger.

"Oh," said Irena, "your eyes are so blue, I just know our child would have the same."

We ate the rice and beans and ham and drank the beers and afterward I explained that I was exhausted and wanted them to go. Irena was alternately coy, sultry, and sulky.

"Let's take a farewell photo together before you both go," I suggested.

"Should I be naked?" Irena asked Magda. They giggled.

"Yes, do it," said Magda. Irena began untucking her top.

"That's not a good idea," I said, "the lab would probably confiscate the pictures."

I put the camera on a chair and set the self-timer. In the picture, Irena is smiling broadly and has one arm around me. I am looking into the camera red-faced and stunned, as if I had just been rapped in the forehead with a ball-peen hammer.

Irena and Magda began to rummage through Congo's things. They opened the sliding door of the Masonite closet, took out his cologne, and sprayed it on one another's thighs, cackling madly with glee. Magda then yanked up Irena's skirt, spritzing her panties.

"Okay, ladies," I said, "it's past my bedtime." I shook Magda's hand. Irena crossed her arms, sullen.

"She's waiting for a kiss," said Magda. "Give her one kiss and then we'll go."

"All right," I said. I leaned in to give Irena a quick peck. She threw her arms around my neck, pulling violently at my spine. I got a toothful of acrid lipstick as she thrust her tongue into my mouth.

"Today's my birthday," she said, "give me a present."

I struggled to disengage myself.

She walked over to my backpack and stood there fingering my possessions. "Give me this baseball hat," she said in a wheedling tone.

"I need that," I said. I was an ambassador of envy.

"But you have this other straw hat."

"All I have to give away are some pens," I said. I rummaged around in the backpack and pulled out the ziplock bag of ballpoints I carried with me to hand out to schoolchildren. Each of them chose one.

"Mine doesn't even write," said Irena, turning pissy again after making her selection and trying it out on the side of her fist. Finally, after replacing the bad pen, I got them out the door. Alone at last, I collapsed on the bed, reeking of cheap perfume.

In the morning, Congo astonished me by appearing, as advertised, at seven sharp. He was still pickled drunk, but calm, and he seemed to have slept and bathed, although his fat face was dotted with unhealthy beads of sweat after the exertion of climbing the slight rise to the house. I had the distinct impression that his breath no longer stank and that the malodorous cloud accompanying him this morning was thanks to the unprocessed alcohol flowing out of his pores.

"The girls already left?" he asked, leering.

"They didn't stay," I said. I don't know why it was important to me for this reprobate to recognize my upstanding moral character. "Would you like to look around and make sure everything is okay? I'm leaving already."

Congo made a cursory inspection of the interior, but he had few possessions, and less worth stealing. He seemed to recognize that I was unlikely to have stuffed my backpack full of his vinyl seatcover remnants, and he waved me away.

Diez

John Sigler

I fled San Miguel de los Baños on a dirt track, cutting due south through remnant pockets of forest. Here, I again saw the *tocoloro*, the Cuban trogon, with its unique tricorn tail. Flycatchers and warblers flitted across the trail and I actually took my binoculars out; it was the first time since Soroa, in Pinar del Río, that I was wearing them around my neck as I walked. I birded my way up some low hills and crossed the ridgetop, descending through cattle pasture with views of distant canefields, the land flattening out again toward the Caribbean Sea, as I arrived at the *central* Jaime Lopez.

Jaime Lopez was a trainspotter's dream, with fields full of chaff-strewn cane cars like circus cages parked on the muddy railroad sidings. Train tracks meandered off across the fields, leading to nowhere except more hectares of cane. Bizarre rusted fixtures, tubes, and funnels collected and concentrated the sweet grass into ever-larger piles of raw stalks waiting finally to enter into the heart of the *central,* where the great smokestack of this rural monster factory filled the air with a thick smell of molasses and hay.

At the highway to the town of Pedro Betancourt, clusters of people stood waiting for rides, holding purses and notebooks and flour sacks over their heads to ward off the sun. Protected by my fine straw hat, I turned and walked along the verge beside the asphalt, but it was burdensome hiking, with too many trucks rushing by, creating gusts of dust and diesel. When a horse-drawn milk-cart stopped and the driver offered me a lift, I gladly accepted. He had a single churn strapped to the back of the cart and we sloshed along for a couple of kilometers until he turned off to deliver it to a community of cane-cutters. I went back to plodding along the highway. It was brutally hot. Shimmering ribbons of heat flowed like mercury over the black tarmac along the road before me.

I finished my last liter of water and stopped at a worn, scorched maintenance depot to refill my canteens. It was a low, green outbuilding, shuttered tight with dark-brown shutters, sitting off the road in a patch of red dirt denuded of all growth by the comings and goings of trucks that filled up there with air and water and diesel, and dumped loads of telephone poles and baling wire on the cracked earth. It had once been muddy—the trucks had left mighty ruts behind—and some truck parts were scattered about near a rusty oil barrel, but there were no trucks, or workers, and the place felt and looked uninhabited.

"*Hola, hola,* anybody here?" I yelled, taking a few tentative steps toward the end of the building, which must have been an office of some kind. "Hey!" I heard back. After a minute, a wiry old guy in a baggy blue tanktop came around the corner. He was all sunburn and sinew, with white hair showing at his temples under an olive gimme cap that he wore backward, with the bill shielding his neck. He was painfully skinny, or all of his clothes were too big, but he had a broad, friendly smile and a welcoming twinkle in his eye.

"Do you have any fresh drinking water?"

"Sure, of course, come on back here." We walked around the building and I got the backpack off and leaned it against the wall to get the bottles out of it. The cement walkway ringing the shed was stained red from the dust, and years of rinsing it off had washed a skirt of mud up onto the bottom of the wall so that the structure appeared to have merged with the ground. I got my bottles together and he grabbed up a mighty wrench.

"The water's over there," he said, gesturing at an array of pipes and goosenecks coming out of the ground across the lot, gargoyles of plumbing stuck there to feed vehicles.

"Is the pack safe here?"

"There's nobody out in this lost and forsaken place except me," he said with a grin. "You can leave your pack wherever you want."

I figured him to be about sixty, but he had a long, sprightly stride, and I struggled to keep up.

"Are you English?" he asked.

"American. Well, my mother is English, so I'm half-English."

"America is like a pillar of strength in the world today. If the United States collapsed, the whole world would plunge into chaos. I'm half-English, too. What do you think my name is?"

"I don't know. Mine's Richard."

"Mine's John. John Sigler. My grandparents on my father's side were British Jews. They came out to Florida, and then they moved here."

We reached the tap, an enormous spigot that might have been used for filling up fire engines. John cranked it open with the wrench, and the gush of water filled my canteens in seconds. I drank one off and filled it again and we walked back.

"Are you just on vacation or are you religious?" he asked.

"Well, maybe a little of both," I said. I had been having a lot of success lately telling people that the point of my walk was to fulfill a *promesa*, that I was making a kind of pilgrimage to El Cobre. This struck people as reasonable and familiar, and I had discovered they were less likely to think that I was insane.

"I'm Protestant," said John. I thought: scratch the *promesa*. "That's why they discriminate against me."

"What do you mean?"

"I have a degree in economics but I'm out here killing myself all alone in this depot. They won't give me a job. Why? Because I'm not a leftist and I'm a Protestant. Look at my hands."

He held out his cracked, cane-cutter palms for inspection. The sky had clogged with graying clouds that crowded and poked at one another, flirting with the rainy season, and coppery dust devils whirled away across the lot. When we got back to the shed, I was reluctant to hurry off. John was friendly and talkative. I wanted to know how the grandchild of expatriate Jews from London had ended up a Protestant in an overwhelmingly Catholic country, wielding a wrench in this desolate place that looked like a film set for a remake of *The Grapes of Wrath*. And after the previous night's fiasco, I didn't want to wait until dusk before I began looking for lodging. I sensed he would offer me a place to stay, no strings attached, if he had one.

"You don't live *here*, do you?" I asked.

"No, I live in the town. It's barely living." He smiled broadly, but his eyes wrinkled at the corners in a twinge of pain. "Richard, you should know that things are terrible here. Terrible, terrible, we are living in misery.

We still have slavery here. In the old days, the blacks wore collars around their necks and ankles; we don't have that any more, but that's the only difference. Yesterday was payday; we were supposed to get paid for five days, but they paid us for four. There's nothing you can do about it. Eighty pesos a week. You know how much a beer bottle of cooking grease costs?"

"No," I said. I was a bit frightened. John was getting agitated. He made his points emphatically and loudly, in the open. He was fearless. Most Cubans I'd met closed the shutters, sat close, and spoke softly when criticizing the regime. I looked around to make certain that there really was nobody there but us.

"Twenty pesos," he said. He opened his arms out from the elbows and shrugged, the international gesture that means, *It's impossible.* "Everybody here lives by stealing, taking this and that, selling here and there. You wouldn't believe it, people work all kinds of marvels just to survive. You see that house over there?" He waved down the road. "They have nothing, they cook with wood. The baby has a belly out to here. Starving. In misery. Richard, I'm a man of God, I can't lie to you. This is the reality, not what you see on television, fifteen thousand people waving flags. They are very good at putting on a show here, but don't you believe it, it's all lies." He paused and mimed pulling off a mask from beneath his chin. "Everyone here has two faces," he continued. "One for the show and one for real."

A child of about ten or eleven rode in through the gates on a beat-up bicycle and parked right in front of us, staring up at me, goggle-eyed. I couldn't imagine where he had come from. I was so freaked out that anyone at all might have overheard John's tirade that I scowled at him. "What do you think you're looking at?" I asked, in the same bullying tone a boy named Thatcher Wert had once used on me in my first week as a freshman in high school just before he punched me in the chest.

"It's okay," said John, to the child. "It's just that we're having a private conversation." The little boy rode off without a word, wobbling out the gate and up the road.

"Don't be fooled," said John. "It's no better here than in Guatemala or Honduras or any of those countries. Eighty percent of the people are in terrible misery while the other twenty percent don't even know what the special period was. They don't miss any meals or lack any medicine."

"I haven't been to a doctor here, but the state medical system sounds pretty good to me," I said.

"Pfft. The clinic here in town doesn't even have needles for injections. If you cut your finger, you have to go all the way to Jovellanos, where they might be able to stitch it up for you with henequen.* The doctors are sending their patients to *curanderos* because drugs aren't available. It's misery. Women are out in the street at eight in the evening trying to get together enough money for a handful of rice for their children's dinner. There is plenty of repression, too. I'm involved in the struggle for basic human rights, with the *Movimiento Opción Alternativa.*"**

At this point, I experienced a moment of complete cowardice. All I wanted was to give John a shake of the hand, snatch up my pack, and get on down the road. The only thought in my head was that some obscure official would arrive at any moment to fill up his radiator and check up on this dissident whom they had banished to this miserable, lonely outpost. Nobody would ever believe that I had just walked in here to fill up my water bottles and stumbled upon this man by chance. I could only be a collaborator, a notetaker fraternizing with the antirevolutionary forces. Why else would I be here, standing amidst weeds clogged with black axle grease and swirling red dust?

"I'd like you to come to my house so you can see how I live," said John. "No refrigerator, no television, the bed collapsing onto the ground because it's riddled with termites."

"I don't think that would be such a great idea," I said. Moments earlier, I had been hoping for just such an invitation. "Don't you think people would wonder what I was doing there?"

"I've had foreigners come before," John said. "People from the Church mostly. But I've even had some Miami types in my home. That has never been any problem with the authorities. They're very scared to make a fuss in front of foreigners."

"Isn't it dangerous for you later, though?"

"I don't care, I'm not afraid. I have nothing; what can they take from me? All they can do is kill me, and I put my trust in God, so I'm not afraid. Once, they came to my house and beat me with sticks and gave me a huge gash on my head. Look here." He took off his hat and separated his hair

---

* A fibrous member of the agave family from which rope and cord are made.
** The "Alternative Option Movement" is an illegal organization dedicated to raising the issue of human rights in Cuba.

with his battered fingers, to show me the scar where they had torn his scalp. "I had blood running down my face and they took me to the prison in Matanzas and locked me in a room for thirty-one days. No toilet, nothing, just a light bulb twenty-four hours a day. The food was on a flat plate they slid under the door. Solitary confinement." He paused. "Look, before the revolution, I know they used to torture and murder people, they used to dump the bodies right here, in the canefields. That doesn't happen any more."

"How old were you when the revolution triumphed?"

"I was eight. We lived right next door to the Jovellanos prison, and I remember as a child hearing the screams of the people being tortured. That has changed, but we are living in terrible, terrible misery. My two brothers are locked up for complaining about the human-rights situation, and I have two sons that they lock up all the time. Not for any crime—after two or three days, they let them out—but they do it again and again, and people talk. 'Those are the sons of so-and-so,' they say."

I took John's photograph. He stood with his legs planted wide, squinting into the sun and smiling his wide smile. He held his fist up in the air in a salute I associate with the Black Panthers. It was funny to see it from this scrawny, old, white guy, his bony shoulders and elbows jutting out like the knobs on a dill pickle.

"You know," he said, "the government offered me the chance to get out, to emigrate to the US. They said, for people like me, they could make arrangements. Because they'd love to get rid of me. But I turned them down. I don't want to leave my own country. Why should I? I love my country."

"The very best of luck to you," I said. We embraced and I hiked away down the road. I was in a daze. The whispering canefields now seemed somehow ominous, and when I reached the Alamar-like concrete block housing schemes on the outskirts of Pedro Betancourt, they looked to me like prisons. I stared into the faces of the townspeople as they peddled past me on their bicycles or strolled the sidewalks and saw only men brandishing sticks in the night and women selling themselves for rice.

South of Pedro Betancourt, the endless fields of cane gave way to endless citrus orchards, forests of orange trees planted in precise military rows. They were part of some two hundred square kilometers of groves that stretch from Jovellanos in central Matanzas south to Jagüey Grande, ending at the borders of the great swamp. On my map, they were pale green, divided into quadrants by orange roads.

The road was elevated above the trees. At the foot of the steep embankment was a broad expanse of grass buffering the orchards. Signs on the telephone poles warned that it was prohibited for any unauthorized persons to enter the groves. I was shaken and wanted to get away from Pedro Betancourt, as if, by reaching a new place, I could escape John's Cuba. So I thumbed rides in open wagons pulled by tractors, jumping into the back to ride from one plantation to the next with orange pickers and commuters piecing their way toward Jagüey Grande, one lift at a time.

"I'm walking across Cuba," I told them, and they oohed and aahed. Nobody asked me why, then, I was traveling in their wagon. I caught another ride with some surveyors in an open-sided bus, but, after driving only a kilometer or two, the driver stopped and the crew got down and headed off into the fields. I left the hard pavement and descended the embankment to walk on the soft grass beside the orange grove. The sun had burned off the clouds and a refreshing breeze teased at the dark leaves of the trees. I walked fast, but I couldn't stop thinking about John. Despite his difficult life and refusal to make things any easier for himself, either by leaving Cuba or simply keeping his beliefs and feelings to himself, he had been irrepressible and joyful. I imagined I would go mad, sitting alone all day in the desolation of his dusty depot. The thought came to me that I was jealous of his faith.

On the highway above me, a large dump truck with the blue license plate denoting a state vehicle roared past and then eased on the brakes, pulling off onto the verge a couple of hundred meters ahead. I saw two men in green fatigues descend from the cab and start walking back toward me along the shoulder. *Shit, someone saw me talking to John.*

They were from the interior ministry. One was brawny and ruddy-faced, and stood looking down at me from the top of the embankment with his hands on his hips, his right hand much too close to the sidearm hanging off his belt. The other one had the complexion of a rotten pineapple and was picking at his teeth, facing the oncoming traffic as if his role was to stand there and protect them from being run over. He was a ferret of a man. With his bad skin, he looked like a narrow version of Manuel Noriega.

I put a huge smile on my face and waved up at them. "Well, hello there, a most good afternoon!" I said, remembering for once to mangle my

Spanish to near incomprehensibility.

The burly one moved his gun hand off of his waist and made a tiny gesture with two fingers, waving me over. I scrambled up the bank, grinning madly, and made a bold, insincere attempt to shake hands.

"What are you doing here?" asked the bigger one. He was clearly in charge, and unimpressed by my friendly bullshit.

"Just walks."

"Why?"

"Just way to see country, meet many peoples."

"Where are you coming from?"

"Excuse, please?"

"Now, where are you coming from?"

"Today, I leaving from San Miguel de Baños," I said chirpily.

"You can't have walked all the way."

My pride was hurt, and my Spanish improved. "Well, I admit I caught a ride here and there," I said, "when I got really tired, but I walked most of it."

"Why are you walking down there next to the trees?"

"What do you mean?"

"It's prohibited. Why don't you walk up here, along the road?"

"I was doing that, sir, but the grass down there is so much softer on the feet. It makes a big difference, especially when one is walking all day long."

He paused the interview to consider this answer, which, I realized too late, had fully revealed my proficiency as a Spanish-speaker. At last, he smiled. I breathed a sigh of relief. Obviously, he had done his military service.

"Wow," he said, shaking his head. "Walking, imagine that. I'll tell you what, we have to make a stop and take care of a little paperwork at the office down the road, but if you don't mind waiting a few minutes, jump in the truck with us, we'll give you a ride."

It seemed to me it would be rude to say no, and worse, suspicious. I was still in a paranoid froth. The big guy urged pineapple-face to get into the back and then slid over to the middle of the seat next to the driver, a mustached fellow in blue workclothes. Once I had wrestled the backpack off and onto my lap in the shotgun seat, we were so cramped together that there was scarcely room for the driver to operate the long gearshift. Every change of the gears threatened to bring the official's healthy sexual function to an unnatural end. We drove a short distance in this fashion, with the frame of the pack jammed against the windshield and vibrating against the glass like a jackhammer, and the driver drily saying *Sorry* each time he saw fit to use the transmission. I responded to the official's questions, which were now more curious than interrogatory in nature, with lengthy, insipid answers, blathering on about how fabulous it was to experience the sights and sounds of Cuba, until his eyes glazed over. After a long stop at the office, he thought better of the travel arrangements and climbed into the back with his cohort. I had also seized the opportunity to put the backpack in the rear, which is how I came to arrive on the outskirts of Jagüey Grande stretched out in comfort in the cab of a citrus truck while two officials from the dreaded interior ministry stood bracing their knees in the back, grasping onto some chains for balance, and making futile one-handed efforts to light their cigarettes in the ripping lowland breeze.

Jagüey Grande is not a small community, but thanks to the sort of bush telegraph that advertises the day's meager excitements in slow-paced places the world over, I was already famous there. The tractor-riders from earlier in the day had arrived before me, and people pointed and whispered as I walked toward the center. At one corner, an old American sedan stood idling, waiting for me to cross, when a man on a bicycle rode up beside the car, propped himself against the hood, and leaned in the driver's-side window. "That's the crazy guy who's walking to Guantánamo!" I heard him say. Through the windshield, I saw the car's occupants pan their heads in unison, following me across the street with their eyes as if I were some spectacular fish swimming by at the aquarium.

The little city is flat and young, and must have sprung up from the sandy edges of the swamp in the 1960s to cater to local orange production. Streets and avenues divide it up into neat squares lined with one-story tropical homes, all of which have pretty tiled porches with potted plants. Many of the porches shelter ornate examples of Cuban rebar patio furniture, benches, loveseats, rocking chairs, and armchairs welded together out of scrap metal, unique, ingenious, and beautiful seating created out of scarcity.

I went to an address that I had found on the Internet, where a woman examined me by peering over the tall garden gate before ushering me quickly inside. In the backyard, a thriving hair salon was doing big business underneath an awning. Women were sitting around reading tattered, old, fashion magazines from Madrid and Berlin, their fresh dye jobs sandwiched into little aluminum foil packets that made their heads look armored. Two hairdressers were clipping and primping away at customers in two barber's chairs, one of them a gay man *working* the caricature of the fruity hairdresser. At first, the woman, Ramona, said I would only be able to stay for the night. She said someone had called and reserved the room for the following evening. The next day, she confided to me that she hadn't rented in over a year, and didn't have the license for it, but, now that she knew I could be trusted to keep a low profile, they'd be pleased to have me for as long as I wished to stay.

After we had arranged the terms, I sat on the patio in the back and ate mangos from a bucket and watched the haircutting day wind down. Ramona's parents lived in the house next door, sharing the yard, and her father came out and joined me. He was one of the few Cubans I met who was as big as I am, well over six feet tall. He had a mighty barrel gut that had once been a barrel chest and was wearing surf shorts and a wifebeater, revealing great meaty arms.

"American?"

"That's right."

"You'll feel right at home," he said. "This is *gusano* central. Every last one of us is sick of it around here." He laughed, a deep rasping chuckle. "And that over there is the number one *gusano* of them all." He pointed to the gay hairdresser, who smiled and shrugged, as if to say, *I can't deny it*. It had not been a homophobic comment. *Gusano* literally means worm, and the word is used in Cuba by government, media, and public alike to refer to Cubans who have betrayed the revolution and fled to the United States. It is a virulent and scathing insult. I had never before heard a Cuban boast of being a *gusano*, adopting the word as a badge of pride, the way a gay man might refer to himself as queer.

I met Carlito, a kid from the neighborhood whom Ramona introduced as almost a member of the family. He was dressed in the latest international youth garb, baggy cargo pants (an extra pocket all the way down by the ankle) and a T-shirt that said *Pervert*, from the terminally hip South Beach streetwear company of the same name. Carlito wanted to know if there were a lot of jobs available in Florida. He had already tried to go twice, once in an open wooden boat with a motor rigged from a pirated car engine. Both times, the boat he was in had been found and scuttled by the

Cuban coast guard. The result of these busts, he said, was that he would never be given a decent job in Cuba. He had wanted to leave because "there are no possibilities here," but now, since the failed attempts, he saw his prospects as even more dismal.

"As soon as I have a little money and a good opportunity," he said, "I'll try again."

Carlito had recently had another run-in with the law and been arrested in Varadero and jailed overnight. Cubans who did not live or work on the resort peninsula were not allowed to go there, presumably because they might hustle, harass, or just sleep with the tourists, endangering the for-eign-exchange pot of gold that the beach represented. Carlito had gone to buy some shoes anyway because all the best dollar stores were there. "Ev-eryone knows," he said, "that Varadero has the best selection of sneakers." He had been stopped on the street and asked for his identity card. In the prison where he had spent the night, he said, were three or four hundred other Cuban youth, all guilty only of having no satisfactory explanation of what they were doing on the peninsula.

Until then, I had resisted giving advice, or saying anything that might be considered encouragement of any kind, to the many Cubans I had met who wanted to leave the country. But my chance meeting with John Sigler had affected me deeply, and I liked Carlito, who had emphatically stated that, no matter what I said, he'd be making another attempt the first chance he got. He had dreams, ambitions, and desires. Even if all he wanted was to earn enough to buy the hottest new pair of Nikes, his burning passion for self-advancement was refreshing. In comparison with Carlito, many Cubans seemed defeated, trapped in a glutinous inertia, unable even to imagine an exit from their status quo. So I showed him the handheld GPS receiver I carried in my pack, thinking that if he could get his hands on one, he'd be less likely to drown.

He saw its utility immediately. All one had to do was plug in the coor-dinates for Key West, hit "Go To," and motor along, following the proper course on the little video screen.

"This is perfect," he said. "I have to get this. Last time, we had a com-pass, but it was useless. The needle was thrown off by the metal of the mo-tor." The boat must have been very small indeed. I pictured Carlito leaning as far out over the bow as he dared, a friend or fellow traveler holding his ankles as he tried to take a reading above the churning waves.

Ramona had a sister in Orlando and a daughter who lived in Hialeah. Her husband's daughter from a previous marriage was a computer programmer in Queens. With so much family up north, Carlito thought he'd be able to get his own GPS.

The entire household had completely disassociated itself from Cuba's "revolutionary society" and seemed to be living in a Miami of the mind. Ramona had a doctorate in mathematics and had been a university professor teaching calculus until quitting early during the special period to enter the far more lucrative field of backyard coiffure. She was so alienated that when I wondered if I might join the family to watch *El rey del ganado* with them that evening, she scoffed and said she'd already seen the entire series on bootleg videotapes obtained for her by a friend in Havana. I wondered what on earth she talked about with her clients while they were under the scissors. But when the time for the soap opera came, they evicted their younger son, who was in the middle of watching a video of some Rambo-style Hollywood bloodbath, from in front of the television. I sat alone in their living room, watching my *novela*, no longer able to pretend to myself that I only did so in order to share and experience snapshots of Cuban family life.

Once

Looking for birds at the Bay of Pigs

So, Fidel says to Pepito: "Pepito, we have to get rid of all the crazy people in Cuba, they're slowing us down, putting the brakes on the revolution. You gotta take care of it for me, just get me a list of whatever you need."

So, Pepito says: "No problem, Chief. To transport them all, I'm gonna need eighty buses and a limousine."

"Eighty buses? That's a lot of lunatics. And why do you need a limousine?"

"*Comandante*, surely you're not just going to ride around in any old *guagua!*"

—Joke making the rounds in Playa Larga

In the morning, Ramona squeezed me in for a fifty-cent haircut, trimming my beard with a precision that hinted at her background in theoretical mathematics. I headed south toward the Zapata Swamp, Cuba's Everglades and the scene of the ill-fated Bay of Pigs invasion.

Clusters of egrets flying overhead hinted at the marshes to come. Beside the road were plantations of scrubby pineapples. Their singed pink fronds sprouted out of the earth in rows, a spiny army of fruits. I heard the piercing cackle of a large woodpecker and found, rooting on the ground in the dust of a dry pasture, Fernandina's flicker, all rich yellow buff barred with black. Tinged chestnut on the face and orange about the eye, it was long-tailed and terrestrial, with colors both more muted and more beautiful than the sharp contrasts of the continental North American flickers. It is a rare bird, endemic to the island, and it would be Cuba's rarest woodpecker by far if not for the tantalizing possibility that the giant ivory-bill still lurks in remnant tracts of Eastern forest.

I was congratulating myself on adding the splendid flicker to my "life list" when I heard the unmistakable squawk of parrot and was able to add another. Above the road, squabbling with the leaves of an ancient shade tree, a pair of rose-throated parrots flashed cobalt-blue wings as they wrestled with the hanging fruit. I watched them for some time. Despite their white foreheads and the lurid pink throats for which they are named, they were well-camouflaged. Unless they grew testy and vocal and fluttered a wing, or abandoned the greenery to inch their way along an exposed branch in hand over hand silhouette, they were almost impossible to pick out against the foliage. At last, a car came barreling down the road beneath their tree and they wheeled off into the sun, yelping.

I soon reached the open swamp. The long ribbon of asphalt weaved before me toward the Caribbean, and I swore to myself that I would walk the entire distance. The previous two days spent crossing the island from Matanzas to Jagüey Grande had included travel by rail, donkey cart, tractor, surveyor's bus, and government orange truck, and I felt guilty. I had accepted rides before, of course, but I had rationalized these earlier lapses away, blaming them on medical and technical emergencies beyond my control. On either side of the road, twin seas of reedy orange stubble stretched to the horizon. The swamp had burned not long before: the base of each reed was black with soot and the earth was ashy. Tiny fresh green shoots peeked out of these scorched reeds, begging for rain and offering hope for the future.

In the marsh, a rise in altitude of centimeters was enough to change the vegetation completely. Here and there, a copse of trees grew up out of the merest elevation, like an island in the reeds. These imperceptible hills were just enough for the roots to survive the wet season without drowning. Cars and great tour buses bombed by, for I was still within day-tripping range of the Varadero Beach tourist enclave, but nobody had walked here in a very long time. The shoulder was scattered with snail shells I guessed might be Pomacea, the only food of the snail, or Everglades, kite, known in the US only from South Florida.

When there was no traffic at all, an awesome stillness descended. Only the faintest breeze stirred the stiff remnant columns of burned reeds, and far, far away, somewhere where the fires had not burned, and there was life, tree frogs called. Their distant chirping reached me as a barely audible chorus, a sort of auditory mirage that shimmered on the very edge of hearing. A crab the size of a dinner plate backed down into its burrow when I approached, blocking the entrance to its lair with a massive beige claw. A man rode past me on a bicycle. The seat was much too low for him; as he pedaled away into the distance, his pointy knees jutted straight out to the sides, pumping methodically up and down like the angular joints of oil derricks.

I passed roadside monuments to the martyred heroes of Girón, slain by the *gusano* invaders of the Bay of Pigs. Gray monoliths and houseplants by the side of the road memorialized Julio Luis Rodríguez González, Raúl Rojas Mendoza, Iluminado Rodríguez Rodríguez, Ramón E. Baez Vázquez, and José Ramón Fuentes Cano. The Kennedy brothers, their CIA and Pentagon consultants, and the enraged expatriate Cuban youth hastily trained in Guatemala for combat believed the Zapata Swamp was the perfect place at which to land and prepare a base before launching the invasion they were certain would crush Castro. But walking here, in the brutal heat, with an unbroken view over the endless gooey muck of the marsh bottom, I could not imagine how the invaders had planned to cross into greater Cuba over this treacherous expanse. Then, as now, only three roads penetrated the swamp to emerge at the coast. From the ground, the plan seemed absurd.

At the end of the road in Playa Larga, I planned to settle in and then track down Orestes Martinez, a guide famous across the Internet as the foremost expert on the Zapata's birds. I had read several trip reports posted on the many Websites that cater to fanatical birders. One explained how to track down Martinez, known as "Chino," who had no telephone, but rarely strayed far from the tiny village of Santo Tomás where he had been born and raised in the very heart of the swamp. He and his brother knew the regular haunts of all the swamp's dazzling specialties: the bee hummingbird, smallest of all the world's 10,000 bird species and now frightfully rare; the blue-headed quail-dove, a brilliantly plumaged skulker of the forest floor, hounded to near-extinction by hunters and charcoal gatherers; the Zapata wren, endemic not simply to Cuba but to this very marsh; and the Zapata rail, another secretive and obscure endemic, "flightless, or nearly so, with completely unknown habits," as my *Guide to the Birds of the West Indies* equivocally put it.

Toward the end of the afternoon, Playa Larga appeared like a mirage at the end of the long strip of highway. I arrived at a junction, a triangular patch of grass thirty-two kilometers from Jagüey Grande. Such distances are routine for, say, avid through-hikers on the Appalachian Trail, and there had been no hills of any kind the entire day, but I felt pride in my accomplishment. I also felt sore and battered. To my left were the beginnings of a beach resort and to my right a few houses stretched around the crook of the bay. I stood there, trying to guess which way I should walk to find a *casa particular*. If I could avoid asking someone's help, I was far less likely to pay a five-dollar surcharge, the steerer's commission for bringing a tourist to a house for rent. Already, in Palpite, the somnolent village I had passed some five kilometers back, a man on a bicycle had offered to ride ahead and "make a reservation" for me at the *casa* of his "very good friend."

Across the grassy triangle, I saw a guy break away from the group of people who were standing and waiting for rides out of the swamp. I began walking with purpose, as if I knew where I was going. He pedaled to catch up with me on his bicycle, and slowed beside me. The man was a classic hustler from central casting. His outfit was the essence of international hoodlum chic; he was wearing camo cargo pants, gold chains, rings, and bracelets, and he sported a ghetto goatee, beard and mustache meticulously trimmed down to fine pencil lines that followed the line of his jaw and made a narrow-edged box around his mouth. He looked like an extra in an East LA rap music video, except he was a tad old for his *barrio* outfit. I couldn't just ignore him, so I paused, and he pulled to a stop beside me.

"You're a birdwatcher?" he asked.

"Yes," I said, guardedly. I wanted to ask him how he could possibly know this, but I didn't want to encourage conversation in any way. Then I realized my binoculars were dangling around my neck.

"Would you be looking for a guide?" he asked. He was older than I had thought, really much too old for the gangsta pose. He reminded me of an off-duty prison guard who has absorbed the fashion esthetic of the inmates by osmosis.

"Yes," I said. "I'm looking for a guide, but, thank you very much, I have a name already, I know who I want to use, and I don't need any help."

"Would you by any chance be looking for El Chino?"

"Yes, as a matter of fact."

"That's me," he said. "Orestes Martinez at your service. I was just over there at the bus stop saying goodbye to my girl. I saw you and thought: 'That guy has got to be a birder.'" He stuck out his hand.

I thought: *Spare me.* At many megabirding destinations in the world's poorer countries, self-taught ornithologists compete actively for guiding business. Whenever some homegrown expert carves out his little slice of notoriety in the guidebooks or web pages devoted to some arcane field, orchid-spotting for instance, or yurt construction, impostors soon emerge. My companion was looking at me strangely.

"Come on, let's go," he said. "I'll take you to a great *casa particular*; it belongs to my very good friend, Nivaldo, the best cook in all of the Zapata Swamp."

All Cubans must carry their *carnet*, or identity card, with them at all times, and anyone who cannot produce it when asked to by the police risks immediate arrest. I thought of asking this man for his, as if I was at home and he had come over to read the gas meter. Looking again at my would-be guide, I noticed his T-shirt for the first time. It was one of those made-while-you-wait shirts, hot-stamped from a photograph at a booth at the mall or state fair. This one had a blurry image of two men in full swamp kit, standing in the bush, binoculars at the ready. Underneath the photograph, in English, it read: "Chino and Angel, birdmen of Zapata."

"Uh, sure," I said, blushing. "Vamonos."

At Nivaldo's house, a couple of pasty, middle-aged Germans were just leaving with their *jinetera* dates, two black teenage girls from Cardenas wearing matching lime-green bikinis. The house was built right up against the bay. Wooden fishing boats were resting above the tideline along the rocky shore and minute waves lapped at the pebbles. Chino and I sat and planned birding logistics, trying to maximize the theoretical number of species I might see over the next few days.

"This is a challenge," he said. "You have no car. I've never had a birder on foot before. The distances between the sites for the specialties are very great."

"Can't we hitch?"

"That's what I would do if I was alone, but you sort of stick out; I don't think trucks are supposed to take tourists. And there is very little traffic to some of the places we need to go." Chino stared at me for a moment. "Do you by any chance have another hat?"

"What's wrong with my hat?" I asked. "I got this from a woman in Matanzas who makes hats for *guajiros*."

"Maybe a baseball cap would be better," said Chino. "It would make us less conspicuous."

In the end, we contracted with Nivaldo to drive us to Soplillar the next morning. He was the proud owner of an early-Fifties American sedan that had faithfully carried him for years to his job as a chef in the tourist hotel at a nearby crocodile farm. He was a corpulent, sweaty man who loved to cook, eat, and drink. He was madly in love with a new girlfriend, and excited and enthusiastic about quitting his job to run his beachfront home as a business. The couple swanned and mooned about the kitchen. Nivaldo, a great ham, enjoyed embarrassing the poor woman with endless floral praise directed as much at us spectators as to her.

"Have you known each other long?" I asked.

"Our earthly bodies have only recently had the chance to meet, but our souls, I feel, have been together throughout all the ages," he said, and then burst into a fit of cackles and enveloped his blushing date in a meaty embrace.

At dusk, hundreds of thousands of mosquitos arrived from some nightmarish corner of the swamp, billowing through the still air in black clouds. The kitchen-dining area was also the garage, and the big sliding door was open to the outside. It was much too late to close it. Short of going to bed beneath a net, there was nowhere to hide from the onslaught. An arm exposed in the air attracted dozens of the infernal beasts, which landed within moments like tiny helicopters descending in unison for a surprise tactical maneuver. As mosquitos go, they were slow and dull-witted, but what they lacked in stealth they made up for in sheer numbers.

I tucked my trousers into my socks and put on my only long-sleeved shirt, a thermal, long underwear top I had brought for sleeping outside and scarcely used. Sweating, with another T-shirt wrapped around my exposed neck, I gobbled Nivaldo's enormous and lovingly prepared dinner in fits and starts. I could only manage quick and furtive forkfuls from the dishes of fried fish, rice, beans, papaya, vegetables, fruit salad, and fried plantains spread out before me on the table. I needed my hands free for vigilant swatting. My ears and forehead were ringing from my own slaps and stinging from the bites, and my palms were bloodied with the carcasses of half-engorged skeeters.

"How do you like my food?" asked Nivaldo, hopping up and down and hugging himself with vigor in a vain attempt to slay the crowds of mosquitos sucking at the softness behind his shoulders.

"Oh, it's great," I said. "But, in all honesty, it's a bit difficult to enjoy the meal."

"I didn't know you were coming, or I would have had the food ready earlier," he said, whacking the back of his neck with a mighty paw. "Tomorrow, you should try and arrive back for dinner in time to eat before dusk. They only come out at dusk." This was true: only half an hour earlier, we had been sitting in peace.

"There's a saying around here," said Chino. "Everything that comes from the north is good. The more revolutionary types get annoyed by that and say that guy is a *gusano*, but we reply, 'What we mean is the *breeze* from the north, the only wind that carries away the mosquitos.' Around here, when the wind blows from the north, the sea turns beautiful and blue."

I wondered which way the wind had been blowing in April 1963 when the Girón invaders landed to establish their beachhead here. Little would be worse for morale on the first day of an invasion than to be ravaged by these incessant swarms of what my father calls "gravy-sucking pigs." I pictured young and inexperienced soldiers, perhaps the scions of exiled land barons, trying to set up camp, already fearful of nightfall in this unknown place, reading every shadow of a palm frond moving on the sand as an announcement of the arrival of Cuba's defense forces, and a trillion mosquitos whining in to feast on their newly arrived blood.

The next morning, Nivaldo hotwired his own car to start it, reaching beneath the steering column to make a connection between two bare, dangling wires. Chino had changed out of his jewelry and sinister sunglasses at his brother's house and arrived wearing a baseball cap that said *Cornell Lab of Ornithology* on it. As we drove off, Nivaldo put on a cassette of the genre they call "discoteca" in Cuba, which is basically fast, bouncy European house music. The cassette deck was only half as old as the car, but something was wrong with it: it played at near double-speed, and we went bombing down the road blaring unintelligible high-pitched adrenaline dancebeats out the windows into the roadside forest. It was just after dawn and the morning mist was rising off the low thickets beside the road.

"We might hear a bird or two out the window and want to stop for a moment," I screamed to Nivaldo. "Could we turn that down just a bit?"

"Oh, sure, I'm sorry," he said, and turned it down halfway, to a dull roar.

Soplillar is a tiny village on the edge of the swamp, where the palm savannah gives way to marshes and reedbeds. We waved goodbye to Nivaldo and walked a dirt track away from the dozen houses making up the community. Chino was attuned to every fragment of birdsong and knew immediately when a new arrival was in the trees nearby. He identified species from the tiniest of monosyllabic chirps, and knew what we were looking for in the foliage even before I was aware that a bird was there to be seen. A scant hundred meters down the trail, Chino heard the liquid chortle of a Cuban vireo and whistled it out of its bush with a dead-on imitation of its call. It flew nearby and craned its neck, anxiously looking for the invader before plunging back into the foliage. It was our first endemic, a good omen.

"We're going to see the bee hummingbird now," said Chino with certainty. He led me to a small clearing and pointed up to a bare, exposed snag. "It's a *jucaro* tree," he whispered. "They love *jucaro* and almost always nest in it. Many times, you will find the male sitting on that snag." In less than a minute, a tiny speck darted in and sat just where Chino had pointed, showing us its steely blue back. I crept cautiously around to the side for a view of the garnet throat glinting in the sunlight. The bird was about the size of a teabag.

It was too easy. "How did you know?" I asked.

"When the male finds a perch he likes, he uses it over and over again. Sometimes for two or three years." This suggests that the male stakes out one territory and watches over it from his favored perch for his entire life; the average lifespan of the larger, migratory ruby-throated hummingbird of the eastern US is thought to be only about three seasons.

Everywhere beside the path was the constant rustle of the *cangrejo colorado*, black and scarlet land crabs that seemed to be forever scuttling off through the leaf litter in a paranoid rush. They were often startlingly loud. Again, I pictured the *gusano* invaders, driven mad by the jungle sounds, dazed by the heat and the onslaught of mosquitos, firing their weapons indiscriminately into the forest after every retreating crab. When Chino and I stood still, listening for birds, the movements of these countless crabs came to us through the warm air like the scrapings of a thousand tiny leaf rakes.

The next day, Nivaldo made a dawn run in his blue bomber, up the road to Jagüey Grande to purchase some of the fresh ingredients that went into his epic spreads. Chino and I got out in Palpite and walked an old logging road west, leaving the sun and the village at our backs. The path was so overhung with branches that it was like walking through a tunnel, and the woods were much darker and wetter than those around Soplillar only some five or six kilometers to the southeast. On either side of the track, the ground was black and boggy, too moist to hold even a crab's burrow. Chino kept up a quick pace to deny the mosquitos a chance but then stopped dead, so that I almost ran right into him.

"Key West," he whispered, referring to the quail-dove of that name. "Let's see if it sings again."

I had heard nothing. We stood in the trail, swatting ourselves softly. There came a low hooting, from no discernable direction, not unlike the vibration of a distance bullfrog. Then we heard another, faster series.

"The second one is a gray-headed quail-dove," said Chino, "the two of them, together!" He prowled up and down the trail, looking for an entry into the bog. I followed him onto the squelchy black forest floor. Quickly, he picked his way through the snarls of angular branches and fallen tangles of trunk and root, listening for more hoots. Little light filtered through the dense and multitiered canopy. Much bigger, and less agile, than Chino, I moved like a bulldozer behind him in my headlong rush to keep up and possibly see the extremely rare gray-headed quail-dove. Branches splintered and exploded beneath my feet, and my huffing and puffing sounded loud and unnatural. To plunge further and further into the woods like this seemed a ridiculous enterprise. No bird that was not stuffed and nailed to a tree could possibly remain in the area after this onslaught of bushwhacking.

"Shhhh," hissed Chino, stopping and turning with urgency to wave me forward with his stubby fingers. There, not ten meters away, in the crook of a low tree, the gray-headed quail-dove was looking down at us, as at visitors from another world. Pumping its tail in dismay, it sat perched and ready for flight but stunned into immobility by our bizarre arrival at its front door. I pulled the binoculars up to my eyes with cautious haste and had plenty of time to appreciate the iridescent emerald sheen on the hind-neck and the eggplant-colored shoulders and upper back. The head was chalky-gray, grading to almost pure white in front, between the eyes. Then terror overcame curiosity: the bird burst into flight, weaving and banking away through the tangled underbrush. We stumbled back out onto the trail, high-fiving and speaking of this excellent sighting in rapturous tones. We were beginning to be friends.

"You know when you came up to me in Playa Larga, when I had just arrived," I said, "I thought you were a *jinetero*."*

Chino laughed. "I kind of had that sense."

"I think it was the sunglasses more than anything."

"I fought in Angola," said Chino. "The worst thing that happened to me while I was there was that I had a goat that I was keeping and taking care of in camp. I had it tied to a tree, but, one day, it got itself all snarled up in the rope. I was down on my knees trying to untangle it and didn't see that there was a cobra there. The goat struggled and the cobra reared up and spat venom right in my eyes. I was blind for three days and spent a month in the hospital. The bright sun still hurts my vision if I'm not careful."

"Did you see any good birds over there?" I asked. "Sorry, I mean, not while you were blinded by the cobra venom, of course." It was a stupid question, the equivalent of asking a Vietnam veteran if he had seen any interesting species of heron while under fire in the Mekong delta. But these are the kinds of questions that spring into the fevered birder's mind. Chino was nice about it. I suspected he had heard worse.

"I saw some things," he said, "but I can't remember, really, I didn't have a book, and, you know, we didn't really have time for that kind of thing."

"No," I said, "I suppose not." It took a moment for me to feel a flush of embarrassment coloring my ears, but Chino had moved on by then.

The trail narrowed to a wet, single-file track. In moments, my trousers were soaked through by the previous night's sprinkling of rain. Beside us, another quail-dove flushed into the thicket in an explosion of wingbeats. Chino said he felt from the sound of the take-off that it was a Key West. He had so much experience with these birds that he could identify them to species from the bulk implied by the noise a bird made lifting off into the bush, the way schoolboys in London's air-raid shelters learned during the Second World War to identify the make and type of aircraft passing overhead by the particular drone of the engine. Moments later, we came upon a male, the partner of the flushed bird, waddling quickly away from us along the path. As it weaved back and forth, I saw its rich ruddy back, iridescent green nape, and crisp white stripe down the cheek before the

---

* *Jinetero*, although the masculine form of *jinetera*, does not mean male prostitute, but refers to the sort of street-smart hustler who attaches himself to tourists to extract a dollar here and there, or to lead them to a *casa* in order to earn a commission. The word is derived from *jinete*, which means jockey.

rotund little pigeon spied a gap in the foliage and, still walking, turned abruptly into the forest.

Quail-doves are plump, undoubtedly tasty, and, despite their shy and retiring nature, too curious for their own good. Perhaps they are a bit dimwitted. Terrestrial pigeons that roam the forest floor in an apparently random and chicken-like search for food, their numbers on all the Caribbean islands have been decimated by introduced predators. Cats and mongeese, but especially men with guns, stick-traps, axes, and chainsaws have all conspired against quail-doves and the forests they live in.

The trail we were walking emerged at the tip of a pristine, glassy lagoon. We sat and had a snack under an enormous *jucaro* tree festooned with Spanish moss. Someone had recently cleaned their catch and the skeletal remains of a meter-long fish with a bizarre reptilian head lay stretched on the ground. Chino said these were the bones of the *manjuarí,* another species endemic to Cuba. He described it as "a living fossil," the giant or alligator gar, *Atractosteus tristoechus*, an archaic fish thought to be essentially unchanged since it first slithered from the ooze in the Carboniferous period some three hundred million years ago. This fish emerged along with the first reptiles, fifty to a hundred million years before dinosaurs roamed the planet and more than two hundred ninety-nine million years before anything much resembling *Homo sapiens* appeared.

"Isn't this a protected area?" I said. "Someone's been fishing here."

"Yeah, they're poachers."

"Do the park rangers do anything about it?"

"In theory, but the situation here is very difficult. That's one of the reasons I'm glad I'm not a park ranger any more. Some rangers will actually tell the hunters to watch out, give them a little helpful warning on days when the boss is going to be out on duty. Then, you know, they collect little favors in return, a piece of meat, or a few fish." Later, I wrote in my notebook the embarrassingly self-evident observation that it is difficult to enforce anti-poaching laws when people are going hungry.

It was a beautiful spot. The water was pristine. Small fish, no bigger than a quarter, with peach-colored bellies and electric-blue heads, lounged centimeters from the shore, then darted away in pursuit of an even smaller, minnow-like fish that had dared to invade their miniscule territory. At the opposite end of the lagoon, families of ducks, or grebes (it was too far away to tell), paddled in the narrow strip of shade where the marshbrush hung over the water. Two ospreys glided over, perhaps looking for a *manjuarí* of their own, and tricolored herons crouched in the shade on logs far across the water. On the horizon, distant reedbeds promised unseen avian treasures.

"If we had a boat, I bet we could see some birds out there." I said.

"There must be one stashed around here somewhere," said Chino. He got up slowly and wandered off to poke around in the bushes. After a few minutes, he returned, accompanied by a young hunter armed with an antique 22-caliber rifle. The dinged and battered barrel was attached to the stock with bits of black electrician's tape. *The birds have a chance*, I thought. He showed us his boat, stashed not ten meters from where we had earlier been sitting, and said we were welcome to use it. He was going on foot into the forest, but, if we rowed only two kilometers from our tree, we'd reach the open swamp and its avian specialties.

"Let's do it," I said to Chino. "That's the way to get out to the good habitat!" He gave me a long look, as if fully appraising my height and weight for the first time.

"I don't know," he said. "Don't you think it might be better if we just had a snooze on the grass before going back to look for the blue-headed?"

"Don't worry," I said. "I'll row. I rowed in college; it's my only sport. I like rowing."

The boat was a little over two meters long, made out of a single, large slab of aluminum sheeting that had been bent and banged into a rough facsimile of a dinghy. It was about the gauge of a disposable pie pan. The oars were triangles of the same, wedged and nailed into slots at the ends of two sticks. These had to be threaded through the oarlocks, which were made from loops of old shoelace tied through a hole in the gunwales. It was an inventive and unseaworthy craft.

The lake was very shallow, and the feeble oars stirred up a cloud of green, clayey ooze with every stroke. We made our way slowly down the lagoon, a light breeze at our backs. On the verge, a black-necked stilt stalked the shallows on the improbably long legs for which it is named. A mat of floating algae harbored a flock of shorebirds. There were a handful of tiny semipalmated sandpipers and a larger bird at the edge of the group, the much less common white-rumped sandpiper. Except for these few waders, however, it was very quiet. We inched our way along.

"I'm sorry there aren't more birds," said Chino.

"It doesn't matter," I said. "There's nothing as tranquil as being out in a boat like this on a lake like this."

"Please let me row," said Chino. "It will wake me up. Your rowing is making me drowsy." I could see that he was reluctant to enjoy being rowed about by his client. "Really, I'm enjoying myself," I said, and it was true. The sun and quiet and gentle lapping of the ripples on the hull were calming. I felt more relaxed and content than I had in months.

We talked about notorious birders that Chino had met and guided, figures from the fanatical upper echelons of the birding elite whom I had only heard about or seen references to on the Internet. I had read about Chino in one of John Hornbuckle's trip reports. Hornbuckle is a British birder who has written many diaries describing his voyages to all the far corners of the globe. His trip reports and those of many others are posted on the Internet and have become an important resource. It seemed whenever I was planning a trip anywhere, I stumbled across Hornbuckle. He was a man who had already been to all the places to which I wanted to go and, when in them, had invariably seen all the birds one could possibly hope to see. I was horribly jealous, all the more so because I found his reports so accurate and useful. According to Chino, "Hornbuckuh," as he pronounced the name, was an excellent ornithologist but "half crazy." After going out hours before dawn and birding without pause all day, he'd then expect to spend the entire night looking for owls and nightjars "if you let him."

"I'm collecting stories about all the crazy birders I've met," said Chino. "I want to write my own book. You will definitely be in it. A birder *walking across Cuba*." He shook his head, bemused. "*Walking!* You are even crazier than Hornbuckah!"

Rounding a bend, we saw what appeared to be a semi-inflated inner tube floating in the water, a puffy black arc extending vertically out of the water. It looked uncannily like those grainy photographs of the Loch Ness monster. Thinking that it was a tire, I realized that other than the bones of the *manjuarí* left beneath the *júcaro* tree, which could scarcely be considered litter, we had seen no sign of man, no trash, no tires resting on the bottom. Because Cuba produced almost no trash. Almost nothing in everyday use was even packaged. Supermarket shopping bags were nonexistent. At home, fifty dollars worth of groceries, double-bagged, went home in two dozen flimsy and toxic sacks.

We rowed over to see this strange object. The sinister coil protruding from the surface of the lagoon turned out to be the bloated, gas-filled middle section of a very large snake. Its drowned head and narrow tail drifted flaccid beneath the surface. I had rowed for an hour. It was time to go back. The GPS reported that we had traveled all of 850 meters from the *jucaro* tree. "We didn't get very far," I said. "It would take us a lot longer to get to the reedbeds."

"Don't worry, I know a place we can reach in a car," said Chino. "Tomorrow, you will see the Zapata wren, and the sparrow. Now, I will row us back. I am falling asleep here in my seat. I insist."

Very, very gingerly, in a sort of dance performed in extreme slow motion, we edged past one another to trade places in the bathtub-sized craft. Chino sat amidships, oars at the ready. I eased my way down onto the triangle of board that was wedged into the stern. As soon as I sat down, the bow lifted out of the water like a very small whale and pointed skyward. For the first time since Chino had climbed a tree to find our position in the swamp, I was looking up at him. The stern of the boat, beneath my seat, was planted firmly in the muck. Chino rowed, but he could scarcely get the blades into the water from his elevated perch. I felt like the fat kid on a seesaw, parked flat-footed on the ground, watching his friend kicking his legs in the air, unable to get back down to earth. After a few minutes of this, I was forced to state the obvious.

"Chino, we don't seem to be moving."

"I feel very bad about this."

"Don't feel bad, I'm the one who's too heavy for this so-called boat."

After carefully changing places again, I rowed us back to shore.

On our way back through the forest, we began to hear quail-doves calling. They had come out again from wherever it was they rested through the long hot days to wander in the post-siesta cool of the afternoon. A ruddy quail-dove flushed from the trail and I saw a quick burst of rust against the green leaves before it disappeared on clapping wings. It was our third quail-dove species of the day.

Chino led us to a place where there was a straight and unbroken view of almost three hundred meters of trail. We were to wait here and watch, hoping the spectacular blue-headed would at last make an appearance and wander out onto the path.

"This is the exact spot where Hornbuckah saw it with me," whispered Chino. "But it's not quite time yet."

I slapped a mosquito on the back of my neck. "Have you ever seen all four species in one day?"

"To be absolutely truthful," said Chino, "no." But then he added cheerily: "Maybe today will be a first."

Mosquitos began to emerge in quantity, and I realized peak blue-headed quail-dove hour would coincide precisely with the daily insect onslaught. I wondered what Nivaldo was cooking. Far down the trail, a brown shape moved out of the woods with a dove-like waddle. We jammed our binoculars to our eyes in unison. The bird meandered aimlessly in the two-meters' width of clearing.

"Key West," I said, in a disappointed tone. I let my binoculars hang back down against my chest. Only that morning, of course, I had been ecstatic to see this species. Minutes later, another one wandered out onto the trail, much closer to us, and then dozily marched back in the way it had come, as if it had taken a wrong turn. We stared intently down the long green hallway. Another half an hour passed before a third Key West emerged, this time from the right side of the trail. It strolled a few meters and then wandered off to the left. It was like watching, in the most extreme slow motion, one of those old cartoons in which Bugs Bunny zips in and out of a long, doorway-filled corridor, eluding Elmer Fudd, who always manages to open the wrong door.

"It's wall to wall with Key Wests out here," I said. "And we're being eaten alive. Let's call it a day."

"Only if you want to go," said Chino, making quite sure we both knew who was responsible for this very un-Hornbucklesque surrender.

In Palpite, a new red rental car was parked in the dirt in front of a small whitewashed house.

"I know that car," said Chino. "I saw it in Playa Larga a couple of days ago. It's this guy Julio I grew up with, visiting from the States. He left in the Mariel boatlift. Look, I'm going to tell him your rental car broke down in Playa Larga and see if I can get him to give us a lift."

The family was sitting around on the porch. I recognized Julio right away because he was wearing a brand-new oversized Tommy Hilfiger polo shirt in screaming red, white, and blue, like a Mondrian painting. When he came down off the porch to greet us at the gate, I saw that he was extremely drunk. Chino introduced us. Julio was wearing a pair of Nike high-tops in butter-colored leather that had just come onto the market before I left New York. I remembered them because they cost $150 a pair.

"An American down here in this fockin' nowhere place? How the hell you end up here?" he said. He laughed, much more loudly than necessary. His English was okay, but his strong Cuban accent and the rum made him almost incomprehensible.

"I just came down to see some birds with Chino," I said in Spanish.

"No shit," he said, sticking to English. "Where ya from?"

"Nueva Yol," I said. "La Gran Manzana."

"I live in Miami," said Julio.

Chino said, "We were just going to go out here on the road and hitch a ride when I saw your car parked here." He gestured at me. "His car broke down. We had to leave it in Playa."

"That sucks," said Julio. "Wanna drink?"

"No, thanks," I said. "We have to get going."

"Hey, man, any time you're in Miami, come by. I live right on the river. Just go to Thirteenth and the river and ask for Julio. Everybody knows me."

"All right," I said. "You have a good stay, and take it easy."

Chino and I walked up toward the road.

"He could have offered us a ride," said Chino.

"He was drunk; I wouldn't have wanted to get in the car with him anyway."

"I guess he's doing pretty good for himself over there."

"Maybe," I said. "But you're doing good over here. You're famous all over the world as the number-one guy for the birds of Zapata." Chino wasn't so sure.

We reached the highway just as a truck stopped to load and unload passengers. The bed was half-full with corn. We clambered up and gripped the rusty back edge of the cab, bracing our legs against the metal floor among the rolling ears. As we barreled down the highway, I watched the last rays of sun flickering through the woods. Over the rushing wind, I yelled to Chino: "This might not be any safer, but it's a lot more fun!"

I arrived back at Nivaldo's just in time to wolf down another of his exquisite meals in a fury of bug-slapping. There was a stiff breeze coming off the water and I took the food out to the little bar set up by the beach. At least there, the mosquitos could only attack from one side, gathering their strength in the wind-shadow to the lee of me. Eugenia, hired by Nivaldo to make up the beds and do the laundry, brought her plate of food out to join me. Within moments, the downwind backs of her thighs turned black with mosquitos. The sight reminded me of a film shoot I once worked on in a lab in a South Florida swamp, where a University of Florida researcher was performing enemas on mosquitos to try and curtail their ability to transmit malaria. He kept his supply in an aquarium with a wire-screen lid to which a hapless, half-plucked chicken was strapped skin-side down, offering up a defenseless supply of live blood. Eugenia's legs looked like that chicken.

In the morning, Nivaldo drove us to a spot Chino said was a favorite of the Zapata wren. We left in the dark for the long drive, almost all the way back through the burnt swamp to Jagüey Grande. In the rosy dawn, blasting Nivaldo's overcranked dance-pop tape, we turned onto a dirt track built atop a dike. On either side were canals full of croaking frogs and squabbling moorhens. Beyond stretched pristine, unburned reedbeds. Chino told me that the fires along the highway behind us had destroyed every wren nest he had been monitoring that year.

The car crept slowly along the top of the dike. "Here," said Chino, finally. Nivaldo eased the 1952 Ford to a stop. We got out stretching our joints and muscles, still stiff with sleep. Nivaldo kicked pebbles and Chino and I looked out over the endless marsh. It was remote and isolated. The car looked very strange in this landscape. I felt as if we were gangsters who had driven out into the countryside to dispose of a body.

"I have to play the tape," said Chino. "Otherwise we have no chance. We will see nothing." The day before, I had refused to let Chino play his birdsong tapes to lure out the quail-doves. My limited experience with bird guides has led me to the conclusion that many birders rely much too heavily on playback to bring birds out into the open. Playing a tape of a bird's song is essentially an aggressive and territory-invading act. The bird responds because the mechanically reproduced call declares a threat to his dominion and food supply, and a challenge to his sexual prowess. While many ornithologists use tapes in their research, and insist that playing them, at least in moderation, does no harm, it is as if you were to arrive on a man's porch and yell through the window that you had come to raid his fridge and carry off his wife. For an extreme skulker like the Zapata wren, however, I would have to push ethics to the side.

Chino's tapedeck was a battered relic that shuddered and rattled like an old air conditioner when he hit the rewind button. The cassette had been played over and over again, and probably copied and recopied down through many generations of tape. It hissed and crackled, sending amplified white noise out into the quiet air of the swamp. Once, perhaps on this very dike, someone had mistakenly pressed record instead of play, so that just before the recorded Zapata wren call, there was a clicking sound and then the voices of a bird-tour group murmuring as they waited. Still, it was magic. No sooner had Chino broadcast the first phrases of the wren's call out over the marsh than a response came back to us from about a hundred meters out in the reeds. We paused. It sang again. We were having a conversation with the Zapata wren. Even Nivaldo was fascinated.

"There, it moved," said Chino, in an urgent, hushed whisper. "Did you see it?"

I hadn't seen anything. I was scanning, desperately looking for a little brown bird in this ocean of brown reeds. Then it called again, closer in. Chino backed the tape up, deftly manipulating the volume control at just the right moment to avoid the stretch of inadvertently recorded conversation. He played a brief snippet.

"There," said Chino. I looked at where he was pointing just in time to see the wren fly out from a hole in the reeds to the end of a long stem about twenty meters out from the dike. It clung there, small and brown and unspectacular, jerking its head around and searching for the interloper. We did not play the tape again, but the bird remained, curious and defensive, flitting from one clump of reeds to another in plain view. We all got, as birders say, "excellent looks."

The breeze rippled the reeds and we heard the Zapata rail call, a series of monosyllabic honks that grew faster and faster until they blurred together and sputtered out. I was getting greedy. "Do you have a tape of it?" I asked. "It doesn't matter," said Chino. "It never responds. To see that one, you must come back in the winter and spend all day waiting in a blind, standing in the water. We get a group of people and drive it toward the blind, you could see it. These old-lady-birders and tour groups don't have what it takes. But you're just crazy enough to do it."

"Thank you, I guess," I said. "Let's try for the sparrow."

We wandered the dike, and I searched the hedgerows for flocks of birds that might include *Torreornis inexpectata*, the Zapata sparrow, a bird that by rights should not carry the name of the swamp, for it occurs in three disjunct and far-flung corners of Cuba, of which the swamp is only one. If we didn't see it, I could walk to Cayo Coco a few hundred kilometers to the east off the north shore of Cuba and see it there. Chino was pessimistic because he relied almost entirely on his ears and had not heard any trace of the sparrow since we had arrived with our wren-playback system. His ear was phenomenal, and he was, of course, correct. There were none to be found, and we headed back to the car. Somewhere further out on the dike, Nivaldo had found a place to turn around. "You know, I'm having a good time," said Nivaldo, stepping on the gas and reaching for the radio. "I sort of see the attraction. I think I could get interested in this."

"Stop, turn that off," said Chino. "Shhh. Stop the car." Nivaldo slowed to a stop again, mystified. We scrambled back out onto the road. Chino pointed at a bush. There, as if waiting for us, sitting on a branch beside the dirt track, was the Zapata sparrow, with its pale yellow belly and fine black mustachial stripes. Chino said he had heard the merest fragment of its call note from inside the moving car, over the noise of the engine, among the frogs and rustling reeds and nasal whistles of blackbirds.

The next day, Chino came to say goodbye as I was strapping on my pack and getting ready to set out on the walk to Girón. He said he hoped I would be back someday to wade in the swamp and look for the Zapata rail. I was going to miss him, my friend, the aging homeboy birdman.

Along the grassy margins of the coastal highway, hundreds of orange and red crabs scuttled away from me on the way to deposit their eggs in the bubbling surf. But some had already begun to lay, even though they had another one or two hundred meters to go through the scrubby limestone underbrush before they would reach the shore. These premature Moms were bubbling with brown roe, carrying along a slimy pile of their own caviar as they rushed to the sea.

To say that I walked to Girón is not quite accurate. I trudged for two hours along the shoulder. Once the sun got up high, the blacktop became a griddle. On the side of the road, flat pancakes of crab roadkill baked in the sun, until the air smelled like the Fulton Fish market in July. When I found myself drinking off the third of my four liters of water before it was even ten o'clock, I clambered back up onto the shoulder amid the crab carcasses and stuck out my thumb. I told myself I had already been along this road with Nivaldo and didn't need to walk it. A salmon-colored *colectivo* taxi, another 1950s American monster, converted to diesel, soon stopped.

"Ay, qué calor," said the woman who slid over to let me squeeze in the back seat. *What heat.* This was a Cuban mantra, a classic conversation-starter.

· "Insoportable," I said. *I can't take it.* "I was going to walk to Girón, but forget about it."

"No, you would die. *Americano?*"

"That's right," I said.

"My daughter is leaving next week. *Le salió el bombo.*" She won the lottery.

There is, of course, no lotto in Cuba. When people refer to the lottery, they mean the visa lottery at the American interests section.

"I don't want her to stay in Miami," the woman continued. She took a wallet out of her pocketbook and opened it to a photo. "After all the terrible things I've heard, I hope she will go somewhere else."

The photo showed a slightly heavy blond woman, smiling at the camera. In a few days, she would be on her way to America with a one-way ticket and one hundred dollars of carefully saved cash.

"She's twenty-nine years old," the woman said. Her voice was filled with anxiety and hope. I didn't know what to say.

"I'm sure she will do well there," I said.

In Playa Larga, there were dozens of places to stay. I found a tidy, air-conditioned apartment and went to the Bay of Pigs museum. Black-and-white mural photographs illustrated the miseries of living in the Zapata Swamp before the Triumph of the Revolution. Blown-up sepia prints showed men in filthy rags standing in front of charcoal pits. The text on the wall said that the cottage industry of charcoal manufacture had been the only work available to these impoverished men, who had been illiterate and unskilled. The next room held poignant reminders of the fallen heroes, simple objects laid out in glass cases. Precisely because the objects were so commonplace and unspectacular, they were powerful reminders of the humanity of the men who had owned them. Here were the comb and house key of Angel Torres Portales, found on his dead body. The identity card from the Havana Riviera Hotel left behind by Dagoberto Muñoz identified him as a "casino waiter." A photograph showed Antonio Pujol, his *orisha* beads visible at the collar of his shirt. This time, they had failed to protect him.

Inside more glass cases were rows of photographs of the militia members who had defended the revolution to their deaths: Giraldo Díaz Pérez, of Pedro Betancourt; Eusebio Cañer Enriquez, "peasant," of Santa Isabel de las Lajas; Wilfredo Díaz Rodríguez, a cattleman from Torriente, in Matanzas. A chart illustrated with facts and figures the lineage of those others, the captured and disgraced invaders, proving them to be the sons of big-money *latifundistas,* large landholders, and landlords. The evil invaders were the descendents of gross accumulators of capital. In the museum was a quote from Fidel dated April 15, 1961, the day after the initial airstrikes against the Cuban air force in San Antonio de los Baños and Havana. He said: "If this aerial attack should prove to be the prelude to an invasion, the country, ready for struggle, will resist, and with an iron hand destroy whatever force attempts to disembark on our soil."

Sitting on her sofabed in her Havana apartment, Miriam had recounted for me her memories from the day of the airstrike, when she was a child in San Antonio de los Baños. She was usually so grim and sour about her life, always dwelling on her daily problems, but when she spoke of that day, she snapped out of her torpor and depression, and her eyes flashed with pride, both in her mother and in the fervor of the people standing up for the defense of the revolution.

"I remember when the planes came," she said. "We all rushed out into the street and looked up into the sky over the city. All along the block, people were coming out of their houses, pulling on their clothes. Some of them had rifles and pistols. My uncle came out with his rifle, they had distributed rifles to all the citizen's militias, and he was firing up at the planes. It was dawn, and my mother, who was really much braver than my father, came outside half-dressed. She stood there in the street pulling on the skirt and buttoning the shirt of her militia uniform. Everyone, the whole town, was ready to go defend the revolution, and when the word came a few days later that they had landed at Girón, people started walking, hitchhiking, anything, any way they could go, everyone heading toward there, to combat the invasion."

Doce

Hiking to Cienfuegos

"In the tropics one must before everything keep calm."
—Joseph Conrad, *Heart of Darkness*

After three hours of walking alone through sunny, dry woods, I felt oppressed by the weight of my solitude. It pulled and tugged at my already overloaded backpack. I had taken a truck inland from Girón to where, on the map, a single track wound through an enticing blob of green wilderness, cutting toward the coast and the city of Cienfuegos. I walked through spectacular, pristine woodland, filled with birds, and should have been happy. But it was always the same. I dreamed of solitude, but then, when I was alone with myself for too long, I thought I was going mad. I became nervous and began to wonder if I had made a wrong turn, although the path was straight and without forks. *I should have reached the coast by now,* I thought. At last, I reached the first clearing I had seen for many kilometers. A mule was grazing at the parched stubble. Civilization. From out of the shade beneath a tree, a man jumped up to greet me. He had a terrible limp, thanks to a gruesome clubfoot. He hopped toward me. I didn't like the looks of him; he had shifty eyes that moved away from mine in mid-sentence as he spoke. "Hello, my name's Alfredo," he said, casting his gaze down to the ground. "Where are you going?"

"To Cienfuegos," I said, and immediately regretted telling him.

"That's far, very far," he said, squinting at me. I could see his yellow teeth.

"I better get going, then."

"I'll walk with you, you might get lost."

"You really don't have to do that."

"I'm going back to the village."

He limped along beside me, coiling and uncoiling a length of tarred black rope. I walked faster, trying to leave him behind, but he just swung his bad leg around to the front that much quicker. He was almost running on his good leg. I asked myself if I was being cruel, and I had the thought that perhaps I was ill disposed toward him *because* of his handicap. There was a sinister desperation in his urgent efforts to keep up with me.

"There's absolutely nothing between here and there," he said, wheezing savagely.

"You know the road?"

"I know it, but it's barely a road. You could get lost along there. Anything could happen to you." He paused. I felt he was considering all the possible horrors I might face. "It's very dangerous along there. You be careful," he continued. He said this as if it were a challenge, not advice, and then looked at me with a strained, sour smile. The wilderness is the safest place in the world to be, I thought, until someone else knows you are out in it.

"They did a tourist in over there by Jagua," continued Alfredo, smiling a little bit more broadly. He paused and licked his dry lips. For effect, I thought. "Murdered him. They say they caught the guy, though. He got nine years." By now, I was almost sprinting down the trail. Alfredo lurched along behind me, sweating.

"Is there any other way to get there?" I asked.

"You best walk up to Cocodrilo and catch the *guagua*."

"I'm definitely going to take your advice," I said. "I'll go to Cocodrilo. Absolutely." It was a bald lie, but I wanted to throw him off the track. We reached his home, a squalid pile made from palm trunks.

"Thanks for all the information," I said, barely pausing to say goodbye. Once alone with his thoughts, I was sure Alfredo would waste no time in lamenting the lost opportunity I represented. How easy it would be to get together a few fellows and catch up to me on the road. Surround me with machetes, grab the moneybelt and binoculars, and roll my fat corpse into the woods, a snack for the ever-present turkey vultures soaring overhead in the hot, still air. I marched fast and sweating, without stopping, through the rest of the village of Guasasa. It was a brown and dusty backwater undoubtedly full of bandits, and I didn't stop until I was well on the other side and back into the deep woods along the coast road.

As I sped past, people called out the usual questions to me from their porches. "Hey, where are you from? Where are you going? Where are you coming from? Why are you in such a hurry?"

"I'm rushing to catch the bus in Cocodrilo," I yelled to as many people as possible as I breezed past, insulting Guasasa's hospitality. When I reached the turnoff, a few kilometers further on, where the hard-packed dirt road to Cocodrilo turned north and a rutted cart track headed west along the coast to Cienfuegos, I realized I had not stopped to fill my water bottles. I was still in a panic. To retreat and give up the ground I had gained on my pursuers was impossible. Surely I would pass at least one more house. With a liter and a half of water to last me the thirty kilometers to Cienfuegos, I turned on to the trail and headed into the bush. Alfredo would lead them the other way, toward Cocodrilo, looking for the American with his shiny backpack full of goodies.

Almost immediately, I heard a motor straining somewhere up ahead on the trail and a minivan crept around the corner toward me, the first vehicle I had seen since getting down from the truck in Ramona, half a day's walk away. It was full of French tourists, a three-generation family filling every available seat.

"Are we far from Playa Larga?" asked the driver.

"Maybe twenty kilometers."

"Oh, my God. Is all of the road as bad as this?"

"I don't know, I didn't come that way. But you are about to come to a village, it should get better after that."

"On the map it looks like a road, but this is not a road; we've been out here for hours. But where are you going?"

"To Cienfuegos."

"*Mais il fait vâchement chaud*," said a woman in the back seat. But it's so extremely hot.

"Do you have water?" asked the driver.

"Not much," I said. "Don't you think I will find any along the way?"

"*Bof*," said the driver, using that solitary dismissive syllable that for the French means, forget about it. "Here, you must take ours." They rummaged on the floor in the back and gave me a plastic bottle that had once been full of mineral water. There were about three fingers of liquid left in the bottom. "I'm sorry, that's all we have. We already drank it all. It's so hot, you know."

It was a nice gesture that did nothing to relieve my worries that I would soon run out. As they drove off, I realized I was going to die of thirst on this savage coast of brigands and bandits. My mind was still racing; I had worked myself into a froth of paranoia. I felt I was becoming unhinged. With my last shred of rationality, I told myself I needed to relax, take a minute, and breathe deeply.

A faint trail led down through the trees to the shoreline, and I got the hammock out and slung it up between two trees. There was no beach here: the shore was a solid skirt of limestone, weathered into a morass of razor-sharp, pint-sized canyons. Below this shelf of rock, which resembled a lunar landscape, the brilliant, infinite turquoise of the Caribbean stretched out to the horizon, twinkling beneath the midday sun. I lay in the hammock and wondered if Cynthia had spent the day looking out at her patch of distant Greek sea, and which one was bluer.

The incoming waves were trapped beneath the overhanging limestone and, with nowhere else to go, they sent vertical explosions of surf rocketing into the air, where the water fragmented into a fine mist and blew inland across the broad width of rock to settle, salty, on my lips. After two hours' rest, I was not sure if the panic had passed or if the further solitude had sent me deeper into madness, but the sun had descended to a much less savage angle. I packed up and hiked east along the limestone. It was slow going, over sharp rocks that threatened to pierce the heavy soles of my boots, but it was worth it to walk beside the roiling sea, the sun at my back and an endless stretch of uninhabited coastline ahead. Every few kilometers, a whittled pole or length of bamboo wedged into the rock showed that fishermen had been here, but except for these abandoned markers, there was no sign of anyone having ever walked this way before.

The pockmarked, channeled rock was riddled with the fossils of sea creatures, shadows of coral and fragments of shell so lifelike that I stopped to pick one up, only to discover that it was part of the rock itself. A shard of brain coral, snapped off and hurled up onto the shelf by some hurricane gale or monster tide, lay nestled in a scoop in the rock beside its twin likeness, a fossil countless thousands of years old.

A zenaida dove burst out from one of the endless hollows and flopped away across the lava-like surface, dragging a wing along the sharp ground.

It looked terrified and badly wounded, pausing in its exhaustion to let one wing hang limp on the ground, until I drew near. It twisted its neck to look at me, goggle-eyed, and then struggled off ahead of me again with laborious jolting movements, flapping desperately all the while, but unable to get off the ground. We continued along the coast together in this fashion, as if I were kicking a soccer ball down the road, catching up to it, and kicking it again until, when we had gone some two or three hundred meters from where it had flushed, the bird flew off, completely healed, into the woods. It had all been an act, an elaborate diversion to lead me away from the nest. The "wounded" parent, stumbling along as if in its final death rattle, had been offering itself as an easy target to me, the predator, drawing me slowly away from the defenseless eggs or chicks that it had left behind in a bowl in the ground. I had found the act so convincing that despite my previous knowledge of the behavior, I had pursued the bird to the edge of the forest, almost wondering if I could help it in some way, and very much doubting that it could still fly.

When the razor-edged rocks began to bruise my feet, I looked for an opening in the impenetrable coastal scrub. The dense twisted branches of bay grapes formed a waist-high canopy and every possible opening was clogged with a tangle of thorns. There was nowhere even to launch a boat along this coast, and doubtless no fresh water beneath the sandy soil behind, so nobody lived here. In one tiny inlet, I finally saw a minute and battered rowboat bobbing in the turquoise calm behind a spit of rock that curved to shield it from the surf of the outer sea. It seemed abandoned until I realized it was tied to rocks, with monofilament fishing line, at either side of the inlet, keeping it positioned in the center of the pool, well away from the crags and overhangs of the limestone. This was undeniable proof that I was not alone on this remote coast, and a twinge of paranoia returned.

I walked away from the coast. Here, surely, a trail would lead back to the dirt track just inland. There was a clearing. A sandy, motorable track came in to the beach from the left, back the way I had come, but angling away from the beach. It would be a minor bit of backtracking. Then, about two hundred meters off to my right, I saw a man standing and looking at me. I felt sick to my stomach, but waved, tentatively. The man just stood there, watching me. At that moment, another one came around from behind a bush; I remember he had on a bright turquoise shirt. When he saw me, he said something to the first man and then immediately began to back away. I didn't like the looks of it at all. Until now, the people I had met in the most remote places had invariably been the friendliest. If these guys were backing away it meant they were up to no good. I didn't want to get any closer, but what would they think if I headed off without a word? That would be even worse.

"Hola," I yelled. "Does this track lead back to the road?"

The first man, tall and gangly, gestured in the air. I couldn't tell if it was a wave of assent or of dismissal.

"Okay, great," I yelled again. "I'll just be on my way, then."

I walked fast, crunching away through the loose sand of the wheel ruts in a cold sweat, my temples pounding with adrenaline. I didn't look back, but, as soon as I had rounded a bend and was out of sight, I stopped to think. "Turquoise shirt" had moved away with a sinister sense of purpose, as if he were going for a weapon. In minutes, they would follow. I needed to think fast. I had to get off the path.

Frantic, I scrambled up a bank and plunged into the forest, using the bulk of the pack to force a gap open in the thick foliage. Brambles ripped at my forearms and snagged on the nylon fabric pack, slowing me down. I was like a rhino charging through the woods, snapping branches under my boots, the pack's frame ramming into the low-hanging branches and the narrow trunks of trees that crowded together, fighting to get their leaves up through the low canopy to the sun. One whipping branch took my hat and I paused, gasping for breath. I was streaked with bark mold and lichen and my arm was bleeding where a thorn had torn the skin. Behind me, the dinner for my night in the wilderness, half a loaf of bread left over from breakfast, lay scattered into crumbs on the forest floor. The plastic bag it had been in, tied to the outside of the pack, was shredded into ribbons. *Calm down*, I thought.

I leaned against a tree for support. Once I was sure there were no barking dogs on my trail and no men crunching their way through the forest after me, I struggled to regain my sense of direction. Although lost and panicked, I knew the road had to be nearby. Beyond a nasty thicket of brambles up ahead, a band of sunny clearing looked promising. I bulled my way through and found myself standing in the track, blinking in the bright sunlight, sure that I was losing my mind. Sighing in exasperation at my own foolishness, I took off the pack and began pulling twigs and burrs from my hair and beard.

The tall, gangly man appeared at once, pedaling an old black bicycle down the lane behind me. He stopped, putting one foot on the ground for balance, and stuck out his hand. "I'm Jorge," he said, as I shook it. "Didn't I just see you by the water there?" He looked skinny, earnest, and harmless.

"Oh, that was you?" I said. "I didn't want to bother you guys." I plucked at the front of my shirt, raining twigs and moss down onto the ground. "I was trying to find a shortcut through the woods," I continued lamely. "I saw your boat."

"We like to fish on the weekends. Me and the guys ride our bikes down here and see what we can get."

"You camp out?"

"Yeah, sometimes we bring the wives and have a real party. Anyway, I'm off to get some baitfish down in the next inlet. Have a good day."

After a few more kilometers, I followed another of the periodic little footpaths back to the beach and strung the hammock up in a grotto of beach grapes for the night, wrapping the mosquito net around it like a cocoon. My hanging camp was perfectly hidden from anyone walking along the shore. I went out onto the rock lip by the water and enjoyed a can of sardines in sauce, mopping up with the few chunks of bread I had managed to salvage from the jungle floor. Far away down the coast toward Cienfuegos, in the binoculars, an enormous, strange domed structure, like a gigantic concrete mosque, broke the skyline. Beyond it, across the water to the southeast, the Sierra del Escambray mountains were just visible through the haze and foam, gray shadows that loomed up into the darkening sky.

From the hammock, I watched a Cuban coast guard cutter cruise past, very close to the shore, searching, perhaps for fishermen like Jorge. Black-market fish and lobster were a big industry in Playa Larga. The beach in front of Nivaldo's house was lined with wooden boats that set out in the middle of the night on clandestine fishing trips among the hundreds of cays out beyond the mouth of the bay. Seafood could be exported for hard currency, so private fishermen were, in the state's view, stealing money from the revolution each time they pulled a fish out of the sea.

At dusk hundreds of mosquitos gathered on the outside of the net, humming madly in their desperation to get at me. I laughed and blew gusts of sardine-breath at them, making them lift up in little black clouds and move off, whining. They seemed to be able to smell their exact distance from my blood, for the thickest concentrations were in places where my flesh was closest to the net. A finger held up in the air just inside the netting brought dozens rushing to the nearest spot, where they jockeyed for position on the other side of the mesh like commuters bunching up to get in the subway doors. The thick litter of crunchy bay grape leaves rustled directly below me. Looking down, I saw a Cuban racer, a meter and a half of black snake, sliding like water through the forest debris, starting out for an evening of hunting.

The advantage of sleeping poorly is that one rises early. Before the pink blush of dawn had faded from the sky, I was on my way. Accompanying me down the track was something more than embarrassment. I felt almost a sense of awe at how completely I had given myself over to fear and panic, abandoning my cherished rationality for paranoid hallucinations only because I had been left alone with my thoughts for a short few hours.

After my days in the swamp, civilization and Cienfuegos beckoned. The city sits along the shore of a vast lagoon, a great natural harbor that empties out into the sea through a narrow channel where the Castillo de Jagua perches on the rock along the narrows. I intended to hike to the castle, where I would catch the ferry across the bay to the town.

All morning, the great gray dome of the mosque came in and out of view on the horizon. In testament to how huge and distant it was, the thing never seemed to get any closer. When I was still many kilometers away, the road turned inland, and terrifying, large signs proclaimed the beginning of a no-access military zone. The mosque, it turned out, was the reactor core of the Juragua nuclear power plant. A low, white building surrounded by a chainlink fence and topped with barbed wire had the rows of a tidy vegetable garden incongruously lined up beside it. On the far side, a man was working in the garden with his back to me.

"Hello, hello," I called out. "Excuse me!" He seemed not to hear.

"Hey, hey, hello!" Finally an ancient and crusty *guajiro* toddled over. He appeared to be wearing the same fatigue outfit in which he had fought the revolution some forty years before. He squinted at me through the wire.

"Do you have any water?" I asked.

"What?"

"Water?" I shouted.

"Sure." He opened the gate and I handed him my canteens.

"I'm hoping I can walk through to Jagua Castle," I yelled.

"You can't walk through this way, we have this blocked off. I'm the guard here. You'll have to follow the road out to the highway"

"You're all alone?"

"That's right."

Somewhere beyond this lonely outpost, there must have been more security in place to protect the mothballed power plant, but, at that moment,
this stone-deaf man puttering about alone in his garden seemed to sum
up the project's decline. He reminded me of Hiroo Onoda, the Japanese
soldier who had stayed on in the Philippine jungles of Mindoro for thirty
years after the end of the Second World War, on guard with his loaded
rifle, unrelieved, and refusing to believe that the battle was over, the war
lost, and the troops gone home.

Looming over the road was a line of great trellises built, rather pre-
maturely, to support the high-tension lines that would conduct the juice
across the country. These rows of pylons, like flocks of mammoth origami birds stretched out in flight, were to have delivered fifteen percent of
Cuba's energy needs. Without any wires strung on them, the metal frame-
works looked naked and ridiculous. Columns of these scaffolds radiated
out across the countryside, but only one was strung with cable, bringing
in to the reactor the electricity needed for its maintenance and upkeep. I
followed a line of them to the highway and caught a lift in the back of a
truck, converted into a bus by means of a welded-on peaked roof and metal
benches.

Juragua #1 is an enormous structure like a gigantic silo or an oversized
gray cement lipstick. It was surrounded by seven motionless yellow cranes,
gathered around it in preening attitudes, like bridesmaids. In the early
1990s, the Soviets had stopped financing its construction, with the reactor
core ninety percent complete. After the insult of abandoning socialism,
they had had the gall to request that the $750 million dollars required to
complete the project be paid in real, convertible currency. One by one, the
army of Soviet technicians training the Cubans and assisting in the construction packed up and went home.

Millions are spent each year just to prevent the work already completed from going to waste, as the salt spray chips away inexorably at the
concrete and the machinery grows rusty and paralytic from disuse. The
vast complex stretches along the highway, outbuildings and hangars and
more cranes trussed up in their own rusty cables, like oversized kits that
have never been assembled. A huge conveyor belt mounted on a truck,

like an oversized airport luggage loader, had tall letters printed on its side. "Putzmeister," it read.

Juragua is a ghost town that never had a chance to be a town, a sort of ghost town under construction. One Cuban, trying to explain the shock to the system that came with the collapse of the Soviet Union and the withdrawal of its favors, described the waste of resources as incredible. Everything was over-engineered, he told me, all the refrigerators and television sets made heavy and indestructible, as if steel were free. He claimed that whenever a piece of machinery broke down, they would just abandon it and order another one from Moscow. Like everything in US-Cuban relations, the power plant has become grotesquely polarized. The Miami contingent and the politicians that represent it in Washington point out that radioactive fallout from a reactor meltdown would, on a favorable wind, take only a few hours to blow across the Florida straits and settle on the southeastern states as a cancerous dust. This reactor, say the last people likely to be invited to visit it, is another Chernobyl waiting to happen.

Logic would dictate that American expertise therefore assist in assuring the reactor's safety and reliability, but, instead, the Helms-Burton Act legally interprets the anticipated but purely hypothetical conclusion of the reactor as an "act of aggression" against the United States. The by-product of its low-grade uranium reaction is ill suited to manufacturing nuclear weapons, but firing up the reactor would be, according to recent United States law, an act of belligerence tantamount to a ground invasion of the naval base at Guantánamo. These maneuvers in turn bolster Cuba's stubbornly held position that safety is not the issue: the US simply wants to crush the island's dreams of energy self-sufficiency under the oppressive jackboot of imperialism.

Going past in the back of a truck, I had no idea that Juragua was the object of such saber-rattling. It looked moribund and post-apocalyptic, as if the arthritic cranes, frozen in place, would never again bend or swivel to haul another chunk of concrete. "They say," said the man on the bench next to me, "that they are about to start work on it again. But, then, they are always saying that."

We came to a ghastly housing complex, two twenty-story high-rises, one nothing more than a shell, the other flapping with laundry. This, my friends on the bus told me, was *la ciudad*, "the city," built to house the Soviet technicians and scientists working on the project.

"The city?" I asked. "What city?"

"I don't know. The nuclear city, I guess."

Trece

Cienfuegos

Cuando a Cienfuegos llegué	When I arrived in Cienfuegos
Y esa ciudad quisé verla	And that was a city I wanted to see
Ya que la llaman la perla	The one they call the pearl
Ahora le diré porque	And now I'll tell you why
Una Cienfuegera me dijo Moré	A Cienfuegan girl said to me, "Moré"
En una tarde de Mayo	One afternoon in May
Allá por Pasacaballos	It was over by Pasacaballos
Con rumbo hacia Rancho Luna	On the way to Rancho Luna
Ella me dió una fortuna, Senores	She gave me a fortune, gentlemen
Y en Cienfuegos me quedé, ya tu lo ves.	And I decided to stay.
—Beny Moré, *Cienfuegos*	

Belching diesel, the ferry from Pasacaballos rounded a small island in the Bay of Cienfuegos. The "Pearl of the South" stretched out low and long and gaudy along the waterfront. It was a milestone of sorts. Cienfuegos, I estimated, was almost exactly a third of the way from Pinar del Río to Guantánamo. I puffed out my chest and looked out over the waters, my hand firmly on the guardrail. There is something about standing on the open bow of a ship, even one putt-putting its way across a glassy, sheltered bay, that lets a man bask in the light of his own adventure-some spirit. *I have walked a third of the way across Cuba*, I thought to myself. In this swell of pride, I conveniently ignored the occasional lapses that had helped me advance.

Far across the water on the starboard side, dozens of horse-drawn carts and old American sedans moved along a waterfront boulevard lined with evenly spaced palms and colonial and neoclassical mansions painted in rich blues and yellows. This was the Prado of Cienfuegos, which emerges from the interior of the countryside to define the arrow-straight spine of the city before continuing tangent to the bay, where it transforms into the *Malecón*. A stroll beneath its colonnaded lengths passes first through the center of the city and then emerges beside the shimmering water.

As soon as the boat had docked, I made my way to the Prado. The roofs of the houses along both sides of the street extended generously from the buildings, creating a shaded pedestrian walkway separated from the street by an eclectic row of quasi-Doric columns. The doorways of the houses were cutouts hinged into grand wooden shutters reaching almost to the ceiling of the arcade, and some were left gently ajar, offering views into the dim salons within. As everywhere in Cuba, life was lived right out on the street. Through the open shutters as I was walking by, I saw a baby having its diaper changed. A few houses down, a bedridden man, at the other end of life, was lying on his side in a hospital bed-on-wheels that had been pushed up against the window to give him a view outside.

Too many of the houses were for rent. I found a room with Jesus and Arelys, a couple in their mid-thirties, my age, but with a twelve-year old son. Arelys was plump, blonde, and bland. She said it was very lucky for her that I had arrived at random ("por casualidad") to rent their room, as a Canadian had just vacated and was flying back to Toronto that afternoon. The room was upstairs, with its own tiny terrace over the interior courtyard of the house. While I was settling in, Arelys came back upstairs.

"I'm very sorry to disturb you" she said. "The Canadian gentleman is downstairs. I assure you I made up the room, but he insists he left something here."

"Sorry, eh," he said when he came in. He had bushy, salt-and-pepper hair and looked about fifty. "I think I must have just left something there under the bureau." He got down on his hands and knees and peered into the gap below the long dresser, and then stuck his arm along the floor, pulling out a small white plastic bag. It didn't seem that he had left it behind so much as stashed it there. I tried to mind my own business but I must have looked at him oddly.

"Its just my bag of trinkets," he said. "Twenty-dollar watches and that sort of thing. To give out to the girls, you know. I had to throw it under there in a hurry. I couldn't let the one I'm with now get a look at it, or she would want everything for herself, you see. She was here when I was packing up."

I found the *jinetera* phenomenon terribly sad. The women who offered themselves to any single male tourist and the teenagers hanging on to the arms of aging European men were a scandal, a constant reminder that the ideals of the revolution were crumbling and that Cuba was for sale. All its antique furniture, books, heirlooms, and grandmothers' jewelry were already gone, everything that was worth selling, up to and including the women. It was so common for women to get married and move to Italy that it was almost a cliché.

Cuban men viewed the monied, foreign johns with a mixture of despair and disdain, but like a Medellín priest with a full collection plate, they were unlikely to complain that there were a few more dollars flowing through the neighborhood. When women like Arelys opened the door and found me standing alone on the doorstep, a look of malaise and apprehension came over their faces. It combined disappointment that I was not a perky young backpacker couple; fear that I would return drunk and belligerent in the middle of the night and bring the worst sort of women into the house; and self-doubt as to whether it had been a wise decision to go into the bed-and-breakfast business. Putting their fears to rest as soon as possible after arriving made relations with the family much smoother, but I also felt a need to defend myself. I found it inexplicably infuriating whenever Cubans assumed that I was visiting their country on a quest for easy sex.

I went downstairs with the Canadian, whose name was Paul, and met his date, Mary, and his translator-guide, an English teacher named Pablo who had quit teaching at a local school "to go freelance," as he put it. It would be difficult to learn English in school in Cuba today, since almost everyone with a solid command of the language seems to have turned, officially or unofficially, to the tourist industry. Mary was clearly a friend of Arelys's.

"She's very new to that world, she's not really a *jinetera*," Arelys said after they had gone. "I hope things are going to work out for her."

"It's never quite clear to me what makes a *jinetera*," I said.

"Well, Mary's a nice girl," Arelys said vaguely. "I think she just likes the attention. But she has to be careful. They have a new law and are cracking down. You know I have to copy down your passport information and present it to immigration?"

I nodded.

"Well, any Cuban that accompanies a tourist, I now have to write down the number of their *cédula* and provide it to immigration. If a girl turns up registered three times with different men, they arrest her and she gets street-sweeping detail, kind of as a warning. Then if it happens again, she goes to jail."

"What happens if you register the tourist but not the girl?" I asked, imagining that this was exactly what had happened with Mary.

"You can't do that. Imagine what would happen if the girl stole something from the tourist and he went to the police. As it is, most of them don't trust the girls and give me all their money to hold so it's not in their bedroom."

"I heard about the *jinetera* prison in Havana," I said.

"There's another one here," said Arelys, opening her eyes wide. She bit her lip thoughtfully. I sensed her civic pride doing battle with the desire to gossip. "Jesus's parents have a farm just outside of town, right next to the jail. It's called Las Tecas. Sometimes, from the farm, you can see the girls working in the fields. They say there are eight hundred girls locked up there. It's terrible to think of all those young girls spending their teenage years locked away."

"How long do they lock them up for?" I asked.

"Two or three years." She said, sighing and shaking her head in dismay.

"They should arrest the men," I said. "If they want to solve the problem."

Arelys laughed at this outrageous suggestion, a possibility so remote that she had never even considered it. In Havana, Miriam had already told me such a thing would never happen; the authorities would never risk jeopardizing the influx of tourist cash, so they went after the supply instead of the demand.

I went outside and sat on a park bench on the pedestrian island in the middle of the Prado with my notebook. "Me, depressed, alienated, how does this affect my views?" I wrote. A young girl I took to be a teenager, walking with a couple of friends who were on their bicycles, stopped in front of me. She was wearing red shorts and a white T-shirt and looked as if she had just come from soccer practice. The friends kept going.

She put a hand on her hip and fixed me with an appraising, sassy stare.

"Where are you from?" she asked, without introduction.

"Right next door," I said. "The United States."

"And what are you doing?"

"I'm writing in my diary."

"We could see each other later."

"I don't think so."

"Why not? Tonight."

"I'm leaving town," I lied.

"All right, bye," she said, hurrying off to catch up with her friends.

I wandered up the Prado along the covered walkway, admiring the handmade floor tiles that paved the arcade. Each house had its own pattern or style in front of it. The flow of horse-carts had slowed to a trickle; they really were for commuters, but many bicyclists peddled up and down the grand, broad avenue on Chinese one-speeds. I had the epiphany that cycling, not walking, was the Cuban national response to the energy crisis and the special period. Nobody ever walked anywhere. What had I been thinking? I was tired of trudging along under the hot sun earning the odd looks of the people I passed along the way. An idea began to take shape. I would make one last mighty effort and hike over the Escambray mountains to Trinidad on foot. From there, near the coast on the southern edge of the range, all the way to Bayamo, well into the Oriente hundreds of kilometers to the east, Cuba was as flat as the Bay of Cienfuegos that stretched out beside me. I would buy my very own Chinese bicycle and ride across the great central prairies of Cuba.

Just off the *Malécon* I found a *paladar.* Someone had converted their small front room into a restaurant, with four tables. Seated near the door were some men drinking beer. One of them leaped up when he saw me and came out onto the sidewalk. "Come in for dinner, come on in and sit down, I have chicken, I have fish, I have pork. I have cold beer."

It was a small, out-of-the-way place that looked almost as if it might have Cuban clients. After hearing these promises of abundance, I went in and took a seat at a table divided from the revelry by a wooden screen. An older, shriveled little man came out from the back somewhere and brought me a menu. Everything was outrageously expensive. I sat there and looked at the menu with distaste.

Cuban restaurants that do not cater solely to tourists often have two almost identical menus, one in dollars and the other in pesos. The peso menu, with complete meals for less than the equivalent of a dollar, shows prices typically a fifth of those on the dollar menu. Usually a decent command of Spanish and the firm insistence that you are aware of this institutionalized clipping is enough to embarrass restaurant proprietors into bringing out the peso menu. I found it unsettling, however, to argue and haggle over the price at the beginning of a meal that had not yet even been prepared, let alone eaten. It rather took away my appetite to see the owner, frustrated and annoyed at his failure to fleece me of my dollars, go storming off into the kitchen to prepare the order we had finally settled on.

The shriveled waiter returned.

"I think I'll just have a beer," I said.

He looked crestfallen.

"You don't want anything?" he asked feebly.

The first man, who had gone back to drinking beer with his cronies, must have been listening, for he came around the side of the screen and gave me a broad, car-salesman's smile. "Things are slow," he said. "You should know that everything on the menu is half price." He thought for a moment. "Except the beer."

The waiter, who was hunched over and seemed to cower like a dog fearful of being hit with a stick, told me that the garrulous, beer-drinking owner was his younger brother. I felt sorry for him. He introduced himself as Fernando. He wasn't really a waiter, he confided, he was a medical entomologist, studying the mechanisms through which insects transmit disease. It just hadn't been possible to go on with his work, given the economic situation, so he had come here to help out. I described camping out along the coast toward Playa Larga amid hordes of mosquitos. He brightened visibly, smiling as if I had given him a wonderful gift.

"Aah," he said. "That's *Aedes taeniorynchus*, we call it the *mosquito bobo*." The stupid mosquito. "It is also known as the black mosquito, or coastal mosquito. They call it the stupid mosquito because you can kill huge clumps of them on your arm with one swipe."

"That's the one," I said, trying to share Fernando's enthusiasm. "It lands on you in a cloud."

"It's not a dangerous species here in Cuba, although it is reported that in other countries the most severe infestations of a similar species have killed cattle outright, just by sucking their blood. The ones that cause the most concern here are *Anopheles albimanus* and *Aedes aegypti*. The *Anopheles* is the vector for malaria in Cuba; they call it *albimanus* because the ends of the legs are white. It is a rural species, and malaria is rare today; almost all the cases reported are discovered to have come from someone catching it abroad and bringing it in: soldiers coming back from Angola with malaria, that sort of thing. *Aedes aegypti* is the one we are actively trying to control. It is the vector for dengue and yellow fever."

I had seen the anti-mosquito patrol in the streets in their gray hospital-orderly shirts, with "*Aedes aegypti* eradication campaign" marked on the shirt pocket. Many houses had stickers on the doors, posted like elevator maintenance reports, where the patrol noted down the results of their searches for jars of standing water and old tires. It was an impressive public-health campaign.

"Mosquitos are so beautiful," said Fernando, with passion. "You look at them under a microscope and you begin to appreciate the taxonomy, and you realize they are truly beautiful insects. It is a beautiful field. Every day, I learned something new." He had transformed into a different person from the battered restaurant waiter, although he was still skinny and shriveled. He looked a bit like his subjects, lean and gangly, with a big Adam's apple bobbing in his narrow neck, and long, skinny fingers that had once focused the knobs of a microscope as he peered through the glass.

"It is a great sadness to me," he said, "that when I left the lab, I had to abandon my huge collection of flies, mosquitos, and cockroaches, all native to Cuba. There are seventy-two species of mosquito in Cuba, and I had collected many of them."

The brother yelled for more beer and Fernando excused himself to go back into the kitchen to fetch some more cans. When he returned, I invited him to sit down at the table and continue the conversation. "My son won the *bombo*," he said, quietly. "He has his interview with the American interests section this coming October. My wife and I are hoping we will be able to leave with him. Do you think it's possible I might find some work with mosquitos in Florida?"

After dinner, I went to the movies. On the Prado were two glorious and palatial theaters almost across from one another. A small, handwritten sign advertised Costa-Gavras's *Music Box*. Another little sign in the ticket window said, "The air turbines are insufficient. Price 80 centavos." The theater was only charging the equivalent of four cents instead of five because the air conditioning was broken.

Inside, it looked as if I had stumbled into an onanist's convention. Twenty solitary men were scattered among the six hundred or so seats in the dim light of the great sprawling auditorium. I wondered if I had misread the date and bought a ticket to a porno by mistake. But pornography is outlawed in Cuba.

The theater was of the kind that no longer exists in the United States, cavernous, with a huge screen. Cuba had not yet caught the cancer of the multiplex, although below the screen, in the passageway in front of the stage, were three huge television sets on wheeled carts. A few more single men wandered in, unsure of whether to sit near the televisions or farther back so that the sets wouldn't block their view of the big screen. Hecklers called out from the back that this film was to be projected on the "pantalla grande," the big screen. Finally, a Chinese woman came in with her son. She was to be the only woman in the audience.

We waited expectantly for the lights to go down. Instead, a skinny shell of a man padded down the aisle to the front and began to address the meager audience in a cracking voice. "Good evening, and welcome," he said. "Please come sit closer to the front," he said to the handful of us who were in theater. "I'm not sure my *a capella* will reach the back." He waited. Nobody moved.

"Some of you may remember," he began again. "In the past, we had the *cinémathèque*. Twice a week, films of quality were shown here. But for reasons we are all aware of, we were forced to put an end to those evenings. Prints of the films grew scarce or disappeared, and the parts for 35mm projection became almost impossible to obtain. No more films were sent from Havana." He looked sad and withered, as if he had let the drastic demise of projected celluloid during the special period affect him personally, and waste him away, like a disease.

"As you know," he continued, "almost all the films we see today are shown on video. But the real cinema...," he paused, searching for a shred of drama as he gestured behind him toward the yellowing screen "...is this. With these Monday evenings now, we hope to revitalize film, showing not just the usual blood and guts, but films of quality. If the evening is a success, we hope to apply to Havana for prints of other quality films that may still be in existence."

The film opened with a long sequence of a family party in which an extreme close-up of the tines of a music box, twanging against its rotating drum, was intercut with images of couples dancing and carrying on. We saw rhythmically edited close-ups of violins being played. You could almost hear the music swelling in the background. It was only after a few minutes, however, that I realized that I couldn't in fact hear the music swelling in the background.

"So it's a silent film, is it?" someone shouted in the dark somewhere behind me.

"I won't be back next Monday," croaked another wag, going for the easy laugh.

The sound crept in, as if the projectionist had discovered a long-forgotten volume knob in his ongoing archeological exploration of the projector and turned it up cautiously as an experiment. A hum of sixty cycles filled the room, issuing out from somewhere behind the screen, a low, hornet-like buzz that obscured the English dialogue, which sounded as though it was being played off of a very old phonograph record that had been cleaned with sandpaper. On the screen, white subtitles in Spanish blended seamlessly into the texture of the print, which was faded and washed out and pitted with a miasma of scratches that went flying past the arc lamp, giving the entire film the patina of an ancient oil painting badly in need of restoration. Between straining to hear the dialogue somewhere within the buzz and static, and squinting to read the subtitles through the snowstorm of scratches, I could just about extrapolate the substance of the plot.

Jessica Lange plays a successful New York lawyer, the quintessentially assimilated daughter of a Hungarian Second World War veteran who finds himself accused of war crimes after forty years of living a peaceful life in Forest Hills. After agreeing to represent him, she begins the agonizing process of confronting his hidden past. It is the late 1980s and communism is collapsing in eastern Europe. Documents that have been locked away in the vaults of the secret police since the end of the war begin trickling out into the world beyond the Iron Curtain.

In Cienfuegos, *The Music Box*, a film as serious as a heart attack, was still good for one big laugh. Lange's character travels to Budapest, to try and pry loose some information that may exonerate her father. In a taxi, sure that her "translator" is really there to keep tabs on her, she suggests that he is working for the secret police. "Nobody likes working for the government," he scoffs. "No money." At this, a chorus of chuckles and snickers rippled through the cinema.

The two projectors had bulbs of very different ages and color temperatures, so that every twenty minutes or so, with each reel change, the entire character of the cinematography shifted between the dim and blood-soaked pink of a lamp on its last legs to a dreamy and ethereal overexposed wash when the bright light from the other projector overpowered the strip of film. Despite it all, the movie was riveting. Even when the film inevitably jumped from the sprockets, and the image froze and shuddered on the screen before blistering into a brown puddle, out of which the light burst like the sun through dense clouds to melt the strip into two pieces, all of us sat expectantly, waiting for the projectionist to get the film back on track, gripping on to our pent-up anxiety and the backs of the seats in front of us.

"Next Monday, I'm not coming," the wag in the back called out again, but this time nobody laughed. When the film ended and I stumbled out onto the Prado, I was not the only one wiping my cheeks with the back of my hand; I was surrounded by men in tears.

The next day, I went to Santa Isabel de las Lajas on a pilgrimage. An inland, sugar-cane town near the central highway, Lajas is the birth- and last resting-place of Beny Moré. A titan among the many legends of Cuban music, Moré is an untouchable cultural hero. His music is the soundtrack of Cuba, and his anthems in praise of Cienfuegos, Lajas, or the waist-wiggling dancefloor skills of Cuban and Mexican women are as beloved on the island as they are in the Cuban Diaspora. He is at least as famous in Cuba as Frank Sinatra is in the United States, and his legend has grown to include a touch of Jackie Robinson: "El Beny," as he was called, was a light-skinned black man, and he is said to have stood up to the color barrier in Havana's 1950s music industry, when black artists were welcome to record, but were locked out of television appearances and select nightspots.

After hours spent waiting with the Cienfuegos *amarillos*, a combination of rides in the back of government trucks got me to Lajas, where the first woman I asked for directions offered to take me to the house Beny had built for his mother. The neighborhood was very black and was literally on the wrong side of some train tracks, where a long, battered freight sat baking in the sun. As we skirted around the train, I asked a man where the train line went. "Esta roto," he said. It's broken.

It was a pious neighborhood. Through the open windows of the surrounding houses, I saw many *Santería* altars, usually on a simple set of bookshelves or a breakfront draped with cloth. They were laid out with strange assortments of objects: bowls and jars and empty bottles and figurines and plastic flowers. Red statuettes of Santa Barbara presided over many of these collections.

The house that Beny built was a simple one-story square structure filling its corner lot. One of his sisters (he was the oldest of eighteen siblings) was sitting on the little porch, sucking on a mango pit. "Go on in and look around," she said, waving to the open door behind her without getting up. I went in while the woman who had brought me chatted on the porch with Beny's sister. I found this remarkable. Imagine going to Graceland, being given the run of the place, and finding nobody even the slightest bit fearful that you might make off with some priceless Elvis artifact.

The living room had been converted into a religious shrine, not so much to Beny as to the saints. Three tiers of blue cinderblocks, painted with the same paint as the outside of the house, made a home for various small virgins, vases of plastic red roses and purple hyacinths that would never wilt, chromolithographs of San Lázaro and some other saints I didn't recognize, a fake Hummel figurine of a somewhat gloomy basset hound, a claw of heliconia, a plate of coins, and some fresh offerings of herbs in glasses of water. These altars were always odd combinations of the sacred and mundane, a mixture between a home chapel and the sort of tchotchke shelf used to display a collection of eggcups of the world, miniature crystal swans, or figurines of elves hauling water from a well and prancing about a tree-stump in a forest glen.

There was nothing remarkable about the house, but I went outside and asked Beny's sister if I could take photographs. "Of course," she said. "Just don't take any of me." She fingered one of the beaded necklaces she was wearing to show her affiliation to the saints. She said she herself had no objection to my taking pictures of her, but one of her saints didn't like to be photographed.

I crossed the tracks and went along the main street. The main plaza, dotted with whitewashed busts of generals and patriots, burned blinding white in the sun. A bar on the corner sold the usual, vicious *aguardiente*. "Where's the cemetery?" I asked the bartender. "I want two shots, one for me and one for Beny. I promise to bring the glasses back."

She laughed, not because I wanted to serve *aguardiente* to a dead man, but at the thought that she would give me her glasses to take away. She poured a double in a plastic cup so flimsy that I had to hold it by the rim to prevent it from collapsing. The alcohol was dangerously inexpensive. Moré had been a great drinker, and he died young, at forty-three, of cirrhosis of the liver.

The graveyard had once been a few blocks outside of town and now was on the edge of it. The gates were open. There was nobody alive to ask for directions, so I wandered through the dense clusters of graves to the far end of the cemetery. Mother's Day had been two days before, and many of the headstones, scorching in the sun, were freshly tidied and decorated with just-wilting flowers. Rusted rebar, bent and welded into crosses, and snapshots, protected from the elements by glass-fronted tin frames, adorned the tombs. The graves that nobody had visited were conspicuous in their disarray, scrubby and plantless and dusty, with dirt pushed by the wind into little piles in the corners of the stones. They were like abandoned vacant lots in this microcosm of a city.

There are many people in and around Lajas named Moré, for the *Conde*, the count who owned the tracts of canefield there, and gave his name to the slaves that worked them, like cattle branded with the name of a ranch. Beny lay next to his mother. Tall gilt letters spelled out the name, and a quote from his lyrics about his hometown, "Lajas mi rincón querido, pueblo donde yo nací" ("Lajas, my beloved corner, the place where I was born"). Like most of his songs, the words and ideas are simple greetings, praises, or boasts, but even just reading those two lines on the tombstone was enough to evoke the miraculous voice that sung them. I tried not to feel self-conscious as I sprinkled *aguardiente* on the ground, the way Cubans and Haitians do when they open a bottle, for the saints, and the dead.

Catorce

A short trip to Mexico

My visa was about to expire. After having extended it once, I had no choice but to leave the country. To get back to Havana from Cienfuegos, I treated myself to the absurd luxury of the Viazul tourist bus. Less than ten of us nestled into the plush velour seats, almost cold from the chill of the air conditioning. On the overhead television, the tepid plot of some Hollywood entertainment unfolded. It was an artificial environment unknown to the average Cuban, as if we were traveling through the country in a gigantic terrarium, aliens that could only move about in a hermetically sealed box containing and preserving fragments of our own distant atmosphere.

After a night in the familiar gloom of Miriam's apartment, I flew to Cancún. The road leaving the airport was lined with dazzling billboards for the Outback Steakhouse, Papa John's Pizza, the Kahlua B52, the Warner Brothers Studio Store Cancún, and Planet Hollywood. An advertisement for José Cuervo Tequila presented festive and exuberant North American college students whooping it up, with the tagline, *Tequila—Huhhhn!*, as if the Cro-Magnon behavior of kids on spring break needed promotion. Another sign advertised tickets for a theatrical revue called "Too Mucking Fuch." By the time we arrived at the bus station, I had decided that perhaps the closed society of Cuba wasn't so bad after all.

Cancún is a cultural vacuum, a hellhole of international high-rise hotels jockeying for position on a once remote and pristine beach. I caught the first bus out for the four-hour ride across the dry and scrubby expanses of the northern Yucatan to the old colonial city of Mérida, where Cynthia and I had spent some time. As I hobbled my way across Cuba, I was holding onto our relationship like San Lázaro's crutch: she was in Greece, and Mérida was as close as I could get to her.

Beside me on the bus, a drunk Mayan explained at great length his indisputable theory that the world today is controlled by the ebb and flow of money. In contrast, he said, during the ancient civilization of the Mayans, the only currency had been time itself. "Tiempo, tiempo, tiempo," he intoned, shaking his upstretched arms at me for emphasis. Gusts of boozy morning breath wafted over me as he repeated his mantra. "Everything was time. *No hay mas!*" There was nothing more. "It's a difficult concept to understand," he finally admitted, before laying his head on my shoulder and falling into a drunken slumber.

After Cuba, Mérida was a riot of commerce. It is probably as lazy and relaxed a tropical city as one could hope to visit, but to me it was a bustling bazaar filled with an impossibly rich cornucopia of goods. Bicycle shops were packed to overflowing with hanging, gleaming wheels and shining spokes. Fabric merchants displayed bolts of cloth in a riot of rich patterns and textures stacked into high teetering piles in the windows. Next to a boutique selling trendy surfer clothing to Mérida youth, a pawnshop bristled with used cell phones. (One ringing in the Cancún airport had startled and puzzled me until I remembered what it was). Shoe stores were everywhere, dozens of them, and copy shops, and stationers and butchers and hardware stores. I stared into the windows in amazement, like a bumpkin on Fifth Avenue gazing at the Empire State Building. Bucolic Mérida and its Mexicans sitting on park benches in the plaza seemed an amazing, throbbing place.

During my four-day vacation from Cuba, I went into almost every one of Mérida's shoe stores looking for a pair of white mules for Miriam. Once initiated as a *santera*, she would wear only white from head to toe for an entire year. I fondled pair after pair of women's shoes until the tiny Mayan shopgirls looked at me with the bewildered revulsion reserved for the fetishist. Shopping for women's shoes is a mysterious, inscrutable ritual subject to its own unfathomable laws, and my fear of failure was too great. I purchased white lace shawls; white pantyhose, size large; and a white blouse, embroidered with white thread, but I concluded that Miriam would have to find another source for her white shoes.

I wasted a day rushing from one Internet café to another and failing to "instant-message" with Cynthia in Greece. I asked without conscious intention at a travel agent about the price of a ticket to Athens and swam in the pool at the Hotel Dolores Alba, where the two of us had stayed. As I was walking out the door to go back to the bus station and the Cancún airport, Cynthia finally called.

"I miss you a lot," I said. "I'm not really sure if I want to go back."

"I miss you, too." We both started to cry.

"I wanted to stay at the same hotel where we stayed together, to be as close to you as possible," I said.

"We had a huge fight there," said Cynthia. "Don't you remember?"

I flew back to Havana. Approaching the tiny closets of the immigration officers with the nonchalance of experience, I slid my passport across the high counter to the almost invisible functionary behind it.

"Is this your first visit to Cuba?"

I remembered the feeble, stuttering obfuscations of my previous entry into the country. I boldly spoke the truth.

"No," I said, "it's actually my third."

From down behind the counter where I could not see came an exuberant and violent flurry of thumps. The official returned my passport. He had stamped it three times, once for each admitted visit, as if the word had come down from on high that Immigration was to make up for the lost years of letting Americans sneak into the country with a wink, to spend their dollars. I stared at the three fresh green squares on the passport page in horror and disbelief. Here was not only the evidence that I had violated the Trading with the Enemy Act, but indelible proof that I was a serial offender.

Back at Miriam's, I considered once again contriving a premature end to my trip, packing up the growing cache of unused items I left with her, and moving to some happier place. By now, I had almost filled her small closet with stupid possessions I should never have brought with me in the first place, dumping more and more items each time I passed through Havana in a desperate attempt to lessen my load.

Miriam always asked when I would be back. This was partly out of concern and friendship, but also because she spent much of her time worrying about whether she would be able to pay the room-rental tax each month. She lit candles and freshened the glasses of water that stood on her altar to the saints, and she sat on her couch with her feet up and her arm crooked across her eyes, fretting while she waited for the telephone to ring, ignoring the television that flickered, incessant and soundless, in the gloomy dark of her tiny apartment.

I never did manage to move. Cuba suffered from a national inertia, a debilitating and virulent malaise that sapped one of all strength and motivation. Miriam had a terminal case, and despite four days in Mexico and promises to myself that I would start afresh and look at Cuba with a new eye, I was still infected.

Miriam was pleased with the white headscarves and pantyhose and understanding about the shoes. "I'll just have to resolve them somewhere else," she said. While she was looking over the newly arrived garments, her neighbor called. She needed a favor.

"Richard, would you help them? They need a foreigner to buy some drugs. They have all the money together and they will drive you there in a car. You don't need to do anything but go along for the ride."

The woman's son had intestinal parasites. She arrived and explained that the necessary medicine was only available at the international pharmacy. Her husband was waiting in front of the building in their battered Lada. She got in the back with her son and gave me the front seat. As he gripped the steering wheel, her husband's hands were trembling. I knew he was worried about being caught chauffeuring a tourist without permission. He was so nervous and tense, I was afraid it might affect his driving.

"I don't understand," I said. "Why is it you need me to come?"

"I have two prescriptions that can only be filled in dollars at the international pharmacy," said the woman. "Only foreigners are allowed to shop there. I'm a doctor, I know these are the only things that will clear up his parasites."

She explained that the UJC, the Young Communists Union, had complained that these pharmacies sold medicine only in dollars. At a recent congress, the group had argued that because not all Cubans had access to dollars, although it was now legal to possess them, the international pharmacies were unfair and promoted unequal access to medical treatment. They had resolved this problem by voting to make it illegal for any Cuban, with or without dollars, to shop at the pharmacies. It was a typically admirable and ludicrous attempt to maintain equality within Cuban revolutionary society. The pharmacies were now "international" in the sense that they sold only to holders of foreign passports.

The boy needed two medicines. One prescription would cost seven dollars to fill, the other fifteen. It was a fortune. "Now you not only need to somehow come up with the dollars," the mother told me, "you have to find a foreigner to come with you and buy the drugs."

Inside the pharmacy, the shelves were stocked with a dazzling array of multivitamins, toothpastes, deodorants, antacids, and suntan lotions as if here, in this dollar-only environment, the American embargo was not in effect. It was like the pharmacies I had seen in Mexico. The cashier wrote down my passport number and gave the woman the medicines. None of us pretended that the medicine was for me, and my signature was a formality.

They drove me back to Miriam's, embarrassing me along the way with their profuse thanks. I was back in Cuba.

Quince

Hitching to Trinidad

"**S**antiago, Guantánamo, who has the list please?" The man called out over and over as he wandered through rows of park benches, their aluminum slat seats worn shiny and smooth by thousands of bottoms. They were packed with aspiring travelers, and just when he had found the list and was about to add his name to it, the crowd surged up off the benches and out toward the highway, where an open-backed eighteen-wheeler had pulled to a halt. Two *amarillos*, five policemen, and a semi-official plainclothes dispatcher attempted to wrangle the crowd as they clambered up a rolling stepladder into the back and, scrambling on the wheel-wells, threw bags of possessions to passengers already over the wall of the container. Moments later, the trailer was packed full and the truck rolled off en route to Camagüey, two-thirds of the way across the country. Because of my friend Reynaldo, I did not catch this ride.

An official response to the transportation difficulties that emerged during the special period, *amarillos*, or "yellows," are government employees. Wearing yellow shirts and mustard-colored slacks, they run hitchhiker way-stations at important highway intersections and on the outskirts of towns. Their job is to oblige state-operated vehicles to stop and pick up hitchhikers, to make sure that people are given rides in the order they arrive in, and to make certain that all vehicles travel full to capacity without being overcrowded. After riding from Cienfuegos to Havana on the luxury tourist bus, I had decided there was no better way to plunge myself back into Cuban life than to attempt the return journey with the *amarillos'* help.

It was one o'clock in the afternoon and I was sitting in the grandfather of all hitching-posts, a great wall-less outdoor cathedral of waiting on the eastern outskirts of Havana. I had left Miriam's at 8:30 that morning: after an interminable ride crushed into a *camello* and a long wait for a lift to the *amarillos*, I had advanced perhaps fifteen kilometers from her apartment. When the eighteen-wheeler pulled up, I stayed where I was on a bench across from Reynaldo, the keeper of the Cienfuegos list, because he was going to Cienfuegos and had signaled to me, with a wink and a calming open-palmed stopping gesture, to wait for a better ride. Because it is an hour south of the central highway on the coast, Cienfuegos is a tricky destination. The turnoff is at a place named Aguada de Pasajeros. Nevertheless, almost all the Cienfuegos passengers had gone on the eighteen-wheeler and would try their luck getting a second ride from the Aguada crossroads. Reynaldo pointed with glee at the list to show how few people were now left ahead of us. He had a complex arsenal of winks and conspiratorial hand gestures he used to communicate with me as we sat across from one another. These bespoke great experience and wisdom in the intricacies of organized hitchhiking. He touched his cheek below one eye, winked, and then patted his chest with the palm of one hand. That meant *watch me and do what I do*. He had taken me into his confidence.

An hour later, Reynaldo made more knowing, calming gestures when another vehicle to Aguada was announced. "Tranquilo," he said. "Be patient. Soon we will get a ride direct to Cienfuegos." The open-sided shed refilled with people and emptied again slowly, like a tide pool. It was like watching geology unfold in real time. I thought of the Mayan man on the bus to Mérida chanting *Time, time, time, there is nothing more*. I ate a last minuscule ham sandwich, purchased that morning in the Vedado. It seemed like weeks ago. I was finally made to understand that Reynaldo was waiting for a particular vehicle, a sand truck known to have brought a load from Cienfuegos to a construction site in Havana. Soon, it would be heading back, empty, he was sure. We were by now the veterans of the waiting room. Reynaldo had become the keeper not only of the Cienfuegos list, but also of the lists of people hoping to get to Santa Clara and Ciego de Ávila. I was the only one who had a pen.

Another huge truck pulled in. It had benches welded into the back and was apparently a private concern, somehow licensed and taxed to charge passengers on a for-profit basis. Now, the plainclothes dispatcher made a great display, rushing about frantically and collecting together a herd of passengers to Camagüey. It was obvious he would receive a kickback of some kind. Reynaldo was disgusted. He made his eyes like slits and made the money sign, rubbing thumb and forefingers together, then pretending to put his hand in his pocket. He tapped one temple. We should be wise and avoid this ruse. "Muy caro," he said. Very expensive. And when they finally announced the price of the "tickets," at fifty pesos—or $2.50 for the five-hundred-kilometer trip—the crowd fell back in horror onto the waiting-room benches like a receding wave. The truck left almost empty.

The day dragged on. The only thing relieving the tedium was the ever-changing cast of characters who arrived from nowhere to sit awhile under the rusted wavy roof. Reynaldo was a night-watchman at a machine shop outside Cienfuegos. Five nights a week, he sat in the yard of a garage under the trees, guarding against thieves; on the sixth day, he went to Havana on the train, smuggling sixty pounds of cheese in cardboard boxes to furnish the over-the-garden-gate pizza industry in the city.

"In the train, it is easy to carry big packages and it is slow, there is never any vigilance," he said. "On the way back home, when all I have in my pocket is the cash, I can take the *botella* and it doesn't matter if I catch rides with policemen, or sit next to soldiers." Reynaldo tapped his forehead to underline his shrewdness. He was friendly and determined to help me. I was weary and growing resentful that I had not pressed on to Aguada when given the chance so many hours earlier, and I blamed him instead of myself. It was by now almost four in the afternoon. Soon, the *amarillos* would go home for the day and there would be no more rides. It would even become difficult to retreat to Miriam's.

At five, a small, empty dump truck pulled in. Above the passing traffic and the wind, I heard someone shouting "Aguada." Suddenly, Reynaldo, and everyone else, leaped up and rushed to the highway, squeezing through a gap in the chainlink fence. A chaotic crush of bodies clambered into the vehicle from all sides. A dozen soldiers in green fatigues scaled the tailgate, jumping into the back with the speed and precision of a tactical hostage rescue. There was no sign of the waiting list or even any pretense that there had ever been a list. Reynaldo had abandoned me as I struggled to run with my huge backpack, and when I reached the rear bumper, he was already in the truck, staking out a tiny space in which to stand. The driver had leaped out of his cab and was stomping on the pavement, red-faced, fuming that the *amarillos* had overloaded his vehicle. A policeman was ineffectually trying to pull some of the later comers back down off the truck. I had one foot on the bumper and the other leg crooked over the tailgate. Two soldiers inside the truck were helping to tug me over by pulling on the pack frame, but one of the *amarillos*—or a policeman, I couldn't see which—had grasped my belt from behind, and I was trapped in a human tug-of-war. "Get off, get off," he was shouting. "It's too crowded."

"I'm with him," I yelled, gesturing vaguely at Reynaldo, who was packed into the crowd in the middle of the truck. This was clearly not true. Our six-hour alliance of winks and gestures had dissolved in moments during the dog-eat-dog survivalist assault on the truck, but the policeman released his grip long enough for me to flop over the tailgate. Only the dense crush of bodies prevented me from falling to the bed and decapitating a woman crouched there. Somehow, I got the pack off and wedged down between my legs, but I could see neither my feet nor the floor of the truck because every available inch was taken up by passengers. The first dozen or so to get in had sat down, but at least ten of us were jammed together on our feet, like hapless spectators at the front of a stadium rock concert. The exasperated driver determined that the only way to prevent even more passengers from boarding was to drive off, and we began to move down the highway at a terrific speed. Holding the pack with one hand, I grasped the precariously low side rail somewhere far behind me with the other. It was excruciating to travel this way, with both knees bent in a skier's crouch and one hand reaching back through the crush of bodies to the metal railing, as if frozen permanently into the sort of contorted position otherwise only achieved when playing Twister.

Aguada was a hundred and eighty kilometers away. After we had traveled about ten of these, my extremities began to go to sleep. I could feel toes and fingers dully tingling with pins-and-needles, but any change of position required a phase of delicate negotiation and barter with fellow passengers, and the whistling wind made conversation impossible. Beside the road rice paddies, palm-fringed lagoons and the thatched roofs of the *bohíos* glowed intense shades of gold and green in the late slanting sun, but it was hard to appreciate the romance. I couldn't decide whether I was more terrified by the speed at which we were moving or more relieved that the discomfort would end sooner if we kept up our blistering pace.

There was little to be done. To distract my body from its agonies, I counted and recounted the passengers. At first, I concluded that there were twenty-five of us but an unattributable foot jutting out of the throng made me repeat the tally. I came up with twenty-six, then twenty-five again, then twenty-eight when I realized one woman had two children wedged before her on her thighs. I had a shouted chat with my nearest neighbor. He screamed into my ear that he was from Santiago, in the Oriente. "It's only a twelve-hour trip if you get a good ride," he bellowed, when I pointed out that Santiago was very far away. "I moved to Havana because there were more jobs, but I go back every weekend this way, to visit my family."

A really great ride in Cuba is known as a *tremenda botella*. The *tremenda botella* takes you almost to the very door of your destination, turning at each fork in the road and passing through every city and large town the way you might have gone had you been driving, and at last finally, amazingly, passing through your own tiny village. My neighbor hadn't been so lucky. He would, hours from now in Camagüey and without the help of any *amarillos*, hope to find a night truck continuing on to the East. After twenty-four hours at his parents' home, he would turn around and hitchhike back across the country to Havana.

In Jagüey Grande, one lone woman got out. Her departure did nothing to relieve our overloaded condition and, a few minutes down the road, something deep within the engine quietly expired. The truck slowed imperceptibly until I realized we were traveling at an almost sane speed. We continued, halfway straddling the shoulder, dragging slower and slower until the vehicle began softly to shudder and the driver pulled to a halt. The highway ran straight and flat through endless fields of cane.

Stiff-limbed and clumsy, the passengers untangled themselves from one another and climbed down to the pavement. We were stranded in a great expanse of nothingness, but it seemed positively jolly to be standing on the asphalt doing careful, exploratory calisthenics, at least compared with the prospect of continuing in that truck. There was a generalized mad, limping rush down to the fence beside the grassy margins of the highway, followed by a great communal urination. The man from Santiago salvaged a shattered length of fencepost, which he put at an angle across the back corner of the truck as a tiny, dangerous bench.

In a Cuban truck of thirty-odd passengers, it would be very bad luck indeed not to find an accomplished mechanic, and all too soon we were moving again. Across flooded fields of emerald rice, a column of black rain reached down to the fields, blurring the landscape into a great gray smudge.

For many kilometers, the storm flirted with the highway, but we never felt more than the spray at its edges, and strange cold gusts that pushed like veins across the hot land. At the Cienfuegos exit ramp, Reynaldo and I got out and stood in the dirt of the shoulder under the gray blanket of the evening sky, wriggling our fingers and cracking our necks. This was the crossroads destination that, six hours earlier, we had ignored at every opportunity, waiting for the Holy Grail, a *botella* direct to the city of Cienfuegos.

"If we don't have a ride by the time it gets dark," said Reynaldo, "we'll have to walk into Aguada. Nobody will stop for us at night."

"Is it far?" I asked peevishly, forgetting that I had already boasted to Reynaldo that I was crossing Cuba on foot.

"Only about two kilometers. The train to Cienfuegos passes through at 9 pm."

As we began to trudge up the shoulder, a blue state truck turned off the highway and scooped us up. It was headed for Cienfuegos. I was so glad that we were actually to arrive that night that I happily paid the extortionate charge of one dollar demanded by the driver.

"I told you we would get a ride," said Reynaldo. "But in all my trips, it has never taken me so long before. I was starting to wonder if we would make it."

"No es fácil," I said. I had left Miriam's house twelve hours earlier. The black night whipped by beside the dump truck. We were in a celebratory mood as we rattled down the road.

"The only thing I don't like here in Cuba," said Reynaldo, "is that I can't freely sell my little bit of cheese."

Standing on the dark wet pavement in a yellow pool of streetlamp at the edge of town, we said heartfelt goodbyes, earnestly wishing one another good luck forever. Our friendship was less than twelve hours old, but it had been forged in a fire of adversity and struggle.

Jesus and Arelys welcomed me like a long-lost son. The next morning when I left, they loaded me up with seven oranges and two mangos the size of melons. The most famous in all of Cuba, Cienfuegan mangos are huge and meaty, each one a meal in itself.

I was facing the brutal hike across the Escambray mountains, steep jagged teeth covered in dense forests, where Che Guevara mustered his troops for the final triumphant assault that had panicked the dictator Batista into flight. Crossing the Escambray, I had decided, would be my last great push as a hiker. I called a number I had for a doctor who rented out rooms in Trinidad.

"Please hold a room for me, I'm on foot, but I expect to get there in three days," I said.

I set out for the nearby village of Caunao, a suburb of Cienfuegos where, with more help from the *amarillos*, I hoped to catch a ride to the base of the mountain range. A guy driving a horse-cart, a *carretero*, stopped for me on the highway.

"How much to Caunao?" I asked.

"One dollar."

I offered fifty cents for a ride as far as the *amarillos*. He agreed, and I got in the cart.

"Take your pack off, you'll be more comfortable," he said.

"Do we have far to go?" I asked, dully. I had passed Caunao before by bus when visiting the local botanical gardens, but hadn't paid much attention. The driver had an epiphany. It had not until this moment occurred to him that I might never have been there.

"In fact, the truth is, you're right, it's not far at all, no need to take your pack off," he said. "I'm not supposed to take foreigners, so do you mind paying me now so that no one will see?"

As soon as I had paid, we reached our destination almost immediately.

"Here you go," he said cheerily, pulling to a halt. We were in the middle of nowhere. In a field beside the road, a torpid cow ceased nibbling at the grass to peer briefly at us.

"This isn't Caunao," I said.

"Yes, it is."

"No, it isn't. We agreed that you would take me to the *amarillos* in Caunao," I said. "This is not an *amarillos* post."

"They're not here today."

"I paid you in advance in good faith to be taken to the *amarillos* in Caunao," I said.

"The fare should be one dollar."

"Then why did you accept my offer of fifty cents?" I asked. "My understanding was that we were both satisfied with the terms. Anyway, the proper fare is five cents."

"I'll give you your money back," he threatened.

"Fine," I said. The conversation lapsed. We sat, immobile, in sullen silence. I stared fixedly out at the grazing cows. Finally, he gave the horse the reins and it began to plod down the road.

We continued in this climate of acrimony, without speaking. After a time, the driver said, "Ya estamos en Caunao." We're already in Caunao.

I ignored him. We passed grand prerevolutionary farmhouses beside the road, and more pastures. After about another kilometer, a sign beside the road finally welcomed us to Caunao. The driver stopped and gestured reproachfully at it, as if it were somehow proof that he had been in the right all along. It was the weekend and indeed there were no *amarillos* to be found at the town square. Nonetheless, within minutes, a truck stopped and waved me to jump into the back.

"Manicaragua?" I yelled. Any vehicle going there would have to pass the turn up to the mountains, where I planned to begin to hike.

"Almost," he called out the window. As I put the pack up into the truckbed, my heavy bag of fruit burst. The driver had no other cargo and drove unburdened at a terrifying speed along narrow and twisting country lanes through the canefields. Mangos and oranges careened across the floor of the truck while I clung to the gutter on the back of the cab's roof. Had Reynaldo been there, he would have made the chopping motion with his hand that he used to express high-speed travel. Fingers outstretched like the blade of a knife and his arm pumping like a sewing machine, he might have shouted "Esto si corre!" Yeah, this one runs! Chop, chop.

The mountains were fast approaching. A geological afterthought surging out of the otherwise placid landscape, the Sierra del Escambray is a cluster of dark and jagged hills that stands alone and anomalous, orphaned by the surrounding flats of the Zapata Swamp to the west and vast expanses of cane and pasture, once jungle, to the east. They looked much steeper than those of Pinar del Río, and seemed to leap out of the ground without warning.

At the base of the mountains, the driver pulled to a stop to pick up another passenger at a turnoff where a narrow sideroad led through the fields to the south and immediately began to climb up the hillside. Far above us, on a sharp ridge, I could see whitewashed houses glowing bright against the bald red earth. Higher still, piney forests turned the mountains a dark, impenetrable green. Somewhere in these heights was the settlement of El

Nicho, a dot on the map where I hoped to spend the night.

"We're turning here," said the driver, twisting his head out the window. "Manicaragua is just a few kilometers more. Any car passing will take you there."

"Is this Entronque de Minas?" I asked. The "crossroads to the mines" was where I had intended to get out and hike up into the hills. "I'm going to El Nicho."

"That's where we're going, to visit our father," said the new arrival. He was the driver's brother, a dockworker in Cienfuegos, going home for the weekend. It was an indisputable *tremenda botella*. I told myself that to get out now and walk would be to slap fate full in the face. Also, it looked like a merciless and sunbaked climb.

As the truck strained up the mountainside, a car full of women and children caught and passed us; when we arrived, the house was full of family. It was a gathering of the entire clan. The patriarch, to add to my luck, was a backwoodsman and amateur cartographer who knew every ridge and tree of the Escambray. He was very hairy, with salt-and-pepper beard stubble and bold white eyebrows, and was dressed in nothing but some tattered khaki jogging shorts and a pair of cracked and shattered rubber boots. His dense white chest hair was sprinkled with trapped sawdust and seeds, as if he had already done a full day of bushwhacking before the kids arrived for their visit. He brought out into the sun of the porch a sheet of plywood on which he had mounted topographic maps of a far superior scale to mine. They were dusty and wormholed and waterstained, covered with meticulous notations of landmarks and trails, which he had added in pencil over the years.

"Three weeks ago," he said, "I came down from Cuatro Vientos in three hours. Walk slow, take some photographs, you'll get there in about five." Cuatro Vientos means four winds, as in *the top of the mountain*. I thought: *Twelve hours, straight uphill.*

The track climbed steeply through majestic upland pines, skirting the Loma Cimarróna, Maroon Hill. The *cimarrónes* were the earliest escaped slaves of the Caribbean, Africans who had fled into the most remote mountains of the big islands to establish autonomous communities out of reach of the plantation-owners. The Escambray has always been a rugged place where the opposition holes up. Only a few years after these mountains sheltered Che's guerilla contingent, anti-Castro counterinsurgents made them their home.

It had been many weeks since I had last hiked even the slightest rise and I was soon gasping for breath. Behind me, the views were magnificent, but I was too exhausted to remember to turn and look at them. Blood pounded in my temples and sweat dripped off my forehead as I trudged, head down, with numbing slowness.

A man with a donkey and a machete was coming down the hill.

"Cuatro Vientros?" I gasped hopefully, keeping speech to a minimum of syllables.

He looked at me, pondering the long odds of my ever arriving in that place.

"Still quite a ways to go," he said, then nodded his head in confirmation of the great distance remaining.

"Much hills?" I asked, rather dimly, given that we were surrounded on all sides by mountains.

"Well, you have a ways to go up here still, then you go down a bit. After that, you go up again. That's quite a hill, honestly, that one. From there, it's pretty much up. You go up and down. Mostly up."

I thanked him for his encouraging pep talk.

"Good luck," he said. He gave the donkey a tug and started down the mountain.

"Okay, then," I said, without much conviction. "Off I go."

The mountains sheltered only a few settlements, tucked onto the less vertical land along the road. In one community, I stopped for water. It had the lovely name of Cien Rosas, a hundred roses, but it was a slapdash cookie-cutter village, a long row of identical tiny clapboard houses like barracks. A grizzled white guy I took to be about seventy was sitting on his front stoop beside a homemade leather-and-burlap saddle leaned up against the wall. He had no shirt on but was wearing a crushed, antique cap, once army issue but no longer of any identifiable color, and he had a half-century's worth of farmer's tan, so that his arms and hands were almost black starting from just above the elbows. Whatever shirt he usually worked in must have had a saggy, stretched-out collar, for the tanned red of his neck drooped down onto his chest like a bib. He was all muscle and sinew and, despite his age, gave the impression of being made out of wire cable. As he spoke, his Adam's apple bobbed up and down and his collarbone jutted out as if the rest of him was hanging from a coat-hanger. His name was José Oliveira Flores, which made him, at least on his mother's side, Joe Flowers from Hundred Roses. I asked for water and he leaped up with tremendous energy and went through the house to the backyard to fill up my canteen. The structure was so small that we conversed through it as he drew the water.

"No water inside," he said. "No pressure." There was no water in the yard either. José gave the canteen to his son, who disappeared up the line of houses in the back.

"Did you fight in the revolution up here?" I asked.

"After the revolution. We fought against the counterrevolutionaries for three years." His eyes sparkled at the memory of it. "It took a long time, but we flushed them all out. *Nosotros defendemos esto hasta el final,*" he said. We'll defend this until the very end. He made a gesture encompassing the land, the mountains, the little row of houses, the revolution. It was a quint-essential declaration of eternal *guajiro* preparedness.

"I don't have very much left," he repeated, "but until the very end."

José's son, Carlo, came out with the water. He was a version of his father in the prime of life, muscles bulging under his skin, the same military cap twenty years fresher, still visibly peaked. I took their photo together. They stand emotionless, with their arms straight down at their sides, people un-accustomed to having their picture taken, in front of the house where they lived together. José sat down again next to the saddle and leaned against the peeling paint of the house and pulled out a cigarette.

"One more picture," I said. "With the cigarette."

"Un guajiro de verdad," he laughed. A true *guajiro*. I felt like one of the idiot tourists I had seen snapping pictures of the oxcart in Viñales.

I asked for a shortcut and they said, as all Cubans always did, that there was one, but that I would get lost.

"Still," said José, "it would be a big advantage. You avoid a truly huge hill."

"That sounds very interesting," I said quickly. "I don't mind getting lost. In fact, I insist on taking the shortcut."

An in-depth father-son analysis of the route followed, but, in the end, José volunteered Carlo to take me as far as a place called Charco Azul, as-suring me that it was no problem at all and even inventing some spurious errand that Carlo suddenly had to do there. We set off at a blistering pace through the forest, following a streambed down along a rocky trail. The stones in the path had been worn smooth by years of feet passing this way.

"When I did my military service, a thousand of us hiked through here," said Carlo. "We went right through, all the way to the Oriente."

"In this heat? At this time of year?"

"At this time of year. Three months and twenty days of hiking." By now, it sounded insane even to me.

I imagined coming upon a marching column of a thousand Cuban soldiers here on this narrow trail, where the afternoon sun dappled through the high trees onto the quiet forest floor. For a moment, I thought I could hear them up ahead. I pictured the two of us stepping out of the way as platoons of men marched by on their basic training for Angola. It was a surreal and awful vision.

In the hopes that talking might slow him to a reasonable pace, I tried to keep up a conversation with Carlo, but the walk had taken on a determined military character that was difficult to shake. I learned that he and José had been waiting for rain for quite some time. We were in a drought. Also, that Carlo wanted to leave the countryside and go to the city.

"There's nothing for me here," he said. Until then, I had thought him a younger but seamless extension of his father. But he shared the elder *guajiro*'s economy of speech and volunteered only that in the city he might find "more opportunities."

We emerged from the forest at Charco Azul, a small collection of houses clustered together along a stream in an idyllic valley. The cries of children playing ball reached us as we crossed the stream on stepping-stones. Carlo pointed through the town at the last mountain between me and Cuatro Vientos. We said goodbye and he brushed off my thanks as if an insect had landed on his ear.

The trail went straight up through the steepest coffee plantation I'd ever seen. The dark-green, oily bushes looked precarious, as if they might snap off and barrel down the mountainside like caffeinated tumbleweeds. It was shadegrown coffee, and the hill was dotted with mighty trees thirty or forty meters tall rising straight up to the sky. On the steepest parts of the climb, they seemed almost to grow parallel to the slope.

Cuatro Vientos was above the coffee zone, along a ridge of pines in the clouds. It was only a few houses, with a tiny hotel for Cubans visiting the breezy heights. The sun blazed against the whitewash of a small row of rooms. Finally, I found three men sitting at a table in near darkness in the shuttered kitchen. I wondered how they could see what they were doing.

"No hay condiciones," called one of them out of the gloom when I asked for a room. There are no living conditions.

"I walked all day, all I need to do is sleep," I said.

"There are no sheets, and no towels."

"I have a sleeping bag and a towel."

"There are no keys for the rooms."

"Do you have anything to eat, then?"

"No," he said. "Better go to Topes."

I saw nobody else in the village. Two guys in a tractor picked me up and took me halfway to Topes de Collantes, along roads that followed the ridges of the mountain range. Standing in the back of the cart, I had views of the Escambray's highest peaks and a distant, blurry vision of the sea.

Topes de Collantes is a spa and resort complex centered on the Kurhotel Escambray, a monumental Stalinist-Brutalist edifice with soft, art deco corners. It is tempting to blame this monstrosity on Soviet influence in Cuba, but the Kurhotel predates the Castro era by decades. Perched on a grassy hilltop, surrounded by lonely, spherical topiaries and endless, wide, bombastic staircases, the building, once blinding white but now stained and blotchy, was a bizarre spectacle. Rows and rows of square inset window frames marched across its surface like so many caves and black tongues of rain stain marred the deco detail. Wherever I stood, the building loomed over me. It is said to be full of all sorts of therapeutic and relaxing opportunities like steambaths, massages, masks, and exfoliation treatments, but the building had the grim aspect of an edifice that, once entered, is only left in death. None of the guests (or patients or inmates) were enjoying the afternoon sun on the lawn or walking down the stately *Last Year at Marienbad* staircases. It would probably have been an interesting and noteworthy place to stay, but I could not even bring myself to ascend the long driveway. I moved on down the road, thumb out.

Louis and Ally, two vacationing graphic designers from Amsterdam, picked me up. I told them I had been walking across the country but that I was going to give that up now and buy a bicycle. I admitted to them what I had barely admitted to myself: I couldn't imagine remaining in Cuba long enough to reach the Oriente on foot, and I wasn't enjoying myself much.

It was another perfect ride. They were staying in Trinidad around the corner from the house where I had made a reservation. Rogelio, the doctor, answered the door.

"Hello," I said. "I called last night about a room."

"We weren't expecting you for three days," he said.

"I moved a lot faster than I expected."

"But you couldn't have walked here from Cienfuegos in just one day," said Rogelio, a bit puzzled.

"No," I said, "I had a *tremenda botella* to start the day off."

I thought with pain of the long string of compromises I had made since first accepting a ride in a horse-cart weeks earlier in Pinar del Río. I tried to feel triumphant instead of defeated. My epic walk was at an end.

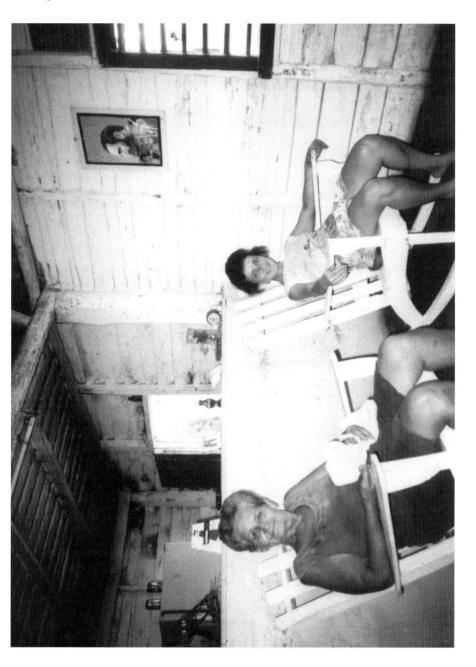

Nieves Batista Abreu and her daughter Betty: "Food is no problem, but our clothes are falling off our bodies. Here, have a banana...."

The Darwinist and the animist.

Dagoberto Manzo: He went inside and returned with a double-necked contraption straight out of a heavy-metal music video, except that it had the lustrous wood and voluptuous curves of an acoustic guitar....

Loretta Acosta: "...stripped of her bangles and beads, she could have passed for a Philadelphia Main Line society matron.

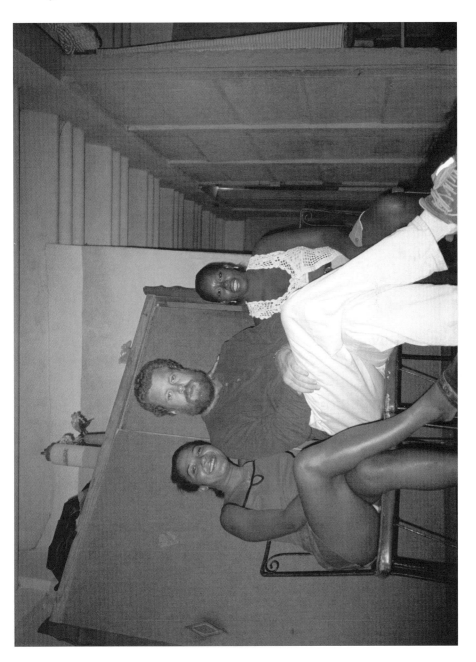

"Let's take a farewell photo together before you both go," I suggested. "Should I be naked?" Irena asked Magda. They giggled. "Yes, do it," said Magda. Irena began untucking her top. "That's not a good idea," I said, "the lab would probably confiscate the pictures."

John Sigler: "You know," he said, "the government offered me the chance to get out, to emigrate to the US. They said they could make arrangements.... But I turned them down. I don't want to leave my own country. Why should I? I love my country."

José Oliveira Flores: "...Nosotros defendemos esto hasta el final," he said. We'll defend this until the very end. He made a gesture encompassing the land, the mountains, the little row of houses, the revolution.

Rigoberto, the septuagenarian bicycle sales agent: He asked me what I liked best about Cuba and after I said probably the music, he invited me over to his house to listen to him play the clarinet.

Angel Placeres Valmaceda: He seemed to have reduced the bike to its last and most minute component....It was obvious to me that the bicycle would never ride again.

The INDER bike-shop squad: Angel at left and "El Vate" with his exuberant handlebar mustache.

Iroko, the house of God tree: To paraphrase Lydia Cabrera, at night such trees are said to pull up their roots and go walking across the land to meet with their neighboring ceibas and gossip.

Eduardo Hernández Gil: The house was minuscule, two tiny rooms entirely given over to his beliefs, with the claustrophobic feel of an overstuffed antique store....Urns, dolls, bowls of stones, chromolithographs, and strings of beads were everywhere.

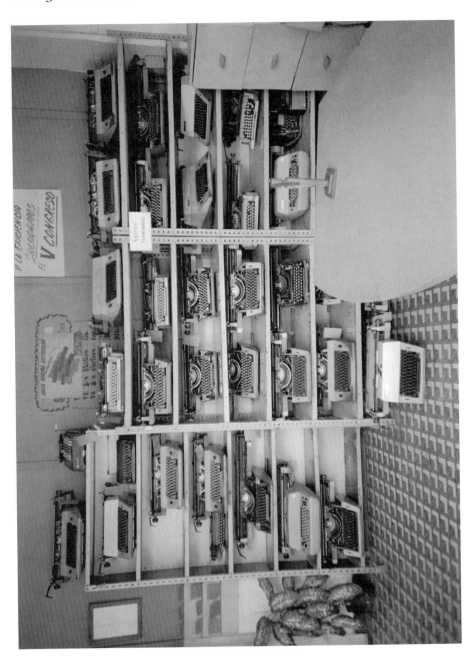

...staring into a time capsule.

The land was as flat as I had pictured it when buying the bicycle back in Trinidad, but I had overlooked the headwind, which is savage, relentless, and exhausting.

Pablo Milanes: "Ou vin salué mwen?" Have you come to greet me? Pablo seemed not to recognize me. I realized it was not Pablo speaking. "Yes," I said.

In Cuba, there will be no transition toward capitalism...!—Fidel

PART TWO
El rey del Ganado

Dieciséis

Zen and the art of bicycle maintenance

The famous brand is in new elegance. The Co. should be in sprits of "industrious, rigorous, perfect and innovation", love "Flying Pigeon" as his life, love customs as the God, try his best hard to the first class in market competition.
—Tianjin Flying Pigeon Bicycle Co., Ltd., Website

A septuagenarian named Rigoberto found the bicycle. He was lingering on a street corner outside the sort of Cuban bar that serves only cheap rum in ersatz containers brought by the clientele. Rigoberto had a tight, wooly white afro and tufts of silver mustache and a pair of goggle-eyed glasses with lenses as thick as a finger, magnifying the sag and age under his eyes. He asked me what I liked best about Cuba and after I said probably the music, he invited me over to his house to listen to him play the clarinet. We sat in battered plank chairs a few feet apart while he played "Theme from Prague." In the dim room, without accompaniment, the music was spooky and very loud. I wriggled to get out of the direct line of fire but Rigoberto followed me with the barrel of the instrument. I felt like a snake being charmed.

"I'm sure I'll locate a bicycle," he said as I was leaving. "I'll ask around."

Even compared with the rest of Cuba, much of which seemed a frozen image of the tropical 1940s, Trinidad felt old and relaxed. The upper part of the town is a UNESCO World Heritage Site, a network of cobblestone alleys quite unchanged since the town's fall from prominence in the 1870s, when the rail system grew in economic importance. Stranded behind the

Escambray without train service, Trinidad was forgotten by progress. I settled into a kind of inertia, watching the street life unfold from the splendid rooftop terrace of Rogelio's colonial mansion, or wandering the city admiring the patina of the ancient pastel-plastered walls.

One afternoon when I had returned to Rogelio's, he said an old black gentleman had stopped by to see me.

"Rigoberto?" I asked. "The musician? He must have found a bicycle."

"He didn't say, he just said he would come back later."

It was typically Cuban not to leave a message, particularly if commerce was involved. But Rigoberto was not very far away and when I stepped out a few minutes later, he spotted me and got up from where he was chatting with a neighbor on a nearby stoop. "I've been looking for you," he said. "I hope you haven't made any commitments with regard to the question of the bicycle."

"No," I said. "Actually, I haven't seen any yet." I had done almost nothing substantive. Rogelio was ostensibly helping me find a bicycle to purchase but, since he was my landlord, it had been a tactical error to tell him I would be staying on in Trinidad until I found one.

"A woman who lives just across the road from me has a Chinese bicycle she wants to sell."

"Excellent, when do you think I could see it?"

"I wanted to make sure that you hadn't found something already, so tonight, when she comes home from work, I'll arrange for it. You would be able to come by tomorrow."

When I went to Rigoberto's the next day, the bicycle was not there, but Rigoberto had a note from the owner authorizing him to pick it up from her *centro de trabajo*, her work center. He said I should wait in his living room. His wife brought coffee and then disappeared into the back of the house. An hour passed.

"Is it terribly far to the *centro de trabajo*?" I said at last, calling out to Rigoberto's wife. Trinidad was small enough that Rigoberto, however old and frail, should by now have been able to walk right the way around it several times.

"I'm sure he won't be long now."

Half an hour later, Rigoberto returned with the bicycle, exhausted. The man to whom the note was addressed had not been at the *centro de trabajo* and Rigoberto had had to walk from one side of town to the other, find the man, get him to sign off on the release, go back across town and fetch it, and then, since he was too old and blind to ride it, push it all the way back up the steep cobblestoned streets of Trinidad.

The bicycle was a Flying Pigeon, the heaviest and sturdiest model of Chinese bicycle. Cuba had imported tens of thousands of them after the fall of the Soviet Union, when the gasoline supply dried up. The thing weighed almost fifty pounds. It was crafted with indestructible solidity out of iron and steel and had a massive triangular kickstand like that of some motorcycles, requiring you to violently pull the vehicle backward and up into the air, leaving the rear tire several inches off the ground. Turning the pedals made the rear wheel go around; squeezing the brake lever stopped it. There wasn't much more to it than that.

"What do you think?" asked Rigoberto, the seventy-two-year-old bicycle agent.

My only fear was the cotter pins. They were both missing the nuts that held them into the cranks and they had been battered and hammered into rusty lumps of metal. It was hard to tell if they would hold the crankshafts onto the bottom bracket for all eternity or give way after the first hard day of pedaling. I shook the cranks as hard as I could. They seemed solid, virtually welded into place by rust and the pressures of having been ridden. "It looks good," I said. "But I'd like to show it to the guys at the INDER to see if they think it will make it to Guantánamo or not. "

We agreed that I'd return at five after the owner had passed by on her way home from work and given her approval to my borrowing the bike and having it checked out. Rigoberto said she wanted sixty dollars. I knew this was was merely an optimistic opener, probably suggested by Rigoberto himself.

As I walked the few short blocks back to Rogelio's house, a kind of jungle telegraph seemed to spread the information that I was about to buy a bicycle. When I got back, the son of a neighbor was waiting for me in the alley next to the house. He was about thirteen and had with him the dismal remnants of a child's bicycle. It had no brakes, a chain rusted into immobility, and a front wheel as wobbly as a Moebius strip. There were no cotter pins at all, so that the cranks, instead of being parallel and opposed, were at right angles to one another. I thanked him for bringing it and pointed out its most obvious defect, the fact that it was entirely unrideable. When I next went out, a man was waiting for me in the street with a Light

Roadster, another brand of Chinese one-speed, light only in comparison to the Flying Pigeon. It was pristine and clean, with none of the rust and chipped paint of the nurse's bike. I didn't even have to ride it to know that it was in perfect working order.

"You can have it for forty-five dollars," said the man. It was uncharacteristic of a Cuban to cut straight to the bottom line this way. He was a hustler, a Trinidad *jinetero* I had seen from Rogelio's rooftop terrace. The guy was a permanent fixture of a stoop just down the block, who whiled away his days whistling and hooting at passing women, only leaping to his feet to attach himself like a limpet to passing groups of European tourists. Usually within a block's walk from his corner, the tourists were trying to shoo him away as if he were an insect. I was sure the bicycle had been stolen to order, or at best extorted from some hapless relative. "I'm sorry," I said, borrowing Rigoberto's elegant turn of phrase, "but, in the question of the bicycle, I have already committed myself."

The next day, Rogelio took me and the bicycle to the INDER bike shop and introduced me to Angel and his brother, "El Vate" (the Bard), the guys, he said, who were in charge of everything to do with bicycles in town. The INDER is a national network of recreation centers and sports facilities for kids, the first rung in Cuba's phenomenal Olympic training ladder. Trinidad's INDER worked the way I thought socialism was supposed to. The two brothers, cycling enthusiasts who had in their youth both ridden the *Vuelta a Cuba*, the Cuban *Tour de France*, presided over a bike shop abuzz with activity. They organized teams of youngsters, coached, led training rides, acted as surrogate parents, and fixed and tweaked the bicycles of the entire town at no charge. Anybody, from Rogelio, perhaps needing a gear adjustment for his new ten-speed, dollar-store mountain bike, to a tear-stained kid whose chain had fallen off, could stop in and be assured of the best service humanly possible. If the work was done by Angel, the repair came with a soft smile and encouraging word; when the mechanic was El Vate, then a guffaw, a ribald joke, or a crippling bear hug sent the cyclist and the repaired bike on their way.

The wall behind the workbench was a riot of bleached and dog-eared images of the brothers in their glory: El Vate curled over the handlebars, his sideburns puffs of afro the size and shape of pork chops, the tendons popping out of his neck in the intensity of a sprint; Angel with a sloppy grin, head thrown back in post-finish-line ecstasy, one hand on the bars and the other reaching up over his head in a cautious wave; *pelotones*, columns of riders in silouette against the canefields, heads tucked and thighs hammering down the pedals, each mere centimeters from the rear tire of the man in front, drafting; team photos and clippings snipped from *Granma*, some with a half-line or less circled in pen or highlighted—a national mention for a local rider made good. In one photograph, only El Vate's head was visible, poking up out of dense, neck-high grasses. In another, next to it, he was lounging in military fatigues in front of a strange bull-nosed supply truck.

"That's me in Angola," said El Vate. "That's the first truck I drove there. It was American."

"How was it over there?"

"Well, once I learned how to talk to the women...."

"Oh yeah? How's your Portuguese?"

"Listen," he said, holding a hand up for silence. "Listen carefully. *Me gustaow la mullhel*." He jutted his head forward dramatically with each word, as if searching for the scent of a flower on a passing breeze.

"I like women" I said.

"You speak Portuguese, too! *Me gustaow la mullhel*," he said again, rolling the words around in his mouth like a caramel.

"You're just saying *me gustan las mujeres* with some kind of Angolan accent," I said.

El Vate howled with laughter. "*Me gustaow la mullhel*, that's all you need to know how to say."

Angel made a list of parts we would need: new brake pads; new chain; bearings and cones; new front tire ("It can be found, it's hard, but if we get one, we'll put the rear tire, which is not so old, on the front, where it won't have so much wear. You have to be inventive."); cotter pins; longer seatpost ("I think I have one at home. I'm going to find it for you."); extra inner tubes; larger freewheel.

"These bikes," said El Vate, "are much better than that crap they're selling in the dollar stores these days. Those are just plastic everywhere, they fall apart the first time you ride them."

"How much should I pay for this one?"

"Not more than thirty dollars, tops."

At 5:30 the next afternoon, I took the list and bicycle back to Rigoberto's. Marta Zuñiga, the owner, wore white nurse-shoes and limped.

She had had a horrible freak accident on the bicycle and now was scared of it. Riding too slowly, she had fallen and the bicycle had come down on top of her, pinioning her leg against the curb.

"I was in a wheelchair for seven months," she said.

"That's terrible," I said. I couldn't imagine how a simple fall could possibly have been that serious. Marta showed me a gruesome scar on her leg where the surgeons had gone in to reattach tendons and ligaments. I tried not to take it as a bad omen.

"I once used it every day to get to work," said Marta, "but I'll never ride a bicycle again. I walk now, even though it's difficult and far."

After this tale of woe, I was unsure how to move forward into the negotiating phase of the meeting without seeming insensitive. I had brought Angel's list of defects as a bargaining chip. No mild-mannered, crippled nurse was going to take advantage of me. "There are quite a few things that need to be replaced," I began.

Marta looked dejected. She stared at the bicycle, which had caused her so much grief. "I always took such good care of it. But since the accident, I lent it to my cousin and before I knew it, he had lent it to a friend and now I'm sure many things are wrong with it. I don't know who let it get so run down."

"It's a wonderful bicycle," I said. "Don't get me wrong. I'm going to ride her to Guantánamo." Somehow, we had reversed roles. It was as if I were trying to sell her the bike.

Rigoberto gave us a bright smile and tried to move things along. "I told the gentleman here that you wanted sixty dollars," he said to Marta.

"I'll have to replace the chain, and the cones and some other things," I said. I felt like a heel, holding the list of flaws in my lap. "I was told it's worth about thirty, or maybe less, but I would pay thirty."

"Oouw," said Marta, as if I had kicked her in the shin, near her scar. "What about fifty? I think I could accept fifty."

"Thirty-five," I said, aiming for forty and a handshake. But the negotiations collapsed and we lapsed into pleasantries for some minutes. Marta had gotten her bicycle at the beginning of the special period through her *centro de trabajo* on a payment plan, at a cost of about a month's salary. The conversation slowed. A crevasse of fifteen dollars separated me from owning this expression of the contemporary Cuban condition.

"I'll take the thirty-five," she said. "I'm never going to ride it again anyway."

I had been ready to pay forty and now I felt cheap. "Are you sure that's enough?" I asked. "I want you to be happy with the arrangement."

"It's okay," said Marta.

She went across the street to get a notebook and I slipped Rigoberto an agent's commission. Marta came back with a half-sheet of paper, which she had signed with her *cédula* number. She wrote: "By means of the present, I communicate to whomever it may concern that I sold the Chinese bicycle to comrade Richard through all legal channels and that the same was acquired by me through my worker's center."

On the corner between Rogelio's house and the INDER bike shop lived a *tapicero*, an upholsterer who I had seen hard at work over an industrial sewing machine or sometimes sitting in a rocking chair in the next-door front room, looking out at the street. I showed him the bicycle and asked if he could make some saddlebags for it. He took measurements and drew out a design on a slip of cardboard, showing me how the bags would slant backward so my heels wouldn't bang into them as I pedaled.

"You're American, aren't you?" he asked.

"That's right," I said. His eyes narrowed.

"I don't think much of your country."

"Have you been there?"

"I'm not interested in going there."

"Well," I said, "there are a lot of things I don't like about my country either."

"What are you doing here?"

"I'm just sort of traveling around, seeing what it's like here."

"I've heard in America you have to pay to go to university. You might be the best student in the world but if you don't have the money, that's it. No more studies."

"That's not quite right," I said. "Really good students are often able to get scholarships, or at least special loans. There are ways. Although I'm sure there are people who want to go to college but can't."

"Here you don't pay anything at all. Nothing." He was getting angry.

"I went to university. I got some loans and financial aid. I had a job. It wasn't so difficult."

"Hmmf," snorted the *tapicero*. "You want an extra outside pocket on one of these bags? Or just a main compartment?"

"That would be perfect, to put maps in." After my lukewarm defense of the American way, I had been afraid he was going to refuse the commission.

The days were ticking by. In the morning, I handed the bicycle over to Angel and we went over the list of parts. In the state store, all the bits we wanted to replace—most of the bike's moving parts—would cost $5.75, less than it would have cost to fix a flat back home. The brake pads were a few cents each, the new chain a quarter.

"Not the inner tubes," said Angel. "They never have them and when they do, they're rotten. *No sirve.* I swear they arrive from China all nicely powdered up with talc but already full of holes. We'll get those on the private market. They're handmade. Absolutely unpuncturable."

"Handmade?"

"I know a man who makes them from old truck inner tubes. They're expensive, but much stronger than the store-bought ones."

The bulletproof gray-market inner tubes would cost two dollars apiece. I gave Angel ten dollars to get started. "Come back this afternoon and I should have her ready for you," he said.

When I returned to the INDER, the bicycle was in pieces scattered around the patio, as if there had been an explosion. One of the advantages of a Flying Pigeon is that it has about as few moving parts as it is possible for a bicycle to have and still move, but Angel seemed to have reduced the bike to its last and most minute component. He was sitting on a stool in the sun struggling with a wheel, his fingers gloppy with grease, an errant ball bearing cemented to the back of one hand like a wart. The rest of the bearings were suspended in a clump of black slime on the bottom end of an overturned tin can. The chain lay flaccid and desprocketed on the dusty bricks, and the chipped brown frame was a sad and contorted wheel-less heap that summoned to mind the pathos and destruction of an auto wrecker's yard. El Vate and the gaggle of prepubescent would-be Olympians that were always hanging about the place had all wisely taken refuge inside. It was obvious to me that the bicycle would never ride again.

"Aah," said Angel, looking up and indicating with a gooey wave that he would not be shaking my hand. "There you are. I'm just changing the cones." I bowed my head and closed my eyes and grabbed the bridge of my nose between my thumb and forefinger. "I'm thinking the bicycle won't be ready today," I said slowly.

"Well," he asked rhetorically, "what is it that's going on here in this country? Some of the parts, Richard, are unobtainable. Not to be found anywhere. What happens? Once in a great while, nobody knows when, a shipment of parts comes from China to Havana and then they get sent out all over the place. Sometimes, they make it here; sometimes, they don't. Trinidad is a small town."

"Do you think I need to look for another bicycle?"

Angel looked at me as if I was out of my mind. "Pffft! We'll just have to be inventive. *Hay que inventar.* One has to invent in Cuba. When I rode in the *Vuelta a Cuba*, we had *nothing.* You constantly had to invent and solve problems. Oooooh, look, look. I have goosebumps. Look how I shiver with excitement just talking about the *Vuelta.*" Angel, who was wearing nothing but the same exhausted and threadbare pair of red cycling shorts he always wore, had indeed gone prickly all over, like a newly plucked chicken.

"Look, these are the new cones," he continued, "and I found a larger freewheel, not new, but it will make it easier to pedal. And here are the new brake pads." I could see at a glance that the brake pads—small, pink, and aerodynamic—were all wrong. The Flying Pigeon, with its Paleolithic system of steel rods, required brake pads almost two inches long that were pulled up into the inside of the rims, not squeezed against their outside surfaces.

"These aren't the right brake pads," I said.

"Come on," said Angel, "they must be." I showed him. He looked unhappy. "Vate," he called through the door of the shop, "these seem to be the wrong brake pads."

El Vate had just finished adjusting something on a woman's bicycle and he came out of the shop with her. We watched her wheel the bike away across the courtyard. There was no denying that she had, in ample quantities, that quality which Dominicans simply refer to as "swing."

"Whoooompf," said El Vate, exhaling with a force that suggested he had been holding his breath ever since the woman's arrival.

"Indeed," I said.

"He's terrible," said Angel.

El Vate made his eyes like slits, full of glee and cunning. He flashed a wicked grin like an amateur Shakespearean actor declaring himself to be evil and curved the back of his hand around his mouth in a mock conspiratorial gesture. "I have four girlfriends." He burst into a guffaw. "But don't tell my wife!"

A kid about twelve wandered into the courtyard, one of the youthful team riders.

"Hello, Miguelito." Angel crouched down until they were face to face. He took Miguelito by the arm. "I need you to do something for me." Miguelito beamed. "You know the other bicycle shop in town? I need you to go to the store right across the street from there—you know the one. Take these and tell them I sent you and tell them you need brake pads for a China 28. And if they don't have them, get the money back. Okay?"

The child soaked it in as if the future of the revolution was being entrusted to his care.

"Now, you come straight back," said Angel, patting Miguelito on the shoulder. "Take my bicycle." The kid was on the bike and out the door in a flash, only pausing to glance through the window of the shop to make sure the other kids understood just how much responsibility he was being entrusted with.

"At least that's taken care of," said Angel.

I looked at the sprawled skeleton of my Flying Pigeon in horror.

"Don't worry, you'll be going for a test drive tomorrow," said El Vate. "My brother more or less knows what he's doing." He collapsed in howls of laughter. El Vate was one of those people who, when asked to please be serious just this once, redoubled his efforts to turn everything into a joke. It must have driven his four girlfriends mad.

As I walked back to Rogelio's, the patriotic *tapicero*, Miguel, called to me from his living room. One of the saddlebags was complete; the other required perhaps an hour more labor. He invited me in to see the work and meet some relatives.

"This is my daughter and my son-in-law, visiting from Havana. Conrad, this is the American who is walking across Cuba."

"Actually, I'm sick of walking, I'm switching to a bicycle."

"What do you think of Cuba?" asked Conrad. I was asked this about five times a day. Miguel was the only Cuban I had met in all my time there who I felt was suspicious of me simply because I was American, so I replied cautiously.

"The people are wonderful," I said.

"What about the government, the system?" asked Conrad.

"Well," I said, "I haven't really dealt with the government, I've mostly been out in the countryside."

Conrad looked at me. "You're very diplomatic."

"Miguel was telling me a little bit about the educational system," I said.

"We're having a little party tomorrow night, I'd like to invite you. The family, a few friends. We're going to try and get some nice fish."

"Con mucho gusto," I said. "That's really nice of you, I don't really know anyone here." I wrote down the address.

Conrad's party was the most exciting thing to happen to my social life since Esther had invited me to the anniversary of her saintmaking. I was still cursing the Havana immigration service for that missed opportunity. Because I had needed a new visa, I hadn't been able to go.

"Rogelio," I said, "I need help. I've been invited to a party and I have no idea what to take." I had no decent clothes either, only T-shirts stained brown by sweat and the cheap leather belt.

"What kind of party is it?" he asked.

"I don't know. Dinner, I guess. It's being given by Conrad and his wife, the daughter of the *tapicero* on the corner, do you know them?"

"A bottle of rum would be fine. It's probably a goodbye party."

"A goodbye party?"

"Yeah, I heard they won the *bombo*. They're going to Miami."

Sitting on the roof at Rogelio's, I heard the sound of a *comparsa* moving somewhere in the grid of streets below the house. I ran downstairs and down the street. *Comparsa* is rump-shaking party music, something like a cross between samba and the rabble-rousing cow-bell riffs heard at hockey games. A typical *comparsa* goes, *Dang-gang-giggada-dang-a-dang-a-diggada-dang-gang-giggada-gang-HUH!*, in which "Huh" represents a massive unanimous wallop on all the drums, introducing a pregnant pause. Here, there is just time for one swing of the hips through the impressively silent air before the whole lively mess churns back into action. *Comparsa* is crowd-pleasing and unsophisticated music that lacks the sinuous complexity of the *rumba*, but is played on the move and on the march, for an ebbing and flowing crowd that wants the instant gratification of an endlessly repeated hook for as long as they choose to join in.

I followed the impromptu parade to the plaza. The square of streets around the little park was throbbing with carnival commerce. At one corner was a ride for the kids. On offer were tricycles for hire, welded together out of bits of tubing and old wagons, no two the same. Some looked like chopped Harleys for toddlers, with long steering columns. *Lechón* was everywhere: dozens of these bronzy, gleaming, spit-roasted pigs were splayed out in the sun on their outstretched trotters, teeth bared in a rictus, the cooked skin stretched tight over their jowls. One pig wore sunglasses. The vendors served up roast-pork sandwiches on gritty little rolls, sprinkled with hot-pepper vinegar, for a few pesos. I spied a man selling popcorn in cones of paper made of pages torn from a old book. Using yesterday's *Granma* for toilet paper was one thing, but desecrating books to sell popcorn was another. I approached his tray.

"One peso of popcorn please." I ate and then untwisted the salty, greasy page. "Marx, Engels" I read along the top margin, "The Supposed Divisions in the International." I went back over to the seller. Compartments in his wooden tray held popcorn, salt, and rectangles of paper. The orange cover of the gutted book rested on a corner of the tray.

"May I see that, please," I said, whisking it away before he could answer.

"Hey," he said. He put his hands protectively over the compartment that the book cover had been hiding from view. It was the till, full of peso coins and a few notes. I had unwittingly opened his cashbox.

"I'm very sorry," I said. "I didn't know that was where you kept your money. I just wanted to see the book cover."

He regarded me with suspicion. "Those are just some old books," he said.

After what he could only have interpreted as an attempt to steal his earnings, I realized I had lost the moral high ground. Nonetheless, I tried to muster as much indignation as I could.

"But this is *The Communist Manifesto*," I said.

"Ehhhhh," he said, reaching over and recuperating his rectangle of cardboard. I'm not sure he even heard my complaint. He flicked his fingers away from his body toward the sky, indicating the passage of much time, and the fleeting nature of all things. "An old book is worth nothing at all."

"You could ride to New York on that," shouted El Vate from inside the shop.

Angel was beaming. "She's ready to ride," he said.

The wheels were trued, the chain was glistening and new, and a huge, long seatpost rose out of the frame, fully tall enough for me to ride the bicycle comfortably. Actually, it was two seatposts. Angel had hammered one inside the other.

"Don't worry, that will never give out," he said. "It was the only way to do it. There are no long seatposts to be had. And I changed the free-wheel again: I found one with twenty teeth. That's the biggest they make. Still no cotter pins, but I don't think that crank is going anywhere. It's rusted on solid."

We had concluded that the bicycle, with my hundred kilos plus back-pack and saddlebags strapped on, needed to be as easy to pedal as possible. This meant having a large freewheel and a small chainring. Angel said he was going to keep looking for a chainring. "Here's my address, tomorrow's my day off, come by my house and we'll see."

He handed me two brand-new inner tubes, thick and heavy as boot leather. They had been made with strips cut from truck inner tubes fold-ed like a sausage casing and cemented under the heat of an electric iron. "Where are the valves?" I asked. Where the valves should have been there were small holes the size of a pencil eraser.

"There are no valves in Trinidad either. You'll just have to use the valves that are on the bike already." I had never seen removable valves before, but Angel showed me how, if I got a flat, the valve could be un-screwed from one inner tube with a wrench and clamped through the hole in the new tube.

"I guess I'm going to need a pump."

"You're in luck, the store that sells bike parts is full of pumps. But the chain I was only able to find from a private dealer. It cost thirty pesos. I'm sorry. What happens is, when spare parts do arrive in the store, people buy them up and then sell them later for more money."

"It's fantastic," I said. "Honestly, yesterday I thought this bicycle was history. You're a phenomenon." I pressed a five-dollar bill into Angel's hand.

"You've already paid for everything," he said. "I got all the parts with the money you gave me before."

"That's for you," I said. "For your time."

"It's too much," he said. "This is a lot."

I went for a long ride, sailing downhill the four or five kilometers to the beach and then following the coast road along the sandy peninsula beside the water. The Flying Pigeon was a tank, but everything worked perfectly. The only problem I could see was that the spring that returned the left-hand brake lever to its proper place could stand replacing. I made a big loop back into town and went to the parts shop.

In the otherwise bare window, a bike pump and a brand new Chinese fender lay on a sheet of newspaper. They looked lonely. Inside, it was as if the store was in the final hours of a going-out-of-business sale. A glass case held the last few remaining wares displayed on cut squares of white paper the size of handkerchiefs. One held a pile of nuts, another five bicycle spokes splayed out like pickup sticks. There was a bicycle pump and one freewheel, sixteen teeth, in a box. To my astonishment, there were half a dozen of the brake caliper springs I needed sitting loose on their own sheet of paper. This seemed to be the sum total of the bicycle department.

"Please," I said with some urgency. I was fearful that these few last items might be whisked away even as I stood there. "I'd like one pump and three 28-inch spokes and one of those brake springs."

"Tranquilo," said the woman. "Take it easy." She turned to the dark wooden shelves behind her and extracted a pump from what I now saw was an enormous stack of pumps, a possibly inexhaustible supply, quite enough pumps to fill all the bike tires in Trinidad, if not beyond. From another box, she took the spokes, which I had asked for simply because of the miracle of them being there. I had never broken a spoke on a bicycle before, but now I would be prepared. She got me a spring from the showcase and totted up my items. The bill came to something like thirty cents.

I went outside and checked the spring against my brake. The two springs, left and right, were not identical. Instead they were mirror images of one another. I went back into the shop.

"I'm sorry, this is the right-side spring," I said. "I need the left spring. I didn't realize they were different."

"We only have the spring for the right-hand side, dear."

"Are you sure? Is that all you have?" I gestured at the meager pile in the showcase.

She brought a box and opened it for me. In it were a dozen more springs, each identical to the one I had purchased.

"Do you want your money back?" she asked.

I decided to keep it, just in case. I wondered which town had gotten the delivery of left-hand springs.

Conrad's party was in a house on Calle Amargura, Bitterness Street. "They've gone to get the fish," said the woman who answered the door. In the long narrow back garden, a few tables were set up in a line, banquet-style. I put my bottle of rum on the table with several others that were already there. Conrad soon arrived with Tomás González and two of the largest red snapper I'd ever seen. Conrad's nephews, two beefy and athletic silent types, were building a fire in a grill at the back end of the garden in an open structure that had once been the stables. Tomás set to smearing the inside and outside of the fish with a thick fresh salsa. He was handsome and full of energy, and reminded me of the kind of clean-cut white Latino found in abundance in Colombian or Venezuelan soap operas. His wife was a stunning beauty who could have been a model in a mail-order catalog. Conrad went and fetched some drinks. Once Tomás had put the fish on the grill, he grabbed his guitar.

"I do everything around here," he said, and laughed. "Cook, clean, provide the music."

As the table started to fill up, I quickly lost track of the guests. Tomás sat at the head of the table and I sat next to Conrad. The many women were gathered in a knot at the far end, nearest the house and the kitchen. Soon, the table was weighted down with pots of *arroz congris*, and cucumber, tomato, and green bean salad. Conrad's daughter—a stunning blonde about twenty in a sort of flowing, white Stevie Nicks-style dress—hugged her boyfriend at the far corner of the table. He was sullen and weepy, and I realized that he would not be going to Florida. His girlfriend was breaking his heart and leaving for Miami and here he was at a party intended as a joyful celebration.

Tomás began to play Mexican *boleros*, one love song after another about heartbreaking loss, abandonment, and tragedy. We hoisted one rum after another.

"To starting a new life," someone yelled out.

"Yes, yes, a new life," we cried out, raising our glasses.

"To you not forgetting about us, Conrad."

"To great friends."

"To our new friend from America, Mr. Richard."

"Thank you," I said. "To my very good and new and wonderful friend, Conrad, I sincerely hope you like it in my country."

Tomás ran and checked on the fish. He played "Lagrimas Negras" and "Bilongo." When it got dark, he put down the guitar and served the fish and started videotaping the proceedings with an ancient VHS camcorder on a long extension cord.

"Tio," said Conrad, looking into the camera and addressing his uncle, "we're having a party with all these wonderful friends. I wish you could be here, I'll be seeing you soon, but all these friends of yours want to greet you, and I want to thank you for all the help you've given us and I wish you could taste this delicious fish. And we're coming to Miami and we're going to be with you soon."

Tomás went around the table like a wedding videographer and let each person send out a greeting to the uncle in Florida. It was dark and candles flickered on the tablecloth and I wondered if the video would be watchable.

"Play some more music, Tomás."

"I can't do everything," said Tomás, but he set the camera on a tripod aimed at the table and picked up the guitar again. One of the big quiet guys played bongo and someone else played *clave*.

We feasted. The women watched us drink.

Conrad tugged at my sleeve.

"It's an experiment," he said. He was well on his way to being drunk. "That's the only way I can see it. The Americans have won the Cold War and now they have Cuba set aside, like an experiment in a laboratory, they have this island in the Caribbean set aside like a little terrarium, and they are just letting it go on, just to see what will actually happen to socialism. That's what I think."

"Maybe there's something to that," I said. I gulped another shot of Matusalem rum. "If the Americans really wanted the situation to change here, all they'd have to do is let a million tourists come down here in their Nikes."

"It's insane. The only logical explanation is that he...," Conrad paused and put his hand to his face as if tugging an imaginary beard, the way all Cubans did when they were going to say something disparaging about Castro, "must be paying off the South Florida congressmen. They've got to be in his pocket. It's the only way to explain why they behave in such a stupid fashion. They're on Fidel's payroll."

"You and your father-in-law must not get along very well," I said. "He seems to me to be a staunch supporter of the revolution."

"We couldn't disagree more, and we have some blistering arguments, but that doesn't mean we aren't family."

"It's too bad he didn't come tonight."

"He wouldn't."

"I'm just sorry the situation is so bad between our countries," I said. "The people get along fine. Look at us. We get along just great. Let's have another drink."

"It has to change," said Conrad. "US-Cuban relations are like a rubber band stretched to its farthest point. It must either break forever or spring back. We are at that point."

We had reduced the red snapper to a mess of bones ringed with salsa and the remains of a bed of roast potatoes. I sucked on my fingers and filled our glasses. Conrad got up heavily and went around the table and took hold of his daughter's boyfriend and dragged him in front of the camera with his arm around the boy's shoulders.

They scrunched down, peering into the lens in the dark.

"Tomás, is this thing on?"

Tomás assured Conrad that it was.

"Uncle, uncle," said Conrad, "this is the *novio* of my daughter. This is a serious thing, uncle. They have been together three and a half years. This is not just a fling; this is serious. You have to help me get him out."

Conrad staggered to his feet. Tomás and I had a drink to avoid weeping. Tomás began playing "Chan Chan" from the *Buena Vista Social Club* album. It's a beautiful song. The whole table sang along while I played *clave*. I forgot that I was sick to death of hearing the *Buena Vista Social Club*.

"It's beautiful," I said to Tomás. I realized I knew all the words.

"You play *clave* like a Cuban," he said. "Hey, get some footage for your uncle of this American playing *clave*." It was time for my closeup. I was glowing with pride. The camera focused on our impromptu little band and I became enthusiastic and made the mistake of trying to sing and tap the *clave* together at the same time. As if a spring had been pulled from a watch, the tune sputtered and collapsed when I butchered first the rhythm and then the lyrics. This was cause for great mirth.

Nobody mentioned that, in a week's time, Conrad and his family would disappear, perhaps forever, to Miami. The video we were making was a surrogate for the uncle it was being made for. It let us invite him to the party, and for one night the videotape stretched like a lifeline across the Straights of Florida. But Conrad was going to stick the video in his luggage and get on a plane, pulling himself over to the other side along the rope and coiling it up as he went.

The *novela* started and the women, wary of the emptying bottles on the devastated banquet table, carried their chairs inside to the living room and gathered around the television. We sang and wept and hugged and drank in the garden. Tomás played the eternal classic, "El Manicero," the peanut vendor. Conrad, his face moist with sweat and tears and rum, sang the *pregones*, the streetcorner calls of the peanut vendor selling his wares. Gripping the table and thrusting his face skyward, he croaked "Maaaaniii, Maanii-ii-ii-ii." We lustily sang out another verse and turned back to hear Conrad's next *pregón*. His head lay on the table amid the refuse of the meal, like a hairy melon. His muscles were loose and relaxed. He had fallen asleep between choruses.

I slept in and then took my hangover to Angel's house. I felt like I had a crack in my skull and the sun had beamed through and sunburned my brain. Angel lived in two rooms on the second floor of a dilapidated house. The ground floor was an abandoned construction site. Part of the façade was bricked over with cinderblocks. I wrestled the iron bicycle up the narrow stairs.

"Sorry about the place," said Angel. "It's all I have. My Italian friend, a rich guy who comes to Trinidad sometimes, he has a really nice bike, he came over one time and he said 'Angel, you live like a pig, how can you stand it?' I felt bad."

"It's fine," I said. It was a squalid hellhole. The floor was rough and sandy raw concrete, the walls unfinished crumbling brick. The roof was a slab of corrugated plastic, green with algae and rotten with holes. For furniture, Angel had an old oil barrel and a table made from a plywood square tacked onto legs of cheap framing lumber. Bike parts were scattered across the floor.

"My wife fell in love with another guy. What could I do? I didn't make a stink, she has the kids, so I moved out. This is what I could find.

"I got you a chainring, a forty-six to replace your forty-eight. Let's slap it on there. El Vate said I was stupid, but I gave my ex-wife the money you gave me. What am I going to do? Those are my kids."

Angel said the money had come just at the right time. He hadn't received his salary in over a month. Another promise had been broken the day before; after expecting to finally collect, he and El Vate had gone home empty-handed. There wasn't very much they could do about it since complaining about not getting paid was considered troublesome and counter-revolutionary activity.

Replacing the front chainring required tapping out the defunct cotter pin on the crank side, for which we had no replacement. Angel had a twenty-centimeter length of railroad track that he used as an anvil. He pounded out the nubs of the cotter pins with a broken screwdriver, banging away at it with another chunk of steel he used as a hammer. In minutes, he had the cranks off. His friend, Edí, heard the work from the street, came up the stairs to see what was going on, and was enlisted to help. Soon, Angel took hammer and chisel to the glistening brass of my new gray-market chain, trying to remove a link to keep it tight on the smaller chainring. I tried not to watch the carnage.

"America, huh?" Edí asked, pushing the bike's handlebars down onto the anvil as if Angel were branding a calf. "Is it true that if they catch you cheating on your wife over there, they cut off your *pinga?*"

Angel regarded the stubby cotter pins as if it had only just occurred to him that we had no others with which to secure the cranks.

"That makes me very nervous," I said. "You think those are still going to hold?"

"I'll show you a trick. You gotta invent. Edí, look in the other room for some salt."

Angel made a solution of salt and water and poured it over the cotter pins, which were sitting loose in their holes in the crank arms. Then he tapped the pins home. The salt would promote rust, locking the pins back into place.

"I have a name for it," I said.

"A name?" said Angel "What, for the bike?"

"Yeah. El Rey del Ganado."

As an official christening, we attached an old horseshoe to the handlebars with a scrap of baling wire, horns up, to hold the luck.

The next day, I took one last test drive, climbing the savage Loma del

Puerto hill on the outskirts of town. It was long and steep. Near the top, I was barely moving forward and when I could no longer stay balanced, I got off and pushed. My heart was pounding, as much from the horrible realization that I was about to ride this iron behemoth across the rest of the country as with the exertion. From the top, it was a flat ten kilometers to the Iznaga tower, which would have been a quick ride if I hadn't immediately gotten a flat. I didn't have my three wafer-thin Chinese wrenches to change the tube with, but two men living in a one-room house beside the road had a blunt screwdriver and spoon and they helped me.

In the village of Manacas, in the shadow of the tower, I left the flat tube to be repaired at one of Cuba's homegrown flats-fixed shops, where rubber is welded together on a heated vise made from an electric iron mounted on a hinge with a long handle to squeeze it down onto the inner tube.

The Iznaga tower is a tourist attraction that looks like a small version of the Leaning Tower of Pisa. There was a parking lot for tour buses and about fifty tables crowded around the bottom of the tower, all selling the same sorts of cotton tablecloths and doilies as the tourist market in Trinidad. Unfortunately, when I went to climb up it, I found there was an admissions charge and I didn't have a dollar, only some small change in Cuban pesos. My appeals for a more socialist interpretation of the entrance fee met with bureaucratic inflexibility.

On the way back to Trinidad, at the bottom of the Loma del Puerto, I got another flat. The outskirts of towns anywhere in the world are good places to find auto repair shops, and Trinidad was no exception. There were three. All were closed. I walked the bike to Angel's house and yelled up at the glassless windows.

"I went to Manacas," I said. "I got a flat. Two, actually."

"What? With those bulletproof inner tubes?" He came downstairs.

"All the repair places seem to be closed, or the man who does it has gone away, that sort of thing. I thought you might know another place."

"Sure, if you want to wait here, I'll take your wheel and spare tube over on my bike and get it done for you."

I handed him the tube I had had repaired in Manacas.

"Te engañaron," he said. You've been cheated.

"What are you talking about?"

"This is not the tube that was in your tire. Your tube was brand-new. This is some old piece of crap that has been repaired dozens of times."

It was time to move on.

"I'm leaving Trinidad tomorrow," I said. "Do you mind stopping by your source and picking me up another spare tube as well?"

Diecisiete

Making saints in Ciego de Ávila

"While bicycling his mind attained a certain passivity, and ideas bubbled up, lingered a while, burst, and vanished."
—R. K. Narayan, *The Painter of Signs*

P acked, El Rey del Ganado looked like a giant armadillo. The backpack frame was wired to the back rack and the new saddlebags bulged with hiking boots, maps, water bottles, and the hammock I had so far slept in for all of three nights. The front wheel threatened to rise off of the pavement from all the weight. I rode gingerly down the streets of Trinidad for the last time. At dawn, there were almost no people about, but, ahead of me on the sidewalk, I saw Marta Zuñiga. Despite her horrible accident, I took this as a good omen. I wanted her blessing for the journey. When I stopped beside her, the bicycle almost fell over.

"Hello," I said, wrestling with the handlebars. "Good morning."

"Good morning," she said. "I thought you were long gone."

"It took a certain amount of time to get things ready, but I'm finally off. Wish me luck."

Skepticism clouded her face. "Better you than me."

Marta admired the horseshoe on the handlebars. Angel had dug up an old pot of paint and painted the horseshoe, fenders, and chain guard a Caribbean turquoise.

"It looks beautiful," she said. She smiled broadly. "The very best of luck to you."

Outside of town, the Loma del Puerto rose off of the coastal plain at a grotesque angle. I put my head down and pedaled. After ten minutes, I had made it at least halfway up the hill, and Trinidad was behind and beneath me. I stood up on the pedals, moving slowly forward. The occasional car or truck, making an early morning run into town, honked encouragement. The crest of the hill was just up ahead.

At that moment, the crankside cotter pin slipped and the right pedal flew forward with a bone-jarring lurch. The feeling was like that of walking up stairs in the dark and miscounting the number of steps combined with the sensation of the stomach rushing up toward the throat that comes when an airplane hits turbulence. I got off and pushed.

Trinidad was three kilometers behind me, all downhill, but I could not face such a defeat, and I refused to even imagine riding up the Loma again. At the top of the hill, I used a boulder for an anvil and began to beat savagely on the cotterpin with a chunk of rock. Sitting in the dust at the side of the highway, I ground my teeth in frustration. I pedaled on, the crankset stuttering. My only thought was of how many more meters I might coax out of the bicycle. Down the road, a man with a brick and a hammer helped me beat the crank back into momentary usefulness. At another farm, when it began to slip again, I borrowed a massive old plumber's wrench and beat it with that.

About ten in the morning, I got the first flat. Soon, my hands were smeared with black grease and my fingers chafed by the thick Chinese rubber. When I finally got the new tube onto the rim, I was almost weeping. With the wheel off, collapsed on his swollen saddlebags, El Rey looked like bloated roadkill. Sitting on the gravel of the shoulder, I closed my eyes, and tried to take deep breaths.

Fifty kilometers from Trinidad, I limped into Banao. By now, the pedals slipped with a sickening thud on every rotation. At the merest hint of a rise, I was forced to get off and push. Most of the able-bodied men of Banao had a turn hammering the cotter pin back into submission; all agreed that the pin was shot and would no longer hold. Nobody had the faintest suggestion of where a new pin might be obtained. Worse, the chain began to slip. I was sure that the chainring itself had bent under all the beatings, and would need to be replaced. I anticipated another feverish week of searching for bike parts in Sancti Spiritus, should I ever arrive there.

As I thunked along, a white-haired old *guajiro* breezed past me on his own Flying Pigeon. Glancing back at my luggage in amazement, he slowed a bit. "These bikes are great for short distances," he said, "but for long hauls, forget it, *no sirve.*"

It was a long, violent, and horrible day. On the outskirts of Sancti Spiritus, I became confused and could not see which way to take to get to the center. I asked another cyclist. He was a kind man, commuting home.

"Follow me," he said, "I'm going there myself." By the first intersection, he had lost me. My pedals simply refused to make the bicycle move forward. The man doubled back.

"What happened?"

"The cotter pin is coming out; I can't go very fast."

"We'll get that fixed. I know a man right near here."

I followed my friend, who rode much more slowly. We stopped at a house. He went in and emerged with a hunchbacked old man chomping on a cigar. He looked the bicycle over.

"You need a new cotter pin," he said.

"I think you're right," I said.

"Don't have one."

"Any idea where I can get one?"

He removed the cigar from the corner of his mouth and crooked his neck up at me. "It's been ages since any cotter pins made it through to here," he said. "Can't help you there."

We crept into the center of town to the state bike repair shop. The mechanic was rail-thin, sour, and surly. He had no work to do but when he saw us, he made a charade of busying himself for a few minutes. He moved a chair a few inches across the floor and went over to a desk and searched for an imaginary paper and moved the chair again.

"Excuse me," I said.

"Just a moment," he said, holding up his hand in well-practiced exasperation.

"No hurry," I said.

He continued to futz.

After some time, he turned to us, slow and droopy-eyed. "Yes?" he said.

"I need cotter pins, badly. The bike won't ride."

He glanced for a bored moment at my bike.

"Cotter pins for a China 28." He looked into my face, emotionless. "I have those," he said.

204

"Wonderful," said my guide, with obvious relief. He had been helping me around town for almost forty-five minutes by now. "You're all set then. I'll be off." He rode away, giving me scarcely enough time to thank him.

The pallid mechanic shuffled off to the back of the shop and opened a padlock on a chicken-wire cage. He returned with two zinc-gray cotter pins and in seconds had tapped out the old rusted nubs with a hammer and replaced them both. He asked for the equivalent of three and half cents.

I rode off. The cranks were factory-tight but nothing had changed in the horrible, shuddering skip of the chainring whenever I bore down hard on the pedals. I rode back to the shop. With profuse thanks for the wonderful cotter pins, I explained the ongoing problem. The mechanic gave me a look that managed to combine anger, disbelief, and tedium.

"The only thing I can see to account for that is that the chain might be a little loose," he said. He fetched a wrench, loosened the nuts on the axle, and pulled the wheel back into the dropouts without a word. Then, he put the wrench down and started messing about with some other chunk of bicycle at the other end of the room.

"That's it?" I said.

He sighed as if I was tormenting him, but did not look up. "That's it, already."

The bicycle rode like a dream. After the interminable day, it seemed a miracle, as if San Lázaro had suddenly broken his own crutch across his knee and gone running down the road. Colonial Sancti Spiritus is a tangle of streets on a hill, undulating in concentric loops around the main plaza. I pedaled around and around, coasting and swooping.

In a household of deranged women, I rented a room.

"Welcome to the house of the *hormigas locas*," Maluna González said to me with a cackle as she showed me in. The crazy ants. Maluna had an arresting shock of white hair on the crown of her otherwise crow-black coiffure, as if she had been hit by lightning. It was not just her hair that was reminiscent of the benign lunacy of the Addams family. Maluna liked to fill a glass of cold water from the fridge and then sneak up on one of her guests and press it against the back of their neck, a prank she accompanied with howls of laughter. Her mother, Estrella, was so vague that any conversation with her took on a surreal quality.

"America," she said. "Hmmn. I have a relative. He lives in....He lives in....Damn, where is that now? Dear," she called out to her harried husband, "what's the name of that place in America where all the Cubans live?"

"Miami, dear," he yelled from the courtyard.

As delightful and refreshing as it was to discover someone in Cuba who could not summon up the name of Miami, it was impossible not to take this as proof of insanity or, at best, willful denial. The word "Miami" was heard on television every day, dozens of times. Elián González, star of the real-life soap opera followed even more avidly than *El rey del ganado*, was even now a hostage, kidnapped by the "Miami Mafia." Every day, the news reported for hours on the Elián saga; every week, another huge rally, carried live from some regional Cuban capital, demanded his immediate return.

Two American cousins, Doyle and Jim, were also staying with the González family. Doyle had come to live in Havana after he "gave up being a loser screenwriter in Los Angeles," and Jim, a rabid photographer, was visiting him for a whirlwind tour of the island. Jim had lots of expensive camera equipment and had shot sixty rolls of film in two weeks. We were all charmed by the madness of the household and spent some happy hours sitting around the kitchen table.

Maluna liked to tell jokes. When she had told one, even our polite laughter was enough to send her into howling giggles. She would then repeat the punchline over and over again.

"Do you know the one about Pepito and the potato-peeling machine?"

We didn't.

"Pepito goes to China to buy a machine to peel potatoes. They have a tabletop model that does a whole crate of potatoes in minutes, but it costs over a thousand dollars, so he goes to the US. They have a much smaller machine that can peel an entire truckload of potatoes in five minutes, but it costs many thousands of dollars. So Pepito goes to Russia. The Russians have a vast machine the size of a refrigerator, but it is only five hundred bucks, so Pepito buys it on the spot and brings it back to Cuba.

"'But does it work?' asks Fidel.

"'Sure,' says Pepito. They throw in a potato, and out it comes, peeled. They throw in a few more. Out they come. So they back up the truck and start dumping potatoes into the machine. Suddenly, red lights flash, whistles go off, a window opens on the side, and a Russian pops his head out.

"'Hey, take it easy,' he says, 'I'm all alone in here.'"

We all laughed, and Maluna went around the room, repeating, "Dale suave, aqui estoy solo," for each of us, to be quite certain that nobody was left out of the hilarity.

Doyle made me nervous. He had thick, loose-leaf notebooks in which he frantically scribbled notes, even while the household was exploding in a distracting chaos of cackles everywhere around him. He appeared to be having endless profound insights, which required immediate transfer to paper. I was so sure that he was working on the ultimate book about Cuba that I was too scared to ask him what he was writing. Doyle wrote fast and large, as if it were an aerobic exercise, wantonly wasting paper in his rush to get his observations down on the page. In contrast, I spent whole days wondering if anything happening to me was even worth writing down, and, when I did write in my journal, I painstakingly covered every square centimeter with tiny black script. Once, I peeked over Doyle's shoulder in time to see him write the words, "going through the motions," and I convinced myself that this was his description of me, his fellow traveler.

Doyle had made multiple trips to Cuba and had owned a variety of Chinese bicycles, including Light Roadsters and a Phoenix. Although traveling by car with Jim, upon his arrival in Sancti Spiritus, he had immediately contracted with Mr. González for a bike rental and had spent whole days pedaling around the outskirts of the city, while I sat in my room and read 1950s American pulp novels (*Gulf Coast Girl* and *To Walk the Night*) that I had found at a used booksellers in the plaza. Doyle had lived in apartments all over Havana and seemed to have been to every town in Cuba of any significance. He was considering staying in Cuba "for up to two years." Meeting him, I felt rather as I think Robert Scott must have, having finally arrived at the South Pole, exhausted and on the brink of death, only to find Roald Amundsen's flag still waving in the frigid winds.

One night, Doyle and I sat up in the plaza drinking beer. We took turns going to the Rapido and buying cold cans of Cristal. I told him I had bought the bicycle because I didn't think I could hack staying in Cuba long enough to walk all the way across. He said he no longer thought he would last two years. "I didn't realize how much griping I'd been doing until Jim got here," he said.

We agreed that the bureaucracy was beyond oppressive. Worse, it was whimsical and hypocritical. Like me, Doyle had been stunned to receive only a fifteen-day extension on his first visa. He had flown to Cancún and returned half an hour later on the same plane. "I would just as happily have paid the two hundred dollars for the ticket directly to immigration and have done with it," he said. "My feeling is, get your next extension anywhere but Havana." Still, we agreed (as we plonked down the dollar equivalent of an average Cuban's weekly salary for each round of beer), it wasn't our status that was the problem, it was all the petty indignities suffered daily by the Cubans that were difficult to stomach.

Between Sancti Spiritus and Ciego de Ávila, the old *central* crosses a series of gentle river valleys. At the first bridge, a rowing coach, screaming instructions down at his passing crew, paused to help me change my first flat of the day. Fifteen kilometers down the road, the front tire went flat again. Already, on my second day of riding, I was down to my very last inner tube. I crossed my fingers and pedaled the five kilometers into Jatibonico, where a flats-fixed guy repaired both tubes and put the best one back into the rim.

"Why did you buy this bike?" he asked. "Why didn't you just go to the *shoppy* and buy yourself a mountain bike?"

"They're crappy. They break down all the time. Cheap stuff," I said.

He looked at the wheel-less Flying Pigeon leaning up against the wall of the garage. "You should have just bought yourself a car."

Somewhere, I passed the midpoint on my journey. For the first time, Guantánamo was closer than Pinar del Río, and I celebrated inwardly. At another bridge, beside the thick and unmoving water of a narrow creek, I met a fisherman named Rayel. He had a Flying Pigeon of his own, with a huge silver fish strapped down to a plank with twine to stop it from bending at the middle and curling down into the bicycle wheel. Rayel called it a *mura*. The river looked small and insignificant and incapable of supporting such a large creature, and the fish itself, already gutted and cleaned, had on its face a look of goggle-eyed disbelief, as if it could not comprehend even in death that someone had managed to catch it.

Rayel was very black, with skin so dark that it had a cobalt-blue edge to it.

"Where are you from?" I asked.

"I was born in Ciego de Ávila," he responded.

"No, I mean originally, where did your father come from?"

"I don't know." He paused. This was not something he wanted to talk about. "Some people say from Haiti."

In the 1920s and 1930s, the vast American sugar-cane plantations experienced a labor crunch. Their solution was to arrange for thousands of temporary guest laborers to be imported from Haiti and Jamaica. Ostensibly required to return home at the end of the *zafra*, many laborers stayed on: in the provinces of Ciego de Ávila and Camagüey, Haitian *bateyes*, residential camps of sugar-cane workers, had endured, virtually as racial enclaves, for decades.

Around his neck, Rayel was wearing a live turtle about three centimeters long. He had drilled a tiny hole at the edge of the shell for a cord, and the turtle hung flat against the chest of his Fila T-shirt, craning its head around and scrabbling gently against the fabric with tiny feet.

"It's alive?" I asked, although it obviously was.

"It doesn't die," said Rayel. "I just stick it in water from time to time and it doesn't die."

"How long have you had it?"

"Tcha," said Rayel, flicking his fingers toward the sky in a hand gesture that means ages and ages.

It was a surreal meeting for both of us. Rayel must have been confused by the direct and nosy questions posed by the red-bearded stranger on a grotesquely overstuffed bicycle, and I, seeing him there standing on the roadside, a Haitian with an enormous fish and a live turtle talisman, could not help but imagine him as a personification of Agwe, the *Vodou* spirit of the waters, master of all things in the fishy domain.

I had no more flats that day, but it began to rain as I neared the town of Jicotea, which, spookily, means turtle. It came down slowly at first, vaporizing immediately on the hot pavement, but then the clouds burst and torrents poured down from the heavens. It was the kind of dense rain that destroys visibility and turns everything pale gray. I tried to take shelter, but I was soaked to the skin within moments. When the rain had passed, I rode into Ciego de Ávila.

"You've got to be Richard," Wilma said from her doorway as I came pedaling up the block. It was a good thing I had called in advance, as I was a bedraggled mess.

Wilma's blonde hairdo and the household she presided over were as reminiscent of 1950s America as her name. In the front room was a television set up in front of rows of chairs, almost like a theater. The room had no other purpose but the unabashed around-the-clock watching of TV. In the evenings, Wilma made snacks and the neighborhood drifted in and out of the front door and gossiped and watched whatever was on.

The bedroom had a wheezing air conditioner and blonde pressboard paneling on the walls. My second-floor terrace overlooking the street was entirely encased in ornate, iron-welded latticework. These floor-to-ceiling grilles are an abundant architectural feature throughout Puerto Rico and the bungalow ghettos of South Florida, but are uncommon in Cuba.

Despite the security I was robbed in the night.

"I hung my shorts on the terrace to dry, and now they're gone," I told Wilma. "They were foul and soggy, but someone seems to have taken them anyway."

Wilma laughed, remembering how dreadful the sodden shorts had been when I arrived the night before.

She shook her head in dismay. "They'll steal anything these days."

Ciego de Ávila has a grand central square, lit at night by dozens of soft, round orange bulbs and filled with shade trees and benches. The night before, these benches had been crowded with snuggling couples. Now, the square was an oasis of calm in the throbbing Mecca of shops that radiated out from the center. A long line threaded out of the moneychanger's booth. These were Cubans waiting to change their pesos into dollars, not the other way around. The wads of pesos earned from serving up pizzas, fixing flats, accepting paying hitchhikers, and selling box lunches over the garden gate all ended up there on the line, which snaked down the sidewalk in mute acknowledgment that the state system was in bankrupt disarray and the only goods worth having had to be paid for with hard currency.

Similar, shorter lines had formed outside some of the dollar stores. In contrast, the few places that held any peso goods were moribund and dusty and reminded me of the last struggling businesses on the ruined main streets of post-Wal-Mart Middle America. These peso stores had the tawdry feel of a place in the final hours of its liquidation sale, when the prices have reached rock bottom and only the last few truly unwanted articles remain. There were dismal arrays holding a few poorly made shoes, uncomfortable even to look at, and rows of empty shelves behind glass-topped counters. The clerks were either much too friendly, as if amazed to have a client, or sullen and curdled from the burden of providing years of customer dissatisfaction. Both types were equally amused by my absurd notion that I might find a pair of men's shorts. Forced to choose between waiting in line to get into a dollar store, and shopping in ghostly peso establishments, I wandered down the block away from the center.

A TV repair shop had massive, partially dismantled Soviet televisions. Empty of people, it had a feeling of immobile calm, like a museum diorama. A man on the sidewalk was loading a television into a wheelbarrow specially lined with fabric padding. The typewriter repair shop was even more like staring into a time capsule. Shelves and shelves of manual typewriters, and a few Soviet electrics, lay awaiting repair. As a happy customer strapped his newly repaired typewriter to the back of a Flying Pigeon and wheeled it away, a man approached.

"May I help you?" he asked. "What are you looking for?"

"I was hoping to find some shorts," I said.

"I think I know a place," he said. "Come on, I'll show you."

We went back down the street to the Atelier de Transformación de Ropa Reciclada a la Medida, which essentially means the "workshop where used clothes are altered to measure." A crowd was pushing and shoving to get into this Cuban version of a Salvation Army store, and a hapless clerk blocked the doorway with his arms, urging calm and letting in two or three shoppers at a time when others departed, as if he were a bouncer at an overcrowded nightclub.

"I told you," said the man. "I heard a rumor that a delivery was going to come in today. Let me see if I can save us waiting." He elbowed his way to the front of the pack. "Mira," he said, "would you tell me if you have any men's shorts that might fit this man?" He gestured toward me. I was a head taller than the throng of Cubans. The clerk shook his head: there were no shorts for men of any size.

Obtaining any basic necessity in Cuba was a matter of following rumors, being inventive and patient, and knowing the back channels. The other Ropa Reciclada stores were not expecting any shipments, had almost nothing wearable on the racks, and were doing no business. I gave up and went to the *shoppy*, the dollar department store. The only shorts I could find was the bottom half of a cabana set, a virgin acrylic, two-piece ensemble of elastic-waisted gym shorts and tanktop, in mud-brown knit with royal blue piping. Back in my room at Wilma's, I tried on my new outfit. I looked like a Bulgarian gangster on an outing to the Black Sea.

To add injury to insult, I discovered that behind my stolen shorts lay a far more serious crime. My soggy sneakers were gone as well. To steal them, the thief would have had to climb up to get the shorts, and, hanging off the outside of the house above the street, spied them on the floor. With three or four meters of bamboo pole or a hook on a string, he must have slid or levered them across the terrace before yanking them through the metal grillework. The sneakers had never been the same since the bogs of the Zapata Swamp. They reeked permanently of sulfur and athlete's foot, but, after my recent shopping expedition, I considered their loss a disaster. I was under no illusion that I would find any suitable replacement in Ciego de Ávila. I went downstairs to report this latest crisis to Wilma.

She looked at me in my Black Sea bathing costume, trying to conceal her amusement.

"I found a new pair of shorts," I said.

"Yes," she said, "I noticed."

"Unfortunately, my shoes were also stolen. They were on the floor, and someone must have stuck a long pole through the grille."

"That's terrible," she said. "Nothing like this ever used to happen. Nowadays, these blacks, they have become like cats." The casual racism surprised me, but not for the first time. While many Cubans seemed to be living in post-racial harmony, this much-vaunted accomplishment of the revolution was little more than a myth in households like Wilma's. After the afternoon rains, I cycled through Ciego de Ávila's neighborhoods. Flat and sprawling, it is not Cuba's most attractive city, full of nondescript blocks of houses of too recent a vintage for their decay to hold much charm. Away from the plaza, there were few trees or green spaces.

Pedaling back toward Wilma's, I heard the unmistakable sound of *batá*. Spectators were gathered around the doorway of a low white house and clinging onto the security bars that covered the windows. I was sure it was a *toque de santo*, a *Santería* ceremony in full swing. I rode on for a block and stopped. I could still hear the muffled thuds of drumbeats behind me, like the distant booming of a high-octane car stereo. I wanted to go back, but what was the protocol? Should I just barge in uninvited?

I wheeled the bicycle back to the yard and leaned it against the wall, joining the knot of onlookers peering in through the window. Inside, a party was in full session. Against the far wall sat the drummers. They were older black men, professionals producing an intense and complex interplay of rhythms with no wasted effort. Drumming is exhausting physical work, but although the drums were very loud, the drummers were among the few people in the room who weren't sweating. They wore hats like baker's caps, but of colored silk, and their arms were a blur from the elbows down. No one was immune to the rhythm, although the crowd was not dancing. A congregation as diverse as Cuba itself moved back and forth in place to the beat. There were two very large black women, nicely dressed, as if for a church social; white girls in the Cuban housewife's standard daily uniform of lycra cycling shorts and colored T-shirt; a man with short bleached hair, purple Hawaiian shirt, and white satin pajama bottoms who would not have looked out of place in a gay bar in Miami Beach; and kids, in cutoffs and flip-flops like mine, weaving through the legs of the adults.

In the middle of the floor, a man who looked as mild and sensible as an accountant was transfixed, sweating, and shaking. He danced, and then shuddered in bursts, as if he were operating an invisible pneumatic drill with his clenched fists. It was a look I recognized from Haiti as signaling the arrival of the spirit, when the earthly body is still struggling to keep its wits about it, trying not to succumb. His tidy moustache trembled, and beads of sweat soaked through his polo shirt, darkening the muted burgundy and teal stripes. Then the man was gone, and *Changó* had taken his place.

He ran like a bus gone out of control, weaving through the crowd as startled spectators jumped back in alarm. Charging like a linebacker, he butted people with his head. He was a bull, bent over at the waist, fists at his temples, insensate, ramming through the crowd. Outside, those of us who were gathered around the window lost sight of him and rushed *en masse* over to the door, then hurried back to our window as he tore back into view on our side of the room. He disappeared somewhere into the back of the house. The drums played on. When he returned, his face was covered in ash and he held an armful of leafy branches. Again, he raced around the room, brushing the crowd with the leaves. This was the work that *Changó* had been invited here to perform, the sweeping away of bad energy, and the congregation stepped up and spread their arms, palms out, to receive a wave of the leaves. Once these blessings were complete, the man was much reduced; he looked wasted and confused; another man led him away, as if helping an invalid down a hospital corridor.

I knew there was going to be a pause in the action because a videographer came out of the house and sat down to smoke a cigarette under the awning of a machine shop at the back of the yard. He had a VHS camcorder on a long extension cord. His soundman came out with a coiled microphone cable and joined him. I wandered over.

"I'm a soundman in New York," I said. "What are you filming for?"

"For the owner of the house," said the soundman.

"You film lots of *Santería* ceremonies?"

"Sure," said the cameraman. "Weddings, baptisms, *quinceaños.** Whatever. Today is more of a favor. People like to have a record, especially of this."

"What ceremony is it?"

"This is a sort of presentation. The way I understand it is after people have 'made their saint,' they have this ceremony and are presented. Today, there are six, I think."

"They present all at once?"

"No, they go one by one. The third one just finished."

"I was just going by and I heard the drums and came in. You don't think I would offend anyone by being here? I wasn't invited."

"I don't think so, I don't think it is private. There are lots of people here."

The drums started again and the team hurried back into the house. I took my place at the window. Inside, the crowd had stepped back from the drums and a procession was shuffling around the room. In the lead was a man carrying a calabash bowl full of liquid. With one hand, he sprinkled drops of it ahead of him on the path. Behind him was the next initiate, a mulatto woman. She wore a tall white turban and a flowing white satin gown and she smiled the rapturous smile of accomplishment and completion sometimes captured in high-school graduation photographs. To either side of her were her attendants, or sponsors, and behind her, like a bridal train, four more people followed in single file.

The little parade circled the room three times and then came to a halt in front of the drums. Here, the attendants released her, stepping back to give her room. The woman began to dance as the drummers and cantors sang and chanted in a language I took to be Lucumí, the African language used in the *Santería* liturgy. Being of African origin, the *santos* are pre-

---

* Fifteenth birthday, celebrated in Latin America like a "sweet sixteen."

sumed to speak Lucumí among themselves, and it is proper to address them in this language. One of the cantors seemed to be in a rage as he bellowed at the saint, his face a hand's breadth away from the initiate's face. He was a man of about thirty with the physique of a shot-putter. The tendons in his neck stood at taut attention, and, as he shouted at the top of his lungs, his face bulged like an exasperated basketball coach pacing the sidelines. He was trying to reach the saint, coaxing it, encouraging it, inviting it to the party by screaming right through the body of the woman standing there and into the other world. Apparently oblivious to this onslaught of sound, she herself did look a bit stunned, as if facing a hurricane wind. Eyes closed, she danced on.

Her dancing, like all the dancing I saw that day, was relaxed and slow, a sort of low-energy, two-step, side-to-side shuffle. If there was a moment when *Obatala* arrived to displace the woman from her body, I did not see it. After she danced her dance, she knelt and kissed each of the three drums in turn, before being helped away by her attendants.

The drums were very special. They were old and crusty *batá* wrapped in ruffled vestments like the fabric skirts hung from the front of catering tables. The *Itótele* was shrouded in red velvet, the *Iyá* in a red and yellow brocade cloak. The *Okónkolo*, the smallest drum, was draped in bright orange satin trimmed with white polyester lace, like cheap lingerie or an outfit from Hooters. In the center of the drumhead, on the skin itself, a ring of some kind of resin formed a bowl-shaped depression or open cone, as if the tip of a volcano was protruding from the drum's upper surface.

Two antique male dolls with white porcelain faces were posed near the drummers. One sat on the floor dressed in saintly white, wearing the green and black beaded necklace of *Oggún*. The other hung on the wall behind them, dressed in a straw hat with red trim, a red peasant shirt, and brown *guajiro* trousers. I was later told that these dolls had been placed there to protect the drummers from bad energy released by the dancers.

A boy not more than twelve was the next to be initiated. He was also dressed in white, for *Obatala*. Because of his age and white robes, I recognized the ceremony much more plainly for what it was, a *Santería* version of confirmation, or baptism. I wondered if his parents had pushed him into it or if, like me after my Episcopal confirmation, he would take the official religious recognition of his adulthood as a get-out-of-jail-free card, a permission slip to no longer attend services. I thought not. There was a festive abandon to *Santería*; people might have come to support their friends and relatives on this important day, but they were also having fun. They drank beer, listened to the drums, chatted, and danced. The capriciousness of the *orishas* guaranteed the unpredictability of the affair. It was an exciting event in the life of the neighborhood, one that would be talked about in the days to come. In that way, it was totally unlike a church service.

The crowd ebbed and flowed; a man I recognized as one of the escorts from the first initiation came outside for a rest. He and a younger man sat down in the open shop under the sheet-metal awning, but he got up and came over when he saw me watching through the grille over the window.

"You like the ceremony?" he asked.

"It's very interesting," I said. "But I have no idea what's going on."

"You don't have to stand outside. My friend is the owner of the house. It's no problem, you're welcome to come in and watch. "

"I have my bicycle. Is it okay to leave it out here?"

"My son will watch it," he said. "Put it over here with ours." He gestured at two bicycles under the awning.

The son's name was Enrique. I went inside with the father, Eduardo, and he took me straight through to the back porch. The man who had earlier been "mounted" by *Changó* was there, slumped over in a chair. He was holding his head in both hands and looked as if he had just run a marathon or was suffering from a migraine.

"That's my *hermano del santo*,"* Eduardo said. "When they ride, sometimes you get a headache afterward. Do you want a beer?"

"Sure," I said. A woman was there pouring beer out of an old bottle into white plastic cups as thin as sheets of paper.

"There's nothing else to drink," he said. "Nobody is supposed to have liquor. It's an offense."

We took our beers and weaved through the dancers to the front room. I hadn't been able to see into it from the outside because all the curtains were drawn. It was empty of people but the floor was laden with cakes, bowls of fruit, and bottles. It was an orgiastic smorgasbord of desserts spread out in front of an ornate altar draped in satin.

"Beautiful, isn't it?" asked Eduardo.

"Spectacular."

---

* Literally a "brother saint," meaning a person who has "made" the same saint as oneself.

"Did you see? One of the drummers is drinking *trago*, I'm very concerned about it. The drummers are supposed to be pure. No sexual relations or hard liquor before the ceremony."

"What happens if they break the rules?"

"It's an insult. Things can go wrong. The drums are very special; they are *añá*. They can only be played with respect."

"What is *añá*?"

"*Añá* means they are *tambores de fundamento*." Fundamental drums. I was mystified.

"I still don't understand," I said.

"The drums are not from here. They come from Camagüey. It costs eight hundred pesos to hire them and the drummers. Plus the transport, and you have to feed the drummers and put them up. It is the major expense of the ceremony. Before it was worse. There were only three sets of *tambores de fundamento* in all Cuba, two in Havana and one in Matanzas. It was very far to get them to come.

"The drums have their own spirits, which live in the drums. Did you see, in the ceremony, the initiates bow down and touch their foreheads to the drums and then kiss them? The little lip on the inside of the drum is how you know they are *tambores de fundamento*."

"What's that for?"

"To give food. You hold the chicken and it picks the grain from there. It's a very long and complicated ceremony to make *tambores de fundamento*."

"I hardly understand a thing," I said. "Would you have any time to explain a little of what happened today?"

"I'll tell you what," said Eduardo. "How about you come to my house tomorrow?"

Dieciocho
At Eduardo's

Mayeya, no juegues con los santos
Respeta los collares....

Mayeya, don't play around with the saints;
respect the beads....
    —Ignacio Piñeiro

Wilma was seated on her favorite chair, facing three-quarters toward the street so she could divide her attention equally between passers-by and the television. Her son was sitting on the floor at arm's length from the screen watching a Steven Seagal video.

"You've been gone a long time," she said. "How did everything go?"

"Great," I said, "I stumbled on a *Santería* ceremony. I am spending the day tomorrow with a man I met there so he can explain it to me."

"Oh? Who would that be?" My hosts in Cuba always wanted to know whom else I had met in their town, to make sure I hadn't been latched onto by *jineteros*, low elements, or swindlers. When discussing my plans, I often felt like a suburban teenager trying to convince his parents that he was mature enough to go alone into the city for the day. "His name is Eduardo," I said. "A white guy, mid-forties, knows everything about *Santería*."

"He lives on Benavides?"

I checked the address. "That's right."

Wilma laughed. "He's my uncle," she said. "You should have an interesting day." The look on her face suggested that the mysterious interests of her guests would never cease to amaze her. She clearly thought Eduardo rather a loon.

I had taken Wilma for a professional housewife, but, as with almost all Cubans, the special period had changed her life and priorities. She told me that she had been a lawyer in Ciego de Ávila.

"You no longer practice?" I asked.

"*Qué va*," she said. "For what? You earn nothing. Maybe twenty dollars a month. In any case, people are convicted based on conviction anyway."

"What do you mean, convicted based on conviction?"

"I mean you can mount the best defense in the world and if the guy bringing the complaint is better connected, forget it. A cop could come over here and go, 'Hey, Wilma, how did you get all that money?' Oh, they sent it to me from *afuera*. 'I don't think so, I think you stole it.' No, no, I would say, but if they don't believe you, off you go. And you will lose your case. Period."

Eduardo was wearing a New York Knicks uniform, a baggy tanktop and royal blue shorts made from space-age, northern-hemisphere fabric. The house was minuscule, two tiny rooms entirely given over to his beliefs, with the claustrophobic feel of an overstuffed antique store. Every available surface lodged artifacts of *Santería*. Urns, dolls, bowls of stones, chromo-lithographs, and strings of beads were everywhere. I entered with the utmost care, fearful that I would brush up against a shelf, shatter some sacred object, and incur the wrath of the *orishas*. Eduardo explained that he shared the house with his wife, but did not live with her.

"She attends me as a wife should. She cooks and washes, but we no longer have *relaciones*. She sleeps there," he said, gesturing toward the fractionally larger back room, which also served as the kitchen and bathroom, "and I sleep here. We have to live this way because we made a *promesa* in front of Santa Barbara to be together until death." Eduardo was not an evangelist, but he assumed that my interest in coming to his house was to learn how to get my own in order. "The first thing you will need to do," he said, "is make an homage to the spirits. Begin with the spiritual plane. Take care of your family spirits, your personal spirit. Put out three, six, or nine glasses of water to give clarity to the spirit. Change them every Friday."

The concept of the personal spirit, spirit guide, or guardian angel probably came to *Santería* through Allan Kardec's writings from the 1860s. His treatises on spiritism, mediums, and communication with human ancestors were very popular throughout colonial Latin America and well-suited for syncretic absorption. In the era when Charles Darwin, Alfred Russel Wallace, and Alexander von Humboldt were roaming the world cataloguing its natural wonders, Kardec presented his philosophies as the scientific discovery of eternal truths. The communication with the spirits of ancestors achieved through seances answered those nagging questions about immortality and the existence of the soul. "By facts and logic," Kardec wrote, "Spiritism dissipates the anxiety of doubt and brings back to faith he who might have lost it, by showing us the existence of the invisible world that surrounds us."

Kardec's presentation of his ideas demonstrated a genius for marketing. "From the moral point of view, Spiritism is essentially Christian," he explained, but "has as its basis the fundamental truths of all the religions." Spiritism was brilliantly inclusive, a proto-New-Ageism carefully explained as supplementary, rather than in any way opposed, to existing religious belief. Those who already have peace of mind and find their existing faith sufficient, Kardec suggests in *Le Spiritisme à sa plus simple expression* (*Spiritism Easily Explained*), might not need spiritism. But who in the world is not plagued by doubts? The doctrine melds tidily into the *Santería* concept of the *Eggun*, tribes of spirit ancestors who come to our aid as recognizable individuals, like Susan Werrell, the spirit that Loretta had identified as watching over me in Matanzas. *Eggun* are not *orishas*, but, rather, spirits or souls of the dead. As Eduardo was telling the story of his personal spirit, his son, Enrique, arrived.

"When I was a child," said Eduardo, "I didn't like the movies or going to the park. I liked the cemetery. That is how I discovered my spirit." He showed me a black china doll dressed up in a blue frock. "Her name is Tomasa Saria Sott," he said. The next object on the shelf was a gourd, filled with sticks and pierced at the top by a railroad spike and knife. "This is her *fundamento*. Her mother, Francisca, brought Tomasa to Pinar del Río, hidden in a trunk, when she was just a girl. When they discovered her, mother and daughter were separated, and Tomasa was taken to Sancti Spiritus and brought up in the household of a Dr. Portuondo. I have been to that house, and to the grave where Tomasa is buried."

"She was a slave? Are we talking about the 1800s here?"

"That's right."

"How do you know all this?"

"She tells her story. Over time, we have pieced it together. I had gone to the cemetery with a bunch of flowers and I saw a woman, a woman of color, with a bucket, and I hurried after her, to borrow the bucket to put the flowers in. Suddenly, she just disappeared. I found myself looking into a hole in the ground. I fainted and fell right into the Portuondos' tomb. That's how I knew she was my spirit. Her day is December 24, and I put out a little tree for her every Christmas."

"She's African?" I asked.

"Haitian," said Eduardo.

"She speaks Haitian," said Enrique. "Fluently."

Eduardo explained that, after he was "mounted" by Tomasa, he never had any recollection of what she had said during her visit. Instead, Enrique took note of everything she communicated and passed on the information later.

"What kind of information?" I asked.

"Well, for instance, certain things you need to do, in order to improve yourself, or your chances in life. Certain steps you need to take." Eduardo explained that the head of the doll was *cargado*, charged, stuffed with grasses, toasted peanuts, and sherry: "things which she asks for." The word, *fundamento*, which had so mystified me the day before, refers to objects like this that have undergone a sanctifying ceremony and become the home base for a particular spirit or *orisha*.

We sat in the tiny space at the front of the house. Eduardo brought dozens of strings of beads from a cupboard and carefully went through them as I wrote down the attributes of each *orisha*, the patterns of the beads on their necklaces, and their syncretic saintly equivalents. "Ochósi," I wrote, "blue and amber beads with orange trim. Equals San Norberto, rules over houses and prisons." People all over Cuba wear these strings of beads around their necks, advertising their affiliation with their ruling *orisha*. Most commonly seen are the alternating green and yellow beads of Orula. Equated with God himself, Orula is remote, but rules over everything.

"They say Fidel made his saint," said Eduardo.

"Which saint?" I asked.

"It's not known. The rumor comes from the 1980s, when he made a state visit to Guinea. It was on television, and our commander and chief was dressed entirely in white robes, including even a hat....I want to show you a photograph," said Eduardo. "Look at this."

It showed a black doll in a billowing blue dress, a large blue urn, and beads and flowers constructed into an ornate bower. A man with long, stringy blond hair and a strained, wild-eyed look stood beside the altar. "Yemayá?" I said, referring to the goddess of the sea.

"In Union City," said Eduardo. Union City is the Hialeah of New Jersey, the epicenter of the New York-area expatriate Cuban community. "That's my brother. Do you notice anything in particular?"

The man looked pallid and unwell. "Not really," I said.

"He left in Mariel," said Eduardo. "We didn't see each other for fifteen years. In fact, we lost contact for quite some time. When he came to visit, he saw my *Yemayá* and he couldn't believe it. They are identical. He sent these photos later, to show me."

"He left in the boatlift?"

"Yeah, almost twenty years ago. It was terrible."

The Mariel boatlift was the most important and traumatic Cuban exodus since the revolution itself. It began in May 1979 when twelve dissidents crashed a bus through the gates of the Venezuelan embassy in Havana and asked for political asylum. A series of attempts by copycat asylum-seekers followed at other embassies, which were placed under guard. For the first time, the contradictions between the glories of the revolution and the people's right to choose, or at least move, were displayed internationally. Then, in March 1980, a Cuban guard at Peru's embassy was shot and killed during an incident in which another bus had attempted to crash through the gates. Castro announced that the guards would be removed and all those seeking asylum could do so freely. Within days, thousands of Cubans clogged the Peruvian embassy. The Carter administration, probably the most vocal one in the twentieth century on the issue of human rights, trumpeted these events as proof of the repressiveness of Castro's system.

Embarrassed and shocked by the number of *Habaneros* who had flocked to the embassy, Castro nonetheless called America's bluff. Boats had already begun sailing to Mariel harbor from Miami and the Florida keys to deal with the embassy refugees. Now, it was announced that any Cuban who wanted to would be allowed to leave on them. The flotilla that followed carried more than 125,000 Cubans to South Florida.

This exodus left psychological scars on both sides. In Cuba, shouting crowds assaulted the would-be deserters. "Undesirables" such as homosexuals and the mentally ill were urged or forced to join the migration.

Families were torn apart. Those remaining behind watched as their departing loved ones were jeered at. Some joined in the jeering. On the Miami side of the water, a state of emergency was declared in South Florida. Arriving Cubans without resident family were immediately incarcerated in "processing centers" at military bases. Riots broke out at Eglin Air Force base and Fort Chaffee, Arkansas, when the American dream began to resemble indefinite detention. In Miami, the Orange Bowl became a tent city for hundreds of disgruntled Cubans whose sponsorship arrangements had turned sour. Hardened criminals from Havana's prisons joined Cuban intelligence operatives salted among the departing crowds, turning the Miami yachts into Trojan horses.

Eduardo said that his brother had had "a lot of problems." When he left, the neighborhood watch committee organized a goodbye party, hurling eggs and rotten fruit at the departing *gusano*. After twenty years, however, the mood in Cuba had changed. Having Marielito relatives now was often a cause for celebration, in no small part because they were a possible source of income. Dozens of Cubans had told me of making the trek to the US interests section in order to put their names in for the *bombo*. Failed *balseros* returned to the island by the Cuban or American coast guard were still officially ostracized. Based on what I had seen, though, their neighbors and relatives prayed for their safety and success. If they failed to reach Florida, the neighborhood welcomed them quietly back and commiserated.

"You know what he told me when he came to visit?" asked Eduardo. "He said, 'I could never live here, you people work too hard.'" Eduardo used the quintessentially Cuban expression, "pasando trabajo," which, for the depth of feeling it expresses in Cuba, might be best translated as "going through hell."

"What does he do in New Jersey?" I asked.

"He receives that public assistance, what do you call it, welfare."

Enrique went to get beer from the local tap and came back with Pedro, the next-door neighbor. Pedro was built like a fire hydrant, with a taut, squat, round body and forearms like hams. He had no neck, just fat folds of flesh at the back of his almost bald head, which was covered with about a millimeter of salt-and-pepper stubble. His narrow yellow eyes and manic sneer reminded me of a chronic steroid-abuser. Immediately, he showed me his brand. On his meaty upper arm was burned an X above the Roman numeral III. The violent, smooth scars ridged the skin.

"I'm a *palero*," he said, meaning a practitioner of *Palo Monte* or *Palo Mayombe*, a strain of Afro-Cuban religion parallel to, but distinct from, the dominant *Santería*. *Palo Monte* literally means "wild sticks," although the wilderness described by the term *monte* is as much a state of mind as an actual place. "This brand indicates that *en mi casa mando yo.*" In my household, I'm the boss. The marks are made during the *rayado*, or striping ceremony of initiation into *Palo*. Pedro made every statement into a challenge and his words rushed out in aggressive bursts. I was sure that he had been a fearsome bully as a child.

"I also work with *palos*," said Eduardo. "*Palo* is a different religion. The *fundamentos* live underground, and the work is done with sticks. You want to see?"

"Of course."

"We have to take our shoes and shirts off," said Enrique, "and roll up our trousers. For respect."

We stripped and rolled up our pants as if preparing to wade across a river.

"No jewelry or other adornments," said Pedro.

"Let's go in," said Eduardo, gesturing to a doorway, curtained with a hanging sheet, leading to what I had assumed was his bedroom.

"Homosexuals are not allowed," said Pedro, with unnecessary venom.

We entered a tiny, dark space that was both Eduardo's bedroom and his "dark room," the place where he worked with the spirits of *Palo*. The bed was against one wall. Had I to sleep there, I would have suffered nightmares. If the rest of the house was like a cluttered junk shop, the *Palo* room was more reminiscent of a forgotten and obscure corner in a long-disused barn, where clumps of sodden hay, bird droppings, and rotten timber collect into fetid and unrecognizable piles. Dried fish and hooves hung from the ceiling. Along another wall, the tops of the *prendas* or *ngangas* emerged from the earthen floor like shattered stumps in a primeval forest. A disagreeable organic odor hung thick and musky in the air. There was nowhere to sit except the bed. We crouched on the floor.

Palo ngangas consist of an iron cauldron, or *caldero*, filled with at least twenty-one sticks from twenty-one powerful species of tree. These, mixed with animal bones, feathers, and earth collected from cemeteries, crossroads, and other loci of supernatural power are bound with chain and buried in the ground. The *caldero* becomes home to a *brujo*, essentially the *Palo* equivalent of an *orisha*, who does the bidding of its human owner.

Eduardo's room held three *ngangas*.

"This is a *Zarabanda*," he said, indicating the largest and most grue-some pile. What I took to be the clump of sticks was barely identifiable. A fence of machetes driven into the ground surrounded it. The entire mess was covered with a foul, black patina of dried blood, egg white, *aguardiente*, and years of candlewax drippings. On the wall above the *Zarabanda* (or *Sarabanda*) was painted a skeleton with a serpent winding its way up a bolt of fire bursting through the top of the skull. A collection of grisly objects hung down from the ceiling like a string of onions. Eduardo ticked them off for me as if they were the ingredients of a stew: goats feet, chicken feet, the feet of a male pig, and a freshwater turtle. These were blackened and greasy with candlesmoke. Chicken feathers dotted the *Zarabanda*.

"What's that?" I said, pointing at a squiggly, dangling object that looked like a freeze-dried snake.

"That's a 'twenty-one,'" said Enrique. He had lighted a cigar and was busily puffing the smoke onto his own *prenda*, a *Chola Wengue*, the *Palo* equivalent of the *orisha Ochún*.

"A twenty-one?"

Pedro made a slithering motion with his hand, miming a snake.

"You mean a *majá*?" I asked, using the common Cuban term for the reptile.

They all turned on me at once, fiercely shushing.

"You can't say that word in here! That word is not permitted in front of the *brujos*," said Enrique.

"That's why, when we are in here, we refer to it as a 'twenty-one,'" said Eduardo.

"I didn't know. I'm terribly sorry," I said, as much to the gloomy clumps of blackened sticks as to my companions. I stood up to leave, contemplating my doom. Pedro gave me a look of contempt.

"I'm sure it's okay," said Eduardo. "Since you are just learning and all."

I told them what I had heard about *Palo Monte*, that it was witchcraft, and that while *Santería* is used to bring good things, *Palo* is used for evil and casting spells.

"Some people would call us sorcerers," said Eduardo, "but we are reli-gious people. You can do either good or bad with both the saints and with *Palo*. God is up there noting everything down, and when you get that telegram to go face that final reckoning, you bear the responsibility."

Despite Eduardo's protestations, the operating principle behind the "work" done with the *ngangas* underlines the comparative amorality of *Palo Monte*. A successfully consecrated *caldero* is essentially a spirit prison, like a genie's lamp. The *caldero's* owner makes demands on the resident *brujo*, or witch, but the spirit itself does not distinguish between good and evil acts. Instead, the *brujos* are delightfully capitalist, unjudgmentally setting a price, for instance the blood of a white hen, on whatever deed is requested of them. Any sense of morality is only dictated by the values of the human owner who commands it.

The grisly aspects of the *Palo* room were calculated to be impressive and disturbing. Although Eduardo was a meek civil servant who worked full time restoring 35mm film prints in the hopes that they would survive yet another screening, he was also a religious professional. The advantage of being the owner of a *nganga* with a reputation is that others will come and pay you to rent it, and, as in any service business, success rests only partly on positive results. Aura and atmosphere are just as important. This terrifying room, and the unbelievable fact that Eduardo peacefully slept away his nights in it, enhanced his reputation as an effective *palero*.

Laid out on the *prendas* were an assortment of charms left by Eduardo's clients, and I asked him what kind of problems he was asked to help with. "It's usually love problems," he said, "but it could be with a *permuta*, moving house, or emigrating." He showed me a bundle, a lumpy object the size of pear, wrapped around and around with red and black thread. It looked mummified. "This one was placed there by a *jinetera* who wanted to go to Germany and marry a tourist she had met. The *brujo* told her to get a gourd and put in it some earth from the German embassy along with earth from the Cuban immigration office, and to write the names of the people who didn't want her to go on slips of paper. She had to put the slips of paper in the mouth of a white chicken, bind up the head, and sacrifice it. Inside that gourd is a bundle. In there are the chicken's head, some important powerful sticks, and the earth samples."

"What happened?" I asked.

"She was successful in leaving and she has been in Germany for four months already."

I felt I understood a little too well the source of the musky organic stench that hung heavily in the room. "How long will that thing stay on the altar?" I asked.

"The object will remain there," said Eduardo, "until she returns to thank the *Zarabanda* or until the *brujo* itself says that it should be removed."

"How much do you charge?"

"It's entirely depending on the ability of the person to pay," said Eduardo.

"I have a *Lucero*," said Pedro, referring to another *Palo brujo*. "It works exclusively for me. No rentals."

Eduardo showed me another charm, a pig's tongue bundled up in a black envelope of cloth and bound with black thread. This had been used in a cleaning ritual along with a bath of grasses. Such *limpiezas* are common in the Afro-Caribbean religions; important herbs, powders, and leaves are mulched with alcohol and water into a purifying salve used to suds away evil spirits and protect the bather. Also hanging on the wall above the *Zarabanda* and the *Chola Wengue* was an *empaca*, a bull's horn, also *cargado*, and with a mirror set in the end. Pedro took it down and thrust it toward me.

"Look in the mirror," he said. "If you don't see yourself, you're fucked."

I did not reach out to take it from him. His hand was moving, the room was dark, and the shard of mirror was small and black. I would argue that it is difficult to see oneself in a mirror held by another under any circumstances, but particularly when its glass surface is dingy with soot and wax and the reflective surface behind is pitted with mildew. But although I bobbed and weaved like a basketball player, I did not see my reflection in the glass of the *empaca*.

Diecínueve

In Camagüey

The province of Camagüey was once a vast tract of tropical jungle, but the ride east along the *central* today runs through rolling, pastoral ranchland. Rows of clouds stretched across an endless blue ceiling like fish scales. An incessant wind bowed the sugar cane down to westward. The *monte* that once covered this land is now fully under man's control. First, the Spanish cleared huge tracts for their *haciendas*, then Americans arrived to gobble up the rest in their insatiable lust for cane. I wondered if the *brujos* were in retreat, or if they somehow adapted to the altered landscape. Where was it that people went to collect the twenty-one different species of sticks they needed to make their *ngangas*?

In Camagüey, the Big Sky heartland of Cuba, the only trees left standing are mammoth bolus-trunked ceibas reaching up toward the heavens, rare and solitary in the occasional field. The land is as flat as I had pictured it back in Trinidad, but I had overlooked the headwind, which is savage, relentless, and exhausting. Riding into it is like trying to push-start a mobile home.

I stopped for water under a ceiba tree. A farmer was leaned up against the trunk, as if he had been waiting for me. My appearance was absurd. My sneakers gone, I was pedaling in enormous, clunky hiking boots. My tight brown shorts looked like the sort of garment French men consider it acceptable to go swimming in.

"You going to Camagüey?" asked the man, unfazed. I nodded, breathing hard. "That's far on that thing. Sometimes I see cyclotourists, but never on one of those bikes. *Estás pasando trabajo.* And most of them are riding the other direction, because of the wind, you know. You want cheese?"

"Cheese? I was hoping you could fill up my canteens."

He pointed down at the ground. Tucked between two of the ceiba's roots, which rose like buttresses out of the earth, was a pie-sized white wheel of cheese resting on a plastic bucket lid.

"That's a big cheese," I said. "I can't carry that."

"I've sold cheese to cyclists before."

I guarded the cheese while he went to fill the canteens. When he returned, I asked him why he didn't set up a table beside the road.

"It's illegal to sell cheese," he said. "It's dangerous."

"So how do you sell any?"

"I watch the cars. If it's a private car that's coming, I pick up the cheese and show it to them, but if it's a state car, or a truck, the cheese stays hidden down there in the roots."

I drank some water and we watched the passing traffic for an opportunity. It was a desperate kind of fishing.

"Look there," he said, pointing back down the highway, "cars like that offer the best possibilities." Far down the road, I could just make out a white compact heading toward us. It was a hazy spot on the asphalt, scarcely identifiable as a vehicle. The man had an eye. "Those are the cars they rent to tourists. This would be a good opportunity, but you can see that there are trucks behind it. I can't take the chance of them seeing me." He looked crestfallen. As the small convoy approached, I saw that everything he said was true. His powers of distant identification were like those of a champion birder. The car whistled past, then two large blue governmental dump trucks.

"How many cheeses do you succeed in selling like this?"

"Sometimes the whole day goes by and one doesn't sell any. But sometimes I sell a certain number." Suddenly he reached down, scooped up the cheese, and jumped up into the roadway. He stretched out his arm to display the cheese. A passenger car coming from the direction of Camagüey was fast approaching. Like a matador with a cape, my friend pivoted with the cheese to give it maximum exposure as the car passed, but the vehicle did not slow. He walked back and laid the cheese back down in the shade between the roots of the ceiba.

"I know it's risky," he said, "but one has to live."

"No es fácil," I said.

At an address I had in Camagüey, a wizened, old woman greeted me at the door with a familiar look of unwavering disapproval.

"Is this Elsa's house?" I asked.

"Elsa's not here. She's in the hospital, she's very sick. I'm her mother."

"I'm very sorry to hear that," I said. "Does that mean you aren't renting rooms?"

"No, we have a room. Elsa's sister is taking care of the business. But it's very difficult. She has *problemas de nervios*." By now, I understood "nervous problems" to be a catchall diagnosis used in Cuba to describe anyone overwhelmed by the stresses and tribulations of daily life.

Despite the unenthusiastic welcome, the room was perfect, and I was exhausted. I opened the double doors to let the sun in onto the ornately patterned tile floor, pulled off my boots, and collapsed on the bed. Moments later, Elsa's mother padded silently down the courtyard and peered into the room.

"You must be very hot and sweaty after such a long ride," she said. "Wouldn't you like to wash up?"

"I plan on that shortly. Mostly, I'm exhausted. I'm just lying down for a moment."

"You must take off the bedspread. It must be very hot."

"I will. It's not too hot; I'm only lying on top of it. I'm not actually going to sleep just yet," I said. I was so tired it was all I could do to respond.

"Let me help you," she said, coming into the room.

"Really, it's okay, I'm just going to rest for a few minutes." *Please stop talking to me.*

She seized the edge of the bedspread like Harry Houdini preparing to yank the tablecloth out from under a heavily laden banquet table. Despite my hundred kilos, she began to tug.

"It's too hot, it's too hot," she said in desperation. "And so difficult to wash."

I rolled to my feet just in time to avoid being dumped onto the floor. I was a sweaty, filthy mess.

The house was pervaded with an aura of dysfunction. Elsa's mother was prone to weeping silently, and I often found her pacing the courtyard, her geriatric face wet with tears. When not weeping, she looked for things to disapprove of. In contrast, Elsa's husband, Henry, had a beatific smile permanently affixed to his face. In the almost two weeks that I stayed there, we had only one conversation. We had it over and over again, however, with only slight variations.

Each time I came into the house, he offered his hand for a sickly, gripless handshake. "Oh, Richard," he said, "how do you like our fine city of Camagüey?"

"I've only just arrived," I said. "But I'm sure I'm going to like it here."

The next day, I said: "Well, I haven't seen so much of it yet, but it seems very nice."

And the day after that: "Oh, it's quite nice."

"I'm so glad," he would invariably reply. "You're enjoying your stay here? I'm so glad." Sometimes only half an hour would pass between one of these conversations and the next.

Henry was dangerously thin and appeared never to eat. While speaking, he always looked away as if at some imagined heavenly object far behind me. His placid smile never wavered. I was tempted to insult Camagüey, just to find out if he was actually with us.

Henry, it's horrible here, unbearably dull. I'm miserable. I can hardly wait to get the fuck out.

Oh, so you're enjoying it, then. I'm so glad.

Elsa was in the hospital suffering from an asthmatic attack brought on, I was told, by the interaction of Ibuprofen with her normal asthma drug. After five days, she came home and lay in bed in a frilly yellow nightgown. Although she coughed and wheezed with the horrible chesty rattlings of a tubercular who seemed to be on the point of death, with me she insisted on maintaining the pretense that all was normal. Whenever I put my head in to ask how she was doing, she urged me to be sure and ask her for anything I needed, proposing dinners and breakfasts and afternoon drinks, although she could not get out of bed.

It was a claustrophobic atmosphere of gloom and denial, and I fit in well. Instead of exploring this large and little visited Cuban city, I went out only in the evenings and sat at the corner bar, drinking too much. I stayed in bed late into the morning, adding to Elsa's mother's disapproval. In hopes that I would find a fax from Cynthia, I went every day to the telecoms office, pestering the woman there until she hated me. And I reclined, paralyzed in a chair on the patio outside my room, leafing through my notebook and complaining bitterly to myself that I wasn't having any adventures worth writing down.

One tearful day, Elsa's mother explained everything. A terrible tragedy had befallen the family. A year earlier, Elsa's daughter, her son-in-law, and two of their three children had died in a head-on collision while driving near Bayamo. Only the infant child, left behind with Elsa for the weekend, had survived. "I'm sick with this," said the old woman. She looked at me and her face was wet. She sobbed, swallowing her words. "My oldest granddaughter....And now Elsa is in and out of the hospital. We are all sick, sick. I don't know how we will ever recover."

"It's too terrible to contemplate," I said. "I'm so sorry." I didn't know what to say. I am helpless at dealing with the grief of others and to this failing was added the insult that I had prejudged the family and determined that they were all lunatics and manic-depressives.

I went out and walked the narrow, curving streets of the city, as tangled and confusing as those of any European ghetto. The houses pressed up against the one-way *calles* and trapped the stultifying heat of Cuban June. Up the block, two old crones were sitting on a stoop. They had a few wrinkled mangos piled into a pyramid on the sidewalk. The women waved me to a stop and one reached up to shake my hand. She had no teeth, and, when we shook hands, she held on fast and reached up with the other hand to tug on my fingers, one by one. It was a sort of quick finger massage that felt as if she was trying to pull imaginary rings from my digits.

"She can see, she can see," said the second of these ageless women, cackling. "She's my mother," she said, but their great age had rendered the years between them insignificant.

Mom was still holding onto one of my fingers. "Give me two pesos," she said. Much to her shock, I did. Much to my embarrassment, she embraced my thigh with both arms and rested her forehead on my knee. I squirmed.

"What do you see for him, eh?" asked the daughter. "Does he have good things in store down the road?"

"Yeah, yeah," said Mom, clinging tight.

She showed no signs of releasing me from her hug of gratitude. Nor did she have anything else to say about what she had seen while pulling on my fingers. I wriggled my leg in hopes that this would inspire her to free me.

"She lives around the corner," said the daughter. "Drop by whenever you want. *She can see.*"

Finally, I was released. It was a most abstract fortune-telling. The woman had looked into my future without any interest in telling me what she saw there.

In Camagüey, I couldn't shake my feelings of uselessness. Although I had no plan, I felt that things were somehow not going as planned. I told myself I needed to get out of the city and ride out and explore the countryside, but I couldn't summon up any motivation. I wallowed in the gloomy climate of Elsa's home.

One morning, I woke to a deafening churn of helicopter blades moving low and loud over the rooftops of the city. Out on the patio, cranked as loud as the street music that booms out of jeeps on New York weekends, I heard a chaos of televisions in the neighboring houses. Snippets of defiant bombastic speech mingled with the cheers of a huge crowd. My first thought was that the long-feared American invasion had begun. Cubans, especially in the countryside, often asked when the US was likely to begin its inevitable military assault on Cuba. I replied that I thought such a thing unlikely; I suggested that Cubans watched too much television. Now, I wasn't so sure. Another chopper beat past, bending the branches of a garden sapling and shivering the leaves of the neighbor's mango tree. I hurried to pull on my trousers.

Out in the street, I heard more televisions blasting. There was a strange auditory phenomenon. Seconds after hearing a shout or cry on television, the same sound echoed out in delay, as if all the distant televisions of the city were reverberating together. I peered through a window and realized what was happening. It was Camagüey's turn to hold a rally demanding the return of Elián González. The helicopters were circling to capture aerial shots for the live television broadcast, and the faraway echo was the actual event, booming out of distant, enormous loudspeakers.

These enormous rallies had become a torment for me and the other viewers of El rey del ganado as one provincial capital after another mounted its mammoth demonstration. Officially, the protests were spontaneous manifestations of public support, but they took the form of carefully scheduled and meticulously orchestrated pageants presenting three essential elements to the public: fiery speeches castigating American policy, the kidnappers of Miami, and the Cuban Adjustment Act; outpourings of emotion and pleas for the safe return of the child, Elián, from mothers or tiny, teary schoolmates; and interstitial entertainments, ranging from *decimistas* rhyming about the standoff to choirs of schoolgirls and *salsa* or jazz combos. All demonstrations were broadcast live and then replayed in near-entirety on the evening news, pushing the start of the soap opera deep into the night.

I followed my ears to the demonstration, walking through empty streets lined with parked *guaguas*. The battered buses had brought demonstrators from every corner of the province. Nearing the zoological gardens, I fought a tide of people streaming out of the rally, each with a tiny paper flag. A grand lawn was transformed into an ocean of Cubans standing in the brutal sun, facing a stage so distant that the people singing and dancing on it looked like red-white-and-blue ants. The helicopters had gone and the mass of humanity was fraying at the edges, but it was an awesome display of propaganda. The speeches droned on and on. Nobody seemed to be paying any attention, although there were identical automated flurries of audience participation at the end of every speech.

"Fatherland or death," screamed a minuscule figure at the distant podium.

"WE SHALL TRIUMPH!" responded the masses, or at least some of those in the front.

"¡Viva Fidel!"

"¡VIVA!"

"Down with the Cuban Adjustment Act!"

"DOWN WITH IT!"

Having arrived by bus directly from their *centros de trabajo,* most demonstrators were technically at work; the many Elián rallies across the nation must have taken a heavy toll on productivity. Attendance, like so much of the people's cooperation in the ongoing revolution, was a semi-voluntary civic duty. Non-participation was frowned upon by bosses and neighborhood-watch-group leaders, and the frowns were noted down and compiled into an implicit accounting of revolutionary fervor. Unless you had a much better reason than usual for not going to work, you were expected to show up at the right time and pile onto the bus with your colleagues.

As soon as they had been counted, and filmed by the helicopters, many people took advantage of the free transportation to enjoy a day in the city. I joined the streams of people flowing toward the center of town. Like the Cubans, I had done the required and put in a brief appearance.

Back on the television at Elsa's, the masterful multicamera production continued uninterrupted, looking just as urgent and crowded as it had before. Again and again, the live editor cut to sweeping aerials from overhead helicopter shots, demonstrating the magnitude and density of the crowd. But the sound of rotor blades was no longer heard whirring above the house. The crowd scenes had been filmed earlier in the day, just after the buses unloaded.

I hung the hammock in the courtyard and lounged, reading Lydia Cabrera's *El Monte*, which I had stumbled on in a Camagüey used bookstore. It is the seminal work on *Palo*. In it, Cabrera, through a compilation of oral histories, describes a fascinating supernatural world so clogged with spirits that "we rub elbows with the dead and the saints every minute of the day." In the view of her myriad informants, every tree and plant is a being with a soul, and the *monte* contains everything necessary for both the preservation of health and the working of evil. Every possible calamity has its antidote or prophylactic in some stick, herb, or weed. In search of a cure for my Cuban malaise, I decided to head for the wilderness.

Veinte

Lords of the ceiba

One of the last patches of forest left of the vast jungle that once was Camagüey is a remnant near the village of Najasa, a few hours bicycle ride southeast of the city. It is famous among birders as the only reliable place to see one of Cuba's rarest birds, a rather drab brown and white flycatcher called the giant kingbird. According to a Hornbuckle trip report posted on the Internet, an ornithologist named Pedro Regalado lived there. With luck, the kingbird might be seen right in his backyard. Another Internet report, posted by a birder whose first language was not English, described Pedro as "a bit of a weird guy, in the positive way." Leaving my enormous mound of luggage at Elsa's house, I stuffed the hammock and a pair of socks into a saddlebag with my birding gear, and rode out to find him.

After two hours of pedaling on a road entirely devoid of traffic, I neared Najasa, a tiny Alamar built in the fields, presumably as some sort of rural resettlement scheme. A roadside stand at the crossroads sold sandwiches of the kind common throughout the country; gritty rolls smeared with ketchup or "pasta," a thin paste made from flour, water, and salt, sometimes with the vaguest suggestion of mashed vegetable. The consumption of one of these nutrition-free snacks was to my astonishment supposed to sustain a grown man through an entire morning of machete-wielding in the canefields.

Famished, I ordered an "embutido" sandwich, as I had already experienced pasta sandwiches and "pan con mayonesa," bread with mayonnaise, and I imagined nothing could be worse. "Embutido" means stuffing or, with any luck, sausage, but the very first bite tasted like dirt. Surreptitiously, I lifted the top half of the roll. The filling was a sprinkling of reddish clay chunks like misshapen ball bearings. I rolled one between my thumb and forefinger and could find nothing to dispel my impression that I was eating a soil sandwich. I popped the hard little ball in my mouth, for a taste unadulterated by the stale bread. The "embutido" tasted acrid and muddy.

Imagining that I was the victim of a cruel hoax, I looked up at the woman in her rickety wooden booth to see if she was laughing. But she was smiling and friendly. I almost expected her to ask me how I was enjoying my breakfast, or whether I wanted another. This was simply what the Cuban worker could afford, the only sort of meal possible on a one-peso budget in post-Soviet Cuba, a sandwich that was neither animal nor vegetable, and was therefore, by process of elimination, mineral.

"Do you know Pedro Regalado, the ornithologist?" I asked.

"I don't think so, but any ornithologist must be at the nature preserve at La Belem. Just keep going down the road."

The road turned to dirt the color of my sandwich, then muddied as it began to rain. Clods of earth clogged the brake pads under the fenders and the tires sent up little spurts of dirty water. Ahead, the low, forested hills of the Sierra de Najasa appeared. The fields here held remnant trees, as if they had been more recently and less completely cleared. They had dense hedgerows and stands of scrub at their edges. At least one majestic ceiba, which Lydia Cabrera called the "house of God tree," was in almost every pasture.

At night, Cabrera writes in *El Monte*, such trees are said to pull up their roots and go walking across the land to meet with their neighboring ceibas and gossip. The ceiba is recognized as a saint, the *orisha Iroko*, and as the tree of the Virgin Mary. In this syncretic legend, Mary fled to a ceiba carrying the baby Jesus, and the tree opened itself and made a hole for them to hide in. For protection, the tree covered itself with fearsome thorns, closed up the hole, and ridiculed their pursuers. In even earlier times, during the Great Flood, the ceiba was the only tree "respected by the waters," and mankind saved itself by climbing to the upper branches of this leafy Noah's ark. "No la fulmina el rayo," notes Cabrera, lightning does not strike the ceiba, nor can the most fearsome hurricane take it down.

Ceibas indubitably have what it takes to be named the holiest of trees. Literal kings of the jungle, they tower into the sky. Their canopy blocks out the sun, and the trunks of the largest specimens are so massive that a herd of cattle seeking shade can disappear behind the trunk. Circumnavigating one is like walking around the outside of a house, but it is not only their size that makes them revered. The trunks of ceibas are studded with an awesome array of fist-sized thorns, not narrow and fragile like the spines of a cactus, but thick, sharpened pyramids of solid wood, as if of a gigantic rose.

A sodden farmer walking with his donkey pointed out Pedro's house and I pushed the bike up the muddy track to the door.

"Buenas, buenas," I called out as I stepped onto the porch. A man that had to be Pedro answered the door. He had a rumpled academic look I knew well from my father, and bright, slightly bulging eyes.

"Hello," he said. "Come on in and get out of the rain. Put the bike up here on the porch. Do you have a lock for it?"

"All the way out here?" Pedro's was one of an odd, isolated row of three houses that seemed to have landed at random in the midst of the wilderness.

"Sadly, it's just as bad; you better lock it."

Within moments, I was sitting in Pedro's living room beside a wall of bird books, changing out of my sodden socks and trying not to drench his couch.

"So what do you need to see?"

"The kingbird, obviously, and the crow." Najasa is also one of the only places to see the Cuban palm crow, restricted to only two small patches on Cuba.

Pedro smiled and made a dismissive gesture with his hand. "Those are guaranteed. If it stops raining, we'll go out this afternoon and see them both. What else?"

"Whatever else there is."

"There are many. I believe this is one of the best places in all of Cuba for birds," said Pedro. "I discovered this site. But the bird tours always come here as an afterthought. Because the ornithologists who lead them come from Havana, and the Zapata Swamp is much closer."

Outside, a torrential thunderstorm had begun. Through the roof, it sounded as if the sky was tearing apart.

"My wife will make us some lunch," said Pedro. "Are you hungry?"

"I'm pretty hungry. In Najasa, I ate the strangest thing at the roadside stand. An *embutido* sandwich. What is that?"

"Oh, no, you can't eat that."

"So I discovered, but what *is embutido?*"

"Honestly, I don't even know what that is supposed to be," said Pedro, getting down a cardboard box of bird specimens from the bookshelf. He handed me a brown sheath of feathers, as light and sad and dead as the leftover cardboard tube at the core of a roll of toilet paper. At one end, a beak jutted out in the unnatural stretch of avian *rigor mortis.* "That's a giant kingbird, the bird I have spent almost all my time studying for the last two years."

I rotated the taxidermist's work between my fingers. "I wouldn't be able to distinguish this from a loggerhead," I said. The loggerhead kingbird is a common forest bird throughout much of the Caribbean. Like the giant, it is dull-brownish gray above and a dusty white below. I opened Raffaele's *Birds of the West Indies* to the kingbird plate. It showed a giant kingbird with a massive, canoe-shaped bill fully twice the heft of the one on the bird I was holding.

"It's really too bad. There are so many avoidable mistakes in that book," said Pedro. "The bill really isn't necessarily any larger than on the loggerhead."

"Nobody consulted you?"

"My relationship with some ornithologists in Havana is not so good. One of the best known of them, I don't know, he seems to have a problem with me."

"But surely you are the foremost expert on this bird," I said.

"Probably. Thank you. Look, I am from Havana, I grew up in the city. I'm a city boy. But I studied to be an ornithologist. How can you be an ornithologist in Havana? The birds aren't in Havana. So I left, to live in *el monte.* Nobody else does that. They all want to stay near the university, so they might be invited to the international conferences. It's how you advance your career here, how you get your papers published, not by staying in the field and actually doing the work."

"But they must come out into the field," I said.

"Sure, some of them I see once, maybe twice a year. They show up with a foreign group for a day or an afternoon, with people paying big dollars to come birding in Cuba, and they say: 'Okay, Pedro, where can we take these people to see the giant kingbird today?' They pass through." Switching to English, he said: "I call them the city birdwatchers."

Pedro took down a book I had never seen before, with an abraded nineteenth-century binding that had somehow survived some hundred years in the tropics.

"The second edition of Gundlach," he said.

Juan Gundlach was the John James Audubon of Cuba, a German amateur scientist who spent fifty years observing and cataloguing the island's birds. I paged through the book in awe. He had made countless difficult trips into every corner of the island in an era when much of Cuba was still a tangled wilderness, and he had seen birds that had become extinct even before they could be photographed, like the Cuban macaw, of which he wrote: "In 1850, it was almost common in the northern portion of the Zapata Swamp, but little by little they have withdrawn into the heart of the swamp, so that in later years I have not encountered any more specimens."

"I had one birder who offered me hundreds of dollars for the book," said Pedro, "but no matter how much necessity there is, I could never sell it."

The torrents of rain finally cleared off. Outside, the sky was still covered with a ceiling of gray cloud, but the air was clean and clear. Bright droplets of water fell from the power lines and the painfully green trees. We rode our matching Flying Pigeons on a muddy track through the fields, binoculars slung over our shoulders. On the antique cycles, riding through the wet wilderness, we looked like a pair of crazed Victorian naturalists.

"I used to ride to Camagüey and back in the same day," said Pedro, calling over his shoulder, "but I'm a little too old for that now." But it was all I could do to keep up with him. Thankfully, Pedro soon stopped at a gate by a trail leading into scrubby jungle.

"Look at the ceibas," said Pedro. "You can tell if they grew up by themselves in a cleared field or if they were part of a complete forest."

"I'm not sure I follow," I said.

Pedro pointed into the field behind us, where a herd of black and white cattle were munching beneath a monster tree. "That tree grew up alone," said Pedro. "That is why it is so round, with branches and leaves going out in every direction." The ceiba had the classic, archetypal silhouette of a child's drawing of a tree: a broad trunk topped by a circle.

"Now, look at that one," said Pedro, pointing at another ceiba in front of us. The trunk rose high up above the ground without branching in the least, before suddenly spreading out at the very top into a broad green mat, like a gigantic parasol mushroom. It was an entirely different shape from the tree behind us. "Even though now it is the only tree remaining, you can see that this one grew up inside a primary forest. Fifty or sixty years ago, this would have been a diverse tropical forest, with as many as a hundred species of tree per hectare. This ceiba concentrated all its effort on getting up to the sunlight, then it spread out, fighting for area at the surface of the canopy."

"Why is it that when these forests were cut, only the ceibas were left standing?"

"Because they look like baobab trees, which were sacred to the Africans," said Pedro. "The country people thought it was bad luck to cut them down." He might have been quoting from Cabrera, writing fifty years earlier. Although her oldest informants, former slaves quite possibly old enough to have been born in Africa, agreed that the ceiba "is not the legitimate Iroko," the tree reminded them of the baobab, and they consecrated it with the African name for that immense tree, "venerated throughout the coast of Guinea."

Pedro opened a gate and we wheeled our cycles along a track marking the border between field and forest. "One big difference between the loggerhead and the giant," said Pedro in a whisper, "is that the loggerhead is really a forest bird, whereas the giant likes the edge habitat, places like this, where it's open. We'll leave our bikes here, but we have to keep an eye out."

We made sure the bicycles were out of sight of the road and leaned them up against a tree. I thought Pedro was rather paranoid about theft until he said he had already had a bicycle stolen while out in the woods doing research. "I can't afford a lock," he said, "so I used to cover the bicycle with brush to camouflage it. But someone must have been watching where I was going and planned the theft. This one is my daughter's; if I lose it, I'll scarcely be able to continue my work."

Suddenly, a loud, three-syllable whistle rang through the forest.

"That's it," said Pedro. His face lit up with excitement. "Do you hear it?"

Pedro pointed through a hole in the hedgerow at the magnificent ceiba, alone and huge in the adjacent field. "On the top right," he said. Sitting on a high branch and surveying its domain, the kingbird looked to me like a larger, browner version of the common, garden-variety eastern kingbird. It was fluffy and a bit bedraggled from the rain. Pedro, I realized, was if anything more excited to see it than I was. For him, the bird was an old friend, but it had lost none of its allure. He knew the precise size of its territory, its habits and songs. Pedro was smiling for almost the first time since I had arrived. He scrambled to pull a battered cassette deck from his backpack.

"We'll bring it in," he said.

"Do you think playing tape disturbs the birds?"

"No. I've established dozens of kingbird territories around here, always by playing tapes. The birds get agitated, but it doesn't seem to do any harm. They apparently guard an area between one and two *caballerías*, which is to say between thirteen and twenty-eight hectares (a *caballería* equals approximately thirty-three acres), so they're huge territories. I theorize that they have a big home range, but then a smaller core part that they defend and protect; I can't be completely sure. It would be much better if I could work with colored bands. Still, I've been able to distinguish the exact extent of many territories because the birds will respond to a tape, but always stop when they reach the edge of their established territory." Pedro cued up the tape and pressed play. The kingbird screeched and tore down out of the ceiba to land in the foliage overhead. It looked about nervously and began to call down at us.

"Not one writer since Gundlach has properly described the call," said Pedro. "Even in Raffaele, the description is of an alternate call of the loggerhead kingbird. Probably because the recording they have at Cornell is wrong. I only found out a couple of years ago when a birder brought a cassette with him of the birds of Cuba. It was published by Cornell, but the call labeled for the giant kingbird is actually the territorial call of the loggerhead. Look, the bird will now go check the perimeter." The kingbird indeed took off in the direction we had come, flying straight out to the edge of the road to perch on a utility wire. "He won't cross," said Pedro. "His particular territory ends right there at the edge of the field."

We grabbed the bikes and wheeled them rapidly back through the mud. The bird had staked out its turf and was checking the edge for intruders. The ceiba in the middle of the field was the kingbird's castle, and the invisible edge of its territory, known only to the bird and Pedro, was uninfringeable. "It always, always nests in a ceiba," said Pedro. "Even if it can only find a ceiba like this one, stranded outside the forest, it will nest there and then fly to the forest edges to feed."

In the pasture to our left, Pedro heard palm crows calling. The sound they made was an unhappy cawing, drawn out and nasal, like a whining parody of an American crow. It was unlike the bizarre chatter of the much more common Cuban crow, which makes an array of watery-sounding clicking tones and, as Raffaele puts it, "gobbling, reminiscent of a turkey."

Far away, at the end of the huge pasture, a small party of the black birds was marching across the cow-munched grassy stubble. Ever-mindful of theft, we pushed our cycles into the field, startling some cattle that loped out of our path at an angle, moving just far enough away to determine, as cows will, that we were not walking toward them with intent. The crows cavorted, leaping up on the *aroma* bushes. Despite their plaintive calling, which suggested a profound misery, they seemed to be rejoicing.

For the non-birder, the joys of seeing the world's smallest humming-bird, or a garish and raucous parrot, are easier to understand than the ap-peal of picking one's way through a wet field clogged with cow pies and thorny branches in order to see a crow. The desire to see and identify a new species, no matter how plain its appearance or boring its habits, is what separates birders from people who simply enjoy walking about in na-ture and seeing what they can find. This need to conquer the new is what makes birding a disease.

I hurried toward the back of the field, keeping the trunk of the ceiba that had grown up alone between me and the birds, in hopes that they wouldn't spook. We leaned our bicycles up against the mammoth trunk, failing, as Lydia Cabrera says is appropriate, to excuse ourselves to the tree. I read later that we should have first spoken to it and said, "With your permission, I am going to walk in your shade." Still, despite the insult, the tree was affording us some protection, since any potential thief would now need to traverse two hundred meters of open field to get at our bikes. We sneaked closer to the crows. A platoon of them was striding across the denuded grass in exploded formation, spread out like commandos, moving from one bit of cover to another.

"That right there is how you know them," said Pedro. "They walk just like us, on two feet." A couple of the nearer birds bolted to the crown of a distant royal palm to mewl and flop about among the loose fronds. We stopped so that the rest of the squadron would not scatter.

"They march around and turn over lumps of dung, looking for some kind of insect in there," said Pedro. "But if you were to see a regular Cuban crow, as opposed to a palm crow, on the ground, you'd realize it doesn't really even know how to walk. In the first place, you almost never see it on the ground, but if you were to, you'd note that it only hops."

On the top of a bush, one bird began to wag its tail with a strange and jerky mechanical motion that I'd never seen in another North American species of crow. "Tail-wagging behavior," said Pedro in English. "This is another example of what I have been talking about. Arturo Kirkconnell, even though he is my good friend, I have to say he is a city birdwatcher. He co-authored a paper that said that this palm crow does not wag its tail. When I read that, I was very surprised. You don't see it every day, but anyone who has spent time with the species in the field would know that, just like the Hispaniolan palm crow, this one wags its tail when it is agitated. I said to him, 'Arturo, I could have told you.'"

We left the crows wagging and cawing as we picked our way around the cowpats and out of the field. Pedro was stubborn, uncompromising, and intense. It was easy to imagine how he had become alienated from the elite biologists of Havana. Although his science was unimpeachable and he had made great sacrifices to pursue his lifelong study of Cuba's birds, he did so on his terms. I was sure that, back in Havana, they called him eccentric and strange and probably worse. Pedro's disdain for the political minefields of academia was proven by his absence, and his reward was a kind of oblivion. Without a telephone or car or computer, Pedro's only connection to the outside world was a post-office box three hours away by bicycle in Camagüey city. His best friends and companions were the birds he studied.

"My best contacts are outside the country," he told me when we were back in his living room. "That makes some people jealous. I have many published and also still unpublished scientific studies, but mostly, it is only possible for me to publish in outside journals. For instance, I've documented the first record ever of the peregrine falcon breeding in Cuba. But it is difficult just to survive."

The house was tiny. Pedro's "study" doubled as his daughter's bedroom. In her mid-twenties and pregnant, she lived at home because there was no housing available for her and her husband. He also lived with his parents, and they only saw each other on weekends.

Pedro's existence depended on the rare visits of foreign birders, to whom he sometimes sold his exquisite illustrations of Cuba's birdlife. He showed me a half-completed painting of a Cuban trogon. "I'm trying to complete my own field guide to the birds of Cuba, but I end up painting the same birds over and over again, particularly the spectacular species like this one, because I have to sell the drawings to survive. This trogon will take a week to ten days of my spare time and I can sell it and we live on that, but it takes up valuable hours when I could be working on the plates for the book." It was too gloomy to think that for lack of a scanner and computer, Pedro had to repeat his work over and over again. I changed the subject.

"What do you think about the ivory-billed woodpecker?" I asked. "I heard in Havana that there's another scientific expedition to search for it on Pico Turquiño."

"I heard about that," said Pedro. "I don't have high hopes. Pico Turquiño is in the south. The reason they're looking there is that there is good habitat, large chunks of unspoiled forest, but I think that area was never part of the original range of the woodpecker. Where I saw it was in the north, nowhere near the Sierra Madre."

"What?" I said. I lurched forward from the couch and almost fell on the floor. "You saw the ivory-billed woodpecker?"

"Only once."

"That doesn't matter. There are only a handful of people alive who've seen it. Where was it? When was it?"

"In the mid-Eighties. I was stationed in the Oriente for many years as a conservation officer. That was where I did all of my work before I came here. The bird was in the area of Moa. Not far from where they found it later."

A sighting of the ivory-billed woodpecker is the ultimate fantasy of any North American birder. A huge and spectacular species that once roamed the swampy bottomland forests of the American South from Florida all the way across the top of the Gulf of Mexico and deep into Texas, the black, white, and red bird has not been conclusively identified on US soil since the Second World War. Although it is enormous and would be conspicuous both by its trumpet-like whinnying call and the plentiful scars of boring and bark-peeling which it inflicts on trees, its evident absence is unacceptable to the birder psyche. The dream that the ivory-bill still persists somewhere in the deepest, dankest Southern bayous has never been extinguished by scientific reports of its definitive disappearance; as recently as 2005, the ornithological establishment was bitterly divided by controversy in the wake of an alleged sighting in eastern Arkansas.

The ivory-bill is perhaps the only bird that made its home exclusively in both Cuba and the United States, but this fact was long ago obscured by the politics of the Cold War. The revolution occurred just before the 1960s flowering of environmental consciousness. By 1962 and the publication of Rachel Carson's *Silent Spring*, the book that first woke up America to the threat of species extinction and environmental destruction, Cuba was our worst enemy in the hemisphere. The great chill in relations froze the flow of scientific information. If anyone thought about it at all, it was downright unpatriotic to imagine that Cuban revolutionary society could harbor ivory-bills, those majestic American woodpeckers that we had allowed to fade into oblivion in our own country. As for the Cuban side, if people were seeing the bird in the forests of the Oriente, they weren't crowing about it.

In 1986, the birding world was rocked by reports of ivory-billed woodpeckers seen in montane forest near the town of Moa in one of the most remote areas of the Oriente. It was the height of the Reagan era, as bad a time as any in US-Cuban relations. Castro was being vilified daily for his support of the Nicaraguan Sandinistas and Salvadoran FMLN, and any hopes that the détente during Jimmy Carter's presidency could fundamentally change relations between the two countries had long since faded. Nevertheless, in February 1985, Lester Short, a woodpecker expert from the Museum of Natural History in New York, managed to mount an international expedition to search the Ojito de Agua area, site of the last prerevolution sightings of the bird. In the Cuban report of the expedition, which Pedro showed me on his kitchen table, Girardo Alayón and Alberto Estrada referred to "fresh evidence of feeding activity in the surroundings of the forest ranger's house, [although] the bird was neither heard nor seen."* Another expedition that fall proved fruitless, but Alayon led a third Cuban expedition in 1986 that conclusively identified a female near the headwaters of the Yanei River at 9:11 on the morning of March 16. The next year, Short returned and confirmed the sighting for any Americans who might have been skeptical of Cuban science.

"My name doesn't appear anywhere in the records of the expedition,"

---

* Girardo Alayon and Alberto R. Estrada, *Proyecto sobre investigación y conservación del Carpintero Real*, Empresa Nacional para la proteccion de la Flora y la Fauna.

said Pedro. "Although my boss told them that I should be a part of it and obviously I was the person responsible for endangered species in the entire area. But they didn't even invite me to join."

"Why not?" I wanted to hear the story although the memory had brought a sour look to Pedro's face.

"I think it was that same person from Havana," he said, "some kind of jealousy, I don't know. I mean, they weren't even ornithologists. I could have been very useful. Alayon was a specialist in spiders and Estrada studied reptiles, they were guys I didn't know, from the university. All I know is that I met Alayon later and asked why I wasn't included. You know what he said? 'Look, I'm really sorry, but I didn't know you. I had heard you were a difficult guy to work with.'"

"So when did you see the woodpecker?"

"It was some time the year before they came."

"Don't you know the date? That seems important."

"I'll check," said Pedro. He went into the study-bedroom while I read Gundlach's account of the ivory-bill. "Every year," he wrote toward the end of his career, "the numbers of this beautiful species diminish, thanks on the one hand to the destruction of the large forests and on the other to the persecution it suffers from hunters, who kill it without making any good use of it afterwards."

"November 23, 1984," said Pedro, handing me an index card on which he had noted the date of his unique sighting. "I had always asked around a little bit to see if the forest rangers or the woodsmen remembered seeing an enormous woodpecker. I remember one guy, for some reason I remember his name, Santiago Poll, he told me in 1979 that in an area called Palmar Churroso, at the headwaters of the Rio Miguel, he used to see the bird when he was out with his father, thirty years earlier. He said that the story told by the black people there—he was a black guy—was that what they called 'the bird with the ivory bill' kept the *llave de los tesoros de la vida y de la muerte* [the key to the treasures of life and death] in its nest. So when they found a nest, they would brick the bird in, leaving just a tiny hole for it to throw the *llavecito* down to them. Of course, the birds just died.

"Anyway, in the early Eighties, a lumberjack named Bernardo Campos went to a forest ranger in Moa and told him that he had seen a huge woodpecker, a bird he remembered from when he was a small child. The forest ranger, I can't remember his name, but he didn't believe the story. Even so, when he saw me, he mentioned it to me. I insisted we go immediately to Moa. We found Campos. He had no reason to lie, and the story convinced me. As soon as I could arrange the time, I went out with Bernardo and searched the area. We didn't see anything, but we found signs and workings on some trees.

"I couldn't just go up there non-stop day after day; I was the conservation specialist for the whole north of the Oriente, but I began a second series of visits as soon as I could. One day, I had just arrived at the woodcutters' camp at La Breña when Bernardo Campos came hurrying in. 'Quick, quick,' he said. 'I just saw them this minute, I was thinking of you.' He was a really strong guy, but he was in his fifties and couldn't run well. I took off running up the hill where he pointed, and what I saw, I'll never forget. Over the ridge, there was a sort of a dip, or a valley, covered in huge trees, and the pair of woodpeckers flew from my right across to my left and down into the valley. It was one of the most spectacular sights I've ever seen.

"I was all alone. By the time Bernardo got to the top of the hill, the birds were gone. So he couldn't corroborate the sighting. He reached me, huffing and puffing, and was as excited as I was, and he asked, 'Did you see them?' And he was so happy that I had."

"Surely the fact that he had just seen them validates the sighting," I said.

"Yes, but still, nobody was with me, and remember: we're talking about a bird that nobody had reported in decades. It was to the point where I was scared to really say anything about it."

"So you didn't tell anyone? How could you not tell anybody?"

"I did tell my boss, and a few of the forest rangers, but before really going public I felt that more work was necessary. I wanted first to learn more. But it wasn't long afterward that I was told about the expedition from Havana. I'm convinced that they'd heard something about it."

"So obviously you didn't tell the delegation when they arrived."

"They had excluded me, snubbed me, in an obvious way. The whole thing disgusted me. I don't think I even got to meet with them before they went to set up in the forest. It's true that I didn't say a word, or give them any information. *Me amargué.* I became embittered. I just about abandoned the ivory-bill at that point. It was soon afterward that I came here to Najasa to work with the giant kingbird."

I spent a miserable night on the couch, gnashing my teeth and slapping at armies of mosquitos. In the interests of traveling light, I had left the mosquito net in Camagüey, thereby guaranteeing that the vampiric insects would emerge in force as soon as night fell. Although Pedro had put the family's oscillating fan in the living room to blow the mosquitos away, there was a power outage within minutes of everyone going to bed. A few minutes later, the current returned, but the fan mysteriously failed to start back up. I pulled myself out of the sagging crater made in the flimsy couch by my ample frame and stumbled across the room. Swatting at my shins and cursing, I punched at the cheap plastic buttons of the fan to no avail. It was impossible to sleep. Finally, as dawn approached, my curses—or an especially loud slap—woke Pedro, who came out into the kitchen in the darkness and wordlessly reset the fan.

In the morning, we birded the refuge of La Belem, pushing the bicycles through the mud of unrideable trails, up hills, through the woods, past abandoned, overgrown orchards. It was exhausting work pushing the iron bikes just as the sun was heating up the day. Pedro remained fearful of bike theft, although we seemed to me to be in a remote wilderness. His tires were as bald as pool balls, but replacing them was an insurmountable expense at the moment. Only the merest stroke of bad luck separated Pedro from disaster.

Flocks of Cuban parakeets chattered overhead and we heard several more giant kingbirds calling. Pedro flushed another Cuban specialty, the bare-legged owl, from a royal palm riddled with nesting holes. As we were making our way out of the reserve, Pedro heard a loggerhead kingbird calling deep in the woods. His face lit up. "I'm going to prove something to you now," he said, pulling the cassette player and a tape from his backpack. "This is the 'giant kingbird' tape from the Cornell Laboratory."

Pedro carefully cued the tape up at low volume, the tiny speaker pressed to his ear. Then he turned it up and pressed play. "Giant kingbird," said an introductory voice in English. The four syllables were invested with gravity and precision. The voice was that of the documentary films of the 1950s in which unflappable, crew-cut scientists wearing white lab coats present absolute truths. It was a voice impossible to disbelieve, the voice of objectivity and knowledge. A few loud and flycatcherish squeaks followed, then a burst of song much like that described in Raffaele as "a chatter resembling that of Loggerhead kingbird but louder, longer, deeper and a bit harsher."

Inside the forest, a bird answered, note for note. Outraged and urgent, it flew closer, not waiting for Pedro to rewind the tape. The chattering grew louder. Now it was coming from somewhere over our heads, near the treetops. Pedro played the call again. The bird dive-bombed us in a low arc, crossing over the track to an exposed branch behind us.

"Loggerhead," said Pedro. He pointed out the bird's most distinguishing feature, the wedge-shaped crest for which it is named. In the bird's agitation, this feature was especially evident. (In Puerto Rico, the bird is called *clérigo*, cleric, because it appears to wear a monk's cowl.)

"I believed you before," I said.

"Still, that's not the same as seeing it for yourself. It's still nice for me to be able to offer the proof," said Pedro.

I suppressed a petty grin thinking of the many birders who, with the aid of the same tape, might have found rare "giant kingbirds" in almost any patch of Cuban woodland, quickly adding to their lists and hurrying on to the next sighting, none the wiser.

Veintiuno

Bayamo botanicals

The road south to Bayamo was as flat as the Zapata Swamp. Ranch-land filled with transient rainy-season ponds stretched in all direc-tions. On either side were oceans of brilliant green sugar cane and seas of rice. Glossy ibises leapfrogged over one another, cadging insects in the cow pastures and flapping in formation across a horizon of yellow bil-lowing grass. The wind was stiff and solid out of the east, and the slightest deviation of the road from its course due south turned the ride into an agony of upwind pedaling. Beside the road, a row of vast white cement letters, in a font I recognized from the *Space Invaders* video game, bade me a farewell from Las Tunas. A mere hundred meters later, as a welcome to the province of Granma, I had my first flat tire of the day. It was the only puncture of the entire trip for which I found a convincing cause other than rubber failure. After suffering all morning from terrible gut pain in this treeless landscape of endless unobstructed vistas, I had squatted behind the *WELCOME TO GRANMA* billboard, using the cover it afforded to make a violent, explosive movement. In my urgency to wheel the bicycle off the road, I had run over a nail.

Twenty kilometers shy of Bayamo, the massive bladed ridge of the Sierra Maestra began to appear at the edge of perception, shimmering like a mirage well above the horizon. The hazy and indistinct blue of these distant mountains contrasted not at all with the sky; the effect was like a tentative first sighting of land from a ship at sea. As I pedaled on, the peaks gained form and contour until they loomed over the marshes.

Granma province is named for the boat that brought Fidel and his guerillas out of Mexican exile to a clandestine landing on its shores in 1956. Once beached, they headed into the hills, and it was in these impenetrable and foreboding mountains south of Bayamo that they nurtured their revolutionary movement. As the mountains loomed ever closer and I pedaled into the outskirts of Bayamo, I got another flat.

I had been trying for weeks to apply basic stress-management techniques to the incessant plague of punctures from which I suffered daily. I took slow, deep breaths and drank from my water bottles as if enjoying a routine rest stop. Only then would I set to the laborious task of removing the axel nuts with flimsy Chinese wrenches and straining my fingers to pull the tire out from the deep and over-engineered steel trench that was the wheel. But on this occasion, I could not contain my frustration. I had eaten only a few roadside mangos that day and was only a handful of kilometers away from family lodging and food in Bayamo. Before flatting, I had already mentally cracked open the first celebratory cold beer of the evening. If I changed this flat, I'd have to replace it with a third stringer of an inner tube, one I thought even more unreliable than the others; if that flatted, I'd have to walk into town. I looked around. A dirt lane off the main road led to a cluster of houses just large enough to support a flat-fixing operation. I decided to seek professional help.

Pushing El Rey del Ganado along the path, I called out like a street vendor to each ramshackle cinderblock house in this dismal exurb. "Hello, hello, does anyone around here fix flats?" A man emerged and indicated a yard, where two drunks were lying in the dust under a tree. They had a bottle perched on a stump.

"*Buenas tardes.* You guys fix flats?"

One of the men struggled to sit up. He gave me a bleary stare. "You have a flat?" he asked.

No, I was just checking, for future reference. "Yes," I said, "in fact, I have two."

The sitting man thumped the prostrate man in the ear with the back of his hand. "There's a foreign guy here, with a bicycle and everything. He has a flat."

The second man roused himself out of his stupor and sat up. "Hola," he said, "we fix flats." He delivered this news with surprised enthusiasm, as if marveling at the miraculous and providential conspiracy of forces that had brought us together.

"So I was told," I said.

"You going to Bayamo?"

"That's right."

"You know it?"

"I've never been there before."

"You're almost there. It's not far to go."

"I'll get there much faster if we can fix my flat."

"We can do that for you," said the first man.

"Great."

"How come you speak so much Spanish?"

"It's so much easier to communicate with the people I meet that way," I said.

The first man got to his feet and, perhaps looking around for support, seized on the bicycle handlebars with an aggressive lurch. "This way," he said, tugging hard on the handlebars in a direction exactly perpendicular to the wheel. I tugged back. "I got it, I got," he said. "We'll take care of it." The second man dusted himself off and grabbed the bottle. I held the bicycle seat upright as we jolted sideways, trying to prevent the whole overloaded contraption from falling over and crushing a saddlebag. My plastic sack of sticky mangos wriggled free and rolled off the back rack and dragged in the dust. A mobile tug-of-war, we made our way between two houses to a low shack in a backyard and leaned the bicycle up against a grease-stained stump that served as an anvil.

"You have a wrench?" asked the second man. "I'll get that wheel off for you."

"I'll take care of it," I said. "You can repair this, meanwhile." I unpacked the flat tube from earlier in the day and gave it to him. He went into the shack, propping open the corrugated tin door to let some light in. A burst of blue sparks and a sizzling, electrical sound followed, as if someone was welding, followed again by silence. I peered into the shack, fully expecting to see an electrocuted corpse laid out on the dirt floor. "You okay?" I asked.

"Yeah, no problem. I'm just preheating the iron." Two wires, unencumbered by insulation, as bare as a newborn babe, led into the shack through a makeshift window slot cut out of the wall. The sparks had apparently come from connecting these to an ancient iron, mounted on a lever, which served as a rubber-welder. "Do you have a pump?" asked the man, coming out into the sunlight and looking around, I was sure, for the bottle. This, he had left inside on the windowsill, inches from the wire strands that led directly from the shack up to the top of a utility pole. I neglected to point it out to him.

"How do you fix flats if you don't have a pump?" I asked.

"Well," said Number One, "sometimes we do have a pump." Sitting under the sun, he had turned sullen.

I handed my pump to Number Two, who managed somehow to thread it onto the end of the valve and fill the tube with air. He proceeded to thrust the air-engorged tube, already lumpy like a string of black sausage from so many previous sad repairs, into a slimy bucket of slops. This bucket appeared to contain a mixture of two-week old rainwater, used crankcase oil, roofing tar, and rotting mangos.

"Aah, here it is," he said finally, somehow spotting a new bubble on the fetid surface after having submerged the entire tube in this foul stew. "Do you have chalk?"

"What?"

"A bit of chalk, to mark the spot." He held his thumb near the offending hole where the air sizzled in its escape from the greasy rubber. Giblets of black ooze dripped off of the tube onto the dusty ground.

"No, I don't," I said in a dark and direct tone. I was growing testier by the moment, although, in fairness, anyone looking at the quantity of baggage strapped onto the back of El Rey might have been forgiven for imagining that I carried with me not only chalk but almost every other conceivable item. The usual procedure for marking the puncture, in this land without chalk, was to stretch the hole slightly and insert a twig, which would then be held fast by the rubber's elasticity.

"That's okay, I'll just hang it here, with the hole at the top." Number Two draped the tube over the doorframe and went into the shack. He reemerged with a jagged bit of rusty metal and began to abrade the rubber with savage strokes. I was sure he would cut clean through the tube at any moment.

"Damn," he said, after several square centimeters of rubber had been chafed raw. "I can't see where the hole was now. Give me the pump again."

By now, I was homicidal and on the brink of a heat-and-fury-induced embolism, but somehow I restrained myself from braining him with the bicycle pump, which, being of prehistoric Chinese origin like the bicycle, was a hefty, solid tube of steel. Twice more, he managed to misplace the puncture. He then asked if I had brought with me the rubber plug to weld onto it. (The possession of such a chunk of processed waste rubber, a pump, and an electric iron are the only essential elements required by anyone wishing to set up a flats-fixed business.) "No," I said quietly, sitting in the dust and holding my pounding temples in my hands. At this bad news, Number One was dispatched to parts unknown, returning much later with a lone, misshapen pellet of black rubber the size of a rabbit dropping. This turd was welded onto my tube, which was duly inflated and proved once again to hold air by submersion in the swamp-like bucket. Then, in replacing the tire on the bike, Number One managed to rip one of the brake pads out of the calipers. At last, after more than an hour of these shenanigans, Number Two made an earnest and delicate attempt to overcharge me by a factor of ten. In a black mood, I pedaled on into the splendid central plaza of Bayamo.

Bayamo was the second city founded in Cuba, but its own inhabitants burned the entire town to the ground after a revolt led by the great Cuban patriot, Carlos Manuel de Céspedes. It is difficult to find a town or village in Cuba without a street, park, or hospital named after this hero who, in 1869, set his own slaves free and led them in an attack on the Spanish. After taking the city, but aware that they could not hope to prevail against an organized and reinforced counterattack, the residents of Bayamo torched their own homes so that the hated Spaniards would only recapture a heap of smoldering ashes.

"You are luking for a room?" asked a man in careful English. He was painfully thin, with every tendon and sinew visible through the skin of his shirtless torso. He was hosing down the sidewalk. Bits of wire and short lengths of PVC pipe held together the lengths of threadbare blue and green hose. Water spritzed and bubbled from the joins, spattering the paving stones.

"Is it your house?" I asked with unnecessary suspicion, in fast Havana Spanish.

He laughed. "Of course. Come in and take a look."

It was minuscule: two tiny rooms, a postage stamp of a kitchen, and a bathroom worthy of a New York City tenement.

"I offer a free trip to the botanical gardens on my motorbike to everyone who stays," he said. "They have the best collection of medicinal plants in the country." This unusual promotion sealed the deal. The next morning, I found myself on the back of a motor scooter zipping through the countryside, the bicycle and its flats forgotten.

José Luis, sitting inches in front of me on the scooter, shouted over his shoulder at me as we whined down the narrow country lanes south of Bayamo. "I love to go to the gardens," he said, "I was an entomologist. Whenever they had something over there they couldn't identify, they would call me up. *Pues*, they still do, sometimes."

"What happened?" I shouted into the wind. We were moving fast through rolling ranchland dotted with clusters of cows. Cattle were so abundant here that José Luis's wife had served me legal beef for dinner the night before. Everywhere else I had been in the country, only nursing mothers and senior citizens received any beef on their ration cards; in Bayamo, beef was miraculously available even on the street-corner pizzas.

"I lost my job. They said I wasn't fit to be a researcher. To be an *investigador*, you must be a revolutionary, they told me. It was the darkest day of my life." José Luis's career as an entomologist had ended when, some years earlier, he had expressed interest in taking his family to begin a new life in the United States. The couple and their children had become pawns in the ceaseless contest between the US and Cuba to portray the other as more evil and self-interested.

In 1994, Castro won a skirmish in the propaganda war by revealing a blatant and racist double standard in US policy, forcing Washington to back away from its long-held stance that all Cuban emigrants would be welcomed into the United States. The crisis began in neighboring Haiti as the military dictatorship of General Raoul Cédras grew daily more savage in its repression of a starving populace. I had seen some of this junta's tactics firsthand while working in Port-au-Prince as a soundman. The routine for the press hordes began with a dawn search for fresh cadavers on the streets of the city. Cruising in jeeps, we looked for grief. Bandanas held to our noses, we warily leaped out to film corpses splayed in the dust, untouched where they had been abandoned by paramilitary assassins the night before, like so many bags of trash. Dust from the unpaved streets clotted their bullet wounds, and some I saw had their hands tied behind them.

In response to daily terror like this, Haitians of every generation set sail for Florida from beaches across the country in whatever flimsy boats they could cobble together. Alarmed by this black tide of refugees lapping up against America's shores, Washington made the announcement, astonishing to many of us on the ground in Haiti, that those risking death to bob about the Gulf Stream in their slapdash plywood boats were not actually victims of political persecution—not refugees at all, actually—but merely economic migrants seeking nothing more than a paycheck. If intercepted at sea, they would be summarily sent home.

In Port-au-Prince, we went to the docks and filmed Coast Guard cutters powering into the harbor to offload a wretched and miserable human cargo of sodden, sulky Haitians who had been picked up at sea. Castro saw an opportunity. As in the Mariel boatlift episode, it was announced that no steps would be taken to prevent the departure of any who cared to leave. Soon, the waters off Florida were clogged not only with illiterate and, of course, uniformly dark-skinned Haitians, but with the well-educated disgruntled of Cuba's revolutionary society. Because of longstanding American policy, however, each and every Cuban was considered a political refugee simply by virtue of having lived in "Castro's Cuba." It was a brilliant ploy by Castro that showcased the hypocrisy of US immigration policy before the rest of the world.

If the enthusiasm that greeted Mariel had come as a stinging slap in the face of the revolution, by 1994, even Castro must have been sure that his offer of a hassle-free departure from the island would find many takers. The grotesque shortages of the special period had by then grabbed the country firmly by the throat. Measures to alleviate the complete lack of soap in the country—just to name one example—had yet to take hold. Each month, fewer and fewer items appeared in the *libreta*. People fondly remembered their last pair of Soviet shoes and wondered where and how they would be ever again be able to obtain vegetable oil.

José Luis and his wife decided to leave. They both had good jobs, he as a research entomologist, she as a bookkeeper, but things were bad and getting worse. An uncle in Elizabeth, New Jersey, agreed to sponsor them and José Luis applied for permission to emigrate.

"I'm a person who thinks things through very carefully," he said over his shoulder on the motorcycle. "I talked it over with my wife and together we decided it was the best thing to do. On the application, you had to include information about your family, your job. Maybe we took too long to make up our minds—I don't know. Everything happens for a reason.

Anyway, we were packed and ready to go. We were ready to say goodbye when word came that the whole thing was stopped. Soon after that, they told me I could no longer be a researcher. I went home and I got in bed and curled up in a ball and cried for a week. My wife said, 'Don't worry, God will help us.' I never would have gotten up again if it were not for her. She is much stronger than I am. *Ella tiene mucha fé*." She has a lot of faith.

"They've told me that *fé* in this country means *familia al extranjero*," I said, shouting into the back of José Luis's helmet. It was an old joke I had heard in Pinar del Río. José Luis laughed. He had rediscovered a positive outlook on life, but, for me, he was yet another one in a string of entomologists, mathematicians, naturalists, and scientists, all expertly trained and passionate about their fields, crushed with disappointment by the realities of the Cuban situation.

At the gardens, a charming eco-revolutionary guide named Imandra explained that the focus was on research and propagation of medicinal plants, especially those disappearing from the wild. Once plants become scarce, she said, they fall out of common use and their place in the oral culture of treatment disappears within a short generation. We walked through cactus gardens and viewed beds cultivated with *yagruma*, *cúrbana*, *manajú*, *rosa adelfa*, and *albahaca morada*.

José Luis and Imandra showed me the Jagüey, an enormous species of strangler fig that grows a lattice framework around a host tree in gray tendrils of solid, woody lace. There is a symbiotic relationship between birds and the Jagüey. After feeding on figs, an adult bird brings food back to its young in a nest hole in another species of tree. The chicks crap out the seeds, which prosper in the remnant nitrogen-rich muck at the bottom of the nest hole, sending up a sprout that creeps out in search of daylight, winding both up and down the trunk, finally engulfing it in *el abrazo de la muerte*, the hug of death, an arboreal equivalent of the Mafia goodbye that can go on for decades. Lydia Cabrera writes of a majordomo in *Palo Monte*, a *ngangulero* who "confessed to me the terror inspired in him by the mysterious and treasonous jagüey, a species of octopus, a vegetable vampire, which embraces and then devours the tree living beside it."

Imandra told us that the point of departure for all the work done at Cupaynicú was the writing of Juan Tomás Roig. His botanical opus, *Plantas medicinales, aromaticas o venenosas de Cuba*, combines scientific descriptions of plants with possible medicinal uses culled both from the international literature and from anecdotal regional reports inside Cuba. The book could be a secular version of the second, botanical half of Lydia Cabrera's *El Monte*; the entries are stripped of all references to *los santos*, the Lucumí spirit masters of the plants. "Enormous tree, native and considered most representative of our flora," he writes of the ceiba. "In Camagüey they use the leaves for baths and in Havana for decoctions....The decoctions are used to advantage against pustules." Roig sifted through folklore and oral history, rejecting what he found to be pure superstition, and then applied laboratory methods in an attempt to find scientific support for herbal remedies, guiding the future researcher down only the most promising trails. Imandra showed us a bed of *albahaca morada*, a purple basil, which Roig found to have "notable anti-diabetic qualities." In 1961, he published a pamphlet for public distribution describing some experiments with the plant and offering free seeds to anyone interested in growing it. "This work," he wrote, "was published in a scientific journal of limited circulation which cannot reach the hands of all the diabetics of the interior and is virtually only known to doctors. Therefore we have decided to publish this leaflet which will arrive free of charge into the hands of those interested so that they may discover the curative effects of the plant...."[*]

Under the sun and among beds of fragrant plants, we were set upon by a plague of gnats. Imandra bent over to pluck a stalk of *albahaca blanca* and handed it to me. It smelled even more like basil than its purple relative. I slapped at my shins. The plant had small, pale leaves the size of a pinky fingernail. I sniffed it and wondered if it would be possible to make a kind of ersatz Cuban pesto with it. "Put the stalk behind your ear," said Imandra, "the bugs can't stand it." It was true. The plant created an invisible force field around my head, and the incessant whining and maddening attacks on my ear canal by the no-see-ums ceased at once. I asked if I might have two more sprigs, which I tucked into the tops of my socks. José Luis found the results hilarious and insisted on taking a photograph of me in which I look like a giant fairy escaped from a high-school dramatic production, or a marine feebly trying to camouflage himself with a few tiny sprouts of weed.

Most of the species that grew in the garden were not particularly rare, and many weren't even native to Cuba. Some had arrived as handfuls of

---

[*] Juan Tómas Roig, facsimile of "La Albahaca Morada, planta a la que se atribuyen propiedades anti-diabeticas," in *Compendio de las Obras de Juan Tómas Roig, Tomo 1*, La Habana, Editorial Cientifico-Técnica, 1983, unpaginated.

seeds smuggled onto slave ships, along with their owners, who had also brought the knowledge of how to use them. Others had come from Europe. I had seen several of them before when Eduardo, in a demonstration of *curandero* knowledge, quickly plucked a dozen species of apparent weeds from his front yard in Ciego de Ávila, handed them to me, and ticked off their medicinal uses.

The ongoing convergence of science and *Santería* was fascinating to me. The renewed popularity of the Afro-Cuban religions, although given nominal government support as a manifestation of national identity, seemed to me a classic symptom of a system in dysfunction. Disillusion with socialism had left a spiritual void that people increasingly searched to fill with the *santos* and their *prendas*; in an earthly parallel, the disappearance of all but the most basic medicines from the peso economy demanded an urgent return to the study and promotion of natural cures based on plants. At Cupaynicú, the quest for curative plants that average Cubans might grow and use on their own was devoid of any mention of the *santeros* or *paleros* with whom much of this knowledge had originated. But the same plants turned Eduardo's scrubby front yard into a pharmacy and Lydia Cabrera's *El Monte*, the unofficial bible of *Palo Monte*, is really a pharmacopoeia.

The plants and trees are the houses of the spirits, who must be asked for permission before their bark, roots, and leaves may be harvested for the benefit of mankind. The *orishas* that control them and live in them must be propitiated and consulted. The *santero*, voodooist, or *palero* healer, when asked from where the knowledge of which plants to use for which infirmities was obtained, invariably replies that it is the *santo* or *lwa* itself that, while "riding," conveys the necessary ingredients and their preparation, speaking through the human horse it has capriciously chosen to mount. From this perspective, the environmental catastrophe mankind is promoting across the globe is an assault on the gods themselves.

Before leaving, we had coffee in the open-sided canteen. "We're destroying the planet," Imandra said. "Soon, it's going to be a world made of nothing but money, without flora or fauna. But we're going to arrive at the day when whoever has the plants and trees will have the power—like in the Stone Age, when those with fire had all the power."

On the way back to Bayamo, José Luis stopped the motorcycle on the side of the road at a place where two farmhouses faced one another on opposite sides of the road. A herd of cows was munching at the grass beyond the fence. "These were the *fincas* of my uncles," he said. "They left. First, one went to Elizabeth; then, a few years later, the other one went to join him." He pronounced it *Leeza-bet*. Elizabeth is almost singlehandedly responsible for New Jersey's bad reputation and freeway jokes. As children in the back seat of the car, my sister and I always pinched our noses to guard against foul chemical odors whenever we spotted the Elizabeth exit signs on the turnpike.

"I wouldn't want to leave this behind and go to Elizabeth," I said.

"As far as I understand, he didn't like the way the wind was blowing. He had twelve and a half *caballerías*," said José Luis. "So, when the agrarian reform came, he was considered a *latifundista*. The law was that they nationalized everything except for your primary residence. That was this farm. But he also had at least one house in town, in Bayamo, so they took that."

"Did your parents think about leaving?"

"My father was loyal to the revolution until the day he died in 1984," said José Luis, with pride.

José Luis was not in the least bit bitter that the two farms had passed from his family into the hands of the people; in that sense, he was still a revolutionary himself. "Around here," he said, "almost everyone supported the revolution, all the middle class, even the business-owners. Because the corruption of the government was total.

"After my parents got married, the uncles gave my father a job as a driver. They had a coffee-hulling machine here in Güisa. Dirt roads went up into the mountains, reaching the coffee plantations. My father drove up barrels filled full of guns or food and medicine for the revolution and came back with coffee. He just waved to everybody and drove on past; they all knew my uncles and their coffee business."

By the winter of 1958, Fidel's handful of men had grown into an organized peasant force with de facto control over much of the Sierra Maestra. It was a textbook case of a growing rebellion. According to José Luis, the Batista government—centralized, arrogant, and corrupt—responded to unrest with terror, the most successful promotion the revolution could have hoped for.

Like peasants across most of the globe, Cuba's small farmers and *guajiros* had little use for government. Their desire was to be left alone as they eked out a living from the land. Any idea that government might provide roads, schools, and healthcare was remote from their experience,

and while the suggestion that the revolution would bring these things undoubtedly helped swell the ranks of the revolutionaries, more important
was the growing climate of government oppression. Many farmers in the
mountains first experienced their government through the arrival of police
or troops sweeping the zone for rebels. Accusations that the *guajiros* were
aiding and abetting Fidel's band, backed by the military's thuggish tactics,
became a self-fulfilling prophecy. Like so many corrupt governments, Batista's collapsed because it declared war on its own people.

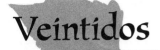

Veintidos
Las Tunas

Décima poets must wear mustaches. So it appeared at least, judging from the abundant facial hair on the aspiring contestants milling around "Las Canturias," the folksy, hay-scattered outdoor stage at the Cucalambé festival in Las Tunas. I sat watching the action from a sling chair upholstered with what had once been the hide of a Holstein, the black and white, bovine Dalmatian pattern adding to the rodeo aura. Regional winners of provincial contests and ex-champions of various national poetry competitions were mingling with the kind of easy intimacy that characterizes the practitioners of any obscure passion. All had spent long hours licking pencil points and wracking their brains in the concoction of octosyllabic odes to *campesino* life while growing extreme mustaches of the sort that demand constant attention and maintenance.

José Luis had agreed to store El Rey del Ganado in his house for me and I had caught an overloaded transport truck back up the road to Las Tunas in order to go to the *décima* festival. Those suffering from stage fright, or subject to recurring nightmares starring themselves making unwanted public appearances, would have cringed miserably at the spectacle. The audience was small, only a hundred or so of us sitting on stumps and calfskin chairs on a soft carpet of fallen bamboo fronds, but we were scornful of failure and critical of success. A full band, deceptively placid in the shade of the improvised stage, tuned their bongo and *laúd*, the twelve-string guitar that jangles along in relentless companionship with the poets. The emcee invited a lady to select the first competitor from papers in a hat, while he in turn selected his opponent. A theme was chosen on another drawn slip of paper: respect, counsel, fable, or some such.

From the moment the theme was announced, the poets stood facing the audience and scouring their brains for the collected improvisations of their lives, trying literally to make the poems of their careers flash before their eyes. The mental contortions were visible, the extreme thinking palpable in the hot air. Each *repentista* had his own tortured style. A seven-foot-tall schoolteacher from Pinar del Río held one elbow rigid at his side, but his hand trembled uncontrollably, his great long fingers shivering dangerously with the violence of a train about to jump the tracks. He was one of the few black contestants. The local favorite of Las Tunas, wiry and cocky with a white cowboy hat tilted back on his head, paced furiously, turned away from the audience, and froze in place, staring at the ground for inspiration before snapping back to the microphone. Others clenched their fists and stared off into blank space for long, brutally uncomfortable moments, or held their temples fast between their wrists as they dredged up verses from the deepest recesses of the brain.

It is not only the adherence to the theme that makes these improvisational battles so challenging. It is the rigid formal constraints binding the poet in the creation of his *espinelas*, as these verses are called after their reputed inventor, the poet and musician Vicente Espinel, born in Málaga in 1550. In his *Diversas Rimas* ("Assorted Rhymes") of 1591, a poem appears in print, apparently for the first time, written in the specific rhyme scheme that still persists today in the Cuban *décima*. In an *espinela*, the ten lines of poetry must each have eight syllables, and the lines must rhyme in a very particular way: the first line rhyming with the fourth and fifth, the second with the third, the sixth with the seventh and tenth, and the eighth with the ninth. If you're having trouble following along, imagine trying to spout such verse off the top of your head. This pattern is generally written abba:accddc, and parts of it are rather older than Espinel. My father, the medievalist John V. Fleming, pointed out to me that the initial abba quatrain, or *redondilla*, doubtless derives from the Petrarchan sonnet, fourteen-line poems written on the Italian peninsula, two centuries earlier.

It is a mystery how Espinel's pattern—and its particular innovation, the rhyming of the fourth and fifth lines—became the gold standard for rhyme schemes. Espinel is better remembered for his novel and as mentor to better poets than for his own verse; even in the *Diversas Rimas*, the handful of *espinelas* are far outnumbered by sonnets, quatrains, and all sorts of other forms. Furthermore, ten-line octosyllabic poems predate Espinel. They abound in the output of the so-called Golden Age of Iberian poetry, and one finds a multitude of different schemes within them. Espinel's Portuguese contemporary, Luis de Camões, who surely numbers among the very greatest of the world's poets of any era, employed a great diversity of them. Yet a poet showing up onstage in Cuba today with any of these other myriad variations would be disqualified. Such a thing would be scandalous, radical.

When performed in competition, there was no denying the dramatic tension of the *espinela*, however it rose to prominence. Behind the poets, the music played on, the tranquil, burbling melodies of the *laúd* driving them like a whip. It was a simple format. After some four bars, the poet stepped up to the microphone and delivered his first all-important line. Once sung, these fateful, first eight syllables defined the shape of the entire ten-line poem to come; later, but very soon, the fourth and fifth lines would be obliged to rhyme with them. The *laúd*, which had dropped out expectantly, announcing the supposed intervention of the poet, began to twang again, the music playing on just long enough for the poet to consider with horror the true depths of the hole he had now dug for himself. Before any time had gone by, it seemed, the *laúd* paused again, demanding the poet repeat, with authority, his first line, and add the second. In these moments, the contestants squirmed and wriggled with linguistic exertion, and their veins stood out on their foreheads like tree roots. I imagined their testicles shriveling and tightening and burrowing back up into their guts in dismay and retreat, as if these grown men had jumped naked into a frigid pool. It was excruciating to watch.

The failures were spectacular, as horrible to see as a triple toe loop crashing down in a squalid heap onto the Olympic ice, or a bird flying into a plate glass window. Lines half-delivered and left hanging in the air for a moment too long met with the prompt resumption of the pleasant, innocuous music, which came like a stinging slap to the face. The audience coughed and moved in their seats when the music went on for too long without any poetic action. Mustached poets groped the air and chewed empty space, emasculated, weeping with frustration after delivering jaw-dropping half sentences that began with authority and poise and then trailed off, lost and unspoken. The representative of Cienfuegos flopped spectacularly; his theme was "modesty." "I'm sorry gentlemen," he finally managed, rhyming, "my nervous state on this occasion prevents me from delivering a timely and proper poem." He expressed this almost modest thought in *décima* format, but it was a prepared admission of defeat to which he had been forced to turn only after endless bars of music had rolled on and on, bland and pleasant, while he stood in gap-mouthed silence, abandoned by the muse.

The poems came too fast, and were abstract and full of difficult words I did not understand, and I regret that I was not able to write down even one. But like late-model country music, they were self-reflexive, speaking of *décima* itself or, in the grand tradition of the form, singing the praises of the *guajiro* life on Cuban soil. They sang of palm trees and thatched huts and eternal friendship and birds twittering in the *monte*. "La décima es la paloma mas bella que he conocido/Es el que fabrica el nido en el arbol del idioma," managed one *repentista*, diverging from his theme to dredge up this flowery metaphor: *Décima* is the most beautiful dove I have known, one which makes its nest in the tree of language.

From each dueling duo, the judges selected one poet to advance to the next round. The other was finished, washed up: a year of back-yard rhyme-writing and bar-stool improvisation had turned sour in his mouth at the crucial competitive moment. The losers stamped off the stage in pointed cowboy boots and punched trees and threw their ten-gallon hats down into the dirt in disgust. It was a linguistic rodeo.

Those advancing to the second round faced the *pie forzado*, literally the "forced foot," in which the final octosyllabic line of a *décima* is drawn from the hat. The improvised poem may be on any topic but must inexorably work its way around to the final line. Here the *espinela* rhyme scheme demands that the sixth and seventh lines agree with the finale. In the strongest poems, the *forzado* will thematically summarize the rest of the stanza. One elegant poem extolling the beauty of a local woman wound up nicely with the metaphoric forzado, "*Linda como flor de Cuba*," pretty as a Cuban flower. It was as if Norman Rockwell had sponsored a hip-hop battle for rhyming supremacy.

I left the poetic spectacle, awash in Spanish rhyming couplets. In the city center, a resident told me with pride that Las Tunas was named for a cactus that had at one time grown around the city in great profusion. This took some time to comprehend since cacti were nowhere in abundance there and I did not know the word *tunas*. Several people spoke enough

English to venture that a *tuna* was in my language a *cack-too*, but I failed to make the intuitive leap that Cubans were just as apt to drop the final "s" in my tongue as in their own. Only when a man in a beer-garden grew exasperated and said that, surely, since I spoke English, I must know that a *cack-too* is a "waterless tree with many sharp spines," did I successfully interpret this translation.

This beer-garden was a hotbed of revolutionary fervor where I spent a drunken afternoon and concluded that at least in Las Tunas the revolution was a grand success. Delicious, cold, and frothy tap beers were on offer, served in glass mugs fashioned from recycled beer bottles. Men in weekend casual clothes bought them as fast as the tap-girl could pour them, drinking under shade trees at rustic benches and tables made from battered slabs of aluminum.

I shared a table with Rodolfo Silva and his son-in-law, Angel Leiva. They had come from the hospital, where Angel's son was admitted "por falta de aire." Because he had been lacking air. He had been having trouble breathing and spent five days in the Puerto Padre hospital before being transferred to Las Tunas a week earlier. "You know how much that costs?" Rodolfo asked me as a conversation-starter. "Not a cent, it doesn't cost anything." Two fat white turkeys, alive but trussed up tight, were hanging upside down like enormous bleached bats from the back rack of a Flying Pigeon locked to the fence near mine. I went to the makeshift bar to buy a round.

"We have a question," said Rodolfo after we had clinked glasses and had a first foamy sip. "If a child in the US has to go into the hospital—what happens?" Cuban propaganda spends a great deal of time comparing its government's export of volunteer doctors to the developing world with the mercenary, golf-playing medical providers of capitalism. Cubans often reminded me that one could fall down and die in the street in the United States and people would just walk past. I felt surprisingly defensive as I attempted to explain the Medicaid safety net and the fiasco that is the American health-insurance system.

"So if you can't afford this insurance or whatever," said Angel, "then they won't let your child into the hospital."

"In the rarest of cases, and that would hopefully cause a scandal. What is more likely to happen is that they send you away and tell you to go to a different hospital, or deal with an emergency and then transfer you. Basically, they waste a lot of time trying to figure out if you have any means to pay. They'll treat you, but then they come after you to get the money."

"It's very simple here," said Rodolfo. "No questions, they just take care of you." It was clear that my waffling defense of the American way had done nothing but bolster Cuba's propaganda message: children were dying in waiting rooms across the USA.

"I have to say, speaking frankly," I said, "many people here have told me that the health system is excellent and you can always see a doctor, right in your own neighborhood, but that any kind of complicated medicine or supplies are impossible to get. To the point where doctors are telling people to go and see a *curandero*."

"Well, that's because of the embargo, isn't it," said Angel.

"I don't know," I said. "Not everything is the embargo."

"There might not be enough resources to go around," said Rodolfo, "but everything is shared equally among everybody. Fidel wants all the people of the world to be happy. He wants everyone to be equal one with the other. He really wants that."

Angel worked at a sugar-cane cooperative and Rodolfo cultivated tobacco. I hadn't seen a tobacco plant since Pinar del Río, some seven hundred kilometers earlier, but Rodolfo said it was such a critical cash crop that there was a government incentive scheme to promote the industry all over the island. "I just got into this business," he said. "It's working out great. They have a certain quota that you must produce, but after that, they buy the rest of the tobacco crop from you in cash. In *divisas*." Hard currency.

"That's the first time I've heard of such a thing in all my time in Cuba," I said. "It sounds almost like capitalism."

"There's a difference," said Rodolfo. "If I have, I'll share it with you. The Cuban will take his last loaf of bread and split it."

"For instance," said Angel, taking one of Rodolfo's cigarettes from a pack on the table, "I don't get paid in *divisas*; I can't afford to smoke. But at the sugar-cane *central*, after we make the quota during the harvest, the extra earnings get divided up among the workers. We have a committee of eighty and we get together and decide how to spend the excess. We might decide to buy a new refrigerator or that the *comedor* needs new tables and chairs."

Rodolfo and Angel assiduously refused to let me buy more than my fair share of beers, endearing them greatly to me. We had about six each; the afternoon was waning. The sky was still a solid white ceiling of clouds, but somewhere a storm was brewing; ominous thunderclaps began to crash their way into our conversation. "One more and we're out of here," said Rodolfo. "We wouldn't go, but we live a ways out of town." We beerily shook hands goodbye.

"Do you think you'll ever be back in Las Tunas?" asked Angel.

After they had gone, I realized I was starving and I bought two tamales to have with what I felt certain ought to be my last beer. Later, I deciphered the scrawls in my notebook: *El tamalero 10¢ @ awesome. They are delicious. IN LAS TUNAS THE REVO IS WORKING!!! You can sit around in a bar wasted as fucks and nobody messes with you in Las Tunas. AVOID BARFING.*

Next day, the bus station was awash with frustrated passengers, broiling in the July sun. I had typically slept in and dawdled over a late breakfast, but the huge numbers of people and their dejected attitudes made it clear that, had I arrived at six instead of ten, I'd have earned only the chance to wait for an additional four hours. People and their bundles and children sat in every patch of shade, lining up in rows in the narrow black shadows cast on the ground by tree branches, like cattle behind the trunk of a ceiba. It was like a crowded outdoor concert, except that, without a stage, there was no focus to the crush.

Behind a heavily barred and grilled ticket-window, a heavy woman who managed to appear both somnolent and harried admitted that they were not selling tickets. There was no transportation. "If transportation comes," she said sensibly, "we will sell tickets." In another line, which wound through a narrow, welded corridor of iron pipe and sheet metal, like a corral, it was possible to buy a *turno*, a scrap of paper that served, like the *último* system, to hold your place in line. Payment would be later, on the bus; the *turno* did not guarantee transport, just your place on the waiting list. Furthermore, *turnos* were only available for trucks going to destinations for which there might actually be departures that day, something unknown, as there were no trucks. The *turno*-seller would not reveal if she based her decisions on mysterious inside information or on the overwhelming preponderance of rumor. Places in a fictive future line for a so-far imaginary bus to Bayamo had not yet gone on sale.

I wandered the crowd asking people where they hoped to go. I wanted to be sure that at least one other passenger in this throng held out hope for Bayamo. People clustered in small grumpy groups by destination. Near a Bayamo concentration, I found an available place to wait where, by virtue of my unique height, I could lean my uppermost shoulder against a tree branch.

"What's happening?" I asked a woman in purple spandex shorts. "It doesn't look good."

"We've been here since morning. It's the *tribuna abierta*," she said. The open tribunal. "In Manzanillo."

"But Elián is already back in Cuba," I said. The open tribunals were the mammoth demonstrations to demand the return of Elián González.

"You didn't hear? They announced that they are still going to hold the tribunals, to protest against the Cuban Adjustment Act."

"But what does the *tribuna abierta* in Manzanillo have to do with transport to Bayamo?" I asked.

She laughed at this naive question. "All the buses are there. From Bayamo, from Las Tunas, to Santiago, probably: they've all been requisitioned to take people to the demonstration. We're all waiting for something to straggle in afterward."

A heavy man dressed in filthy burlap came past us, working the crowd for coins. He had a cardboard *Cerveza Bucanero* box with a few coins in it and a statue of San Lázaro. Fat and shiny and red-faced, he had the same damaged, twisted face as so many of New York's mentally-ill homeless. He was emulating his patron saint, who always wears burlap and is portrayed as indigent and wounded, with festering sores on his shins. The burlap sugar sacks gapped at the edges, revealing a round, unhealthy belly. He twitched crazily, with sudden jerks and ticks. His costume was neither a ruse nor a marketing ploy. The man, in losing his mind, had absorbed the guise of San Lázaro, perhaps from Cuba's national *Santería* subconscious. He believed that he was the personification of the saint.

Around the edges of the crowd, like sharks trying to separate a straggler from a swirling school of fish, freelance dispatchers for the ancient prerevolution gypsy cabs roamed, calling out destinations. I heard Bayamo several times and spoke with the man. At thirty pesos, $1.50, he had only one taker out of this mass of humanity. I told him to find me if the places started to fill up.

"Nobody will take you for thirty pesos anyway," he said. "It's too risky. You should just rent the whole vehicle." Anyone who took me from here was breaking the law, and this, of course, incurred a surcharge. For ten dollars, I could be on my way at once. I decided I would wait. How better to understand Cuba than to wait?

A blind peanut vendor gingerly picked his way through the crowd, selling nuts wrapped in little twists of white paper. "La espera te desespera pero el maní tostao te quita esa anxiedad," he said with a poetic flair appropriate to the home of *décima*. "La espera te desespera y te da anxiedad, pero el maní te la quita." The waiting drives you to despair and makes you anxious, but toasted peanuts relieve those symptoms. "El maní le quita el desespero que la espera le da," he went on, turning the sentiment into a tongue-twister of a *pregón*. Peanuts relieve the desperation that waiting causes.

Sadly not, I thought, and went off to find the Bayamo taxi shill. He connected me with a daring young man with a yellow Lada. Braulio agreed to run the gauntlet of checkpoints with a tourist in the car for six dollars. "I can't let you get into the car here," he said. "Go down to the end of that block and try to stand hidden, off to the side." I turned my back on the baking, waiting crowd and slinked away down a tree-lined street. On the corner, with nothing to do, like a spy, I waited with my dollars to again buy my way out of Cuba's daily dose of discomfort.

When it arrived, the Lada was full of people. A man and his son were trying to claw their way across the Oriente on this worst of all possible travel days, trying to reach Guantánamo. A woman who had moved east to Ciego de Ávila was headed deep into the Sierra to visit her family. Visiting family was always the number-one reason for travel in Cuba. Carrying me around was like driving cocaine up the New Jersey Turnpike; Braulio faced a $1,500 fine and the possible loss of his car, or so he had said in the delicate negotiations. I crammed into the back and tried to keep a low profile, a big man with a big red beard in a tiny car.

On the highway, we started to see oncoming trucks full of demonstrators being driven home from their participation in the "spontaneous manifestation of the people of Manzanillo to demand revocation of the Cuban Adjustment Act." Dozens of open-backed trucks were full of youth waving tiny paper Cuban flags at us as they passed. At the turnoff to the city of Manzanillo, a heavy police presence controlled the flow of traffic. Waved to the side and stopped, we parked in a row of vehicles, watching from a few hundred meters back as an endless convoy of trucks poured out from the Manzanillo spur.

What Cubans do in the unlikely event of a highway traffic jam or other stoppage is get out of their cars and ask around for other rides that may ultimately get them closer to their destinations. All my fellow passengers descended to wander back down the row of stopped vehicles. Five minutes later, they returned to grab their belongings and announce that a truck behind us that had come from Camagüey, thereby avoiding conscription into the Manzanillo propaganda, was going straight through to Santiago if they ever opened up the road—and thank you and good luck to you and good afternoon.

Braulio and I sat in the car. "Do you mind slouching down a bit? Try and sort of hide behind the seat," he said. He told me that he had a six-year-old son, the same age as Elián, also named Elián, and that he had put his name in for the *bombo* four years ago. He laughed. "Lately, I thought maybe of trying to arrange a trade," he said. "My Elián for their Elián." We tried to imagine the intense negotiations that had transpired during the long days when Elián's father, Juan, had kept the world in suspense after being reunited with the boy in Washington.

The key issue that had reinvigorated all of Cuba with nationalist and revolutionary fervor, the reunification of father and son, had been accomplished. For months, the *tribunas abiertas* had been demanding the son be returned to the father. After the US Federal stormtroopers had done just that, a new set of compelling arguments had needed to be devised to explain why Elián and his father, together again at last, must return to Cuban soil rather than, say, get a movie agent and a lease on a condo in Santa Monica.

The shots of Elián's empty schoolroom desk and his grieving classmates in their burgundy scout-scarves were given new emphasis on the nightly news. Psychiatric experts were called to the screen to discuss the corruption of Elián's mind by capitalism and the need for him to return to school as soon as possible to relieve the traumas he had experienced. Braulio imagined Fidel on the line with Juan in Washington, describing the amenities at the new and comfortable house that the Gonzálezes *padre y hijo* would be given in Cardenas. I suggested that Hollywood was no doubt calling with huge offers for the rights to Juan's story and that Bill Clinton had probably stopped by to explain how the right book deal could help you turn over a whole new financial page in your life.

"If I were him, I wouldn't have come back," said Braulio.

"I heard maybe he was scared that if he didn't, he might have an accident." This cynical view had been expressed to me in Camagüey by a drunk and disgruntled Angola veteran, the self-appointed busboy at a beer garden.

"You mean they'd kill him? I doubt that." Braulio paused as the traffic started to move. "*Pues*, of course anything's possible in a problem this big. It would really have looked bad for Cuba if he didn't return."

The rest of the cars around us on the shoulder drove out, but we stayed put. Two hundred meters up ahead, three soldiers peered into the vehicles as they went by. A hundred meters up on the shoulder, another soldier walked slowly in our direction. I was alone in the car with Braulio and we were the last car, remaining behind as if we had broken down. "I'm not sure what to do," said Braulio. "I could just drive through, and if they wave at me, I'll pretend not to see them."

"They must have a police car or something," I said. "They'll follow you if they want to. Do you want me to just get out here? You could turn around and go back and I'll wait a while and then walk up. I'm sure they'll stop a car and get me a ride."

"No, I agreed to take you, I can't leave you here," he said, peering up the road with discomfort. "My father gave me this car," he went on in an elegiac tone, as if anticipating its confiscation.

"We can't just sit here, they've let everyone else go." At any moment, the soldiers would come to see why we were still parked there.

"Lie down on the seat more, and pretend to be asleep."

"What if they look in? That would be even more suspicious."

"I'll tell them you're a sick tourist and a policeman back there stopped my car and ordered me to take you to the hospital in Bayamo," said Braulio.

"What if they separate us and interrogate us?" I asked. I was far more nervous than Braulio, who stood to lose his car. "Tell them I don't speak any Spanish at all, and you haven't been able to communicate with me."

This froth of anxiety proved anticlimactic—once again. I lay down in the back of the Lada, holding my stomach, as Braulio drove slowly past the checkpoint. Another hundred meters and we were in the clear. Forty minutes later, we were in Bayamo, pulling up in front of José Luis's house. Braulio had forgotten all about our close shave. He gave me his card and offered his chauffeur services for any excursions I intended to make, anywhere in the Oriente.

Veintitrés

A really good cup of coffee

I recall when I left a little town in North Carolina
I tried to escape this music
I said it was for the old country folks
I went to New York
Got slick
Got my hair made, heh–heh–heh
I was cool, heh heh
I was cool
But I had no groove, no groove
I had no groove,
But here it comes!
   —Funkadelic

"**M**ango, mango, yuma!" A strapping teenager was yelling at me from the side of the road. Too exhausted to respond or even wave, I was moving so slowly I feared the bicycle would topple over. Bayamo was behind me. I was in the mountains at last, fighting uphill. "Yuma, yuma, mango." He waved his mangos in the air. *Yuma* is street slang for America, perhaps because of "the frequent mention of the town of Yuma, Arizona, in westerns."* I didn't have the energy to respond to this linguistic oddity. Sweat poured off my forehead, salt stinging the corners of my eyes.

---

* "Alludes to the United States of North America," writes Carlos Paz Perez in his *Diccionario Cubano de términos populares y vulgares.* "Santiesteban proposes two possible origins: the frequent mention of the town of Yuma, Arizona, in westerns or the phonetic similarites with the term 'United' (Yunay) which begins the name of that country."

I was praying I would soon reach the town of Aguacate, which means avocado. I believed Aguacate to be at the top of this murderous hill. I imagined Angel and El Vate urging me on as if I were climbing the Pyrenees in the Tour de France. Instead, two oldtimers, *campesinos* sitting in the shade, cackled at me: "Better move a little faster there, sonny, there's a long way to go yet." Men sprang out of the bushes clutching huge and oddly shaped avocadoes like lurid green bludgeons. Instead of cheering spectators, the roadside was filled with jeering vegetable salesmen who charged out of the shadows thrusting grotesque fruits at me, yelling *aguacate, aguacate,* while foremost in my mind was the desperate hope that around the next bend, I would arrive at last in a town named Aguacate.

Finally, the top. A heartwarming sign read, *Highest point on the carretera central 319.89 meters.* The landscape was typical of the Oriente, with waves and waves of mountains and archetypal vistas I recognized from old album covers of Cuban music. Groves of royal palms shot up from sun-furred ridges and simple thatched huts nestled in the hollows beside tidy clearings. Below the road, a river bottom I took to be the headwaters of the Rio Cauto was thick with dark epiphyte-laden trees protecting the watercourse.

At Palma Soriano, I turned onto the old highway to Santiago. After one more savage climb, the road wound downhill and passed before the Caridad del Cobre, the holiest shrine in Cuba. An enormous rust and beige chapel, it is built on the edge of the copper mine that paid for it and for which it is named. Pilgrims who have made *promesas* make their way here from every corner of the country, some on foot, but I coasted past, in a hurry to reach Santiago, Cuba's second city and, for me, a kind of musical Mecca. Like Cienfuegos, Santiago has a great natural harbor. The mountains abruptly slide into the sea and cobblestone streets twist and turn over an uncooperative and tortured geography. Some of its streets are so steep that they give up in the middle of town, becoming broad staircases.

Santiago in July is as hot as the Caribbean gets. Shielded from the cooling effect of the Atlantic by the mountains of the Oriente, the city is like an oven. As if recognizing that it is pointless to expect productivity under such conditions, *Santiagueros* give the entire month over to music and dance. I had arrived just in time for the aptly name Festival of Fire, a weeklong orgy of Caribbean music. On the evening of my arrival, the Parque Céspedes was thick with an expectant crowd milling about and waiting for the music to start. The terrace of the dollar hotel along the uphill edge of the park was crowded with tourists eating dinner. Groups of Cuban youth trolled the wide, paved walkways that cut the park corner to corner. Roadies checked out the sound system, shouting "Uno, dos, probando" into mikes set up on a large stage in the middle of the street. An entire block along the side of the park was closed to traffic and converted into an outdoor dancefloor.

Up the block, music poured into the street through the tall French doors of the Casa de la Trova. I walked up the hill following the sound. An old man gripping the barred windows looked in from the outside while a pair of kids barely tall enough to reach the sill jockeyed for window space. A passing couple paused in their evening stroll long enough to break into a few quick dancesteps, the guy giving his girl a twirl as they laughed and moved on up the street. Inside, an all-woman *son* band played to a packed room: the music wafted out into the street like the scent of baking bread. The Casa de la Trova is a legendary venue, a sort of Grand Old Opry of *son*, the ancient and delicious music most characteristic of the Oriente.

Stripped to its classic essence, *son* requires only a *tres*, *clave*, a bongo, *maracas*, and a *marímbula** for the bass sounds. These instruments were all easily made at home on the farm, so no outlay of capital was required for a bunch of friends to get together and play, sitting on logs in the back yard or gathered around the kitchen table with a bottle of rum. The *son* is at the heart of all the music known today as *salsa*. In *The Latin Tinge: The Impact of Latin American Music on the United States,* John Storm Roberts called it "perhaps the oldest and certainly the classic Afro-Cuban form, an almost perfect balance of African and Hispanic elements." It is a sound that has changed little since the 1920s; the last major innovation in the instrumentation was the addition of a lone trumpet by Ignacio Piñeiro to create his still famous Septeto Nacional.

I saw at least fifteen *son* bands in the weeks I spent in Santiago. They played in the park, at the Casa de la Trova, and the Casa de las Tradiciones. Many of them were traditional sextets, without trumpets. The musicians came from every corner of the city, or from Guantánamo or the outlying towns of Oriente. None of these bands played songs from the *Buena Vista*

---

* A wooden box or plywood crate with an oval or circular hole cut out of one side for resonance. Flat, spatula-like blades of iron, like gigantic versions of the keys on an African thumb piano, are mounted over the hole. The player sits on the box and and plucks the metal keys between his knees with a rubber pick, often cut from an old tire.

Social Club album, even though the best numbers on that record are also *sones*. This was a tremendous relief. Elsewhere in Cuba, wherever it was even possible to avoid the dreaded scourge of Eurodisco, the *Buena Vista Social Club* infected the repertory of local bands with the same cancer of popularity and tourist expectation that obliges every tiki-hut beachfront bar from Ecuador to Thailand to play only Bob Marley. Everyone loves Bob Marley, and everyone loves the *Buena Vista Social Club*, so there was often little else to be heard. By the time I had arrived in Santiago, I felt I never wanted to hear the *Buena Vista Social Club* again.

That night, I wandered through the city, soaking in music. In the park, a family quintet from Las Tunas played sweet, soft country *son* on acoustic instruments, including a *marímbula*. An enormous woman in a flowing Senegalese wax batik *boubou* and New Orleans voodoo-child makeup fronted an Afro-percussion ensemble from Trinidad and Tobago. A group called Canyambu performed *son* with bamboo instruments, thumping different lengths and widths of cured cane against the ground to beat out the percussion parts. The bass was a meter and a half of *caña brava* that resonated with a primeval swampy thud each time it was brought down against the stage. The "bongo" player manipulated two much shorter bamboo pipes, pumping them up and down like pistons and rapping their bases against a stool in front of him. Even the guitar and *tres* had lacquered bamboo surfaces. The front man was rail thin and at least seventy years old, very tall, with improbably long arms that seemed to reach almost down to his knees. He sang with the slightly nasal and rasping quality characteristic of Oriente *soneros*, a Cuban version of a lounge singer's cigarette-and-whiskey-drenched voice that spoke of hard years spent toiling in the *monte*. In a song called "Carbonero," he sang of having once been a charcoal-cutter until the revolution came and did away with the very idea of such a horrible and inhumane job.

My favorite of all was a group that didn't even play *son,* introduced by the emcee as an ancient, unbroken family tradition. They took the stage with instruments I had not seen anywhere else in Cuba: a half-meter-long, Dominican-style *güira* like an oversized cheese grater, scraped with long, fork-like tines; the jawbone of an ass, its teeth loose and rattling in the bleached skull; a jugband bass, one lone string fixed to the end of a flexible stick with its foot attached to an overturned bucket; and homemade kettle drums like something out of an American revolutionary war diorama.

The music began with the plaintive moan of an accordion, introducing something like a twisted, percussive, Napoleonic square dance. It was slow and deliberate antique music that reminded me of the Haitian *contredanse*, which was both a parody and imitation of French courtiers dancing the *quadrille* in the salons of their plantations. In Haiti, such music is still played in the farthest corners of the mountains, out of reach of modernity, complete with a caller yelling out the centuries-old *do-si-dos*. This band was not made up of Haitians, however. They were all white Cubans, and their music was sublime, with a hint of tango added by the accordion. "This is deep, deep shit," I wrote later in my journal. "Get a tape recorder over here right away."

In front of the band, as the musicians played one mesmerizing and largely instrumental number after another, two women danced unaccompanied on the stage. They were, if not frumpy, about as far from the contemporary hardbodies of MTV as I could imagine. They wore floral print dresses and had thick calves. Instead of over-choreographed sexual gymnastics, these two housewives took strange, small, shuffling steps and wriggled their shoulders to the beat, sometimes engaging the audience but largely dancing as if off by themselves. Behind them, the accordion rode plaintively over the plodding rhythm, beat out on what looked like carved-out logs. The percussionist ratcheted the rattling teeth of the equine jawbone with a short stick and played a strange jerky pattern on the *clave*, totally unlike the 2-3 and 3-2 of *son* and *guaguancó*. A huge crowd cheered them on.

The shorter of the women danced in a self-absorbed trance, as if alone in her kitchen, without any self-consciousness, so that, watching her, I felt like a voyeur peeping in at a window, although she was onstage in front of a thousand people. She was visibly pregnant. Looking out at the audience with a warm, enigmatic smile and taking up a microphone, she urged the people at the front of the crowd to join her onstage for a dance. "No sabemos," they said into the lowered microphone, laughing and bashful. *We don't know how.* But coming from Cuban youth, this could only mean we don't know how to dance *like that.*

"I don't either," she said, making a small gesture with one hand as if to demonstrate her inability. But it wasn't true. She was not offended that nobody would join her, and she continued her surreal solo shimmy. It was a tableau worthy of David Lynch: the music melancholy and dirgelike, the dancers almost ecstatic and carried away to some other land by the mild rhythms.

As soon as the set was over, I hurried around the park and made my way to the backside of the stage. "I love your music," I gushed to the first band member I came upon. "What's the name of your band?" His name was Francisco Escalona, and he told me that the band was called Guasimal. "We're all members of the Escalona Rodriguez family," he said. "From Manzanillo."

"I've never heard anything quite like it," I said. "What kind of music is it?"

"It's not music of a certain type. The family has been playing together for over one hundred years. I don't know; this is the kind of music we play."

There are no available recordings of Guasimal, and I was already plotting a recording session in my mind. Francisco said he thought one song had once appeared on a compilation of some kind. "We have videos in France," he said. "But we are workers, we only play music sometimes."

"Well, I loved it," I said. I had rediscovered the joy of being a fan.

"We are very unhappy with the performance," said Francisco. "What you saw is not the whole spectacle."

"I thought it was great."

He shook his head. "We didn't have the coffee."

"The coffee?" I thought I had misunderstood.

"Usually we would have coffee and a *molidor*." It was a word I didn't know.

"You mean to drink?"

He mimed the beating of coffee beans in a mortar and pestle. "Usually, while we play, the women make coffee. First they grind the beans, then they carefully mix in the *guarapo*,* and then cook the coffee and serve it to the audience while we are playing. We play so that the women will be happy while they work making the coffee." This sounded, if possible, even more surreal and wonderful than the spectacle I had just witnessed. "I'd like to see that." I said.

"You should. Without them making the coffee for us, we are uninspired. The music is not the same. We have all been depressed by this since

---

* Sugar-cane juice.

we arrived. We have talked to the festival organizers several times to explain the situation but they still haven't been able to get the coffee we need. Perhaps they will have some for us when we play tomorrow. At home, we would also have a roast pig."

"I hope you get the coffee," I said. I scribbled down their festival schedule and promised to go and see them at their next gig in the patio of Santiago's branch of the UNEAC.

It was a fantastic explanation for the making of family music. The players and cooks formed a circle of mutual encouragement ensuring both that the coffee would come out sweet, smooth, and made with love and that the music would be played with energy and enthusiasm. Everywhere in Cuba, coffee was the currency of hospitality; upon being invited into any house, the first question was likely to be, "Would you like to drink coffee?" Guasimal elevated this caffeinated greeting ritual to sheltered heights worthy of some remote Amazonian tribe. Hearing Francisco describe their typical "performance" at home in the backyard, I felt like an anthropologist given a window onto an obscure rite.

The music was still going strong when I crept home, exhausted from the sensory overload of so much music. That night, I heard the *clave* in my dreams. I awoke to the sound of places being set on the wrought-iron table outside my window, underneath a jasmine-and-honeysuckle-scented bower. I joined my neighbors, a middle-aged Danish couple, for breakfast. They were music fans, and had always wanted to see Cuba. "There's a band that is very popular in Denmark the last years, which we like really a lot," said B, the wife. I didn't quite grasp if that was her entire name, or if she was only known by an initial. "It's called the Buena Vista Social Club. Perhaps you know it."

Like most Danes I have met, they had an unassailable belief in the superiority of their own society and political system. "Scandinavia is changing now," said B's husband, Paul, wistfully. "It is slowly becoming much more like southern Europe." I said something to the effect that I had come to Cuba in the hopes of finding a viable alternative to the ravenous capitalism of the American franchise and its strip-mall culture; they promptly invited me to come and stay with them in Copenhagen should I ever find myself in Denmark.

"Last night, we saw several times the police bothering innocent Cubans, just because they were talking with foreigners," said B. "First, we made friends and had very interesting conversations with some Cubans, but as soon as we went out into the street, they turned their backs on us and ignored us to walk in their own party. And we wondered why, but then we realized that they are worried all the time about the police watching."

Cuba needs the tourist dollars, but they don't want Cubans to interact with the tourists. The excuse is that the aggressive *jineteros* will cause visitors to have a bad experience. I told B and Paul that I had been eating dinner in a restaurant on the corner of the park the night before when a dozen French youths had come in, almost too drunk to walk, and occupied a banquet table in the middle of the room. Within minutes, they were screaming at the top of their lungs, breaking glasses, crashing rum bottles down on the tabletop, and generally behaving in a manner that would have guaranteed their prompt ejection from almost any eatery I have ever been to anywhere else in the world. Two Cuban women with them, evidently employed by the tourist agency that had brought these ugly French to Santiago, looked terrified and unsure of what to do. The rest of the diners tried to wither the almost violent party into submission with increasingly overt nasty looks. Outside, a policeman patrolling the block stuck his head in the door, checking on the situation at the loudest, most boisterous moments, and many of us hoped he would intervene.

The man sitting nearest me at the end of the long table began to rhythmically bang his empty beer mug against the tabletop as if participating in a prison riot. At the far end of the table, two or three from the group were trying to shout one another into submission when two Cuban men slid in the briefly unmanned door to greet their "old friends." The Cubans approached the table open-armed, as if meeting long-lost family members at the airport.

"Remember me? We met each other yesterday," one said. They were sober and well-dressed. Although this is classic *jinetero*—a man you have brusquely refused to buy black-market cigars from the day before sees you again and greets you more warmly than if you were his oldest customer—another blind-drunk Frenchman grinned broadly in recognition and extended his hand to shake, without getting up from the table. It seemed in fact that they did know each other, but before they could even shake hands, two patrolmen rushed in from the street, seized the two Cubans, and hustled them outside before the rest of us even had time to hope that they had come to remove the boorish French. B remarked that it was only a matter of time before this gross double standard would alienate Cubans and turn them against visitors. "Cubans are being treated like second-class citizens in their own country," I concluded.

At the UNEAC, the Escalona-Rodriguez family took the stage in front of an intimate crowd of fifteen intellectual, afternoon beer-drinkers. I sat at a table in the little patio with my beer and waved hello to Francisco. The UNEAC presenter explained that the band existed as part of the family ritual of making coffee, but that, unfortunately, there was no coffee to be had because of Cuba's difficult situation. "Normally," he said, "the coffee would be ground in time to the music, with rhythmic strokes, and sweetened with *guarapo*." He explained that the one-string standup bass was usually built as a permanent installation in the yard of the family house, with the stick affixed in a hole in the ground. "Such an arrangement is obviously not very portable," the presenter said, "so the bass you see here enables the band to travel around."

During the show, the stumpy pregnant woman with the Mona Lisa smile again danced with herself, holding her distended belly firmly and tenderly in one hand, as if it were the back of her dance partner. She was wearing pale-blue overall shorts, a green-and-white floral print top and a bizarre, knitted white hat like an Islamic skullcap. I again found her captivating. She danced for the handful of people on the patio with just as much spirit and enthusiasm as she had for the much larger crowd in the plaza.

Solely by virtue of my having come just to see them, we were now friends. During the set, the presenter came and joined me. He explained that he was one of the original founders of the festival. It had since become a huge monster that needed an entire staff to operate. He had given it up and was now in charge of the functions only at the UNEAC. "Incredible stuff, isn't it?" he said. He was a wiry hipster with greasy salt-and-pepper hair. "Fantastic. Music that hasn't changed in a hundred years. I just had to have them come and play here."

"There's something strange and wonderful about them," I said.

"There are thousands of questions about this band to which I don't have the answer. Have you seen them do their thing with the coffee?"

"Unfortunately not."

"You must see that to get the whole experience. Apparently, there was some fuckup and they thought the festival was going to provide the coffee and the festival says the band should have brought their own coffee with them. It's things like this that made me disengage myself from the festival."

"It sounds ridiculous. How much does coffee cost, anyway?" I asked, looking up at the stage. "I love how she dances."

"You're in for a disappointment, then: they're only dancing because there's no coffee. Normally, the women would be working the whole time to prepare it."

After another sublime and surreal set, Francisco and Angel Escalona came down from the stage and joined us on the patio. "You were great again," I said.

"Well, thanks," said Francisco, "but I didn't think so. We're a little tense because of the problems with the coffee. We're leaving in three days and still haven't done a complete spectacle."

"Why don't you look for someone *with possibilities* to help you get some?" asked the presenter, all but jerking his thumb in my direction. This went right past Angel and Francisco. They were far too country to pick up on even this unsubtle hint. The presenter raised his eyebrows meaningfully a couple of times while I envisioned the cash hemorrhage represented by a twenty-kilo burlap sack of premium Sierra Madre coffee beans. I squirmed uncomfortably. Friendships and associations in Cuba so often, and quickly, take on a commercial character. But Francisco shrugged his shoulders. He knew nobody with possibilities.

"Maybe tomorrow they'll have some for us," he said.

"I wouldn't count on it," said the presenter. He opened his eyes wide and looked at me. "*Mira*, think carefully. I really think you could *find some-one*. Maybe a foreigner. *With possibilities*." We both laughed a bit nervously. To my amazement, Angel and Francisco still had no idea what the presenter was suggesting. "I might be able to help," I said at last. "How much coffee would you need?"

"Let me ask." Francisco called over the divine, pregnant dancer.

"How much coffee is required?" I asked her. I very much liked the idea of being her patron and benefactor.

"Just a little bit, a handful. Just so we have some to demonstrate."

"Does it have to be beans?"

"No, just one packet of ground coffee would be fine. We can put it in the mortar and pretend to grind it up."

Even after almost four months in Cuba, I was staggered that all the stress and anxiety, and incomplete performances that had plagued Guasimal's participation in the festival, might have been relieved with a small bag of coffee. Unfortunately, I had no money. After buying a couple of beers, I had nothing in my pockets but a few ludicrous Cuban pesos. I announced that I'd be pleased to purchase a two-hundred-gram packet of ground coffee for the band to use during their last performances. We agreed to meet the next afternoon at the venue for their next gig, a small park at the uphill end of the old city.

When I arrived the next day, the group was waiting for me; the gig had been cancelled, but nearby was a place where coffee might be available for purchase. It was something like a café. We waited outside on the sidewalk while Francisco went in and began an interminable negotiation. I knew he was explaining the band's predicament in excruciating detail. He emerged at last.

"It's quite irregular, the guy says," he said. "They really just serve cups of coffee here. Brewed. But he's going to help us out."

I cut to the bottom line: "How much?"

"*Pues,* one dollar will get us what we need." I handed him a dollar. The rest of the Escalonas and Rodriguezes and I waited while Francisco went back in and completed the under-the-counter transaction.

That night, at the Casa de la Trova, I was treated like a VIP. When the band arrived, I was standing in the back, watching one of a string of superlative *son* bands. Angel Escalona took me and escorted me to the front row, to a seat they had reserved especially for me. As I settled into my place of honor, the delicious, pregnant, dancing housewife waved to me. She was fussing with a small portable aluminum stove, wrapping a box around it to stop the fire from spreading. She put an enormous aluminum mug of water on to boil. As the band played, the women pretended to grind the already ground coffee, pounding it in the *molidor*, a wooden mortar and pestle almost waist-high. They pulled down on the arm of the *guarapo* squeezer, tugging at a long lever that crushed a rod of fresh sugar cane until the beige juice dribbled down through a dugout slot carved into a chunk of tree. The audience, seated in rows at the rather staid Casa de la Trova, had no idea what to think. They were rapt. The women stirred the *guarapo* directly into the water as it was coming to a boil and then brewed the coffee Caribbean-style, pouring the sugarwater through a long, brown-stained coffee sock.

The music accompanying this extended ritual was bouncy and uptempo. The tunes were the same ones I had already heard at the other gigs, but surfing along on the magnificent coffee aroma and waves of mutual love and support that were emanating from both sides of the stage, the music lost its melancholy, Lynchian quality of antique darkness. The presence of the coffee made the men happy, and they played with more energy, as if they had already drunk it.

As the audience applauded, the pregnant Mona Lisa brought me the very first serving. It would be wrong not to write that it was the most delicious cup of coffee I've ever had.

Veinticuatro

Something in the air

"The stink of black sweat is called *grajo*. It is a terrible thing because it is as contagious as the flu. All you have to do is pass beside a black guy with *grajo* and you catch it! But there is a remedy that completely cures it; you look for a cow that is lying down and you push at it a little bit so that it gets up, but without getting enraged. Then, as soon as you are certain that the animal is not too feisty, you lower yourself down and get underneath it, between the feet, to catch the vapors of sweat that the animal sweated when it was lying down. It seems like an incredible thing, almost laughable, but I have tried it each time when I get hit with *grajo*, for which I seem to have a special attraction since birth; it hits me like flies go for sweets. Maybe I have some black in me without knowing...."
—Pedro, 61, *campesino*, in *The Medical Folklore of Cuba*

After a few days in Santiago, I moved house, although the place I was staying was one of the most spectacular homes I had rented a room in since my arrival in Cuba. Its enormous interior patio was quiet, shielded from the hustlers of the street, and dripping with tropical plants. Metal tables and wrought-iron chairs spread throughout the courtyard gave it the feeling of a private, personal café. But the owner, Angel, was stingy, and he sat all afternoon, morose, at a chair in the doorway of his part of the house, drinking. He was grumpy and unpleasant. I determined that for once, rather than suffering the accommodations and acquaintances fate had dealt me, I would spend an afternoon visiting *casas particulares* and choose one I really liked. The *casa* I picked was on a side street, just off of one of the steep arteries that plunges downhill into the harbor of Santiago. The proprietor, Maruchi, was an enormous *santera* with a dyed, blonde crewcut, as bulky as an East German shot-putter and with a personality big enough to match. Her place was virtually next door to the Siboney recording studios, where countless Oriente musicians have put their music down on tape.

When I went back to the first house to collect my things, I found the owner half in the bag. Weeping, Angel said to me, "Richard, this house has suffered a terrible calamity."

"I'm terribly sorry," I said. "What on earth happened?"

"I haven't wanted to mention it to our guests, to avoid them suffering our troubles, but just two days before you arrived, my wife died suddenly. *Un infarcto.*" A heart attack. "Now, there is nobody to take care of the boy."

"That's terrible. I'm so sorry. And, um, actually, I've been meaning to talk to you: I'm going to be leaving today. I'm moving on."

I slunk away, feeling guilty for judging Angel and abandoning the household in its time of need and wondering why despair and gloom seemed to dog my trail.

The moment the *casa particular* business was legalized, Maruchi had seen an opportunity. Although living in a nasty cement apartment block at the time, through sheer force of will and perhaps with the help of her spirits, she had effected a Byzantine triple *permuta*. *Permuta* means trade, or exchange, which, in Cuba, refers to an official process by which people manage to move house. Thanks to a grave housing shortage in the country, young married couples often end up stuck with their parents for years. Divorced couples continue to live together, and the home life of single children drags deep into adulthood. The *permuta* system attempted to enable mobility. Through it, for instance, a family might trade their house in Santiago for an apartment in Havana. A couple that had split up might leave a prime location or a large property in return for two apartments. To secure her house, Maruchi had split up the original residents, many of whom were no longer on speaking terms with one another. After finding them all new places to live, then reshuffling the inhabitants of those apartments to everyone's satisfaction, she finally managed to barter her way into the sort of colonial property that she might rent out to tourists; I shared her hospitality and leafy courtyard with Roger and Lillian, a couple from a tiny village in the Swiss Alps.

Her house remains my ideal vision of a tropical home: a spacious, cool, dark salon at the front, shuttered to the clamor of the street, and then all the other chambers arrayed along one side of the garden in a row, with access only to and through the garden. All the way at the back, beyond the patio and bowers draped with tropical plants, was a covered outdoor kitchen, conveniently close to the livestock pen. The only drawback was a funky odor said to waft through the garden.

"Sometimes it is very strong, sometimes faint. Sometimes it is not there at all," said Maruchi, lighting incense sticks and tucking them into the potted plants hanging in the garden. She attributed the mysterious odor to her powerful African guardian spirits, who, she claimed, manifested only in an olfactory way. Between Maruchi's Doberman steaming in the sun, the pig lounging with its slops in the pen, and some raucous pet parrots crapping on the stone tiles, I was never certain that I detected any inexplicable odors.

"It smells like woodsmoke," said Roger.

"It is the smell of black man's sweat," said Maruchi.

Roger and Lillian were spending a month taking *salsa* and *son* dance classes in the mornings and Afro-Cuban drumming lessons in the afternoons. In the evenings, the three of us tourists ventured out onto the hot streets of Santiago to the Casa de las Tradiciones, where Roger and I stood, wallflower cuckolds, listening to the sublime music and buying cold beers for the local dancefloor demons who had cut in to sweep Lillian off her feet and force her to demonstrate her new skills.

Despite their similar names, the Casa de las Tradiciones was quite different from the Casa de la Trova. The latter was a famous institution, one of Santiago's must-visit locales; it was listed in every guidebook. Somewhat absurdly, the main room was lined with chairs; audiences sat as if at the theater to watch one of the world's great dance musics performed. The Casa de las Tradiciones was more like one of those restaurants where all the chefs at the other restaurants go to hang out when their shift is over. It was ostensibly for members only, although foreigners willing to pay the one-dollar cover were generally admitted. Whatever musicians dropped by or were to play on a given evening crammed themselves against one wall in what doubled as the living room of a residential house some fifteen minutes walk off the beaten track. The barman dispensed beers from a little nook in a corner of the room that might once have been a telephone closet, and a dozen dancing couples were enough to fill the dancefloor, crowding the band. I never tired of the place. After long evenings of smoking hot *son*, we staggered back home up the dark streets of Santiago.

Maruchi worked at yet another *casa*, the Casa del Caribe. A Santiago cultural institution devoted to Caribbean studies in general and the Afro-Caribbean religions in particular, it is on a posh tree-lined street formerly inhabited by Santiago's economic elite, a stone's throw from an enormous mansion abandoned by the Bacardí family, who took their name and rum recipe to Puerto Rico after the revolution. I had been driven through this neighborhood on my only other visit to Cuba, a four-day junket sponsored by the tourist board accompanying a friend's Australian photographer girl-friend to write a piece about the joys of Santiago for Qantas's in-flight magazine. At the time, we'd been shown one opulent mansion after anoth-er converted into a kindergarten, old-age home, health clinic, or cultural center. At the Casa del Caribe, we had attended a *Vodou* ceremony led by Haitians from a former cane-cutting community in Ciego de Ávila. It had been a coincidence to find that Maruchi knew everyone associated with the place. She told me that her interest in becoming a *santera* was a direct result of her job there.

I relaxed in her garden for days at a time, blaming my persistent lassi-tude on gut pain and diarrhea that had become chronic and wearying since my first stomach troubles in Bayamo, but also coming to the realization that my trip to Cuba would soon be over. Maruchi boiled an empty spirulina container to sterilize it and then took my stool sample to a nearby clinic where a doctor friend worked. The next day he came to see me. I had noth-ing, he said, worse than a classic case of traveler's diarrhea. He tried to refuse the ten-dollar-bill I pressed into his hand. "I know a lot of doctors have left the country," I said. "With the salary you earn here, *no es fácil*."

"I'm conflicted," he said. "A colleague of mine left a conference in Mex-ico City a few years ago and walked across the Rio Grande. He already has his own practice and just now sent me some photos of the swimming pool he is building in his back yard in Houston." Besides my diarrhea, I suffered from the growing certainty that I had had all the solitude and socialist stag-nation I could stomach. I decided to stay until my visa expired, but I gave up on visiting Alto Songo, La Maya, Mayarí, and the other obscure corners of the Oriente made legendary to me by the lyrics of songs I had listened to back in New York. (Rather like Miriam's son, Rodolfo, who sat in his room mouthing the words of Led Zeppelin songs and dreaming of another world, I had played my collection of crusty Cuban vinyl over and over, trying to imagine each village and landmark.) I even abandoned my plans to visit the area where Pedro Regalado had seen the ivory-billed woodpecker more than fifteen years earlier. At a bare minimum, I wanted the closure of reaching Guantánamo, which remained for me the most malignant of the tumors poisoning the Cuba–United States relationship. So close to the end, however, I felt no urgency to move on. Just about everything seemed best postponed until tomorrow.

If I couldn't bring myself to continue the journey, I did at least manage to get out of the house and wander the sloping streets of Santiago. One day on the way to the Casa del Caribe, I came across a *yerbero* selling leaves and bark and herbs out of an open-sided truck. He was a ruined old guy who peered at me through a broken pair of eyeglasses. The spectacles were held together at the hinges with filthy blobs of melted candlewax that reminded me of the residue coating Eduardo's *prendas* on his *Palo Monte* altar. His clothes were balding and stained from years of chopping and juicing magical herbs. I asked for *yerba luisa*, the lemon vervain that Imandra had advertised as a powerful tool against upset stomachs back in the Cupaynicú Botanical Gardens.

"You find any of that and I'll give you a gold medal," he said, bundling a fat handful of foliage in a strip of yesterday's newspaper. "It's been years since any of that came around."

"Are a lot of herbs disappearing?"

"Lots of them. The youth today aren't concerned with this stuff," he said. As he turned to add the bundle to a pile behind him, I heard him muttering, "Una medalla de oro, medalla de oro."

In a Santiago used-book stall, I had stumbled on a copy of *El Folclor Médico de Cuba*, a nine-hundred-page oral compendium of *remedios caseros* (household cures) collected in 1961 and 1962 at the dawn of the revolution. It was as stained and worn as my mother's ancient copy of *The Joy of Cooking*, with crumbling and browning acid-paper pages that only added to its aura. On the cover was a drawing of a woman smoking a cigar as she shredded herbs at a rickety wooden table.

José Seoane Gallo, the compiler, identifies four distinct Cuban occupations concerned with medicinal plants. The *santero* is a professional who reveals plant cures and their recipes only as a medium after "bajando un muerto," literally lowering, or calling down, a dead person. Although the *santero* might choose which *orisha* or spirit to invite based on the needs of the client, he is only the physical vessel for the saint's visit. The spirit or soul speaks through him, both to diagnose and prescribe.

A *curandero*, or healer, also charges a fee for his services, but "works with his own power, without dead or spirits," drawing on knowledge often passed down through the generations to heal with plant remedies and prayers. Faith is still crucial to the cure: "...note that in relation to what I do the important thing is not the remedy that I send them to drink or do, but the prayer which I make. It's not my opinion that I have a special grace; what I have is a great ability to make the sick person believe that he will be cured if he puts faith in what I do to him and what I tell him to do."

Botanists, or *botánicos*, are both the least spiritual and least commercial group, being composed of amateur-scientist mountain men who spend their lives in the *manigua* and are able to identify every plant and tree in the wilderness. They freely share plants from their collection in the same way, apparently, that so many people had helped me, as "when someone arrives at an unknown house to ask for a glass of water to calm the thirst on a long hike. This makes them the natural enemy of the *yerberos*, who would sell their own soul, were it worth anything...."

According to Gallo's informants, the *yerbero* is little more than a dealer who fills prescriptions; his clients are both those seeking the ingredients for a cure and those who purchase herbal offerings to place on the altars of their *orishas*. "Armando, age 54, of Camagüey" told Gallo that there are only two bits of knowledge one needs to know to be a *yerbero*: "The first is to know what sells on a daily basis, so as to always bring those with me. The second is to know where the plants are, the ones that sell daily and the ones that don't, so that I may go looking for them when there is a demand, or if I run out of the ones I have."

Since the muttering *yerbero* had no *yerba luisa*, I bought the only plant I knew how to use, a long fat stalk of aloe to smear on my mosquito bites and sunburn. On the next block, a guy sitting on a stoop spied the aloe spear in the bicycle basket and called out to me: "Mira! Asi que tu ere' un brujo. ¿Va' a hacer una brujeria?" Which means: I see that you're a witch. Are you off to go cast a spell?

Perhaps he was right, since the Casa del Caribe was presenting a series of simulated religious rituals in their yard as part of the ongoing festival, and the house was given over to a museum exposition of "Popular Religions with Room of *Orishas*." The entrance fee was one dollar, or three dollars for those who wanted to have the exhibits explained to them. I said I didn't need any explanations. Nonetheless, a large woman accompanied me through the gallery. She was wearing a flowing Senegalese wax batik *muumuu* and dozens of color-coded *orisha* necklaces. In the *orisha* room, I looked at a collection of very finely worked clay figurines dressed in tidy doll-clothes ensembles, each matching the color scheme of the *orisha* they represented. They were the size of Barbie dolls. San Lázaro was like a black Ken with a crutch, a nice-looking guy who just happened to be wearing a tailored burlap vest. My guide struggled mightily not to explain anything to me.

The room given over to *Palo Monte* held an enormous "Sarabanda" remarkably like Eduardo's in every respect but one. It was odorless. In this museum-like setting, the vast amorphous blob of blackened encaustic was indistinguishable from an artwork by Joseph Beuys. Beside it, adding to the illusion that it was all part of a late-1980s Soho gallery installation, the "ingredients" of the *Sarabanda* were laid out in a row on the floor; piles of earth in little pyramids, presumably collected from "the four corners"; rocks with magical powers; chunks of scrap iron, including a horseshoe; and a neat clump of straw. Missing were the chicken feet, dried fish, and snake skeletons.

"These are only some of the ingredients," I said to my guide.

"That's right, some of them are secret," she allowed.

It was all too tidy, like the unattainable perfection of chopped vegetables laid out at the beginning of a cooking show. The dolls and their pristine finery were unlike the hodgepodge of chipped crockery, dried flowers, plastic toys, cheap, stained chromolithographs, and bowls of rocks that made up most home *Santería* shrines. It felt like spin control; *Santería* was being marketed, and, like real-estate photographers, the organizers had made choosing the right angle their top priority. But I found this endearing because it made me feel certain that those behind the exhibition were believers.

Veinticinco
Cuban Vodou

"...I have these roosters because when I received my *santo* years ago, he demanded roosters.

"Yeah? He asked for roosters?

"Ah, you don't know anything. Sometimes they ask for goats, sheep, black hens, boa constrictors, doves. But they also take things away from you. For instance, I can't ride bicycles or motorcycles or drive cars. The religion is very complicated."

—Pedro Juan Gutierrez, *Tropical Animal*

Pablo Milanes was writhing on his back in the dirt, stabbing at his own stomach with two long knives. As his hands pumped up and down like a sewing machine, the sharp points of the knives made deep dents in his belly. He appeared desperate to eviscerate himself, but the raw steel would not puncture his flesh.

Only minutes earlier, I had been enjoying a relaxed chat with Milanes (who is unrelated to the *Nueva Trova* singer of the same name) and had even invited myself to his home in the mountains. He is a famed *gangan*, or *houngan*, a *Vodou* priest from high in the Sierra Madre between Santiago and Palma Soriano. Friends of friends had given me his name in Havana, and I had read about him in *El Vodú en Cuba*, the book published by the Casa del Caribe in which I had first learned of the deep Haitian connection with Cuba's Oriente. I had already stopped by the Casa del Caribe several times to try and find him during the Festival of Fire and now finally he and his *lakou** were presenting a ceremony for *Papa Legba*, the gatekeeper spirit

---

* *Lakou* describes an extended family group that lives together in an almost self-sufficient cluster of houses, sharing land, fieldwork, child-rearing responsibilities. Often, the patriarch of

who stands at the crossroads controlling the doorway between this world and the spirit world.

I had asked Pablo the difference between *Papa Legba* and *Eleggua*, the Cuban *santo* who fulfills much the same function. Like his Haitian homonym *Legba*, *Eleggua* is always the first to be saluted in any ceremony—the other spirits of the pantheon can only be reached through him, with his acquiescence. *Eleggua*, Pablo explained, is the guardian of the *portail*, the doorway. But *Legba* has the key. "Yo pa mem lwa, me yo mache ansem," he said in Kreyol. They are not the same spirit, but they walk together.

I scribbled this in my notebook.

"You're writing?" asked the *gangan*.

"I hope that's okay."

"Sure, why not? Keep writing. I write also, in the earth."

"What?"

"My father taught me to write in the earth. With seeds."

Pablo's brother, Tato, appeared and gave me the *houngan* hug. This a double embrace with one arm low and the other high, tight enough for your cheeks to touch. The Milanes brothers must both be in their seventies, but Tato almost squeezed the air out of me. I had forgotten the hug came in two parts, first to one side and then to the other, so when Tato released me and switched his arms to left-high/right-low for a second squeeze, I floundered. My arms bobbled up and down as if I were on a date going in for a clumsy first kiss, erasing any Haitian credibility I had fostered by speaking cautious Kreyol.

They nonetheless invited me into their office-for-the-day, a dirt-floor thatched shack set up in the yard of the Casa del Caribe to serve as a temporary *kay mistè*, which literally means "house of mysteries." This is where the *lwa*, the spirits or *mystères,* hang out to do their works. Pablo had a table set up with the usual paraphernalia: an ancient mountain of candlewax from countless candles that had guttered out and flowed like lava; bottles of rum; a box of ash for making *véve*, the complex and sacred symbols of the *lwa*, drawn on the ground by letting the pale dust trail out between the thumb and forefinger—another way, I realized, that Pablo "wrote in the earth"; chromolithographs in frames behind pitted, dusty glass; and *kleren*, the homemade white lightning of Haiti, cane alcohol flavored with herbs,

---

the *lakou* is an older *houngan* like Pablo.

roots, and leaves.

Tato uncorked the *kleren* and dribbled some alcohol on the floor for the spirits. The bottle was crammed full of unidentifiable brown organic matter, as if someone had cleaned out several years of leaf litter from a gutter and stuffed it down into the neck. He poured a healthy shot into a plastic cup and passed it to me. The booze tasted earthy and bitter, but with a perfumed hint of *Agua Florida*, the cheap cologne much beloved by the spirit world and used around the globe, from Hindu rituals to the *ayahuasca* ceremonies of Peruvian shamans. A small chip of purplish wood floated on the surface.

"How many different things are in there?" I asked.

"More than a hundred herbs and roots, mostly roots," said Tato, wiping his lips with the back of his hand.

In Haiti, the late *houngan* and painter André Pierre drank astonishing quantities of *kleren* out of a bottle like this, and nevertheless survived to the ripe old age of about ninety. When I visited him once as part of a film crew, he told us he had had the same bottle for sixty years. Since at the time he was drinking out of a 1970s-vintage gallon Gallo wine jug, I was skeptical. But I was taking him too literally; when the bottle breaks every decade or so, shattering on the ground after one too many or just cracking in half from overuse, the mystical roots and other funk are collected up, brushed off as best as possible and stuffed down the neck of another bottle. "Claro," said Tato, when I told him about André Pierre's eternal *kleren* bottle. "Gen zèb kap bay fòs kat san, senk san zan. Yo p'ap janm pèdi fòs yo." There are herbs working to "give force" for four hundred or five hundred years without ever losing their power.

I liked this suggestion that *kek zèb* that had been brought from Africa centuries ago were still hard at work today. These endlessly topped-up bottles filled with vegetable matter are like the bottomless stews of a medieval cookpot, never removed from the fire, with its ingredients added day after day and year after year. Sipping from Tato's bottle was like drinking out of a terrarium, but with the advantage that, in its mystical aura, flourished the delusion that consuming very strong, home-distilled rum is excellent for health and well-being. When we had filmed him, André Pierre, never far from his huge bottle, had commanded total respect from all who entered his expansive family compound despite being in his late eighties. Tato was muscled and solid, with a thick neck and a boxer's features.

"I think I'll have a bit more of that," I said.

Two *babalawos* from Havana came into the hut and saluted Pablo with a seamless flurry of origami hugs. They looked to be in their thirties. Their stiff and formal greeting was like something out of a bad western confused with the Biblical tale of the three kings from the East. One of them said, approximately, *We have heard wondrous tales of your great powers, which have reached far across this land to our distant neighborhood of Guanabacoa.** Tato poured them each a glass of *kleren*. There was a further ceremonial sprinkling of the ground with alcohol. The men went on in this vein: *We of Guanabacoa consider ourselves mighty in these arts and yet we have traveled all this far way to watch and observe you in complete respect and silence. Do not take our visit lightly but please be sure that we mean only good by being here.* Pablo greeted this starchy proclamation with an amused look. "I'm pleased that you have come. Stay as long as you like. We will begin soon, out here in the yard," he said, escorting them out of the hut. When he came back in, he said: "Guanabacoa is very strong."

"It's obvious that you're very busy," I said, "getting ready for the ceremony and all that. I'm hoping afterward I may travel back with you both to Pilon del Cauto and talk some more."

"That's possible. You should see my farm," he said. "I've been a farmer since I was a boy."

I did my best to firm up the invitation; once the ceremony got underway, Pablo and Tato were going to be more than busy when the spirits arrived to displace their minds and occupy their bodies. Pablo is ridden or mounted by *Gran Bwa*, literally "Big Tree," the *Vodou* spirit in charge of the forests, a preeminent *lwa* in the Congo rites of Haiti. It is from *Gran Bwa* that permission must be obtained before cutting trees or otherwise exploiting the forest. "He is the supreme *mystère*," writes folklorist Harold Courlander, "whose good will or eccentric whim determines the fortunes of all men." In *The Drum and the Hoe: Life and Lore of the Haitian People*, Courlander also notes that *Gran Bwa* is very hard on his human steeds, an observation Pablo confirmed later, when I went to his home in the mountains. For his part, Tato is mounted by *Bawon Kriminel*, another powerful *lwa* associated with the tribe of the *Gèdés*, *mystères* that hang out in cemeteries and generally make nuisances of themselves, crashing festivi-

---

* A suburb of Havana.

ties dedicated to other spirits and sexually harassing the guests. *Kriminel* is much revered in south coastal Haiti, where the Milaneses' father had come from.

It is the *lwa* that do the actual work of *Vodou*, giving counsel or medical advice, feeding or bathing the members of the *lakou* or congregation while in human form. I went outside to wait for their arrival. People were filtering into the yard and the drummers had staked out a semicircle in front of the *kay mistè*. A black goat strained against a short leash, skittish and uncomfortable and, I thought, fully aware of its own imminent demise.

The ceremony began unannounced with a smudging ritual. An elderly assistant with a shovelful of hot coals and burning herbs went around the yard and wafted smoke into each corner, to rid the yard of malevolent spirits. Once the courtyard was cleansed, the drumming started and the *hounsi*, female *Vodou* initiates from Pablo's troupe, began to dance. They wore red or white headscarves, turquoise blouses, and long, black cotton skirts with a broad yellow ruffle. José Millet, one of the authors of *El Vodú en Cuba*, got up and stood in the middle of the yard facing a small audience of foreign visitors. "What you are going to see," he said, "is a family *Vodou* ceremony, a *manjé mort* or 'feeding of the dead,' in which the *cofradia Vodou* of Pablo Milanes will honor their ancestral spirits." But the crowd was busy getting out their video cameras, and his simulcast, delivered like a basketball announcer, was a distraction from the proceedings.

The *hounsi* danced in a relaxed and almost lackadaisical manner, as if unwilling to use up their energy too early in the day. Capricious, the *lwa* may descend at any time to mount a steed, but often there is a building of intensity in the dancing that announces their imminent arrival. The dance and drumming both serve as invitations to the *lwa*, but the dancers pace themselves, gradually feeding off one another as the energy spirals upward. Early writers on *Vodou* invariably used sensationalistic words like "frenzy" to describe the moments leading to possession, and those looking for a logical explanation of the phenomenon have argued that the physical exhaustion resulting from hours of nonstop dancing leaves the body ripe and vulnerable to the community's power of suggestion. As often as not, however, those swept away, struck down, and temporarily dispossessed of their bodies are marginal participants in the dance. Sometimes, they are bystanders who have not danced at all.

The spectators gathered in a bunch a safe distance from the dancers, like cows in the rain, instinctively seeking safety in numbers. I was reminded of the *Santería* initiation in Ciego de Ávila where I had lurked cautiously outside the window until Eduardo invited me in. We uninitiated have no idea how to behave at a ceremony. Should one be hushed, as if entering a church? Will it provoke a scandal to dance uninvited? In a poorly defined ritual space that is usually little more than a bare room or dirt yard, where to stand to ensure that one will not be swept up in the proceedings? Where is that man going with that machete? Clustered in a tight group, the audience kept their cameras at the ready. I counted a knot of ten videographers, standing shoulder to shoulder, a frenzy of filmmakers.

Pablo and Tato came out and began to dance in front of the *hounsi*. Pablo had put on a sort of red and black yin-yang dress shirt, all black with a red stripe to the right of the buttons, and all red with one black stripe on the left. He had long strings of beads draped crossways under his arms like bandoliers. Later he explained that this is his work uniform, the colors of *Gran Bwa*, put on when he is to be mounted by the spirit.

I missed the moment when Pablo went away and *Gran Bwa* arrived to take his place. I remember Pablo suddenly lying on his back in the dirt going at himself with the knives as the videographers jostled to document the happening. The display with knives, common in *Vodou*, serves as proof that human has been displaced by supernatural: no man could survive such a jabbing and cutting and hacking without being punctured and beginning to bleed. Those ridden by the *lwa* often draw the length of a machete blade across the tongue, walk on hot coals, or hold their hands or face over the flames of candles. Courlander writes that those ridden by *Gèdé Nimbo* are known to rub their tongues and eyes with hot pepper.

Tato brought a sequined bottle of rum or *kleren*, and sprayed a mouthful of it in a fine, explosive mist over his prostrate brother, welcoming the spirit with a hazy cloud of alcohol. We were in the presence of *Gran Bwa*. The *lwa* are called to earth to work on man's behalf. They come at our urging from their home, imagined as *en ba dlo*, beneath the sea, in a kind of black Atlantis, the location of *l'Afrik Ginen*, the mystical motherland of Africa, the paradise remembered to which slaves believed they would return in death. *Vodou* faithful are known as *sèvitè*, servitors, those who attend to the spirits, but the relationship between man and *lwa* is reciprocal and businesslike. The *lwa* are in part honored with expensive parties, fine wine, cakes, fruits, and tobacco for the same reasons lobbyists in Washington treat members of Congress to gala dinners, cognac, and cigars: to flatter, influence, and persuade those more powerful than themselves into doing their bidding.

Presented with a huge pot of fried chicken, *Gran Bwa* began to eat his fill. Many *lwa* have terrible table manners, and *Gran Bwa* ate like a hyena. He pulled chunks of chicken from the pot and tore them apart with his hands, stuffing them into Pablo's mouth bones and all, as if the humans around him would at any moment tempt fate and snatch the platter away before he was satisfied. Soon Pablo's hands and face were covered in grease. He pulled bones out through his teeth and cast them on the ground. But the *lwa* are first and foremost providers; after this theatrical display, *Gran Bwa* distributed pieces of chicken to those gathered near him. Soon, a *hounsi* took the pot from him and continued serving the crowd.

Tato took short, stubby candles and set them up on the ground in two rows, like miniature, flickering landing lights on an airport runway. The goat was petted and stroked and massaged and bathed with a mixture of herbs and perfumed *kleren*, as if to sooth the acrid taste of fear out of its blood. Fragrant and clean and glossy black, cosseted by Pablo's sons and nephews, and adorned with lit candles stuck onto the points of its horns, the goat was to meet its maker in style.

Nothing has given *Vodou* a worse reputation in the world at large than the use of animals in ceremonies. The drama and theatrics surrounding ritual killings in *Vodou* and *Santería*, and the use of the blood, which is often poured onto the *prendas* or daubed on the foreheads of congregants, have throughout history been exploited to revile and suppress Afro-Caribbean religions generally. This is especially true today, when so few consumers of Chicken McNuggets or Big Macs are likely to have ever seen a chicken killed and cleaned and plucked, or a cow slaughtered and butchered. But the deaths of animals in *Vodou* come as fast and as painlessly as in any abattoir, and the meat is almost always cooked there and then, and eaten communally by the congregation. Even the common use of the word "sacrifice" to describe these practices is a misnomer: nothing is "sacrificed," except perhaps our contemporary national illusion that boneless chicken breasts magically appear in the supermarket without any actual killing being involved.*

A racist and sensationalist tendency, so strong that it might better be described as a tradition, runs through popular treatments of Afro-Caribbean religion. One has only to think of the countless voodoo exploitation movies cranked out with regularity by Hollywood, going back at least to the 1932 horror classic, *White Zombie*, inspired by books like William Seabrook's *The Magic Island*. Consider two examples, bearing in mind that both are simply descriptions of the slaughter of a chicken, an act that occurs in the modern United States under the far more barbaric conditions of factory farming more than ten million times a day. "Her face was distorted with frenzy," writes Hesketh Prichard in 1900. "Her excitement was horrible; she pressed the bleeding neck to her lips, and, when she slowly withdrew her hand, stood for an instant fixed and immovable, her lips and teeth stained red." In *Voodoo Fire in Haiti*, a 1935 effort illustrated with his own prurient woodcuts, Richard Loederer seems to have felt the need to go Prichard one better:

> The scene was diabolical. There stood the naked negress, her sweat-streaked body glistening in the ruddy firelight, and at arm's length she held a terrified black cock, the very symbol of Satan, squawking and flapping its wings, while the feathers flew in all directions. An awful sickness gripped me. I felt as if I were looking into the very depths of evil....

> [T]he Mamaloi pushed the bleeding neck into her mouth and sucked the blood out of the twitching body. Her teeth were dyed crimson. Blood ran over her chin, her throat, her breasts, and down her thighs.

Both Prichard and Loederer's lurid fantasies were purported to be nonfiction and eyewitness accounts.

At the Casa Del Caribe ceremony, the goat was brought, kicking and resisting with all the stubbornness goats are known for, to the landing strip prepared by Tato. Once there, as if hypnotized, the animal was overtaken by a certain tranquility and it stood rigid, as if at attention, even seeming to extending its neck for the knife. *Kriminel*, with one swift stroke of a

---

* I should mention here that while the killing of animals that will not later be eaten is rare, it is not unheard of. I once witnessed in Haiti the slaughter of a dog, whose body was buried in a pit "inhabited" by the *lwa Kriminel*. This rare and extreme offering was considered such a taboo even within the *lakou* that our documentary film crew, although allowed to observe, was strictly prohibited from filming.

machete, severed its head clean off.

To judge by the enthusiasm that greeted these labors on our behalf, nobody in the yard harbored the slightest doubt as to the legitimacy of the proceedings. Having killed the goat, which the *hounsi* took away for immediate butchering and cooking, the two spirits retired to the *kay mistè*, and, before I had quite noticed what was happening, a long polite queue formed at the doorway of the little hut, as if at a church potluck supper the buffet line had suddenly been declared open. There seemed to be more people waiting than had been in the yard observing. Never mind that the ceremony was only a demonstration, presented under the auspices and according to the schedule of the Casa del Caribe, with José Millet providing a live blow-by-blow like the voiceover narration of a documentary film. It was a tourist ceremony, but none of this mattered. *Gran Bwa* and *Kriminel* were in our midst, at work for hours, doing *despojos*, cleansing us of our evil influences with a laying-on of hands. When my turn came, I approached *Gran Bwa*. He took my right hand and dragged a line down the inside of my forearm from the crook of the elbow with a smooth stone, then across to the other arm and across my body in front of the shoulders. He made cross marks with the stone at these joints and crossroads of the body, then slapped away the evil at each point, putting his palm there and hitting the back of his hand the way a doctor taps at your chest. He did my forehead, then turned me and hit again, behind my shoulders. He took a big swig of *kleren* and blew it in a fine mist onto the front of my T-shirt. Then, although seated, he did a little dance in place and then spun me, first to the right and then to the left, urging me to discard my evil with a sort of skyward waggle of the fingers like something out of morning television aerobics. A final mighty fling of the wrists directed the last of these bad influences away and over the table/altar over which the goat's head was now presiding. Like the other participants, I emerged hushed and invigorated from my brief audience with the spirit.

Driving to Pilon del Cauto in the rattletrap state-provided bus with Pablo was like accompanying an elected official on a celebratory tour of his political stronghold. After turning off the old central highway to begin the long climb up into the mountains, every *campesino* sitting on his front porch or walking along the road appeared to know our bus and our business and greeted us with a wave. Pablo sat in the front in the shotgun seat, behind the broad flat windshield. His return waves combined equal parts greeting and acknowledgment. Once or twice, he stopped the driver to hold a quick conference out the side window of the bus. At one stop, he was given a gift of a fighting cock, an immaculate white bird whose scarlet comb and gullet stood out like blood against its snowy feathers.

When we had climbed many kilometers uphill to where the air turned cool and the road turned to gravel, Pablo got up from his seat and came to find me at the back of the bus. "You must sit in my seat now, to view the countryside," he said, leading me up to the front. "We have a lot of foreign visitors, Tato and I. We've found it is better to be clear on one point. Sometimes, Tato has a visitor; sometimes, the visitor comes to see me. Who were you planning to visit?"

"I was given your name originally in Havana, so you, I suppose. You don't live in the same place?"

"We have different *fincas*. So you'll be coming with me to my house, then." A man sitting on his porch waved to us. Pablo returned the gesture as we drove past. I asked him if he had ever gotten involved in politics by running for some kind of office.

"That's not for me," he said.

"It looks like you're friends with everybody."

"If I can help out, I do. My house has electricity. You'll see. That's because of me, for instance. The electricity didn't always reach so far. I fought for years for that. Sometimes, you help yourself and everybody wins. People have asked me to do this or that office, but I'm not a smart guy like that. I always turn them down."

"You're not interested?"

"Hay un dicho: el loco y el bobo no tiene enemigo," said Pablo. There's a saying: the lunatic and the simpleton have no enemies. "In the field of life, I'm a simpleton." Switching from Spanish to Kreyol, he offered a Haitian proverb containing the same wisdom: *Neg sot pa hipokrit.* The simpleminded man is not a hypocrite.

The road wound up a steep valley carved by the uppermost reaches of Cuba's mightiest river, the Cauto, which drains most of the north slope of the Sierra and widens out as it flows west through the flatlands around Bayamo. The headwaters are on Pablo's land, not far from the sea as the crow flies, but on the wrong side of the ridge, so that the water flowing past his house takes a long and circuitous route across half the Oriente to finally dump into the sea hundreds of kilometers away. At a ford in the river, Pablo surprised the driver by telling him to stop in midstream. "Open the door for me," he said, and stepped out of the bus into the water. He looked around at his feet and then bent down to pick up a rock. Pablo got back on and handed it to me. It was gray and smoothed into an oblong from years in the water.

"Now you have a rock from the Cauto," he said. Pablo had a way of speaking that was invested with weight and wisdom. I put the rock in my pocket for safekeeping. But it was irresistible to think of it as a powerful object. Soon, I took it out again to squeeze it and look at its different angles, the way a boy who has caught a fly ball at a baseball game can't resist pulling out his prize and staring at it.

Pilon del Cauto, the end of the road, was a hamlet of four or five buildings in which the road was rutted to near-impassability. The few of us left on the bus got off and the driver began to negotiate a cautious and tricky K-turn on the narrow, gullied road. Slowly, he drove off, back the way we had come, leaving us in motorless quiet.

"That was the store where my father had credit," said Pablo, gesturing at the building in front of us. "We walk from here. Say goodbye to Tato."

Tato and I exchanged hugs, and he said maybe he would walk down the next day and visit us. I followed Pablo up a dirt track that quickly entered open, healthy forest.

"How did your father end up here?" I asked.

"They cheated him. He came in 1920 from St. Louis du Sud.* They told him there was lots of work here, that you could make Cuban pesos and take them back and buy Haitian money at the end of the season. But then, when they got him here, they said he owed lots of money for the passage."

"They still do the same thing today in the Dominican Republic," I said. "In the sugar plantations, where only Haitians work, they bring the laborers across the border and put them to work and then, on payday, they say, 'You owe us such and such for the machete you used,' and then the next week, they tell them, 'You owe us this amount for rent,' and soon the workers are in such debt to the plantation store, where the owners charge twice as much for everything, that they can't leave."

---

* On the south coast of Haiti's western spur near Aux Cayes, a short boatride from Santiago across the dangerous Windward Passage.

"My father left. He went to work for some French who had a coffee plantation, then fell in love with my mother and got married. I can't remember under which government, but came a time when they said, let's send all the Haitians back to Haiti. At this point, my father had a little piece at Caoba on the French *finca*, so he said to my mother, 'I don't have anything else to give you, you take the land,' and he went down to a friend's place who had some sugar cane. He said, 'Goodbye, I'm leaving,' but his friend said to take it easy and wait and see, that maybe the whole thing would blow over. He stayed there and worked for awhile and, in fact, the moment passed."

We were trudging our way uphill through the forest. Pablo had his fighting cock under one arm. Here and there, we passed small thatched houses painted in the rural Haitian style, eggshell blue with a flourish of red diamonds down the door. At a tall, thorny tree, Pablo stopped. "This is the *mapou* tree, where we do *Petro* ceremonies," he said. The *lwa* of the *Petro* pantheon are the "strong" or "hot" spirits of *Vodou*. It was a ceiba, the trunk dense with thorns. At the base, a row of savage scars wrinkled the bark into folds.

"What are these marks?" I asked.

"That marks the *compromiso*." The obligation. "They are made by the saint himself, during the ceremony, with a machete, to mark the number of years before the next time we must pay tribute."

"This is your land?"

"I have a part, my brothers have a part. All this was my father's land. When he went back to get my mother, the French were trying to evict her. They said Haitians couldn't own any land. That was further down. My father brought her up here. *No había nada.*" There was nothing here. "This was pure *monte*, solid jungle. He built a little *bohío* in the woods and went down to work the sugar cane. Every two weeks, he would walk up here on foot and bring food for her. At that time, there were two boys. Each time, he would clean out a little more forest and plant *vianda*, cassava, plantains. He put in a little coffee.

"One year, he got together about six *quintales** of coffee and took them down to the store I pointed out to you. For years and years, that was the

---

* A quintal was originally equivalent to 100 pounds, or about 46 kilos, but, in today's usage in the metric system, it refers to 100 kilos.

only trading post. A guy named Agustín. He got to be great friends with my father. Dad sold him the coffee and went back down to the sugar-cane fields. The next time he came up, the owner of the store came to him and said, 'Milanes, I am going to give you credit because I can see you are a serious person. You borrow what you need.' And from there, my father went, expanding, getting more land, planting more coffee plants.

"I remember one year, he said, 'This year, we are not going to get one single thing at the store, I want to put every penny into the farm.' We got sugar cane to sweeten our coffee and we went down to the beach and collected our own salt and ground it ourselves in a mortar. That year, we lived completely off of the production of the *finca*.

"My father couldn't even write his own name. But you'll see. I have mangos, tangerines, coffee, coconuts that I planted, *zapote, ñame*."

I struggled to keep up with Pablo, who displayed the same energy he had in the *Vodou* ceremony, striding ahead of me up the hill despite his age. As best I could tell from his indications, he owned most of the land we could see, a chunk of forest and plantings that reached from the Loma del Pilon—a large, knob-shaped hill in front of us—to the Loma del Camaron, "Shrimp Hill," a ridgebacked mountain to our right.

"Is your father still alive?" I asked.

"He died in 1985. At the age of one hundred and five. He outlived his great friend, Agustín. Although my father had stopped doing business with him years ago."

"Because your father stopped shopping at the store?"

"No, that was understood, this was another time, years later, when they were *compadres*. My father had strong ideas about how things should be done, how you conducted your affairs, and he felt Agustín had insulted him. They used to get together to drink coffee and play cards. But one year—at this point, my father had lots of people working—I guess maybe he had borrowed more than usual, expenses were high, maybe he owed 2,000 pesos and change, and perhaps Agustín started to get a little nervous. One day, Agustín came up to the house as usual and they were sitting around having coffee. Finally, Agustín said, 'Hey, Milanes, when are you going to start bringing in the coffee so I can pay down your debt?'

"My father, Manuel, looked at him and said they were just drying it now and he would bring it in soon. But, instead, Dad went down to the bank in Palma Soriano and said he wanted to open up a line of credit. They were real bankers and they said, 'Well, well, maybe, let us come out and look at your place and see if it's worth anything.' They came and looked and said they would give him 70,000 pesos in credit against the land and future coffee production. My father took 30,000 in cash and went straight to see Agustín and said, '*Saca me la cuenta.*' Tote up my bill. And Agustín said 2,000 and whatever it was. So Dad said to my older brother, 'Pay him.' My brother pulled out this big sack of cash and started counting it out. Agustín had never seen anything like that. 'No, no,' says Agustín, 'I don't want your money, I want your coffee.' Manuel Milanes said, 'You are my friend, and you insulted me. You never ever came to my house before to ask me to pay my credit. I am still your friend and I am happy to buy from you, but from now on, I pay cash.' After that, my father always sold his coffee to the bankers in Palma."

The Milanes house lay on a slope between the two hills, on a bald patch of brown earth in the shadow of the Loma del Pilon. It was a family compound in the African style. In the main house, Pablo and his wife lived with one of their daughters. A son and his wife and sons lived fifty meters away, sharing this clearing in the forest. To one side was the pigpen, full of fat and healthy porkers that had churned much of the yard to dust with their trotters. "Tomorrow," said Pablo, "in honor of your visit, we will roast a pig." Just outside the kitchen window was the *kay mistè*, the family *Vodou* temple that served as *Gran Bwa*'s office. Like many rural Cuban homes, Pablo's was a simple large room with a polished cement floor. Sunlight glinted between slats cut from outward curving slabs of palm trunk. One half was the living room, with a television and chairs, and the other half was divided into a row of sleeping quarters just large enough for beds. These bedrooms are tiny because they are used for nothing but sleeping; most of life is lived outdoors. There were at least three generations of Milaneses in or around the house at any moment, and I found it impossible to keep track of everyone.

Next morning, I began to realize just how much time Pablo spent displaced from his body. In the thatched, open-air court outside the temple, two clients were already waiting, as if outside a doctor's office. One was an intense, grim man with love problems. His woman had accompanied him to Havana on one of his weekly trips to sell home-cured hams and then, once arrived in the big city, had left him. He had traveled the hundred and twenty-five kilometers from Guïsa to Santiago the previous day after hearing that Pablo was there. Missing him, he slept in the bus station, caught a 5 AM bus to Palma Soriano and another back to Dos Palmas, the intersection. After catching a ride to Pilon, he had walked up to the house. After my attempts to hitchhike and use public transportation, I understood this journey to be one of great sacrifice.

Pablo emerged and invited him in. I sat with Mirta, who had left on foot from a place called Tercer Frente, Third Front, at 4 AM and walked up to Pablo's. She had made the mistake of sleeping with a man without first removing her *resguardo*, the protective packet she wore around her neck. *Gran Bwa* had crafted it for her on a previous visit and explicitly cautioned that it must be removed during sex. "All this comes from Haiti," said Mirta, by way of explaining why she had traveled so far to see Pablo. "Let me give you an example. These rings," she said, wagging her fingers, "you can make copies of them and take them off to Venezuela, but they will just be copies, not the original. Haiti is the original." I remembered Eduardo's personal spirit, Tomasa, was Haitian and, when she mounted him, he spoke in Kreyol. In Havana, an elderly couple had invited me for lunch and shown me a doll on their shelf inhabited by another Haitian spirit. Fidel, I was told, was raised by Haitian nursemaids and exposed to the powers of the saints at an early age. The sense I had was that Africa is the source and that Haiti is one step closer to it.

It was two and a half hours before the door to the *kay mistè* opened and *Gran Bwa*'s first visitor emerged. "He says you should go in," he said to Mirta. The man looked ashen, as if he had been through a great ordeal.

"How did it go?" I asked.

"We'll see if I get results. That's the only thing that matters."

"What happened?"

"I have to get going. I have a long way to travel." With that, he picked up his bag from the courtyard and strode out of the compound, leaving me sitting alone awaiting my appointment. The intermittent sound of a small gourd-rattle, or *asson*, came, muted by the palm slat walls of the temple. Pablo was calling *Gran Bwa*. I went to the kitchen for a drink of water. "Sometimes he spends all day in there," his wife said, looking out the window.

At last, Mirta came out, looking radiant and bubbly. The visit with the spirit seemed to intensify the mood and temperament brought to it. "You can go in," she said. "Bye. Good luck!"

Inside it was dim. Narrow slats of dusty sunlight projected through the palm-frond walls. "Ou vin salué mwen?" Have you come to greet me? Pablo seemed not to recognize me. I realized it was not Pablo speaking. "Yes," I said.

"Merçi," said the spirit, embracing me with the ritual *Vodou* hug. I wasn't sure what to say to a powerful African spirit. *I've been terribly depressed so I came to Cuba to wander around and now I miss my wife terribly. Well, she's not really my wife, but maybe she ought to be.* I realized this was the closest I had ever come to psychotherapy. *Gran Bwa* picked up a deck of cards and handed me a bottle of perfume and then chastised me for using a back-and-forth rubbing motion to apply the perfume to my head and arms. He demonstrated that the correct procedure is to brush up and away only, flinging off the bad spirits. *Who the hell is this guy? He doesn't even know how to anoint himself with perfume.* He held out the deck of cards.

"Fe siy pa'w," he said. Make your sign.

"What sign?"

"Make that Christian sign," said *Gran Bwa*, with a dismissive wave. He seemed a bit testy, as if unaccustomed to visitors ignorant of proper *Vodou* etiquette. I was very nervous. I made a quick cross-like gesture over the outstretched deck of cards, like an exhausted pope at the end of a long day of babies. We sat beside a low table that served both as altar and *Gran Bwa's* desk. The spirit dealt fifteen cards out into a straw basket. "People are jealous of your work; they want to take over your business." *They can have it,* I thought.

"Sometimes you go to sleep, but then you wake up in the middle of the night and you can't sleep again," observed *Gran Bwa*. "Why is that?" I had experienced chronic insomnia since falling ill in Haiti two years earlier. Although not being able to sleep is a truly horrible curse, I had long since accepted sleeplessness as just another aspect of depression. I tried to remember if I had told Pablo about this problem. I wasn't at all sure that I had.

"M'ap bay yon remèd pou sa," he said. I'm going to give you something for that. *Gran Bwa* appeared to speak only Kreyol and I wondered how his other clients managed. With great care and precision, the spirit tore a page from a notebook on the altar, then tore it again to trim it into a square. In red crayon, he drew seven tiny X-marks.

"Write your name seven times next to the crosses."

I wrote, "Richard Richard Richard Richard Richard Richard Richard."

"Surname?" said *Gran Bwa*, in an exasperated tone.

"Fleming Fleming Fleming Fleming Fleming Fleming Fleming," I wrote. My supernatural encounter was turning into a parody of Cuban bureaucracy.

No sooner had I completed the form than *Gran Bwa* used his crayon to draw a definitive, broad X across my names. It was most unsettling. Gray smoke from the burning charcoal of the pig roast pushed through the slat walls, floating and swirling in the fissures of sunlight. The twin X-marks became intertwined snakes; beside them, the spirit drew something that looked like a sword. With great care, he dribbled onto the paper an ornate flag-like pattern in dots of candlewax.

"Do you have a *pyès?*" he asked, using, I thought at the time, the archaic word *piastre*, which referred to the original Franco-Haitian *gourde*.* Too awestruck to enter into a debate with a spirit on the history of currency, I dug into my pocket for coins, unsure in the chaos of Cuban currency whether to provide *moneda nacional*, *divisas*, or *pesos convertibles*. It was immaterial to *Gran Bwa*, who added two coins I didn't recognize to the one I gave him before placing the little pile in the middle of the square. With the tip of a knife, he piled on a white, crystalline powder, perhaps salt, and then a sprinkling of a rusty reddish dust. He sealed the square of paper around the money and bound the bundle round and round with lengths of red and black thread. The amulet completed, he took a swig of *taffia* and blessed it with a blast of alcoholic spray.

"Give me a candle."

"I don't have a candle," I said.

"You must bring a candle. Run, look for one."

I hurried out of the dim shack and was blinded by the bright sunlight outside. Pablo's wife was in the kitchen. "Do you have a candle? He says I need a candle," I said.

She provided one, and I took it back in to *Gran Bwa*. He prepared it by slicing it partway down the middle, packing the cleft with more of the powders, and melting it closed again. Before going to bed, I was to put the charm, or *wanga*, on a clean white plate beside the bed, light the candle on

---

* The word *pyès* is still in common use in Haiti today and may simply be derived from the French "pièce."

the floor, fill a glass of water, tap three times on the plate, drink the water, and "mande sa ou vlé," essentially, make a wish.

The session continued. *Gran Bwa* braided together the thorny, whip-like branches of the Lazarus plant (*Mimosa pudica*), known in Cuba as *dormidera*, the sleeping one, and in Haiti as *mouri leve*, "dead-and-got-up," and thought to have supernatural qualities because of the way its leaves close up on themselves when disturbed. He twisted them into a tight disk, which he also sealed and bound with red and black thread. This I was to place near the door of my apartment, to protect the household. From the low table behind him, covered with chromolithographs, bottles, and bits of cloth, he passed me a plastic bottle filled with cheap violet perfume, and stuffed with leaves, roots, and herbs. This I was to use as often as possible as a *despojo*, cleansing myself of evil. I was to replenish it with rum and perfume. The spirit removed a long necklace of clay beads around Pablo's neck and put it over my head. By the time I got up to go, I was laden down with amulets and unguents as if I had been shopping in a boutique specializing in talismans. I carefully placed these in a corner of my luggage, along with the stone Pablo had selected for me from the bed of the Rio Cauto.

Trapped between observation and participation, awe and skepticism, I had failed to present *Gran Bwa* with any concrete problems to solve on my behalf. In essence, for him, it was a wasted trip. I had no mystical epiphany. Instead, I had watched the workings of the spirit with the same lack of understanding and fascination that I brought to an aquarium. After a morning of consultations, Pablo was exhausted; it was not, I realized, that his soul was off somewhere relaxing or resting while *Gran Bwa* occupied his physical shell. Anyone who has seen a spirit arrive to ride its servant has witnessed the extraordinary inhuman contortions and sweaty, pulsating spasms that pummel the body in the transition from human to *lwa*. An endless stream of visitors from all over the country, all seeking *Gran Bwa*'s supernatural intervention in their problems, demanded Pablo's daily displacement by the spirit, and so, in his case, the process had become routine and streamlined: a few prayers and rattles of the gourd in the *kay mistè* sufficed to call down the *lwa*. *Gran Bwa*'s arrival was announced with a mild shudder, if at all, but it was nonetheless tiring to be jerked back and forth between the world of the dead and our own, day in, day out.

"I was very scared of this," Pablo told me after waking up from a nap, "when I was young and the saint first started to mount me, and took me and carried me up into the *monte* in the middle of the night and left me there. Or I would come to myself in the cemetery, or find myself there in the woods at midnight. But, after a while, you get used to it. To the point where I would be riding my horse and be mounted by the *lwa* and not fall off." I asked him if he had any memory or consciousness of the long periods he spent displaced from his body.

"Sometimes, it is as if I can see something," he said, "as if you were watching something from a very far distance or hearing about something happening to someone else."

"I was talking to the girl that was here this morning, and she said she had to come, because she had slept with a man while wearing her *wanga*."

"Many times, you find that people arrive in a panic because they did not do this or that thing that the spirit told them to. But then you talk to them and there is always something else. They have some other problem they need to solve, something they need to talk about." It sounded to me like psychotherapy by another name.

The next morning, in the last dim gray of the light before dawn, Pablo woke me up and walked with me back down through his patch of forest, making sure I caught the bus back to Santiago. "If you can," he said, "send me some red and black crayons, the big ones. They're impossible to get here, and I'm running out."

I arrived back in Santiago in time for the ceremonial end to the Festival of Fire, a triumphant, dense, and joyous conga line of a parade that wound through the steep streets of the city and down to the waterfront. It was so densely packed with people that not a single musician was visible in the passing throng. Instead, the music seemed to issue magically forth from the crowd, an organic crush of humanity bouncing to the beat along the Parque Céspedes underneath a sea of multicolored umbrellas. The hapless police could only smile and tap their feet as the procession took an apparently unscheduled turn.

After the parade, exhausted participants wandered the streets in a state of almost post-coital collapse, dragging their instruments as they stumbled down the cobblestones in ornate, bedraggled costumes, triple-tiered hats tucked under their arms. Trailing their streamers on the ground, they wiped sprinkles of glitter off of their faces with the backs of their hands in the crisp, flat, early evening light that comes only after a cleansing rainfall. It is light that the Caribbean palette is designed to capture, and the walls glowed, turquoise and pink and orange. Ancient ladies with countless wrinkles and endless stories perched in the grilled window alcoves watching the street. After the ecstatic unity of the crowd, the disbanding was bittersweet. I have never been to Rio de Janeiro, but the wilted and half-costumed participants splayed out resting on the curbs of Santiago reminded me of photographs of the end of Carnival.

Back at Maruchi's, El Rey del Ganado, leaning up against the garden wall, was as exhausted as the spent paraders. Its front tire splattered with parrot guano, the bicycle looked sullen and reproachful. From the third day of my epic "walk," when I accepted a horse-and-buggy ride, to the hitchhiking, trainriding, and cycling that had followed, I had done nothing but sell out. I realized I didn't have the will to ride my trusty companion the final stretch east. As a sort of farewell, I took some photographs of the bicycle and then removed the painted turquoise horseshoe that adorned the handlebars. Hoping to save El Rey from death by rust and neglect, since lack of use is by far the most dangerous condition a bike ever suffers from, I proposed to Maruchi that she keep it and rent it out to tourists.

"I want to hire a car to take me to Guantánamo," I said.

"It's ugly, and heavily militarized," she said. "Why go?"

"I want to talk to someone who worked on the US naval base."

"Well, you should know that if you start asking questions about the base, you will have somebody watching you for sure," she said. Unfazed by the obscure demands of her visitors, she went on. "Whatever. Hopefully, you won't even notice. You can take a *colectivo*."

PART THREE
Driving to Guantánamo

Veintiséis

A picnic in Guantánamo

"When the first Americans arrived, I thought I was going crazy. Those men, all dressed the same, talking like dogs, something I didn't understand, shouting, drinking....

Later I learned what that was, an American, the United States, but, at the time, I didn't know there were Americans, that there were Chinese, I didn't know how to read, I didn't even know the letter 'o.'"

—Josefina Rodriguez, *Guantánamo Bay*, an oral history

On a Saturday morning, I packed myself into an overstuffed, geriatric, brown Land Cruiser. Blasting down the central highway through the lush rolling hills of the Oriente, we passed a couple of cyclotourists in matching his and hers spandex ensembles, slogging their way uphill into a fierce headwind, a spectacle I regarded with grim fascination and took as the sad justification for the latest in the long string of capitulations that had marked my journey.

The city of Guantánamo seemed neither heavily militarized nor particularly ugly; it was hard to imagine the city teeming with prostitutes and fouled by drunk American seamen urinating in the streets as it was supposed to have been forty years earlier when the US navy abruptly recalled all of its personnel back to the base forever. Walking along the main street, dotted with impromptu curbside restaurants setting up their sound systems for the Saturday night "Noche 'Guantanamera,'" it was impossible to sense that only miles away to the south lurked a mammoth American military facility. When I arrived at the home of Osmaida Castillo, a *casa particular* that Maruchi had called for me, the family was having a heated discussion about the dual robberies of a pocketbook and bicycle, crimes that had the whole city gossiping and up in arms. They paused long enough to welcome me and fill me in on possible leads, for Maruchi, despite her warnings, had then, in classic Cuban fashion, explained every detail of my trip to Osmaida, a stranger, over the phone.

"They say there is a scenic overlook with a view of the whole base," said Osmaida. "Pero a nosotros no nos dejen ir." But we are not allowed to go there. "I heard there is even a restaurant up on top."

"I know about a retired guy, a guitar teacher, who worked there all through the Sixties and Seventies. Supposed to be, he has $150,000, but he can't get at it," said Dionis Castillo, "because the US government told him unless he leaves to live in a capitalist country, he cannot start to receive his pension."

"I'd like to meet that guy," I said, "and how can I find out about the restaurant?"

"Hijo," said Osmaida, to a boy of about ten who was playing in the front room. "You know Ramirez, the guitar teacher in the house near the corner down there? Run, go tell him to expect a visitor. An American who wants to know about the base."

The continued existence of a US naval base on Cuban soil is a geopolitical oddity so bizarre as to beg incredulity. Guantánamo is the last remnant of the pernicious Platt Amendment, a piece of legislation imposed on Cuba by the United States at the end of the Spanish-American War, in 1901. Even the name given this war was an act of historical revisionism, for the United States only stepped into the fray after three painful years of Cuba's battle for independence from Spain. In return for agreeing to then pack up US troops and bringing them home to American soil, Congress demanded "the right to intervene for the preservation of Cuban independence [and] the maintenance of a government adequate for the protection of life, property, and individual liberty," and insisted on the sale "or lease to the United States [of] lands necessary for coaling or naval stations, at certain specified points." The deep internal contradictions of this document, which lauds and applauds Cuban freedom and independence from all entities, except the United States, were forced down the throats of Cuba's constitutional commission and enshrined in the new country's constitution.

The US claimed rights to the use of the natural harbor at Guantánamo in perpetuity, and it was not long before the terms of the Platt Amendment

were being used as a pretext by Washington to oppose any Cuban legislation unfavorable to US business, such as protection for Cuban labor. This
made for a not-very-independent independence, and Fidel Castro was far
from being the first Cuban leader to be upset with America's heavy foot-
print on the island. It was, in fact, during the *de facto* rule of the dreaded
dictator Batista that the Platt Amendment was finally jettisoned in 1934.
Only Guantánamo persisted, with a new lease limited to one hundred
years, at the bargain rent of $4,000 a year. Legend has it that, since the
revolution, Fidel has never cashed the annual check.

Mrs. Ramirez was expecting me. In fact, I imagined the entire city
knew by now that a gringo was on his way to talk to the old guitar teacher.
She let me into the front parlor, a small living room that might once have
been a garage. A Polski Fiat, one of the tiniest cars ever produced anywhere in the world, consumed most of the room. It was covered with a
ratty old tablecloth, the way I had seen other Cubans drape their Soviet-era
television sets to prevent sun damage. José Ramirez sat beside the car as
swirls of fine sandy dust danced in a shaft of sunlight that illuminated the
stubble of his grizzled salt-and-pepper head. There was dust everywhere:
on the threadbare furniture and on the head of the little bust of José Martí
on the bookcase. Ramirez took my hand and greeted me, then put on a
pair of glasses that secured behind his ears with a makeshift assemblage of
copper wire attached to a length of shoelace. The parked Fiat served as a
kind of filing cabinet; peeling back the tablecloth to open the petite passenger door, he removed from the seat an ancient stack of classical LPs and a
folder full of moldering papers. He showed me a Department of the Navy
Certificate of Supervisor Development Training dated 31 March 1954.

"I worked on the base from 1945-1973," he said. "They gave me the
car to reward me for my service."

"When did you last drive it?" I asked, failing to wonder how the US
navy of the early 1970s might have gifted him a Polish miniature sedan.

"Some years now," he said.

"I understand you don't receive your pension."

"They say at some time in the future." He took out an envelope with
a familiar American-eagle graphic under which was printed, "Official US
Government Business Penalty for Private Use." Inside was a green and
beige "Civil Service Retirement Schedule" covered with complicated bar
graphs showing the ratio of years worked to percentage of salary to be paid

out yearly upon reaching retirement. Another inexplicable document filled with clauses and subclauses and exemptions and subheadings explained the eligibility of civil servants to receive pensions. "I filled out everything they sent me and sent it back, but I haven't heard anything," he said. I had the sense that this lone attempt to satisfy the navy's administrative requirements had occurred a very long time ago.

"I worked in electrical maintenance," he said. "First, they had a diesel generator, and then they used sea water to generate current."

"What was it like?" I asked. "I mean, it must have been kind of strange, working there after the revolution."

"It was kind of like a town. There were six thousand people living there. There were carpenters, machine shops. Before, some of them even lived here. One lived right up the street. Well, they all had to go back to live on the base. They all went, every single one."

Despite the precipitous collapse of Cuban-American relations, the Cubans who worked on the base before the revolution were allowed to continue. It was rumored that two or three residents of Caimanera, a village closed to visitors and actually abutting the base, still went to work every day, all these many years later.

"At first it was okay; I could get in my car and drive from here right up to the electrical shop. But it got more and more difficult, with relations deteriorating. I had to get up very early every day, to get public transportation, and then walk for a mile through 'no man's land' to reach the base. I started to have problems, my ankles were swelling." In 1973, at age fifty-two, it got to be too much. He smiled, holding in his lap a crumpled 8 x 10 photograph showing the 175 employees of the electrical-maintenance department sitting in front of their hangar in 1954.

"That's all there is to tell," he said.

"I hear you're a guitar teacher now."

"Well, I was, but I'm retired."

"Retired twice."

"Yeah, once from there, and once from here." He laughed. "At least I get my pension here."

A young man squeezed into the room and sat down with us.

"This is Naftali, a former student. He is now in Havana studying classical guitar," said José. Naftali explained that he was on a three-month vacation back in Guantánamo and that he was in the habit of stopping by to visit his old *maestro*.

"Please, play something for our visitor," said José.

Naftali tuned the guitar and then began to play Hector Villa-Lobos's *Prelude #1*, plucking long vibrating notes that hung in the air with the sun-filtered dust. It was an exquisite performance, and, in that moment, all my self-inflicted solitude, all the abandoned plans and lonely hours of trudging and pedaling while my relationship with my impossibly distant girlfriend withered (in short, the countless uncompleted projects of my life), and even the infuriating and frustrating dozens of homemade bicycle inner tubes I'd changed beside the road, as well as the tragic, chronic, contagious, and terminal depression of my only Cuban anchor, Miriam, all welled up inside of me and I began to cry.

Bulbous tears bubbled down both my cheeks, but, in the bliss of the music, José, and perhaps also Naftali, had forgotten I was there. José had let his chin fall forward onto his chest and closed his eyes, as if to sleep.

As I walked back along the main street, dozens of versions of "Guantanamera," perhaps the most famous *son* of all time, played from the speakers set up along the road. There were techno versions, Euro dance versions, reggae versions, and traditional *guajiro* versions, but nowhere were any tourists sitting to eat, except for the two cyclotourists, dining in their colorful cycling jerseys. With, I knew, only one day left before they would reach Cuba's easternmost tip and complete their journey, they glowed with accomplishment and gabbled like lovers. I hurried past, only to find their bicycles leaning up against the wall in Osmaida Castillo's living room. "We have more guests," she said. "A couple. On bicycles, no less! Didn't you say you rode on a bicycle to Santiago?"

A chauffeur named Cesar was waiting for me. Osmaida had put the word out that I wanted to go to the Mirador de Malones, the scenic overlook above the Guantánamo Naval Base. "What happens is," he said, "it's only open for tour groups. It's in a secure area. But if you want to go, I will try and find the man who takes the groups and can unlock the place." We agreed on a fare of forty dollars, plus a five-dollar entrance fee and $3.50 for drinks at the restaurant, the various charges kept separate to compensate all concerned parties.

In the morning, Cesar came to pick me up in his Lada, accompanied by Frank, the tour guide and keeper of the keys. We took, I thought, a southeasterly direction from the city center, soon turning off the highway onto a rutted asphalt track that ran through a desert landscape that looked similar to parts of Arizona. Soon we reached the first gate, announcing the *zona militar*, the edge of the first level of the military cordon that Cuba maintains around the base. Huge, red cement tanktraps littered the ground like an enormous game of jacks. Frank unlocked a chainlink gate and we passed through, pausing for him to relock it behind us. There was still no sign of the base. The track began to wind up a steep hill clogged with thornbush and cactus. Frank explained that the road up the mountain was hidden out of view from the base. Near the top, he got out to open another gate.

"Aqui estamos," he said. We're here. A small plateau on the top of the hill was dotted with chairs and tables shaded from the blazing desert sun by lengths of camouflage netting suspended overhead. The tiles of the pavilion were painted in a garish yellow and green parody of camouflage. It was the first and only evidence I had encountered that the Cuban authorities had a sense of humor. I started to laugh.

"You like it?" asked Frank. "Wait until you see the view." He walked me to the edge of the pavilion, beyond the tables. Stretched out below us on the valley floor was the entire naval base, bounded on two sides by the dry hills of the Oriente and on the third by the Caribbean. One of those permanently installed, heart-shaped, coin-operated binoculars used by tourists at Battery Park to observe the Statue of Liberty—stamped *See Coast Viewing, Alabama*, it had somehow snuck through the trade embargo—offered, at no charge, close-up viewing of what looked like nothing so much as a satellite photograph of a tract-house development on the outskirts of Phoenix. An expanse of scrub and cactus divided the buildings from a perimeter road dotted with Cuban guard towers. Tidy rows of single-family barracks curved over a hill and Frank indicated a turquoise low-rise apartment block "for bachelor soldiers." He knew, he said, the use of every building. There was little action; on this lazy Sunday morning, one lone, late-model, pickup truck navigated a pristine blacktop road between the tiny houses. A distant American flag waved in the sea breeze. I imagined that I could sense the throb of a thousand air conditioners humming below us in that surreal vista.

Following the routine of his group visits, Frank went and busied himself raising the shutters on the snack bar. Soon, Cesar, Frank, and I were drinking cold beers together at our own private mountaintop resort looking down into Guantánamo Bay. Short in distance, it was a view across so many willful misunderstandings, so much saber-rattling, intransigence, mutual paranoia, and literal hot air that the ordered rows of buildings below us might as well have belonged to another solar system. I mumbled the usual platitudes I dusted off each time I was in a conversation bemoaning the awful gulf between our two countries: look at us here, having a beer together, we just met and we're already friends, so what's the problem?

Frank pointed to a building all alone at the edge of no-man's-land. "The commander of the base and the general in charge of the local Cuban military get together every two or three months down there," he said. "To sit down man to man and have a drink and maybe try to avoid any unpleasant incidents, make sure that whatever situation might arise doesn't escalate." He gestured at an expansive neighborhood of Quonset hut warehouses. "It started with the *balsero* crisis in 1994, when they built those and filled them with Haitians, and then Cubans, and then they *had* to talk. I guess they got along more or less, as people, and decided to continue their meetings." Not long after my visit, it was these buildings that were replaced or reinforced to create a concentration camp and torture center used for the incarceration of hundreds of Muslims held indefinitely without trial or charge, thereby eroding forever the moral high ground the United States had once held in the now quaint and antique ideological struggle with communism.

In the bay itself, a perfect natural harbor, was moored what I took to be a navy frigate; the only other ships appeared to be a couple of pleasure boats laying at anchor.

"Let us know when you've had your fill," said Frank, wandering off to join Cesar under the shade of a marabu tree near the car.

Under the circumstances, I can't say that I felt a great sense of accomplishment at having finally reached Guantánamo, but I allowed myself a feeling of contentment that, after a fashion, I had completed my journey.

"Hey Cesar," I said. "I've seen enough. *Vámonos.* How much more would you charge to drive me all the way back to Santiago?"

Epilogue

It was time for me to go. The final days of my second visa extension were fast running out, but, more important, I was out of energy. I was battered, and weary of hearing the same complaints repeated in town after town. It seemed that everyone was reduced to working some tiny, pitiful scam to try and survive into the next week. The triumphs of the revolution were fading banners fraying at the edges, and the government that waved them had become for so many an adversary that they tried to outwit with petty crimes or obstinate apathy.

I opted to take the train back to Havana, hoping for a last in-depth conversation with the "the people of Cuba," or a final insight inspired by riding the rails the length of the country. Instead—I should have learned by now—I found that those paying for their fare in hard currency were herded together into a single isolated train car, a sort of luxury ghetto of foreigner tourists. I spent much of the ride annoyed by a joyous cluster of friendly Dutch students.

On my last day in Cuba, as I sat on the edge of one of Havana's postage-stamp-sized parks, I had that final and quintessential encounter. A man, about my age, came walking down the sidewalk toward me with his wife and toddler daughter. When he saw me, he paused, letting his family continue on down the street without him. After looking up and down the block for unwanted observers, he approached, holding in front of him a small, blue briefcase. "Excuse me," he said, "but would you be interested in some fresh fillets of fish?" He tapped the briefcase. "I have them right here."

It was little different from the pitch of a Senegalese watch salesman hawking counterfeit Rolexes on Fifth Avenue, but the opportunism and hope in that man's face, and the shame that made him urge his wife and child to continue on, summed up for me in that moment the pathos of the daily Cuban struggle in the post-Soviet era. The image has stayed with me.

Are the majority of Cubans suffering under a thick blanket of totalitarian oppression? Certainly not. But I found that the effects of enforced equality were stultifying, even soul-deadening. I had lost count of the many Cubans who had whispered their dreams to me, explaining that they had entered their names in the visa lottery at the US interests section. The lowest-common-denominator egalitarianism, the crushed ambitions and hopes, inspired thousands to put their name in for the *bombo*, a lottery in which one chanced only to win a trip into the unknown, reviled north, a journey requiring the abandonment of friends and family at home in a society that placed a higher premium on the value of family (in marked contrast to our political rhetoric of "family values") than almost anywhere I have ever been in my wide travels. Despite the prisons full of teenage girls guilty only of lending themselves to too many adventuring foreign men, and others holding indisputable political prisoners, the most scandalous jail in today's Cuba is, to our great shame, the American base at Guantánamo Bay, where hundreds of detainees languish indefinitely, unprotected by the same laws, standards, and guarantees that the United States holds up as exemplary of all that is lacking in Cuba's revolutionary society. One can scarcely conceive of a more effective means of eroding the moral high ground so often claimed by Washington. Guantánamo had not yet become a concentration camp for would-be terrorists when I stood looking into it from the surrounding hills, but I had chosen it as my goal because it was already a metaphor, the expression of all the foul acrimony that clouds Cuban-American relations like a poisonous gas.

I went to Cuba not as a socialist, but probably as one of those Americans who viewed the island through rose-, if not red-, tinted glasses. From the outside, the little island nation seemed to offer a last hope that there might, in fact, be a viable alternative to the rampant, self-destructive consumption and cultural mediocrity of the median American lifestyle. Castro was for me a certain kind of hero, a man who had poked David's pinky finger into the Goliath eye of innumerable American presidencies and lived to tell the tale. But after some time in the country, I began to feel that, almost fifty years on from the revolution, there was little more left to it than this; at times, watching television or reading the newspaper, it seemed that the only claim to legitimacy being made by the state was its unswerving, valiant opposition to the great Northern imperialist evil. There was no problem that the state media (and I never found any other kind) was incapable of blaming on the embargo, or US policy, or the capriciousness of America's leaders in Washington and Miami. I imagined offices of brilliant Cuban journalists gathered together to brainstorm, picking apart even the most inconsequential issues and looking for the angle that would point an accusatory finger at the United States.

No wonder, then, that faced with this propaganda monolith, it was impossible for the Cuban people to take the excellent advice of Prof. Joaquín DiHigo in Matanzas, who had suggested to me that his friends, neighbors, and countrymen should better compare themselves and their standard of living to the squalid horrors of Haiti or Honduras rather than gazing so fixedly north across the straights of Florida.

If this book is in part the chronicle of a gradual, almost osmotic, personal disillusionment with Castro's politics, it is also, I hope, a celebration of Cuba's rich culture, one staggeringly varied and vibrant for an island and population so small. Already, for me, the maximum expression of the fertile collision between Africa and Europe that has resulted in so much wonderful music throughout the Caribbean basin and the rest of the slave coasts of South America, Cuba's hugely disproportionate musical contribution to the world was driven into my ears almost daily, even if the touristic exigencies of the economy demanded that every corner-bar *conjunto* play endless variations on the instant canon of classics freshly immortalized by the Buena Vista Social Club. That families sat together after dinner and played music for one another instead of retreating in front of a PlayStation® or Game Boy® was impressive enough. That their efforts were so often sublime and accomplished was inspiring.

The Muñequitos de Matanzas, essentially an extended family only three or four generations removed from Africa, bring together a mind-blowing array of drumming talent; it is to Cuba's credit that they each receive a state salary, meager though it might be, simply for doing what they do best. Their fifty-year tradition of *rumba* purity is more than doubled by the two-family time machine of Guasimal's curious, primeval coffee-grinding music. But what most impressed itself upon me, what I remember more than these recognized ensembles, were the evenings like those that I spent with Gerardo and his family in Santa Cruz and at Conrad's long, drunken, and weepy goodbye party in Trinidad. Playing music with and for a guest was an organic part of each evening, as natural as eating.

Of *décima*, I knew next to nothing before arriving in Havana and running across *Palmas y cañas* on Miriam's television. This ancient Spanish battle-poetry is not uniquely Cuban, and it has been preserved and kept vibrant in regional variants throughout much of Latin America, but once I learned to recognize it, I began to see how pervasive it is across Cuba's literary and musical spectrum. It seemed to spring up wherever I looked or listened for it. It was buried in the vocal stylings of old Beny Moré and Orlando Contreras recordings and popped up in countless iconic *guajiras*. The demands to "bring Elián home," shouted from the stages of dozens of anti-imperialist demonstrations, were delivered as *décimas*, while holders of this same poetic flame gathered in Miami to craft anti-Castro poems of octosyllabic verse. There was Cuban pride and tradition and resilience in all of this. It fascinated me: everyone had a poet in the family. It was impossible for me not to see in it a source of the rap music I had played as a nightclub deejay in New York, which, despite its commercialization, remains at its heart competitive improvisational poetry set to music.

Stumbling through the country by any means necessary, lonely and gloomy and with my aspirations diminishing almost daily, I was plagued with the thought that my dark mood was clouding my view of Cuban society. And doubtless it did. But I made no particular effort to seek out those equally glum Cubans with whom I seemed inevitably to end up; was it a coincidence that I met and stayed with so many depressives and sufferers from the generic complaint of "nervios?" Misery may love company, but, in fact, I met so many fundamentally dissatisfied, glum, and distressed Cubans that I myself often started to feel better by simple comparison.

I worried less about my objectivity after I blundered by pure chance into the outpost where John Sigler sat watching over a wasteland of pipes and plumbing, sprouting out of a remote plot of red dust. It was a pivotal moment in my experience of Cuba. John was neither depressed nor glum. He was angry. His guileless patriotism gave his story instant credibility; there was no imaginable reason for him to mislead me, and several for him simply to keep his own counsel. I have not changed his name, so convinced am I that he would stand publicly and avow his position. In any case, he and his family are well-known to the Cuban authorities. The brothers whose incarcerations he described to me were imprisoned again, following a 2003 purge of dissidents brilliantly timed to run deep inside the pages of the world's newspapers while the media were focused exclusively on the initial attacks of the Iraq war. Casual googling turns up an Amnesty International report of one Guido Sigler Amaya in the Combinado del Este prison; his brother, Ariel Sigler, is locked up in Ciego de Ávila. Both have been sentenced to twenty years and are considered by Amnesty to be prisoners of conscience.

John, who had refused the free ticket into exile that so many other Cubans were desperate to get their hands on, and who spoke to me about his visits from "those people from Miami" in a tone that made it quite clear he did not share their agenda, is for me a brave and heroic figure. I see the abuses he has suffered and continues to suffer as attacks on a patriot and a man of extraordinary principle. After our meeting, I never quite emerged from beneath the dark shadow of enforced conformity cast by his persecutors.

But I also do not think of John Sigler as a typical Cuban. He did not fit comfortably into the spectrum of people I met on a daily basis, who ranged from those so disgruntled and frustrated that they had already attempted to row to Florida, right through to enthusiastic cheerleaders for the revolution like Conrad's uncle, who made my bicycle's saddlebags. But with the notable exceptions of Rodolfo, the tobacco entrepreneur, and his son-in-law, Angel, with whom I spent an afternoon in a beer garden in Las Tunas, the cheerleaders invariably had the dogmatic, rabid enthusiasm of New York Rangers hockey fans. There was little room for discussion or analysis, and their conclusions seemed always to have been arrived at not by some intellectual process, but by rote. The rowers, on the other hand, had carefully considered their options. They had agonized over leaving friends and family, made long and complicated plans at night, built boats in secret, hoarded fuel, scrounged antique tractor motors, and done their best to adapt them for use in the tropical Atlantic. They risked their lives and professional futures in dangerous and unseaworthy craft. Others not as brave or foolhardy but equally anxious to leave simply made the trip to the special interests section in Havana and hoped that their number would come up.

The punitive and bureaucratic kneejerk reactions to the grave problem of brain drain were to me one of the most oppressive aspects of the Cuban system. Once people like Carlito, the would-be Miami-beach surfer I met in Jagüey Grande, and José Luis, the skinny ex-entomologist from Bayamo, were identified as wanting to leave Cuba, they were cut off, ostracized and marginalized in ways that could only increase their bitterness and resentment and intensify their desire to get out of the country. In the Mariel boatlift, treating the departing like traitors and sending them off with rotten tomato- and egg-throwing mobs was a spectacle that, however disgusting, seemed to present a Cuba and a revolution united against selfish turncoats and cowards who would float away to the shores of the enemy. But after years of post-Soviet austerity, the petty punishments meted out by supervisors and functionaries served only to alienate people from the system. It was as if there was a black book in which your name could be written down at any time, stopping your career cold, for the crimes of dreaming, aspiring, desiring.

The terminated and frustrated, stuck on the island and paradoxically locked out of the careers for which they had trained, were only one aspect of the internal component of the brain drain. From mosquito experts turned waiters and calculus professors offering haircuts, to lawyers running bed-and-breakfasts and English teachers pimping *jineteras* to single male tourists, it sometimes seemed that, like Jessica Lange's Hungarian handlers in *The Music Box*, nobody was left who could make ends meet working for the pitiful state salary, whether they loved their jobs or not.

Between the revolution's remaining fanatical boosters and those frantic to leave Cuba at any cost were, of course, most of the Cubans I met. Families like that of Fredis, Marta, and Esther regularly humbled and overwhelmed me with their generosity. The *santera*, her biology-professor sister, and their tiny, skinny, white friend Artemis really did seem to be living in Castro's much-touted post-racial society. Later, however, I was surprised by a casual racism in many conversations with whites. Increasing crime, in what Cubans remembered as an almost crime-free society, was always attributed to blacks, usually migrants from the east. The Oriente was said to be poorer, more backward, and lazier. Often, these characterizations really meant *blacker*. It was like the United States, without the whitewashing of political correctness.

Cuba was full of contradictions like this, of issues and problems that had been outlawed or legislated away by the revolution with varying degrees of success. The great literacy campaign of the early 1960s, in which Miriam was still very proud to have participated, was a phenomenal transformation of Cuban society; a few decades later, the country I traveled through was full of people overqualified for the most sought-after jobs: those in the service industry catering to the almighty tourist dollar. Depending on who was asked, the famous Cuban healthcare system was either a paradigm for free, public medicine or a scheme in tatters and suffering from widespread shortages of even the most basic first-aid supplies. The volunteer doctors Cuba sent abroad to alleviate suffering in the East Timors and Nicaraguas of the world were either national heroes or, in the alternate, dark and cynical view, privileged opportunists who would likely never return, as they were said to be making mountains of hard currency seeing patients on the side. Although the grotesque gulf between the richest and the poorest, now apparently taken for granted across most of the globe, didn't exist in Cuba, emigrés, once considered traitors, were now a lifeline, their remittances often marking the difference between struggling households and those comparatively thriving in the new hard-currency economy.

The reader, still on board after so long a journey, surely deserves to know if I was enlightened. Unfortunately, since I never knew quite what I was looking for, I can scarcely claim to have found it. My flirtations with *Santería*, *Palo*, and *Vodou* combined the uncomfortable voyeurism of anthropology with my lifelong quest to comprehend, and perhaps share, the faith of others. Despite my own best efforts, however, I remain baffled. As jealous as I was of many Cubans' enthusiasm and ability to ease their lives with such practices, I was never able to escape my own rationality.

Nonetheless, both Esther in Artemisa, and Loretta, the blond, patrician *santera* who read my palm in Matanzas, suggested that my walk across Cuba was a mission of some kind, a pilgrimage. Like San Lázaro with his crutch, I leaned on this conceit when I found that those I met along the way found it much more credible than whatever else I could come up with. But my dabbling in Afro-Caribbean religions was not the stuff of personal revelation. Sometimes, when crouched shirtless in Eduardo's gruesome grotto of a bedroom, or in the captivating presence of *Gran Bwa*, summoned before me to do my earthly bidding, I experienced the sort of contact high that nonsmokers get from spending an evening with a bunch of potheads, but much as I would like to report my epiphanic conversion to an ancient West African faith, that is not how this story ends.

But little is more expressive of a culture than its faith. In Haiti, the cliché has it that ninety percent of Haitians are Catholic, but one hundred percent are *Vodouists*. One meaning of this observation is that, as with Judaism, it doesn't matter what you believe or practice because the religion is indissoluble from the culture. For a Haitian to deny *Vodou* is virtually to deny his identity. The situation is quite different in Cuba, whose heterogeneous racial hodgepodge more closely resembles that of the United States than the rest of the Greater Antilles. I met white *santeros* and black *santeros*, newcomers to the religion and oldtimers. Someone like Miriam, a youngster at the time of the revolution who grew up to become a Communist Party militant, seemed clearly to be replacing a failed and bankrupt faith with another, more individualistic and active one. Maruchi, another white female recent initiate, had instead "converted" in a context of government support and even enthusiasm at the Casa del Caribe: *Santería* studies, and by extension *Santería*, are today worthwhile pursuits, sanctioned by the state's official cultural institutions. Eduardo, and certainly Pablo Milanes, were in essence professionals. Eduardo supplemented his salary as a restorer of old 35mm film prints by calling up the spirits in his cauldrons to intercede, on a cash basis, in the problems of his clients. Pablo, as vessel for *Gran Bwa*, was like a psychotherapist, listening patiently to the issues of his visitors and offering, by way of closure, some magical resolution to wind up the session. For all of them, faith was working, bringing them solace, or structure, and certainly income. In comparison, I felt I had little faith of my own. Nonetheless, through the strong and often strange beliefs of the disparate characters I met across the country, I came to feel that faith itself is as necessary to the healthy human organism as oxygen.

The revolution, for so long and for so many a repository of that faith, and personified by Fidel Castro, was losing adherents. But at what point will that fading belief reach a tipping point? The question I was repeatedly asked once back in the United States was what would happen when Fidel was finally gone. Well, as this book goes to press, he has actually left: after suffering an extended illness and lengthy recuperation punctuated by a boom-and-bust cycle of rumors of his death, he reappeared just long enough to definitively hand over power to his brother. Raúl, who countless Cubans told me would never be tolerated, has effectively taken over leadership of the country. So far, the foundations do not seem to be trembling. The legalization of hard currency, which introduced real disparities into Cuban society, nonetheless helped ease the worst deprivations of the special period, and, in recent years, Venezuela's Hugo Chavez, Miami and Washington's new bogeyman, has also helped to fill the void left by the Soviet collapse. The absurd American embargo, a policy that benefits no one save a few Havana propagandists, lingers on; it is tempting to subscribe to the conspiracy theories of my *bombo*-winning friend, Conrad, whose drunken contention was essentially that Cuba is a sort of communist terrarium kept around by Washington as an experiment.

While in Cuba I agonized over the thought that my experience was too mundane even to bother writing down. I put myself under pressure, from which no voyage should have to suffer, to have adventures, insights, and encounters. Obsessed with "understanding the reality of the country," as I put it to myself, I insisted on the absurd proposition that I should live the same life as Cubans lived. This impossible and highly selective endeavor brought me guilt whenever I pulled out my dollars to relieve my burdensome situation and inspired me to heights of miserliness and stubborn anger whenever Cubans suggested that, horrors, I hand over more of them than a Cuban would for the same goods or services. I refused to see myself as a tourist on vacation. No Cuban, of course, could really see me as anything else.

After four months in Cuba trying desperately to be Cuban, I was finally mistaken for one only on my way home. In Santo Domingo, slurring one word into the next, dropping my Spanish terminal consonants like a Cuban hick, and wearing shorts and Chinese sneakers from the dollar store in Santiago, I was sent by a Dominican immigration officer to see his superior, so convinced was he that I was a Cuban carrying a false American passport and trying to sneak into the United States. This seemed a great irony. The superior officer, however, was not fooled. He asked me what I was doing in his office, scoffed, and waved me on my way.

Once in the United States, I was revolted by my almost physical urge to visit Wal-Mart, the flagship of franchise pollution, a store I have always avoided, blaming it for the destruction of small-town American culture. I felt I had to go somewhere where obtaining a screw, a battery, a gasket, or a bicycle inner tube did not require careful scheduling, inside information, family contacts, and an interminable bus trip. I wandered the aisles in awe, confusion, and ambivalence.

In New York, I returned to work recording sound while working on this book. I was often in Union Square, where some old friends and loyal clients ran a small production company. Standing on the street outside their offices, or on the north side of the square, directly in front of the Barnes and Noble there, was frequently to be found a man with a bicycle and card table, selling a book of his own. Never before or since have I seen a self-published author hawking his work in quite this way, with tireless dedication and perseverance, but as if a book were a glass of lemonade. It was both admirable and pathetic; he seemed to have set up shop permanently, and was there all through the long, hot days of that next summer. Intent on writing, I tried to ignore him; his presence was uninspiring and seemed a bad omen for an aspiring author. I paid the man little attention until, one day, my friend, the cameraman Kevin Cloutier, and I were loading cases of video equipment into a van, and we remarked on the man's entrepreneurial spirit. "You know what his book is about, don't you?" asked Kevin. I didn't. "He rode that bike around in Cuba for a while and wrote about it."

Notes on some sources of inspiration

The literature on post-revolutionary Cuba is vast, and as grotesquely polarized in general as any other manifestation of Cuban-American relations. Books on Castro's imminent demise have done battle for shelf space with paeans to the Caribbean socialist miracle since the earliest days of the revolution. I found little to hold my attention. On eBay, I purchased everything from imposing turn-of-the-last-century volumes promoting US interests in the Spanish-American War to ecstatic examinations of the new Cuban socialist economy to lurid anti-Castro screeds from Miami. I read few of them. I imagined, absurdly, that I might write a non-political book about Cuba.

Once I arrived in Havana, however, I discovered in musty, peso-denominated bookshops a fascinating literature so different in its intent and presentation that it seemed yet more proof that the country exists in an alternate, parallel universe. The qualities that led a book to be published here in the US—marketability, compelling narrative, entertainment potential, even the prospect of actual sales—appeared to be completely excluded from the Cuban editorial process.

The most fascinating publications were themselves a creation of the revolutionary project, odd volumes tucked away in the many used-book shops of Cuba's cities. Browsing the brittle paperbacks on these shelves, among manuals outlining the breakdown of parts for a specific model of Soviet tractor engine and histories like *United Fruit Company: Un caso del dominio imperialista en Cuba*, a 435-page analysis of the pre-revolutionary evildoings of the banana importer that became Chiquita, were gems that sparked my imagination and suggested many of the threads I tried to follow on my way through the country.

Although there are notable exceptions, like the work of the patriarch of Cuban ethnography, Fernando Ortiz, and his sister-in-law, anthropologist Lydia Cabrera, it was after the revolution that a body of writing emerged to valorize the common working man. The peasants, *guajiros*, cane-cutters, and former slaves who made up the bulk of Cuban humanity before 1959 had been treated only as raw, disposable labor, their customs, interests, and intellectual pursuits often ignored or discarded as insignificant. But as educated youths like Miriam went out from the cities to "alphabaptize" the illiterate masses in Cuba's revolutionary literacy campaign, they must have heard countless stories worth writing down. No wonder, then, that after Castro took power, Ortiz's favored mode of ethnography, oral history, flourished.

Miguel Barnet's still controversial collaboration with the 105-year-old Esteban Montejo offers eyewitness testimony to Cuba's slavery days and the battle for Cuban independence. That it has been published in English both as *The Autobiography of a Runaway Slave* and *The Biography of a Runaway Slave* suggests some of the nature of the controversy; for me, however, the book's power lies in the immediacy of the African culture it describes: dance, music, religion, and a complete cuisine just arrived by ship and then filtering inexorably into broader Cuban society.

For Montejo, whether living in the barracoons or the forest, there was little distinction between botany and medicine. For a time, he lived literally in the great wilderness of Lydia Cabrera's stupendous, double-barreled *El Monte*, in which, through countless interviews, she exposes the spiritual, mystical, and medical perspectives of the *palero* before compiling the information gathered into an exhaustive alphabetized *botánica*. Her collected wisdom on the ceiba tree inspired me to daydream of an environmentalism based on the sanctity of plants; more important, it underlined the preeminent place of herbal healing (so easily overlooked in the sensationalism of ceremony) in the Afro-Caribbean religions in general.

El Vodú en Cuba—Joel James, José Millet, and Alexis Alarcón's book on the *vodou* practiced in Cuba's Haitian enclaves—is not an oral history, but it leans heavily on the testimonies of marginalized informants, including people who, like Pablo Milanes's father, lived on in Cuba long after their sugar-harvesting contracts had expired, disenfranchised and at risk of deportation. That a Haitian world thrived inside Cuba captivated me. Also useful was Natalia Bolívar Aróstegui and Valentina Porras Potts's *Orisha Ayé: Unidad mítica del Caribe al Brasil*, which catalogues the African spirits in their varied manifestations from Cuba through Hispaniola and the eastern Caribbean right down south to Bahia.

In *El folclor médico de Cuba*, José Seoane Gallo compiled interviews from the province of Camagüey in 1961 and 1962 into a 900-page volume of traditional medicine, superstition, and hearsay taken straight from the proletariat's mouth, without any editorial intercession remarking on the religious or medical validity of the fascinating, but often preposterous and contradictory, cures his informants had offered up for everything from warts to impotence. My copy of this book, published on the cheapest paper in 1984, is already yellowed and crumbling, its brittle pages at risk of disappearing forever with the knowledge they contain.

Guantánamo Bay, by Rigoberto Cruz Díaz, was another exciting bookstore find despite its evident propagandistic intent. Herein are compiled the testimonials of ex-hookers, dancing girls, bartenders, and hustlers liberated by the revolution from the indignities of working in the service industry of Caimanera, the village turned Bangkok-like den of iniquity under the influence of the adjacent US naval base.

These books were my companions, weighty and sometimes wacky tomes that weighed down the backpack or the bicycle until I finished them and mailed them off to Havana. My only constant companion was *A Guide to the Birds of the West Indies* by Herbert Raffaele and collaborators. Despite the authors' failure to exploit Pedro Regalado's decades of ornithological field experience, the book is a superlative guide to the birds of the region that, somewhat sadly, has rendered the earlier guide by James Bond, for whom the *espión* action hero was named, obsolete. In Najasa, I was lucky enough to hold in my hands Regalado's cherished copy of the second edition of Juan Gundlach's *Catálogo de las aves cubanas*. The first edition, in which the Cuban macaw is not yet extinct, was reissued in facsimile in Valencia in 1996.

I saw so many lizards on my journey that, upon my return, I sought out Lourdes Rodriguez Schettino's *The Iguanid Lizards of Cuba*, a beautiful and detailed work from which I learned both that Cuba is an important center of iguanid biodiversity and that I had failed to note *any* of the field marks useful in identifying the abundance of species I had observed.

Juan Tomás Roig's *Plantas medicinales, aromaticas o venenosas de Cuba* was not useful for identifying plants in the field, but served as an excellent resource for reading about the many plants and herbs that were pointed out to me or appeared in the pages of Cabrera. Roig is as revered in the sphere of Cuban botany as Ortiz is in its anthropology.

Those captivated by the *décima* will find hundreds in *Los trovadores del pueblo*, Volume I ("no Volume II ever appeared," a Havana used-book dealer told me), in which Samuel Feijóo compiles more *espinelas* than even the most gluttonous consumer of *guajiro* verse could ever hope for. One can only delight, after all, in so many palm-thatched huts and crowing cocks welcoming the misty dawn. *Décima y folclor* by Jesús Orta Ruiz (the *décimista* El Indio Naborí) traces the history of the *espinela* from Espinel's Golden Age Spain through its expression as a cry for Cuban independence right through to the revolution when it ceased, he says, to protest.

I'd like to believe that had I never read Philip "Felipe" Pasmanick's article, "*Décima* and *Rumba*: Iberian Formalism in the Heart of Afro-Cuban Song," I might nonetheless have recognized this ancient poetry irrepressibly pushing its way up through every lyrical crevice in Cuban music. Without it, however, I rather fear the form's ubiquity would have passed me by. Originally attracted as a nightclub deejay to the rhythmic power and dancefloor groove of Cuban music, I largely ignored the lyrics. Reading Pasmanick gave me the rare gift of an entirely new perspective—for which I owe him a debt of gratitude—on a musical form that I already loved.

Those wishing to dig into the diversity, origins, and context of the island's incredible breadth of music will likely never find a better book than Ned Sublette's *Cuba and Its Music: From the First Drums to the Mambo*. Unfortunately for me, it was published after I had already traversed Cuba, so I was only retroactively enlightened, but hearing the Muñequitos de Matanzas recordings Sublette released on his record label, Qbadisc, in the early Nineties put Matanzas on my Cuban itinerary from the very start. Ned Sublette was also kind enough to look over the chapter on the Muñequitos, Matanzas, and the *rumba*, and suggested many helpful corrections. Fernando Ortiz's *La "clave" xilofonica de la musica cubana: Essayo etnografico* was also indispensable to that chapter.

Ortiz's *Nuevo catauro de cubanismos* was a useful dictionary for trying to understand Cuban Spanish, which shows tendencies toward becoming its own language, as was Carlos Paz Pérez's *Diccionario cubano de términos populares y vulgares*, with its more contemporary collection of the kinds of things one tends to hear on the streets.

About the author

Richard Fleming is an inveterate traveler, photographer, amateur musicologist, sometime deejay, and self-described "rabid birdwatcher" long enamored of the music, culture, and wild places of the Greater Antilles. Since his graduation from Princeton University in 1987, his work as a sound recordist in documentary film has taken him to the farthest reaches of the globe. He's been around the world with Kofi Annan, flown missions over Kandahar with the US army reserve, followed Imelda Marcos on the presidential campaign trail in the Philippines, camped with geologists in Antarctica, and sweltered on a nuclear aircraft carrier plying the waters of the Persian Gulf. When not on the road, he lives in Brooklyn, New York. *Walking to Guantánamo* is his first book.

A note on the type

Walking to Guantanamo was set in Bembo, the modern expression of the most beautiful and enduring typeface created in the age of the incunable. The punchcutter Francesco Griffo worked in the great Venetian establishment of the printer-scholar Aldus Manutius in a brilliant partnership unique in printing history. His numerous typographical designs are characterized by their dignity, clarity, and reforming classicism. Griffo entirely abandoned the Gothic forms of medieval book culture to find an inspiration in the monumental inscriptions of ancient Rome. Griffo died in 1518, but his influence on the typographical efflorescence of the later sixteenth century was enormous. The great French family of Garamond types derives from his inspiration. Bembo takes its name from the first book in which it appears: the *De Ætna* (1495) of Cardinal Pietro Bembo. The cardinal was himself a considerable humanist scholar, and his little book was an account of his investigation of the famous Sicilian volcano. Thus, Bembo may be said to be particularly appropriate for travel books about hot and potentially explosive places.

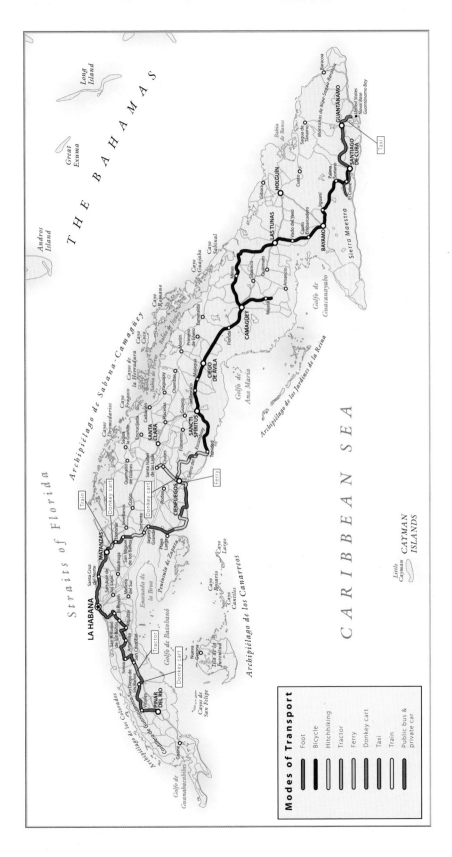

THE BAHAMAS

Long Island

Great Exuma

Andros Island

Straits of Florida

Archipiélago de Sabana-Camagüey

CARIBBEAN SEA

Little Cayman CAYMAN ISLANDS

LA HABANA
MATANZAS
PINAR DEL RIO
SANTA CLARA
CIENFUEGOS
SANCTI SPIRITUS
CIEGO DE ÁVILA
CAMAGÜEY
LAS TUNAS
HOLGUÍN
BAYAMO
GUANTÁNAMO
SANTIAGO DE CUBA

Sierra Maestra

Golfo de Guacanayabo

Golfo de Batabanó

Archipiélago de los Canarreos

Archipiélago de los Jardines de la Reina

Taxi
Train
Donkey cart
Donkey cart
Ferry
Tractor
Donkey cart

Modes of Transport

Foot
Bicycle
Hitchhiking
Tractor
Ferry
Donkey cart
Taxi
Train
Public bus & private car